25

D1108338

Christmas
and Charles Dickens

"Christmas Eve at Mr. Wardle's." An illustration for *Pickwick Papers* by
Hablot Knight Browne. (By permission of the Charles Dickens Museum,
London.)

Christmas
and Charles Dickens

by

David Parker

AMS PRESS, INC.
New York

Library of Congress Cataloging-in-Publication Data

Parker, David
  Christmas and Charles Dickens / David Parker.
    p. cm. —(AMS Studies in the Nineteenth Century; no. 34)
    Includes bibliographical references (p.) and index.
    ISBN 0-404-64464-3 (alk. paper)
    1. Dickens, Charles, 1812-1870—Knowledge—Manners and
customs. 2. Dickens, Charles, 1812-1870—Knowledge—
England. 3. Christmas stories, English—History and
criticism. 4. England—Social life and customs—19th century.
5. Christmas—England—History—19th century. 6. Christmas
in literature. I. Title. II. Series.
PR4592.M25P37   2005
823'8—dc22

2005043618
CIP

All AMS Books are printed on acid-free paper that meets the guidelines
for performance and durability of the Committee on Production
Guidelines for Book Longevity of the Council on Library Resources.

AMS Press, Inc.
Brooklyn Navy Yard, 63 Flushing Ave. – Unit#221
Brooklyn, NY 11205-1005, USA

MANUFACTURED IN THE UNITED STATES OF AMERICA

To Daniel and Michelle,
Clare and Jonathan,
who are repaying
the pains of parenthood,
and adding to its pleasures.

When Dulness, smiling – "Thus revive the wits!
But murder first, and mince them all to bits;
As erst Medea (cruel so to save!)
A new edition of old Æson gave;
Let standard authors, thus, like trophies borne,
Appear more glorious as more hacked and torn.
And you, my critics! in the chequered shade,
Admire new light through holes yourselves have made.
Leave not a foot of verse, a foot of stone,
A page, a grave, that they can call their own;
But spread, my sons, your glory thin or thick,
On passive paper, or on solid brick. . . ."

Alexander Pope, *The Dunciad* 4.119–30

CONTENTS

PREFACE

Between 1978 and 1999 I was the curator of the Charles Dickens Museum, on London's Doughty Street.[1] Every year, during the weeks before Christmas, I would be interviewed by journalists eager to make something of the association between Charles Dickens and Christmas – newspaper journalists, radio journalists, and television journalists. And every year one or more of them would remark at some point, as if no one ever had before, "You could say, couldn't you, that Charles Dickens was the man who invented Christmas?" To begin with, tamely, I agreed. It was the received doctrine. But as the years passed, I found it more and more difficult to square this notion with the evidence. So I tried, with diminishing success, to find polite and encouraging ways of saying, "No, you couldn't." This book has grown out of those efforts.

"The man who invented Christmas" is a phrase coined by F. G. Kitton, just over a hundred years ago. It has rooted itself in Anglo-Saxon consciousness with all the uncompromising persistence of a computer virus. There is no getting it out, it seems, without extraordinary pains, and it is always likely to come back. It takes nerve to dismiss so deliciously mischievous a notion, and it is hard not to feel it effort wasted anyway. Even if anyone listens this Christmas, by next there will be enough who have forgotten such drab advice, or who never heard it. And there are those who will never heed it.

Not a few of them are Dickens scholars. Among such, it has become customary to hedge the notion about with more and more qualifications, to disguise it sometimes, but rarely to abandon it entirely. Acknowledged experts in the field have shown a remarkable capacity for ignoring not only the testimony of the historical record, but also what Dickens himself says on the subject. Some, of course, are incorrigible. It is an enticing notion for those who subscribe to the theory that everything is repeatedly reinvented, Christmas not least, if not by Dickens then by someone else. But not everyone wants to get tangled in such intellectual thickets, and evidence against a proposition still convinces some.

It is not only zealous theorists, however, who need reeducating. Most native speakers of English know something of the Gospel stories, have at least a vague notion of the role of the early Church in founding a festival upon them, and some knowledge of Christmas customs in succeeding ages, but that has not quelled an eagerness to suppose that somehow or other A Christmas Carol precipitated a fresh start in English ritual life. What happened in the distant past is one thing, many today like to believe, but before A Christmas Carol there was widespread indifference to Christmas, after it almost universal enthusiasm.

This is simply untrue. From the late sixteenth century, to be sure, new attitudes toward Christmas began to take shape, in some quarters enthusiasm dwindled, and by the early nineteenth century the festival was being neglected by many opinion-makers and leaders of fashion; but the old delight in it, usual for centuries before 1600, never died out among the majority of the population, and certainly not in the milieu into which Dickens was born. He – with many others – rekindled seasonal rejoicing only among a minority. No rekindling was needed for the majority.

The Christmas books, the stories about Christmas, and the Christmas episodes in other works by Dickens, all in fact grow organically out of a living festive tradition. At the beginning of his career as a writer, Dickens was responding to Christmases he had experienced since his birth in 1812, and it is clear they had impressed him deeply. But like not a few of his contemporaries, not a few members of the previous generation or two, he drew upon more than his own memories. It is not enough, therefore, to study those books and stories and episodes as literary monads, or to relate them only to Dickens's other books. If Dickens cannot be said to have invented Christmas in any intelligible sense, the relationship between his books and the festival needs to be rethought, and a clearer understanding of the history of Christmas in England is called for.

Detail is necessary. Dickens scholars have rarely paid much attention to historians of the subject, and have certainly lagged behind authorities in the field like Ronald Hutton who, in recent years, has assembled a history of the English ritual year more copious and meticulous than any previous history. His findings need to be recognized, and more work remains to be done. Even Hutton's work, I venture to suggest, can be augmented and corrected. For the purposes of this study, at any rate, a greater effort of the historical imagination is needed to determine how English people felt about Christmas as ritual customs changed. Attention is overdue to nuance, ambiguity, irony, and error in some of the source material.

But what above all is needed – and what I have tried to supply – is patient interpretation of historical sources and of Dickens's own writing, free of perverse preconception. Many preconceptions stem from the reductive habit of mind the twentieth century was prone to. But we also need to put aside vague assumptions, rarely supported by reliable contemporary testimony, about Christmas and Nonconformity, for instance, or Christmas and evangelicalism, or Christmas and middle-class hegemony. I offer, therefore, a history of the festival in England from its inception up to Dickens's own day, an analysis of Dickens's writings on it, and an explanation of why it is that both history and writings have been misunderstood.

Every great culture singles out a time of year to be looked upon as the marker of progress and the turning point; as the moment when the previous year is wound up, the next embarked upon; as a moment to be celebrated with ceremonies, feasting, and gifts. The Chinese have Chinese New Year, Hindus Deepavali, Muslims Eid – the end of Ramadan, by Malays appropriately termed *Hari Raya*, the Great Day. Christmas Day is the Great Day for most English people, devout or not.

Dickens was devout, and became more so during the course of his career. Much of this book dwells on the more secular customs of Christmas, but I am mindful, as Dickens was, that they are underpinned by religious doctrine, and that the festival is, at bottom, inescapably religious. Readers are entitled to know where I stand on such matters. Let me say to begin with, then, that I am a tranquil and uncomplaining atheist, not in principle hostile to Christianity – or to its benign aspects at any rate – least of all to the traditional Anglicanism to which Dickens finally became reconciled, and in which I was brought up. But I have never been able to subscribe to Christian theology, or to any other, for that matter.

Yet I do not feel this disqualifies me from tackling the subject. In some respects, I am tempted to think, it gives me an advantage. Piety often has an appeal and dignity of its own, but this is not to be identified with literary achievement, nor is piety a guarantor of such achievement. Distinctions of this kind, and the judgments they permit, are more easily made by the uncommitted.

I do not mean to disparage the Christmas myth, I should say. It is endowed with a deep psychological, not to say biological, validity, making it powerful for believers and unbelievers alike. People shaped by any culture probably feel much the same about their own culture's fundamental myths, but it is hard to think of anything more elemental and unquestionable than the rejoicing expressed in the words, "Unto us a child is born! Unto us a son is given!" And what could be more dazzling than the supposition that the chief problems of life are solved, the turning point of history reached, through the birth of a single child? It is dazzling not least because, in perfectly undoctrinal ways, it is true. The birth of a child is always, or always should be, a new start, a moment of hope, a promise of problems solved, an earnest of continuity – of immortality even, if no more than genetic. Every child is a potential savior. And a birth is a moment for wonder, and love, and tenderness. A religious myth that exploits all this cannot but be powerful.

The story of Dickens and Christmas, however, is to be contained within a history neither of festival nor of literature. It is a story of an English institution and an English writer, and of their effect upon each other. For all that he in no sense invented it, Dickens did change Christmas. More than anyone else, he was responsible for adapting the way we think of it to changes in sensibility that yielded the modern era. He left so distinct a mark upon the festival, moreover, that he can never be far from our modern understanding of it. And Christmas did change Dickens. Writing about it as he did profoundly affected the development of his art. This is the story I propose to tell.

Kingston University

ACKNOWLEDGEMENTS

Dickens and Christmas is a subject I am often asked to speak on. I have had to cultivate intelligible views on it. What I say in this book, however, began to take shape on a particular occasion – my delivery of a lecture in Santa Cruz, during the 1995 summer school of the University of California Dickens Project. The Dickens Universe, as it is known, was devoted to Dickens's Christmas books that year. The Dickens Project, under the directorship first of Murray Baumgarten, then of John Jordan, has provided me with stimulation over the years – not only in 1995. Funding from the Friends of the Dickens Project has enabled me to travel to Santa Cruz and to participate in the Universe. I am grateful both to the Project and to its Friends, for the part they have played in the gestation of this book.

Others people and institutions have played parts too, and to them I am equally grateful. My continuing involvement with the Dickens Museum has been indispensable. Andrew Xavier, my colleague for many years and my successor at the museum, has been unfailingly helpful in making the collections available to me, as has his deputy, Florian Schweizer, and the museum librarian, Donovan Staples. The Trustees of the Museum have generously allowed me to use images from its collections for the frontispiece of the book and on the jacket.

I have received especially valuable encouragement, advice, and information from Michael Allen, Anthony Burton, Robert Patten, and Michael Slater. When he was director of the Bethnal Green Museum of Childhood, Anthony Burton curated an exhibition, "Dickens's Christmas World," on display there between 1 December 1993 and 16 January 1994. His exhibition plan and notes have been an invaluable resource for me.

Other useful advice has come to me from Ian Bradley of St. Andrew's University, the Clerk of the Worshipful Company of Butchers, Mark Cronin of Saint Anselm College, Frank Fricker of the

Canterbury Dickens Fellowship, Fred Guida of Connecticut College and Quinnipiac College, Avril Horner of Kingston University, Peter Jones of Friends of the Classics, Mrs. N. C. McClintock, Christina Mackwell of Lambeth Palace Library, and Lillian Nayder of Bates College.

The email bulletin board, the Dickens List <DICKENS-L@LISTSERVE.UCSB.EDU>, operated by Patrick McCarthy of the University of California, Santa Barbara, is a virtual senior common room for Dickensians, where useful tips are to be had for the asking. I have asked, often, and been rewarded.

For information about records of Christmas celebrations, I contacted scores of historic houses throughout England, and received a gratifying response from owners, archivists, county records offices, and the various organizations now running such establishments. Many replies simply told me that no data of use to me had survived, but experienced researchers know how useful it is to be warned off a wild goose chase. Among those who provided me with positive information, I must mention the following: Rosemary Baird of the Goodwood Collections, John Fryer-Spedding of Mirehouse, Keswick, Alison McCann of the West Sussex Record Office, Lord Neidpath of Stanway House, Lord Petre of Ingatestone Hall, Barbara Powlesland of the Somerset Record Office, Nick Ralls of the National Trust, Sir Reresby Sitwell of Renishaw Hall, Anne Smith of the Sherborne Castle Estates, and Henry Tempest of Broughton Hall.

The information about Chinese customs, Chinese history, and Chinese literature, provided in chapter one, was assembled from a variety of sources, with no system of romanization in common for Chinese words, Chinese names, and the titles of Chinese literary works. To minimize bewilderment among readers, Zhang Yang and Zhang Ling have assisted me, not only by transliterating appropriate terms into standard Pinyin, but also by advising me which terms, from dialects other than Mandarin, should remain spelled as found.

Some passages in this book are recycled from material published elsewhere. Part of chapter four is adapted from my article "John Dickens and George Franklin: Five Letters, 1839–41," which originally appeared in volume ninety-nine of *The Dickensian* (2003). I am happy to acknowledge this. AMS Press is kindly allowing me to rework copyright material from two of its own titles. Part of chapter seven is based on material first published in my article "Drood Redux: Mystery and the Art of Fiction." This appeared in volume twenty-four of *Dickens Studies Annual* (1995). Sections of chapters four, five, six, and seven of this volume, develop material which first appeared in my book *The Doughty Street Novels* (2002).

1

LITERATURE AND FESTIVAL

In 1964, on 22 December, the day of the Chinese winter solstice festival, *Tung Chih*, elaborate ceremonies were performed at the Khoo clan house in Penang, the Khoo Kongsi. Led by the president and the trustees clad in ceremonial black, clan members paid homage to their ancestors. New tablets representing souls of the recently deceased were installed at the ancestral shrine. Pork, duck, chicken, crab, fruit, and Malay-influenced *Nonya* dishes were offered at the shrine, together with Chinese wine. Devotees sampled the food and drink as a way of encouraging their ancestors to consume the spiritual essences necessary for the souls of the dead. Ritual ablutions were performed, joss-sticks were lit, kowtows were made.

At the same time, on the permanent open-air stage opposite the Kongsi building, a troupe of Teochew players performed the opera *Liu Guo Da Feng Xiang* (*Appointment of a Premier by the Six States*). This is a drama which invites spectators to applaud respect for ancestors, and suggests that such respect brings good luck. At key moments during the day's proceedings, opera and ceremony blended, and players in character entered the shrine to pay appropriate homage (Wong 116–18).

It was a typical *Tung Chih* celebration. Nor is the winter solstice the only Chinese festival at which performances of opera play a part. In Malaya and Singapore, for instance, they are important too on the sixth day of Chinese New Year (Wong 47), and customary during the *Kuei Chieh* Hungry Ghosts festival.[1] Troupes of players make themselves available at such times throughout the Chinese world, wherever there are large, well-established Chinese communities and performances of classical opera are permitted. Many temples and clan houses, like the Khoo Kongsi, have a permanent stage for such performances. Where that is lacking, a temporary stage is erected. Opera is used to intensify rejoicing and, when the festival has the religious significance most do, performances take on the status of adjuncts to worship, or of homily.

The connection in Chinese history between the cycle of festivals and literary texts, both dramatic and lyrical, is an ancient one. The *Shijing* (*The Book of Songs*) is an anthology of verses composed between the early Yin Dynasty and the middle of the Chunqiu period (1401–570 BC), and popularly believed to have been compiled by Confucius himself. He was always zealous to promote correct ritual observances, so it is fitting that, among the 305 poems in the book, the most ancient are taken to be the group of forty sung by dancers at sacrificial rites performed in regal and aristocratic households, honoring ancestors, and celebrating the harvest (Lai 27–35). Some can be puzzling, until we see they were intended to accompany ritual dancing:

> We gather and gather the plantains;
> Now we may gather them.
> We gather and gather the plantains;
> Now we have got them.
>
> We gather and gather the plantains;
> Now we pluck the ears.
> We gather and gather the plantains;
> Now we rub out the seeds.
>
> We gather and gather the plantains;
> Now we place the seeds in our skirts.
> We gather and gather the plantains;
> Now we tuck our skirts under our girdles.
> (*Shijing* 8)

Later writers composed such poems, too. The *Jiuge* (*The Nine Songs*) is a set of sacrificial songs by Qu Yuan (born c. 343 BC), the earliest Chinese poet known by name. These suggest some loosening of the tie with liturgy. Perhaps written for sacrifices to the goddess of love, some have the intimacy of love lyrics (Lai 69–71). But for centuries the formal connection with festival occasions and religious observances remained paramount. In the Tang Dynasty, conservative writers such as Liu Mian protested against the rise of poetry entirely unconnected with ritual and expressing only personal sentiment (Lai 169).

Inevitably, Chinese literature developed as others have. Literary texts came to be valued as such, not just as adjuncts to festivities. But many writers remained alert to this ancient connection, and to the powerful emotions it tapped. A tradition arose, for instance, of writing poems to mark the Chinese New Year. The Song dynasty poet Su Shi (1037–1101) wrote about the traditional reunion dinner of New Year's Eve, when members of the family who can do so gather piously in the old family home. *Biesui* is about seeing out the old year with feasting, *Shousui* about the vigil kept by family members till dawn, and *Guisui* about the poet's sadness at being prevented by official duties from joining his family for the festivities (Wong 63). The Ming poet Wen Zhengmin (1470–1559) wrote an entire cycle of such poems, New Year after New Year.

A discourse on Chinese literature and Chinese festivals may seem an oblique way of approaching the subject of Christmas and Charles Dickens, but it can be justified. Among overseas Chinese communities, ancient customs at annual festivals can be observed in detail today, changed perhaps, but scarcely diminished by the centuries. The connection has been preserved, at least between dramatic literature and festivals, without interruption or any need for pious revival. There is something to be said, too, for considering the connection between literature and festival in the most ancient, continuous civilization on earth today, one with little or no influence on practice in the West. There can scarcely be a better way of substantiating a universal connection.

Just how universal it is should be especially apparent to students of Charles Dickens, who will find it hard not to see his sentiments about Christmas foreshadowed by Chinese precedents. Respect for ancestors as such can hardly be said to have played much of a part in Dickens's life, but reverence for memories of the beloved dead certainly did, especially at Christmas time. Fair-minded Confucians would applaud the narrator of "What Christmas is, as we Grow Older," when he advises that, on Christmas Day, we should turn our faces to the "City of the Dead," and "from its silent hosts bring those we loved, among us." "Lost friend, lost child, lost parent, sister, brother, husband, wife, we will not . . . discard you!" he declares. "You shall hold your cherished places in our Christmas hearts, and by our Christmas fires . . . "

(*Christmas Stories* 22–23). *Mutatis mutandis*, it is a very Confucian sentiment.

As a lover of Christmas customs, Dickens would have found much that was familiar to him in Su Shi's poems about the Chinese New Year's Eve dinner. The Cratchits' Christmas dinner (*Christmas Books* 48–54) is described with joy and reverence paralleled in *Biesui*. The poet's longing to be with his family, in *Guisui*, is echoed in *Pickwick Papers* when the narrator speaks of Christmas transporting "the sailor and the traveller, thousands of miles away, back to his own fireside and his quiet home" (*Pickwick Papers* 367).

There is another revealing parallel, too, between the story of literature and festival among the Chinese, and the story of Christmas and Charles Dickens. Even while members of the Khoo clan in Penang were celebrating *Tung Chih* in 1964, in Beijing a politically beleaguered Mao Zedong was secretly circulating among his most ardent supporters a list of what he called "reactionary bourgeois authorities." One name on the list was that of the writer Wu Han, in whose play *Dramas of the Ming Mandarin* Mao detected covert criticism of the Great Leap Forward of 1958, which had resulted in widespread famine. A hostile review of the play, perhaps ghosted by Mao himself, was obligingly published by Yao Wenyuan in November 1965. In it, the term "cultural revolution" is used for the first time. This began the process that led to the launching of an official Cultural Revolution in 1966, which precipitated ten years of political, economic, social, and cultural turmoil in China, during which the traditional cycle of festivals was all but abandoned and the classical opera transformed into something barely recognizable as such. It is still too early to say whether the festivals and the opera in mainland China will permanently recover from Maoist iconoclasm, and to what extent that iconoclasm was an expression of more profound changes in Chinese society.

As I shall show in the following chapters, Christmas in England was subjected to iconoclasm just as implacable, expressing an equally radical determination to reshape society. The effect of this was less severe than is often supposed, but it did mark the beginning of a new phase in the history of Christmas, which persisted for a hundred and fifty years. Dickens was among those who initiated the phase that succeeded it.

But the chief purpose of my discourse on things Chinese, I repeat, is to show how universal the connection between literature and festival is. Despite lack of mutual influence, there are innumerable parallels between China and the West in this respect.

When we turn to Western traditions, we repeatedly find examples of festivals, rituals, and ceremonies, both secular and religious, not merely prompting literary activity and sustaining it, but actually giving birth to literary forms.

Tragedy is a prime example. It arose before 570 BC in ancient Greece, probably at festivals in honor of Dionysus, the god of wine – the god indeed of tragedy, as he was later to become (Easterling 44–53; Levi 173).[2] During early festivals, amid wild jubilation appropriate to a celebration of wine, dithyrambic choruses were performed – group dancing, singing, and chanting, that is, boisterously commemorating myths (Easterling 37). As time passed, the festivals became less of an excuse for dissipation, the performances more complex, ordered, and decorous. Plays that we can recognize as such evolved, investigating the relationship of men and women and the gods. The dancing, singing, and chanting group, the "chorus," was retained, to take part in the action and to comment on it, but around 534 BC an actor was introduced, to play solo parts, to engage in dialogue with the leader of the chorus, and to report events supposedly occurring off stage (Levi 173). The innovator was Thespis, who acted, it is said, in the tragedies he had written (Winnington-Ingram 259). Aristotle tells us a second actor was added by Aeschylus (525–456 BC), and we know Sophocles (495–406 BC) added a third. Each actor would normally have played several parts. Using three meant that, at any one moment, intricate human situations could be represented (Aristotle ch. 4; Winnington-Ingram 258).

Festival organizers made the writing of plays competitive and, for those judged best, awarded prizes of goats, which were sacred to Dionysus. For the same reason, the chorus dressed in goat skins. The very word "tragedy," it is believed, is a record of the genre's origin in Dionysiac festivals. The Greek word *tragoidia* means "goat-song" and, without such an explanation of its origin, it is hard to see how it would have made sense or been of use.

The ode, too, evolved thanks to ancient Greek festivals. The term originally meant no more than a song performed by a dancing chorus, and it was used to describe the choral element of the drama (Goldhill 127–28). But the chief influence on the development of the form as we know it today was the Hellenic games at Olympia – the greatest of the Greek athletic contests, and a religious festival as well, documented from circa 824 BC, but believed to be even more ancient. The games were held every four years in the sacred grove of Altis, near Olympia, originally round an open-air altar dedicated to Zeus and, from the fifth century BC, near a temple housing Phidias' colossal statue of the god. Each victor at the games was awarded only a wreath made from twigs of an olive tree growing next to the temple. But on returning to his own city, he could expect to be rewarded with special privileges and fêted with elaborate victory celebrations featuring a performance of a type of ode known as an epinikion. Simonides of Ceos is known to have composed an early example for an Olympic victor in 520 BC, and mastery of the epinikion by Pindar (c. 518 to c. 438 BC) made this kind of ode a model for the development of the form (Segal 222–35).

King Hieron of Syracuse, Pindar's patron, won a horse race at Olympia in 476 BC. This victory inspired a combination of eloquence and calculation in the poet:

> . . . I must crown that man with the horse-song in the Æolian strain. I am convinced that there is no host in the world today who is both knowledgeable about fine things and more sovereign in power, whom we shall adorn with the glorious folds of song. A god is set over your ambitions as a guardian, Hieron, and he devises with this as his concern.
>
> If he does not desert you soon, I hope that I will celebrate an even greater sweetness, sped by a swift chariot, finding a helpful path of song when I come to the sunny hill of Cronus. For me the Muse tends her mightiest shaft of courage. Some men are great in one thing, others in another; but the peak of the farthest limit is for kings. Do not look beyond that! May it be yours to walk on high throughout your life, and mine to associate with victors as long as I live, distinguished for my skill among Greeks everywhere. (Olympian Ode 1)

Its origins gave the form an enduring function. For two and half thousand years the ode has been used to celebrate remarkable people, things, and events and the poet's personal response to them.

Nor was it only the festivals of classical antiquity that gave rise to European literary forms. Claims – perhaps too bold – have been made about religious origins for medieval romance, particularly for the "matter of Britain," as it was known – the Arthurian stories and others linked with them. Jessie L. Weston's influential study, *From Ritual to Romance* (1920) argues, for instance, that the maimed Fisher King of the grail legend, the land in famine, the bleeding lance, and the jeweled cup may all be traced to a Gnostic text echoing ancient pagan fertility rites. More recent scholarship is cautious about this, and content to link the legend with classical and Celtic myths featuring horns of plenty, magic cauldrons, and other such wonders. These may or may not have been connected with pagan ritual. No one can say for certain.

There is no doubt whatsoever, though, that some of the deepest roots of English drama are to be found in performances honoring a feast of the Christian Church. Throughout much of medieval Europe, miracle plays, morality plays, and mystery plays evolved under Church sponsorship. The ecclesiastical authorities were often half-hearted in their support, and eventually performances became substantially free from ecclesiastical control, but clerics, nevertheless, played a major part in shaping the plays (Happé 10).

The English vernacular mystery plays include some of the most powerful medieval dramas of which texts survive. They depict such biblical subjects as the Creation, the Fall, the murder of Abel, the Nativity, and the Last Judgment. They may have been developed from the liturgy itself, certain elaborations of which became, in effect, Latin playlets performed by churchmen on church premises, complete with characters, dialogue, set, props, costumes, and stage directions (Woolf 3–24). But the mystery-play writers seem to have drawn on other sources too, including religious lyrics, vernacular sermons, and apocryphal legends, together with such secular customs as processions, dances, and folk plays (Woolf 25–38; Cawley xxi–xxv). In tapping such sources, they greatly expanded their dramatic range.

Take the *Secunda Pastorum*, or "Second Shepherds' Play," for instance, in the cycle put on in the Yorkshire town of Wakefield. It is a

Nativity play, the shepherds' worship of the Christ child is mingled with broad comedy, yet the writer contrives to make this strikingly appropriate. One of the shepherds, Mak, is represented as a thief. He steals a sheep from his fellows, takes it home, conceals it in a cradle, and tells them when they visit that it is a baby to whom his wife has just given birth. At first the deception succeeds, but it is exposed by the tender heart of the third shepherd:

> *3 Pastor.* Gyf me lefe hym to kys, and lyft vp the clowtt.
> [*Takes a peep.*
> What the dewill is this? He has a long snowte!
> *1 Pastor.* He is merkyd amys. We wate ill abowte.
> *2 Pastor.* Ill-spon weft, iwys, ay commys foull owte.
> Ay, so!   [*Recognizes the sheep.*
> He is lyke to oure shepe! (Cawley 58–59)

Mak, however, is treated mercifully. Tossing in a blanket is the only punishment his fellows inflict upon him. And the play closes with the shepherds adoring the Christ child:

> *1 Pastor.* What grace we haue fun!
> *2 Pastor.* Com furth; now we are won! (63)

The inventive comedy and the dramatization of the Gospel narrative both focus upon the mystery of birth and the unlooked-for forgiveness of transgression. They resonate together powerfully.

The occasion of the mystery plays was the feast of Corpus Christi. Some plays in certain places were later transferred to other festivals, but most seem to have originated with Corpus Christi. Established in 1317 by Pope John XXII to promote the Eucharist, the feast was initially marked in England chiefly by ritual processions (Hutton, *Merry England* 54). In many towns and cities these swiftly evolved into pageants, as they were known: at first, the carrying in procession of images or tableaux; by the early fifteenth century, performances of plays by craft guilds, probably under the overall direction of a religious guild.

In certain places – Chester for instance – there were performances on three successive days. In some towns and cities, such as Wakefield and

York, stages were constructed on wagons, which could be drawn to suitable sites around the municipality, and possibly even moved during the festival to allow plays to be performed at different sites (Hutton, *Merry England* 40–44, 58–59; Cawley xxv–xxvii).

During the Reformation, mystery plays were bewilderingly banned and revived in England in response to shifts in the theological wind, until performances were finally discontinued altogether. Corpus Christi is scarcely a feast recommending itself to Protestants. But in Kendal, Westmorland, a Corpus Christi play survived until 1605 (Hutton, *Merry England* 82–83, 98, 155). It seems safe to conclude that few of the Elizabethans who established the English secular drama on so firm a footing would have been without memories of such plays.

The mystery plays, though, were not the only festive customs to influence what the Elizabethans staged. Court ceremonies and more popular festivals are both echoed in Shakespeare's works, for instance, and there is evidence to suggest that some of his plays grew directly out of such celebrations.

Dramatic performances had long been used in the royal court to mark festive occasions. Another way of marking them was a custom known as the "disguising," which had evolved out of the amalgamation of various ancient rituals, and which may have been performed in altogether more plebeian circumstances as well (see pp. 33–34 below). It took the form of a procession of individuals in appropriate disguises, parading through the great hall, performing symbolic actions in dumb show, and dancing with each other. During the sixteenth century, under Italian influence, this in turn evolved into the more stylized masque, eventually an elaborately staged show, preceded by a short lyrical drama, and concluded with farewell speeches and songs. There was usually a theme, mythological or allegorical. Masked figures continued to mime actions appropriate to the theme and to dance with each other, but now they also selected dancing partners from among the spectators. The entertainment was usually designed not only to mark an occasion, but also to compliment some significant person or persons involved, to whom appropriate gifts might be offered. Music became more complex, costumes more gorgeous, texts more dense and allusive. Spectacular effects were introduced, and ambitious sets too, changed with elaborate machinery. A late refinement was the anti-masque, a clownish performance preceding the main masque and contrasting with it. Masque and drama, in effect, began to converge in court ceremonies.

Echoes of court entertainments are to be found in Shakespeare in such features as dumb show (*Hamlet* III.ii), the advancement of plot through song (*Two Gentlemen of Verona* IV.ii), masked dancing (*Much Ado about Nothing* II.i), elaborate transformations (*The Tempest* III.iii), and clownish dramatics (*A Midsummer Night's Dream* V.i). *The Tempest* features a masque as such (IV.i), as does *Love's Labour's Lost* (V.ii). The latter, indeed, may have been entirely modelled on the masque. The quaintly artificial plot, the pageant of the Nine Worthies (V.ii), and the concluding songs of the cuckoo and the owl all suggest as much (Pattison xlvii–li).

A Midsummer Night's Dream, though, whatever it might owe to court rituals, plainly owes more than a little to a popular festival: the midsummer watches held on 23 June, the eve of the feast of St. John the Baptist, taken to be midsummer's day. In late medieval and early Tudor England people feasted, on this occasion, decorated their houses with greenery, and in some places decorated churches, too. The origin of the word *bonfire* is to be found in the great fires of bone it was customary to light. The evil-smelling smoke thus produced, it was hoped, would protect populace and crops against the infections of late summer and early autumn. There was usually a royal bonfire at Westminster, and evidence suggests others were sponsored by the aristocracy and the Church.

Many towns and cities put on ambitious celebrations. The City Corporation in London, together with the livery companies, organized torchlit processions through the streets. In 1521, the procession featured five pageants on wagons: "the Castle of War," "the Story of Jesse," "St. John the Evangelist," "St. George," and "Pluto," which incorporated a serpent spitting fire. There were also a model giant called "Lord Marlinspikes," morris dancers, naked boys dyed black representing devils, armoured halberdiers, and a gorgeously clad King of the Moors, sheltered by a canopy and set off with "wild fire" (Hutton, *Merry*

England 37–40).

There were country customs too. Parishes organized feasts known as midsummer ales. Girls inspected the herb "midsummer men" (*Sedum Telephium*), to divine from the leaves the fidelity of their lovers. Giddy behavior was excused as midsummer madness. Customs associated with the first of May were in fact practiced for an entire season, up to July, and especially at midsummer. Greenery for decorations was gathered before dawn from the woods and meadows. There was dancing. Mock kings and mock queens were crowned. Games were played. Dramas were performed. And, to bring matters full circle, these country customs were mimicked and elaborated by the royal court itself (Hutton, *Merry England* 27–34).

It has been suggested that *A Midsummer Night's Dream*, probably written in the mid 1590s, was commissioned to be performed before guests at a great wedding. The play concludes with three weddings, one of them ducal. Prior to this, the audience is entertained by the romantic misadventures of Hermia and Lysander, Helena and Demetrius. The Oberon and Titania story and the play-within-a-play of Pyramus and Thisbe also focus upon the vicissitudes of love. But none of these features are unusual in Shakespearean comedy, and there is no actual record of a performance of the play at a wedding. There is clear evidence, moreover, of its being performed on the public stage by the Lord Chamberlain's Men (Wells 13–14).

If a wedding was the occasion of the first performance, it must surely have been a midsummer wedding, because the play is unmistakeably rooted in midsummer festivities. The title alone prompts the audience to think of them, but so do other details of the text, not least the many references to summer flowers in bloom. It is hard to believe there is no appeal to a festive frame of mind, and apparent that a first performance at any other time of the year would have been an opportunity missed. Titania's great speech in act two, scene one, picks up and enlarges upon the prophylactic motive of the midsummer watches. "Since the middle summer's spring," she tells Oberon, their dissension has had evil consequences:

> ... the moon, the governess of floods,
> Pale in her anger, washes all the air,

> That rheumatic diseases do abound.
> And thorough this distemperature, we see
> The seasons alter; hoary-headed frosts
> Fall in the fresh lap of the crimson rose;
> And on old Hiems' thin and icy crown,
> An odorous chaplet of sweet summer buds
> Is, as in mockery, set. The spring, the summer,
> The childing autumn, angry winter, change
> Their wonted liveries; and the mazed world,
> By their increase, now knows not which is which.

In act four, scene one, Theseus, his bride, and his courtiers repair early in the day to the woods to perform an "observation." Finding the young lovers asleep there, he turns to midsummer customs for an explanation:

> No doubt they rose up early, to observe
> The rite of May; and, hearing our intent,
> Came here in grace of our solemnity.

There are fewer overt allusions in the play to midsummer customs, however, than parallels, unmarked as such but distinct. We see the fidelity of lovers being tested, bewitchment resulting in mad behavior, gorgeous mythical beings performing magical acts, celebrations uniting court and commoner, and a final blessing, in Oberon's song, promising the principal characters good fortune and protection against "the blots of Nature's hand" (V.i). Shakespeare's art transforms all into a freestanding unity but, for those who care to look, the customs of the midsummer watches are detectable.

The title of *Twelfth Night* is meaningless unless we postulate an origin for it in Twelfth Night festivities. Nowhere in the play is Twelfth Night, Christmas, or Epiphany even indirectly alluded to, let alone mentioned. The play was written sometime between 1598 and 1602. Leslie Hotson argues for a first performance at court on 6 January 1601 (Hotson passim). Other scholars suggest the same day the following year (Campbell 902). It is quite clear that, although *Twelfth Night* is not about the festival, it is appropriate to it.

6 January is Twelfth Day, the twelfth day after Christmas. It is the feast of the Epiphany, which commemorates the coming of the Wise

Men to Bethlehem (Matthew 2), the baptism of Jesus (Mark 1), and the miracle at Cana (John 2). Originally Twelfth Night was the name given to the night of 5 January, also called Twelfth Eve. But the following night soon came to be called Twelfth Night, too, and by the second half of the seventeenth century the name was more commonly used for the night of 6 January. The two days together were known as Twelfthtide in Shakespeare's time, and were celebrated as the final phase of the Christmas holiday. Inevitably there was feasting, featuring on this occasion a special Twelfth Cake. Tokens were hidden within it. Discovery of a bean or coin bestowed on the finder the role of mock king or queen. Games of chance were played. In great establishments there was pageantry – spectacles of various kinds, masques, and plays. Something seems to have persisted, in the celebrations, of the Roman festival of Saturnalia, in which the established order of things was sportively overthrown.

It is in this respect that *Twelfth Night* is appropriate to the festival. Identities are confused. Repeatedly, people are not what they seem to be. Deception, delusion, disguise, madness, and the snares of love compose the theme. Feste, the clown, insistently reverses the natural order of things, declaring, for instance, his preference for enemies over friends:

> *Duke.* I know thee well. How dost thou, my good fellow?
> *Feste.* Truly, sir, the better for my foes and the worse for my friends.
> *Duke.* Just the contrary; the better for thy friends.
> *Feste.* No sir, the worse.
> *Duke.* How can that be?
> *Feste.* Marry, sir, they praise me and make an ass of me; now my foes tell me plainly I am an ass; so that by my foes sir, I profit in the knowledge of myself, and by my friends I am abused . . . . (V.i)

Audiences of the time would have enjoyed an additional joke, rarely possible in modern productions. Elizabethan professional theater companies were entirely male. The actor playing Viola, who masquerades as Cesario, would have been a boy pretending to be a girl pretending to be a boy. There could scarcely be a greater opportunity for absurd and ribald fun, appropriate to Twelfth Night.

Throughout recorded history, then, festival has been a nursery of literature. That is scarcely surprising. After territory and language, festivals are what define a community.[3] Festivals demand forms of celebration: ritual, feasting, games, spectacle, and every kind of artistic activity, not least the production of literary texts. Poets in ancient China and tragedians in ancient Greece wrote works for festivals because that is what poems and tragedies were for. There was little choice in the matter. Those who prepared the texts of medieval mystery plays did so because the occasion of Corpus Christi and its sponsorship by the Church imposed tasks upon them or gave them opportunities that they might not otherwise have had. Shakespeare evoked festive tradition in his plays not because he had to, to be sure, but because he saw it as a way of centering those plays upon ritual cycles which gave the community he wrote for its identity. Not all festivals yield literature, nor do all such texts celebrate festivals that are thriving, but the strong relationship between festival and literature can scarcely be denied.

It rarely is in the case of Dickens and Christmas. In the minds of many, though, the normal relationship is reversed. Festive rejoicing, it is suggested, did not give rise to Dickens's writings: Dickens's writings gave rise to festive rejoicing. That way of putting it suggests two propositions in competition. As a matter of fact, they are by no means mutually exclusive. It can be shown that Dickens was inspired to write by Christmas, and that his writings inspired others to celebrate it. But this, I imagine, is the prevailing pattern when festivals give rise to great literature. The problem in the case of Dickens and Christmas lies in the eagerness with which one of the propositions is denied. A substantial recent biography of Dickens declares him "to have almost single-handedly created the modern idea of Christmas" (Ackroyd 34). It is a common claim. However much the assertion is qualified, many want to believe that Christmas, or "the modern Christmas," or "Christmas as we celebrate it today," was brought into being with little help, out of nothing or next to nothing, by texts Dickens wrote.

As a hypothesis, granted, it is neither contradictory nor absurd. Were there any truth in it, we should be compelled to admire a remarkable achievement, and to honor Dickens for it. But there is no truth in it. We can explain why, for more than a hundred years, many have believed it to be true, but we can see that Dickens himself believed nothing of the kind. We can see that he felt his writings on the festival were related to Christmas, much as Su Shi's poems about the New Year's Eve dinner were related to Chinese New Year, or the tragedies of Aeschylus were related to the festival of Dionysus. Christmas, and Dickens's writings upon it, conform to the normal model for the relationship of festival to literature. Despite claims to the contrary, they are no exception to the rule.

In the following chapters I shall show how, more than two hundred years prior to Dickens's birth in 1812, enthusiasm for Christmas dwindled among some groups of English men and women, and how in some quarters this lack of enthusiasm persisted. For a century or so before 1812, many fashionable people had been behaving as if the more secular customs of the festival, if not the religious ones, were anachronisms, delighted in only by the vulgar, best forgotten, and soon to disappear. Christmas did all but disappear from the literary record during much of the eighteenth century. By the early nineteenth, some writers were beginning to lament its decline and predict its extinction. Others, however, continued to rejoice in the festival, but theirs are voices posterity has overlooked or neglected. They spoke for the unfashionable majority. Christmas had become a festival more plebeian and bourgeois than patrician. It was looked forward to eagerly and celebrated ardently more by the have-nots than by the haves. But it was nonetheless thriving. The evidence for this is elusive and not always easy to interpret, but it is there for the finding, as I shall show.

Towards the end of the nineteenth century, a generation of Dickens enthusiasts allowed itself to be deluded by the predictions of the extinction of Christmas made decades earlier. It was a generation with no personal memories of the early years of the century, dazzled by Dickens's achievements. By the end of the eighteenth century, it argued, few took notice of Christmas. Dickens's efforts alone revived the festival in the hearts and minds of the populace.

The argument was given its classic form just over a hundred years ago. In 1903, a magazine called *V. C.* published an article by F. G. Kitton entitled "The Man Who 'Invented' Christmas." It was Charles Dickens, Kitton announced. A founding father of Dickens studies, Kitton (1856–1904) should perhaps have known better, but the sources he examined must have seemed persuasive, and he may well have been moved by the wish to be thought waggish that has moved so many since. Although he is apologetic about it, his joke was daring and seductive at the beginning of the twentieth century, however shop-soiled it is by repetition now. This lapse apart, as a student of Dickens Kitton was zealous, systematic, and constructive. As a writer and as a collector, he laid the foundations for subsequent Dickensians to build upon. Perhaps that is why many Dickens scholars look upon his article respectfully, or at any rate indulgently.

The ground was laid for Kitton's joke over a period of about fifteen years. One writer, in 1888, asked readers to believe that their way of thinking of Christmas was "entirely the result of those tales which Dickens used to publish at Christmas-time, and more especially of 'A Christmas Carol'" (Francillon 351). Another, in 1889, declared that Christmas, "as we know it and enjoy it and wish it to each other, was created by Charles Dickens" ("An American's Reminiscences of Charles Dickens" 359). Kitton himself, in his introduction to an 1890 facsimile of the *Carol* manuscript, suggested it was to Dickens that readers were "principally indebted for the popularization of such kindly charities, reconciliations, and the gracious sympathies that rightly belong to that period of the year" (Kitton, *Carol* iii). In 1904, the year after Kitton's mischievous joke was published, we find a writer agreeing that Christmas was "a mere literary survival, kept up for Dickens's sake" ("The Novelist of Christmas" 50). By 1906, another pioneer Dickens scholar, J. W. T. Ley, had no doubts on the subject. "Beyond question," he announced, "it was Charles Dickens who gave us Christmas as we understand it today" (Ley 324).

In chapter 3, I shall show how mistaken these views are. A quite different picture is yielded by a more careful evaluation of the sources these writers used, and a consideration of sources they did not. For the moment, though, it is enough to point out how, despite superficial appearances, what Kitton and his generation supposed is not confirmed by Dickens's own contemporaries. They were astonished by Dickens's impact upon Christmas practices, but did not suggest he inaugurated anything. It was intensification that they spoke of. Thackeray, for instance, held that the *Carol* "occasioned immense hospitality throughout England; was the means of lighting up hundreds of kind fires at Christmas-time; caused a wonderful outpouring of Christmas good feeling; of Christmas punch-brewing; an awful slaughter of Christmas turkeys; and roasting and basting of Christmas beef" (*Works* 13: 292). Just after the *Carol* was published on 19 December 1843, Jane Carlyle told how it "had so worked on Carlyle's nervous organization that he has been seized with a perfect *convulsion* of hospitality, and has actually insisted on *improvising two* dinner parties with only a day between. . . . I do not remember that I have ever sustained a moment of greater embarrassment in life than yesterday when Helen suggested to me that *I* had better *stuff the turkey* – as she had *forgotten* all about it! I had never *known* 'about it'!" (Carlyle 143).

Neither Thackeray nor Jane Carlyle were suggesting that what they describe were novelties learned entirely from *A Christmas Carol*. In circles they had admission to, Christmas traditions may have been neglected by many, discontinued by some, but they were perfectly well known. Only six days elapsed between the publication of the *Carol* and Christmas Day 1843. It would have taken more energy than even the early Victorians possessed to master a complex set of entirely unfamiliar customs in that time. Thackeray evidently recognized what Dickens had been writing about. As Scots, the Carlyles could be forgiven some ignorance of such matters. The Kirk was hostile to Christmas festivities, and Christmas Day was a working day in Scotland. But if Jane was ignorant of the mysteries of stuffing, her servant had only forgotten them.

By 1843 Dickens was admitted to the same circles as Thackeray and the Carlyles. Like them, he could claim membership of the social and literary elite. But, thanks not least to his modest origins, he had a more detailed knowledge of Christmas customs practiced in humbler circles, than most members of that elite had. More than a love of Christmas prompted him to write *A Christmas Carol*, but he did not invent a festival in order to do so. It was substantially his enjoyment since childhood of a key festival in the lives of most English people, that gave rise to the Christmas books, the Christmas stories, and the episodes describing Christmas celebrations in other works. Festival rejoicing had the effect upon Dickens that it has so often had on writers throughout history. From the rich brew of custom, sentiment, and doctrine that belongs to a great occasion in the calendar of a community, from his awareness of urgent current issues, and from themes which concerned him throughout his career, Dickens distilled literary texts that celebrate the occasion, address the issues, and explore the themes.

Although he allowed himself to feel he was making significant contributions to the festivities, nothing Dickens wrote suggests he thought he had changed Christmas at all, let alone "invented" it. He was aware of the view, common before the 1840s, that Christmas was in decline, and he permitted himself one dry, ironic reference to it (see p. 132 below). But his Christmas writings show, repeatedly and consistently, that he felt himself to be responding in them to popular traditions, time-honored and vital. And he was right to feel so. Much evidence for this will be presented in subsequent chapters. For now, let one piece suffice.

Dickens's 1848 Christmas book, *The Haunted Man*, is set back a decade or so in the past. A key character is said to have attended Peckham Fair, abolished in 1827 (*Christmas Books* 381 and n). Dickens knew his London and loved popular entertainment. He would not have written carelessly about such matters. Milly Swidger is represented as a young woman who has attended the fair since her marriage. The allusion, then, must be supposed a deliberate invitation to readers to imagine the action of the book taking place before 1827, or not much later – during the 1830s, let us say. Milly's father-in-law repeatedly declares himself to be eighty-seven years old, and is said to have an unimpaired memory. Among the memories he finds most cheering are those of many a "merry and happy" Christmas. He remembers Christmas celebrations "and all the merry-making that used to come along with them," from his infancy, his schooldays, the early years of his marriage, and his maturity (384–87). Dickens expected readers, then, to see nothing amiss in memories of a series of joyous

Christmas celebrations, unbroken between the 1750s and the 1830s, give or take a few years on either end. This is not at all consistent with what Kitton and those who think like him would have us believe: namely, that in 1848 readers would have supposed Christmas virtually defunct until five years previously, when the publication of *A Christmas Carol* had triggered a sudden spectacular revival.

Some caution is necessary, perhaps, before this interpretation is accepted. Am I not making too much out of incidental details? I do not think so. *The Haunted Man* is about the part memory plays in creating and sustaining moral identity (see pp. 240–61 below). It is unlikely Dickens would have risked jeopardizing his theme by inviting readers to accept memories contrary to what he and they supposed the facts to be. He gave old Philip Swidger his Christmas memories, because he believed such a character could have such memories. As we shall see, he consistently wrote of Christmas as an ancient festival with unbroken traditions.

Indeed, he saw his Christmas writings as just one contribution to a great annual occasion marked by practices, the vitality of which he only reflected. Some of his Christmas books and stories have Christmas as their theme. Others were written simply to be read at Christmas. All, though, were intended to intensify the rejoicing. Just as Greek tragedians had written plays for the Dionysiac festival, so Dickens wrote tales to take their place alongside the feasting, merrymaking, and other customs, which make up Christmas. His chosen medium of prose fiction gave him access to a wider audience than any dramatist could hope to reach – although theater audiences were not excluded. Eager playwrights swiftly adapted the Christmas books and stories for the stage.[4]

In 1847, because of demands made upon him by the writing of *Dombey and Son*, for the first time in five years Dickens found himself unable to produce a Christmas book. In his frustration, he told his future biographer John Forster how loath he was "to leave any gap at Christmas firesides which I ought to fill" (Forster, bk. 6, ch. 1). He felt he was failing in his duty towards Christmas. It was a great cause to which he ought to submit himself, not just an opportunity his imagination had chanced upon.

We cannot understand that great cause, however, without understanding its history. And to understand the history of Christmas in England, it is necessary to go back to its beginning, which is what I shall do in the next chapter.

THE ENGLISH CHRISTMAS, 598 TO 1660

The feast of the Nativity was invented by theologians, probably in Egypt around AD 200. The Gospels of St. Mark and St. Luke make much of the birth of Christ, but Scripture does not call for believers to celebrate it. It is scarcely surprising that early Christians chose to, though. Christianity is founded on the notion of revealed truth. The Nativity, inevitably, is seen as the first public earnest of that revelation. It would have been clear, moreover, that such a feast had enormous potential for proselytising.

Evidence suggests that by 336 Christmas was being observed in Rome on 25 December. The day seems to have been chosen so that the Christian festival could compete with the pagan festival of *Natalis Solis Invicti*, thanksgiving for the rebirth of the sun. The Church authorities evidently felt the pagan festivities were too seductive, and needed a Christian rival if converts were to be attracted to the infant faith, waverers not enticed away. So the birth of Christ was offered in place of the rebirth of the sun. No one can dispute the success of this counter-attraction, but the uncanonical status of the festival was going to prove problematic. To imitate a pagan model was shrewd policy, but it was hotly disputed at the time, and throughout the history of the Church pagan origins have been something to quarrel about (*Catholic Encyclopaedia* 724–27).

The first recorded marking of the festival in England was on Christmas Day 598, when St. Augustine is said to have baptised 10,000 converts in Canterbury.[1] His mission to Britain had landed in Thanet on the Kent coast the previous year. Between the fourth and the sixth centuries the pagan cultures of northern Europe had exerted a powerful influence in Britain at the expense of Romano-British culture, substantially Christian. Pagan Anglo-Saxons had settled in the east and the south. The centers of Celtic power, and Celtic Christianity, had been pushed to the west and the north. Augustine had been sent by Pope Gregory I to revive the Church and to convert pagans. His attempts had met with no more than modest success to begin with, until he won over the king of Kent, a powerful chieftain, with influence well beyond his own territories.[2] The king's decision formally to convert was probably motivated at least as much by politics as by religious conviction. The legitimacy of royal authority, and relations with Christian powers on the Continent were among the issues at stake. But all worked in Augustine's favour. As Dickens himself put it, "King Ethelbert, of Kent, was soon converted; and the moment he said he was a Christian, his courtiers all said *they* were Christians; after which, ten thousand of his subjects said they were Christians too" (*Child's History* 20).

Having formally Christianized Kent, Augustine set about Christianizing its culture. There are reasons for believing he would have encouraged the evolution of Christmas festivities out of the Saxon winter solstice festival. Gregory I urged him to adopt a gradual approach in weaning the English from pagan practices. Whenever possible, he advised, sacrifices to pagan gods should be adapted into the slaughter of animals for feasting, in celebration of Christian instead of pagan festivals (Bede bk. 1, ch. 30). A sign that this policy was followed is perhaps to be found in the fact that, throughout England by 900, "Yule," the Anglo-Saxon name for the winter solstice season, had become synonymous with Christmas.

An anecdote related by William of Malmesbury suggests the festival was popular by the beginning of the second millennium – although regarded differently, perhaps, by clergy and laity. It tells of young men and women dancing and singing in a churchyard on Christmas Eve 1012, and of their being miraculously punished for their impiety by a priest whose devotions they disturbed (Sandys xiv). By 1100, at any rate, it seems virtually everyone in England was celebrating Christmas vigorously, both in church and out of it (Palmer and Lloyd 96).

Forms of celebration had grown up around a substantially enriched myth. The narrative it is possible to piece together from the Gospels was, over the years, imaginatively augmented. The midwinter date of the feast, chosen out of pure expedience, was absorbed into the narrative and, in northern European versions, winter weather became a feature.

St. Luke's account of Mary's laying the Christ child in a manger, "because there was no room for them at the inn" (2.7), was taken a step further. The stable, unmentioned in Scripture, entered the narrative, becoming the setting for the birth itself and for key subsequent events. Room was made for the ox and the ass, thanks to a fanciful reading of Isaiah 1.3. Fleeting questions recorded by Mark (6.3) and Matthew (13.55), about Jesus being a carpenter, or the son of a carpenter, were elaborated.   Joseph became an undisputed carpenter, Mary an undisputed carpenter's wife.

Much was made of St. Luke's story of the shepherds (2.8–18). The "good tidings of great joy" were told to them first, it was urged. They were the first to visit the Christ child, and the first to spread the news. Christianity was recommended to those without wealth or influence by representing the Holy Family as long-suffering plebeians, the Nativity as a revelation first made to the poor and the powerless, first understood by the poor and the powerless.

But there was also a way of representing the Holy Family and the Nativity, attractive to the rich and the powerful. St. Matthew's Gospel opens with a detailed genealogy of Joseph, tracing his descent from Abraham and King David (1.1–17). Matthew subscribes to the notion of the virgin birth (1.18–25), but he does open the way for representing Jesus as someone born, however questionably, into a royal line.

It is Matthew, too, who records the story of the "wise men from the east" following a star to Bethlehem, birthplace of the "King of the Jews" (2.1–12). This is an uncomfortable reminder for King Herod of the prophecy of Micah: "And thou Bethlehem, in the land of Juda, art not the least among the princes of Juda: for out of thee shall come a Governor, that shall rule my people Israel" (2.6). By the sixth century, in western tradition, the wise men, previously unenumerated, had become three in number, to correspond with the gifts they present to the Christ child: gold, frankincense, and myrrh (Matthew 2.11). And they had been promoted to kings, through association with such texts as Psalms 72.10: "The kings of Tarshish and of the islands shall bring presents: the kings of Sheba and Seba shall offer gifts."

The fully elaborated Nativity myth is extraordinarily rich. With all the details the Gospels provide, and all the imaginative additions, it became a narrative in which almost everyone could find something to recognize, someone to identify with. It is centered upon a mother, a father, and a child. The appeal of this needs no explanation, but more than this was offered. Thoughtful preachers and poets constructed a cluster of compelling paradoxes. The Christ child was human and divine, defenseless and all-powerful, plebeian and royal. The complexity of the myth made it easy to select the way Christmas was to be understood and celebrated. It has enabled different eras, different kinds of society, to take what they have wanted from the festival, and to leave alone much that did not suit them. It can be made a feast in which the family has pride of place, or a feast for the entire community. It can be made a feast honoring the poorest and humblest members of society, or a feast rejoicing in kingship and authority. It can be all of these, just some of them, or something else altogether.

From an undetermined era in the early middle ages up to the last decades of the sixteenth century, the unchallenged expectation was that everyone in England, high and low, would celebrate Christmas joyously, elaborately, at length, and – above all – communally. It was a time for everyone to be sociable, hospitable, and merry – especially the rich and powerful, who had a particular duty to be hospitable. An early carol declares this duty, and prescribes appropriate behavior for those taking advantage of hospitality:

> Now make we mery bothe more and las,
> For now is the time of Cristymas.
> Now every man at my request
> Be glad and mery all in this fest.
>
> Lett no man cum into this hall,
> Grome, page, nor yet marshall,
> But that sum sport he bryng withall;
> For now is the time of Cristymas! (Pimlott 18)

There is an omission here, though, worth remarking upon. The instructions are addressed to men only. They are typical in this respect. This could be used as a pretext for denouncing patriarchy, or as the starting point for investigating gender relations in medieval society. I propose to use it for neither, but I do want to draw attention to this silence about women, as an indication of something that distinguishes the Christmas celebrations of the middle ages and the Tudor era, from the Christmas celebrations Dickens was to document.

The silence, it should be said, is not a sign that women were excluded from the festivities. They are featured in the elaborate formal celebrations described in the fourteenth-century poem, *Sir Gawain and the Green Knight*. There are women at King Arthur's court, and in the household of Bercilak de Hautdesert. One of these tests Sir Gawain's susceptibility to seduction during the Christmas season (*Sir Gawain* pts. 2 and 3). She does so, however, only on her husband's instructions. The issue at stake is honor between men. What she would have done had Sir Gawain been more susceptible is not disclosed.

The poem is in fact an indispensable document for anyone wishing to reconstruct the medieval Christmas. It paints a vivid picture of how it was felt the festivities should be conducted in a royal court and a great household. It is not to be supposed they regularly featured the beheading of a gigantic green knight, with a return match (away) a year later but, fantasy apart, the poet was plainly striving to depict the ideal courtly Christmas. The festival evidently opened with a great fish feast on Christmas Eve (a fast day), and for the rest of the season there was playing of games, jousting, hunting, dancing, singing, and feasting (*Sir Gawain* passim).

Enthusiasm for the festivities remained undiminished well into the Tudor era. In 1557 that source of advice on every point of behavior, Thomas Tusser, was probably the first, in so many words, to exhort his readers,

> At Christmas play and make good cheer,
> For Christmas comes but once a year. (Tusser 37)

The twelve days of Christmas was a phrase much used, but celebrations in fact routinely lasted at least fourteen days, from Christmas Eve on 24 December to the feast of Epiphany on Twelfth Day, 6 January – in the Middle Ages regarded by many as a more important feast-day than Christmas Day itself.

Enthusiasm persisted in fact, if patchily, through to the reign of Charles I. In 1632 the traveller William Lithgow clearly felt he was bestowing high praise when he commended "The best, and most bountiful Christmas-keepers . . . that ever I saw in the Christian world" (Lithgow 475). If something wistful is detectable in his words, there were reasons for it.

Over the centuries many special traditions came to be associated with the festival. Feasting lay at the heart of it. Payments for banquets during the Christmas season are a perennial feature of medieval household accounts (Hutton, *Merry England* 55). Christmas eating and drinking was not, strictly speaking, sacramental, like the mass or the Jewish Passover supper, but it seems to have been all but mandatory. It is scarcely surprising that something so enjoyable should have been popular, but perhaps the injunction to eat echoes the conversion of sacrifice into feast that Gregory I urged on Augustine. Not only did people eat plentifully; not only did they eat special dishes: they celebrated doing so in ritual song.

> The boar's head in hand bear I,
> Bedecked with bays and rosemary;
> And I pray you my masters be merry . . . .

Thus go the words of the Boar's Head Carol. "Pray God send our master a good piece of beef," adjures the Gloucestershire Wassail. "Pray God send our master a good Christmas pie" (Bradley 311, 372).

King John's Christmas feast of 1213 is the first of which any detailed record survives. It was prepared with 27 hogsheads of wine, 400 head of pork, 3,000 hens, 66 pounds of pepper, 15,000 herrings, 10,000 salt eels, two pounds of saffron, 100 pounds of almonds, plus spices, pheasants, and partridges unquantified (Pimlott 21–22). Doubtless there were many mouths to be fed, but plenty was the object. "As many mince pies as you taste at Christmas," declares one old saying, "so many happy months will you have" (Kightly 75). It is sympathetic magic at work: enjoy good fortune and plenty now – good fortune and plenty will continue to be your lot.

The same spirit was still in evidence more than three centuries later. On Christmas Eve 1551, in his great mansion-house, Ingatestone Hall, the Tudor statesman Sir William Petre supped on ling, salt cod, whiting, plaice, eggs, butter, and pies made with warden pears. On Christmas Day, his household and his guests dined on boiled and roast beef and mutton, goose, pies, roast loin and breast of pork, capon and rabbit. For supper there was mutton, pork, rabbit, woodcock, and venison pasty. Generous meals were served throughout the festival, culminating on Twelfth Day, when the most splendid dinner of all consisted of boiled and roast beef, legs of pork and veal, veal loin and breast, an entire pig, pasties of beef, mutton and venison, rabbit, capon, partridge, woodcock, teal and larks (Emmison 308–14).

Certain dishes became traditional fare. Turkey, of course, was not introduced from North America until the sixteenth century, though it quickly became prized as a Christmas dish. Traditions connected with the boar's head are much more ancient. It has been suggested that the boar's head ceremony has roots in Norse fertility rites. We know for certain, at any rate, that in 1289 a boar's head graced the Christmas table of the Bishop of Hereford (Hutton, *Merry England* 55). The Christmas feast of the Corporation of London featured one from 1343 at the latest, when the lord mayor called upon the Butchers' Guild to supply a boar's head every Christmas Day in perpetuity (Billington 100). John Aubrey supposed the tradition had been important enough to leave a mark on English surnames. The name Bowles, he believed, "came from an Office of bearing or carrying a Bowle w^h a Bores head to a Ld Abbot's or a great lord's table on some festivall day at Christmas" (Aubrey 141).

The first record of Christmas pies dates from the late fourteenth century. These seem to have been predecessors, not of mince pies of which there is no mention before 1600, but of Yorkshire pies: boned, diced, simmered, white meat, served cold, moulded in its own jelly.

Plum broth or pottage or porridge is recorded as early as 1573, but it is not until 1670 that we find a reference to plum pudding, a recipe for which materializes in the mid-1700s, and which seems to have outstripped plum porridge in popularity only at the end of that century (Pimlott 23, 47, 69).

During the fifteenth century, sugar became more widely available, sweet puddings and cakes consequently more popular. In 1479, a Norfolk gentleman, Richard Cely, wrote a letter to his brother in London, asking him to procure three or four pounds of sugar for their mother's Christmas baking (Pimlott 23). English cooks learned the French art of confectionary. Feasts at the manor houses even of the small gentry, from this date, began to include elaborate confections contrived out of pastry and sugar, in the shape of ships, castles, and other fantasies (Palmer and Lloyd 97).

The emphasis on eating and drinking at Christmas, thoroughly endorsed by Dickens, is sometimes denounced as vulgar by critics who overlook the importance of feasting in sustaining a sense of communal identity and pride. Feasting at the winter solstice has particular social and economic significance in societies close to their agricultural roots. The significance must have been very plain within the all but self-sufficient economic unit of the medieval manor. In northern Europe the days are short in late December, and there is little to be done in the fields, less to be got. Harvest is past and spring planting not yet begun. Quite apart from being its own justification, a feast then declares the community to be united and successful, more than capable of coping with the demanding rhythms of the agricultural year. There are fresh foods which will not keep indefinitely, and which have to be eaten up. There are animals for which there is insufficient feed, which have to be slaughtered. There is much game which can be hunted without prejudice to breeding. But doing all this according to plan, and consuming preserved foods profusely as well, is a sign that the community's resources are abundant, are being well managed, and are being shared as they should be. Midwinter feasting is defiant conviviality, when the season prompts fasting. Even after economic developments have distanced a community from its agricultural roots, its unity and success can be reaffirmed by a feast at the most dismal time of the year, when all without is cold, dark and barren, all within warm, bright and plentiful.

Closeness to the economy's agricultural roots helps to explain the emphasis placed upon communal rejoicing at Christmas time during the middle ages and the Tudor era. The festival was marked by a variety of customs, but its sine qua non, contemporary texts make clear, was communal feasting and revelry in the great hall of whoever had authority over the community. Christmas songs repeatedly allude to the "hall," and invoke blessings on the "master." This, plainly, was what defined Christmas festivities for most people who thought about it. And it continued to define Christmas for many, long after revels in the master's great hall had vanished into the past.

The early festivities we know most about are the great feasts (in every sense of the word) that took place in great establishments: the royal court, palaces of magnates, manor houses, religious foundations, colleges, guilds, and the like. This is not just because records of such tend to survive. Festivities reflected the structure of society. For all their erosion later in the period, principles for which there is no better term than feudal shaped the social order, and the festivities affirmed those principles. Above all, they affirmed the hierarchical relationships between men, sustained by obligation and loyalty rather than payment, that characterized feudal society. That is why, in surviving texts, women are marginalized. At Christmas, men looked to their masters for hospitality – or were encouraged to do so. With the exception of nuns, doubtless, women were encouraged to rely on their relationships with men for festive enjoyment.

Records certainly show that some landlords and other great patrons kept Christmas on a magnificent scale. During the Christmas season of 1551 at Ingatestone Hall, according to a surviving account, Sir William Petre feasted many "strangeres." Up to twelve additional messes – 48 diners, that is – were served at any one time in his great hall. These included not only "6 messe of the towne & of them that brought presentes," but also "2 messe that cam unbydd." Most guests fed are recorded by name only, and almost all of them were male. Women are never named, and are often enumerated carelessly: a list of male "strangeres" is now and then terminated with the phrase, "& moste part of theyre wives." Even the occupations of some male guests are indicated. Among them were bricklayers, millwrights, carpenters, laborers, a smith, a curate, a tiler, a mason, a tanner, and a butcher. And there were usually groups of the poor, of "strange felowes," of boys and "yonge folkes."

Toby Matthews, archbishop of York, was among those who upheld the reputation of the lords spiritual, even as customs were beginning to change. He hosted six feasts between 26 December 1624 and 3 January 1625,[3] feeding a hundred people at just one of these (Emmison 309–14; Hutton, *Merry England* 178).

These great feasts, under patrician direction and sponsorship, affirmed the permanence of the status quo. They were time-honored rituals, and ritual was privileged in the medieval and Tudor celebration of Christmas. Texts about Christmas extolled ritual: ritual in the broadest sense – that is to say not just formal ceremony, but doing the right thing in the right way at the right time. Time, moreover, was understood to be cyclical, as much as sequential. Narrative, which inevitably asserts change at one level, characteristically resolved itself into ritual. Stories – even the Nativity story itself – were told or dramatized repetitiously, as figures in a pattern, against the background of an unending present. In carols of the era, we notice, the present tense is dominant: *Puer nobis nascitur*, people sang. What should always be done was as important as what, contingently, had been done. The imperative mood is foregrounded: *Benedicamus Domino*, people sang (Bradley 365–67).

In theory, at any rate, social arrangements we tend to think of as feudal ensured that almost everyone could claim hospitality in the hall of a master. In the country, whether he did so or not, the landlord was expected to hold open house – to entertain all comers in his great hall, throughout the twelve days, if not for longer. In towns and cities corporate bodies organized festivities. Municipal authorities were active, craft and religious guilds even more so. As towns grew, guilds strove to supersede for their members the authority and the hospitable role of feudal manors and great households (Jones, *Poulters* 69). They sought to outdo each other in the splendor of their halls, and the magnificence of their feasts. The London Salters' Company, during the reign of Richard II, was famous for feasting annually on a Christmas pie made with pheasant, hare, chicken, capon, partridge, pigeon, rabbit, the liver, heart, and kidneys of sheep, eggs, pepper, salt, spice, vinegar, pickled mushroom, and broth (Huelin 165).

Records of the guilds' celebrations only underline the predominance of collective and public rejoicing over domestic and private. As late as the early seventeenth century, in London, the Fellowship of Masons, it seems, positively required members to attend the Christmas Day revels, and demanded punctuality, too. In 1627, for "coming after the time of prayer on the quarter day for Christmas quarter [i.e. Christmas Day], according to a late order on that behalf," Daniell Challoner was fined a shilling. In 1634, the guild was paying for links to light members home after the revels. Night would evidently have fallen by the time they were ended (Conder 151, 161).

The guilds were not the only urban institutions to organize revels.

The Inns of Court provided jollification in London, not only for benchers and students: yeomen, valets, and "strangers," too, were entertained to feasting, games, music, dancing, and masques. There was even hunting: hounds were set upon foxes and cats inside the great hall. By the middle of the sixteenth century, there were daily feasts throughout the festival in the hall of each Inn, served with great ceremony, according to strict precedent. On Christmas Day itself, there were services in each Inn chapel, and a boar's head ceremony before dinner (Cantacuzino 64–68). The custom of staging masques after dinner persisted until 1614, when William Brown's *Ulysses and Circe*, the last to be written and performed by members, was enacted at the Inner Temple. Perhaps the ever more elaborate demands of the masque form were becoming too much for law students, but by this date the Inns' revels were degenerating anyway (Prest 154).

The Inns of Court were prominent among organizations given to choosing a Lord of Misrule at Christmas, an anarchic alternative "master," set to preside over the establishment in order to organize the revels, and to precipitate as much folly and indignity as possible, paradoxically affirming hierarchy by inverting it – demonstrating, that is to say, just how secure it was. Who was chosen as Lord, and how, varied from institution to institution. Sometimes he was a senior member of the organization, sometimes – to make it more outrageous – a junior member, and sometimes an incongruous outsider. Sometimes he was selected by the top person in an establishment, sometimes by members of a governing body, and sometimes democratically by all members. The earliest surviving record of this tradition dates from the fourteenth century. It evidently flourished in the fifteenth and sixteenth centuries, in noble households, in some municipalities, and in the royal courts, particularly those of Henry VII and Henry VIII. Oxford and Cambridge colleges began to follow the tradition in the late fifteenth century: the first student Lord of Misrule was at Merton College in 1485. And the tradition was adopted by the Inns of Court early in the sixteenth century (Hutton, *Merry England* 9–10; Pimlott 27).

The custom may have been copied from a church tradition. Some religious houses appointed Abbots of Misrule, but the more ancient tradition seems to have been that of the Boy Bishop, chosen to preside over services, to preach sermons (written specially for him), and to go on visitations, throughout Advent and the Christmas season, but especially on St. Nicholas's Day, 6 December, and Holy Innocents' Day, 28 December. The tradition was being followed in York Minster by 1220. Edward I heard vespers conducted by a Boy Bishop in 1299. Edward II rewarded a Boy Bishop with ten shillings in 1317. Religious houses took up the custom. Durham Abbey first appointed a Boy Bishop in 1303. They were even to be found in schools and in parish churches. In the fifteenth century, the Mayor and Corporation of London attended services conducted by Boy Bishops in St. Nicholas's Church, Cole Abbey. The practice was banned by Archbishop Cranmer, revived under Queen Mary, and finally suppressed during the reign of Elizabeth I (Hutton, *Merry England* 10–12, 53–54).

Grandees and powerful institutions dominated Christmas celebrations then, but they did not monopolize them. As the economy developed and diversified, small masters as well as great began to provide hospitality for dependants and neighbors. Halls were a feature of all medieval houses offering more than the barest of shelter from the weather. The homes of substantial yeomen and the town houses of prosperous tradesmen incorporated halls, evidently designed for hospitality as well as for family use. Once yeomen had evolved into prosperous farmers, they were expected to accept responsibility at Christmas time for their servants, laborers, and poorer neighbors. In towns and cities, servants, apprentices, and journeymen looked to their tradesmen masters. They were formally required to do so, in fact. Laws enacted by Henry VII and Henry VIII banned the common people from playing games such as dice, cards, tennis, and bowls, except during the Christmas season, and then only in their masters' houses, or under the supervision of their masters (Sandys xxv–xxvi).

And if the feasts provided in such establishments did not match those in the great halls of landowners, they must nevertheless have been welcome. During the thirteenth and fourteenth centuries, a Christmas goose, capon, or chicken was normal fare for the nascent middle classes, plus bustard or other wild fowl, meat dishes, home-brewed ale or cider, and fine white bread, still a luxury (Pimlott 23).

There were customs, too, which everyone, rich or poor, could enjoy, in quite other settings, with little regard to patronage. These were to become important in providing continuity, as Christmas evolved. The great hall was decorated at Christmas time, but so were more modest homes, and churches too. Holly, ivy, rosemary and other evergreens were used, as they had been in pagan times, and were in the woods for the taking. Virtually all churchwardens' accounts for urban churches, in the Tudor period, show money being spent on Christmas greenery, probably more because it had to be fetched than because it had to be bought.[4] But few towns or cities were so big that families could not fetch greenery for their own homes. John Stow declares that, in the London of Henry VIII, "every man's house" was decorated with holly and ivy at Christmas time (Hutton, *Merry England* 6).

Entertainments of one kind and another were enjoyed by high and low at Christmas. Plays, performances by jesters and acrobats, and music, were all popular. There is a record of costumes being procured in 1348, for the court of Edward III in Guildford: *ad faciendum Ludos domini regis ad festum natalis Domini celebratos apud Guldeford* (Sandys xviii). During the Christmas season of 1509, Henry VIII's first as monarch, the royal court was entertained by three plays and a concert of music. On 28 December 1551, Sir William Petre welcomed "4 singeres & pleyeres that cam from Margetting" to his supper table. Religious houses and municipal corporations often hired the same sort of entertainers as the court, the nobility, and the gentry. Even parishes sometimes hired troupes of players, or staged amateur productions of their own in the village church. Little is known of the plays enacted. Many of those performed by professional troupes may simply have been popular plays from the repertoire, but some, certainly, were Nativity plays. One such was acted annually before the fifth earl of Northumberland. Although there is no evidence for it, it would have made sense for towns and cities with Corpus Christi mystery cycles to put on the Nativity plays at Christmas as well (Hutton, *Merry England* 7–8; Emmison 311).

Evidence also points to another kind of dramatic performance, plebeian more often than not – the mumming play. Mummers, all amateurs, went from house to house enacting their show. In towns there were sometimes public performances in open spaces. The players were often masked, and sometimes the sexes exchanged clothes. When troupes were all male, as often they were, some dressed in women's clothes anyway. After the show was over, there was usually a procession, and a collection was organized for the mummers, or rewards given in the shape of food and drink. Mumming plays, presumably of a superior kind, were acted before Edward III in 1347, Richard II in 1377, and Henry IV in 1400.

It is not clear, however, what it was that mummers performed. Some evidence suggests that the earliest performances on record were no more than the ad hoc "disguisings" discussed in chapter 1 (see p. 9 above), but at some stage the action may have begun to resemble what we find in the mumming plays collected during the nineteenth and twentieth centuries, in the belief that they were relics of an ancient folk drama. These latter-day mummers' plays were performed chiefly in villages – some still are – using texts transmitted orally, modified by performers over the years.

Research, however, has revealed no evidence of plays of this type before 1738, and indicates that they flourished between 1780 and 1900, thanks not least to printed chapbooks (Hutton, *Merry England* 8; Brand 244). Most of the stories enacted in them derive from tales first published in Richard Johnson's *Famous Historie of the Seaven Champions of Christendome* (1596). Their flavour is that of the Middle Ages or the Renaissance, to be sure, rather than of the Enlightenment or the Romantic era. They usually tell of heroes like Robin Hood or St. George. And a spirit of burlesque predominates. Clowns are featured, even a comic Beelzebub. The death and revival of a character or characters is central to them. In the play of St. George, of which there are many versions, the hero boasts of his deeds, and challenges opponents, such as the Turkish knight and the dragon. After the ensuing combats, the doctor is called for and revives the slain. It is tempting to see echoes in this of ancient rituals celebrating the resurrection of the year, but that is not to suppose the plays to be directly descended from such rituals, or to have been extant much before 1600 (Hutton, *Merry England* 9; Pimlott 26).

Just as mysterious as the mummings were the hognells, hogglers, hogans, hogners and hoggells, as they were variously known, who in the fifteenth and sixteenth centuries, in various parts of the country, chiefly at Christmas time, went about the parish, and contrived to be given money (Hutton, *Merry England* 12–13). The custom can probably be identified with the ritual of "hodening," performed in the early nineteenth century on the Isle of Thanet, according to William Hone. One member of the party of revellers carried the severed head of a horse on a pole, covering himself with a horse-cloth and working the jaws with a string. Others rang handbells, and sang carols or secular songs (Hone 1: 1642-43).

Wassailing is better documented than either mumming or hoggling, and there is little mystery about what wassailers did. Guarded against disappointment by a bowl they carried with them, filled with hot ale and roasted apples, and spiced with such dainties as eggs, sugar, nutmeg, cloves, and ginger, wassailers went around their neighborhood, singing Christmas songs, and asking for money, food, or drink. In fruit-growing districts it was the custom to wassail orchards, to promote good crops. The tradition seems to have been especially popular among young women. Wassailing songs, several of which survive, make demands on listeners tunefully. But there was more to wassailing than begging. Carols were sung as well (Hutton, *Merry England* 13–14).

Although during the fifteenth century Christmas carols were developed into an elaborate, not to say courtly art, they seem to have been widely popular for centuries. Some philologists derive the word "carol" from the Greek *choros*. They were indeed often sung as accompaniment to dancing in a way reminiscent of the Greek chorus (see pp. 5–6 above). The earliest surviving English reference to the carol, dating from around 1300, seems to indicate no more than a round dance. This is perhaps less surprising when we consider that not all of the early songs called carols are devotional. Some are about the tribulations of love, some are satirical, some comment on topical issues. The first Christmas carols seem not to have been designed specifically for singing in church. One custom that did grow up in church, though, was the singing of carols to accompany dancing around the crib. This was not something Church authorities were at first always happy about.

Perhaps all this is explained by the probability that carols celebrating Christmas were introduced into England by Franciscan friars, noted for exploiting popular customs and carrying religion beyond the church door. The earliest known English carol text, "A child is boren amonges man," is first recorded in notes for a sermon written by a friar before 1350. Under Franciscan influence, the carol seems to have been appropriated for religious purposes, to express, in the vernacular, a new interest in the humanity of Jesus, most strikingly and movingly marked, perhaps, in examples that take the form of lullabies to the Christ child. Theology and worship are typically played down, in favor of the plain Nativity story, narrated, dramatized or, sometimes, just obliquely touched upon.

Between 1400 and 1550 the carol became firmly established as a Christmas custom, practiced chiefly outside church. A predominant form evolved. Most early examples are divided into short verses alternating with a refrain, usually a couplet. It is a light, easy, folk-song-like form, which must have made a welcome contrast to more solemn kinds of Latin devotional song, and which suited carols to performance in secular settings, by people of every rank. The fact that carols, when not purely in English, are often macaronic, a mixture of English and Latin usually, is a token of the way they bridged the secular and the sacred, the learned and the popular – something observed and imitated in the centuries to come. Dickens was plainly mindful of the strong narrative element in carols, and of the way they reconciled secular and sacred.

Many early carols are skillfully written, and of great power. A few tunes survive from this period, plus about five hundred texts. Among those that have survived are "Adam lay ybounden," "A child this day is born," "A virgin most pure" and "On Christmas night all Christians sing." Some, such as the Coventry Carol, "Lully, lulla, thou little tiny child," were evidently sung, not just at Christmas, but during Nativity plays in the Corpus Christi mystery cycles (see pp. 7–9 above). Some, such as the Boar's Head Carol, are resolutely secular in sentiment. And some, like the Cherry Tree Carol, unrecorded till the nineteenth century but believed to be of great antiquity, tell of apocryphal miracles only loosely related to the Gospel narratives (foreshadowing Dickens and *A Christmas Carol* in this respect).

During the later middle ages the church capitulated over carols, and incorporated them into the Christmas liturgy. How, is intriguingly described in a sixteenth-century poem:

> Three masses every priest doth sing upon that solemne day,
> With offerings unto every one, that so the more may play.
> This done, a woodden childe in clowtes is on the altar set,
> About the which both boyes and gyrles do daunce and trymly

jet;
And Carols sing in prayse of Christ, and, for to helpe them
    heare,
The organs answere every verse with sweete and solemn cheare.
The priestes do rore aloude; and round about the parentes stande,
To see the sport, and with their voyce do helpe them and their
    bande. (Sandys cxx[5])

More Christmas music for all was provided by the waits, groups of
musicians employed to play about the streets. They had evolved out of
companies of watchmen who sounded the hours on trumpets and other
wind instruments. Waits played in the courts of Henry VI, Henry VIII,
and Charles I, but towns and cities employed companies, too. York was
doing so by 1272. The Norwich waits were famous, and can be dated
back to the early fifteenth century. The original waits had no special
connection with Christmas. They played throughout the year, for all
sorts of occasion, but Christmas was one of the times their skills were
called upon. By the fifteenth century, they were a familiar spectacle in
towns and cities at Christmas time (Pimlott 28; Crewdson 105, 132;
Scholes 1103).

For all that the medieval and Tudor Christmas was dominated, then,
by the great feast in the master's great hall, other customs were
practiced, too, often free of feudal patronage. This would prove
important.

Christmas in England, many suppose, is no longer celebrated as it was
in the middle ages and the Tudor era, because of attitudes fostered by
the religious disputes of the sixteenth and seventeenth centuries.
Nothing more clearly demonstrates the errors monocausal history is
prone to. Change in festive customs can be detected well before those
religious disputes even started. The communal Christmas in the great
hall, under the patronage of the master, was an ideal already giving way
to a more complex reality during the later middle ages and the earliest
years of the Tudor monarchs. Feudal principles and actual practice were
diverging. During the second decade of the sixteenth century, we
discover for instance, the earl of Northumberland and the duke of
Buckingham welcomed only clerical dignitaries and gentlefolk to their

Christmas tables – no one of lower rank (Hutton, *Merry England* 7). They were selecting their guests by class, not by community.

One event more than any other loosened the feudal ties binding communities together: the Black Death, which first reached England in 1348. It triggered a population decline which continued for a century at least. The shortage of labor thus caused led to a widespread substitution of money payments for feudal dues, and opened up a market in labor to which the peasantry responded eagerly. This precipitated both geographical and social mobility. In manors all over the country, at Christmas time, the landlord would have found himself formally responsible for ever fewer of the villagers. And ever fewer of the villagers would have looked to the landlord, according to ancient custom, for their Christmas festivities. There were disincentives, in other words, both to offering and to accepting hospitality.

Little wonder, then, that many landowners, so manorial accounts show, ceased to keep open house throughout the Christmas season. They began instead to organize entertainments on specific occasions. They became more attentive to neighbors of their own rank, relatives, friends, and tenants, less attentive to laboring people and the poor. For the latter, if they were lucky, hospitality was replaced by charity. They had to be satisfied with gifts of food, drink, and fuel (Hutton, *Merry England* 178).

Such charity had long been a Christmas tradition anyway. Feudal lords who wished to be respected gave such gifts to many kinds of recipient: to those they were unable to entertain personally; to those they could have entertained, but chose not to; and sometimes to those they did in fact entertain. Records for instance show that, on one occasion in the thirteenth century, servants put to watch over a manor belonging to St. Paul's Cathedral, during the Christmas festival, were each given a white loaf daily, a cooked dish, and a gallon of ale. The thirteenth-century lord of a Somerset manor, each Christmas Eve, gave his shepherd a white loaf and a dish of meat – plus another loaf for his dog, presumably inferior. On Christmas Day, tenants of the manor were given two white loaves, a mess (or stew) of beef and bacon, with mustard, chicken, cheese, as much beer as they could drink, and fuel for cooking (Pimlott 21). Whether they were also entertained in the lord's great hall is not recorded. But thirteenth-century records indicate it was usual for villeins to be excused from work on their lord's land during the twelve days of the festival (Hutton, *Merry England* 241).   The unaccustomed leisure, and gifts of good things, would have enabled them to be as festive at home as its condition allowed.

In towns and cities, parishes and guilds performed the charitable role landlords did in the country. At Christmas in 1632, the London parish of All Hallows gave away sixty-five and a half stone of beef to the poor. In 1639 the London Ironmongers gave eight shillings to the parish, to buy faggots as fuel for the poor (Huelin 167). Both beef and faggots, presumably, would have been consumed in the homes of the poor.

But donations of food, drink, and fuel were, for many recipients, gradually being replaced by gifts of another kind. Some suppose that the giving of gifts to children at Christmas time was a tradition established to commemorate the wise men's gifts to the Christ child. The earliest records, though, suggest that gifts were given to adults, and that they passed up the social hierarchy rather than down it. The custom may derive from feudal dues. Villeins were expected to bring gifts to the Christmas feast their lord provided for them (Hutton, *Merry England* 241). At court, gifts were given by inferiors to superiors on the first of January.   At a later date, it became the custom for clients and dependants to present gifts to those from whom they received or expected patronage. In 1551, as we have seen, the powerful Sir William Petre entertained, among others, "them that brought presentes" (Emmison 312). In 1622, George Wither published a poem about contemporary Christmas customs, entitled "A Christmas Carol." It includes the lines:

> Now poor men to the justices
> With capons make their arrants.
> And if they hap to fail of these
> They plague them with their warrants.

By 1600, the term "Christmas book" was being used for a written record of gifts received. If you gave capons to a justice, I suppose, you would try to make sure he entered them in his Christmas book.

Eventually the process seems to have become reciprocal, however, and finally to have been reversed. A custom evolved of giving food and money to servants and tradesmen on 26 December, blending the old largesse of food, drink, and fuel with something more appropriate to a money economy. A distinct custom was developed for the gift of money, that of the Christmas box which, in the nineteenth century, gave Boxing Day its name. By the later middle ages, the term "Christmas box" had come to mean an actual box, often made of earthenware, in which money was collected for servants, apprentices, and the like, and which was finally broken open on 26 December. They could spend the money how they chose, free of the whim of the donors.

Christmas was being devolved and domesticated. We can only suppose that some poorer folk were celebrating it in their own homes during the middle ages and Tudor times, but early Stuart sources begin to be explicit about this. Wither's "Christmas Carol" declares,

> Now all our neighbors' chimneys smoke,
> And Christmas blocks are burning;
> Their ovens they with bak'd-meats choke,
> And all their spits are turning.

By 1622, Christmas was being marked in every home, this clearly suggests. Where once the sine qua non of the festivities had been communal revelry in the master's great hall, now it was becoming private enjoyment around the family fireside. We can perhaps attach significance to the fact that early seventeenth-century texts are the first to refer to the Yule or Christmas log or clog or block, burned on the hearth during the holiday. There are suggestions that the tradition can be traced back to the fourteenth-century, or earlier. It may well be that lords of the manor burned Christmas logs in their great halls. But the custom would clearly have stimulated more general interest once each family spent the greater part of Christmas by its own hearth.

The switch from hall to hearth was the most far-reaching change of all in festive customs. In the twenty-first century, it is easy to see an emphasis upon Christmas around the family fireside as something cloyingly cosy, but no great effort of the historical imagination is needed to penetrate irrelevant images. There is nothing accidental in the fact that *hearth* has always been used as a metonym for *home*. It was the essential core of the home. Well into the eighteenth century, moreover, probably the majority of English homes had only one hearth, in a room serving as both kitchen and living room. Between 1662 and 1688 a hearth tax was levied on English households. In the dwellings of those sufficiently prosperous to pay, each hearth was taxed, but the poorest families were exempted. Even so, the largest category of those liable lived in houses with only one or two hearths (Hey 213–15). At Christmas time, in a home with only one hearth, the vicinity of that hearth would normally have been the only warm place in the house. For sixteen hours a day in southern England – for more in the north – it would have been the only place at all well lit. And of course it was where festive fare was prepared and consumed.

It is not enough, though, to dwell only upon the physical comforts afforded by the hearth. Christmas in the master's great hall had been an occasion for male networking. Now the festival was moving into territory where females presided – where women cooked, and served, and made decisions. However patriarchal their assumptions, only exceptionally stupid men could have failed to see that their comforts substantially depended on letting the womenfolk organize matters.

It took centuries for this change fully to be appreciated. Arguably, it was Dickens himself who finally set the seal upon it. In his Christmas writings, the central role of women at Christmas time is taken for granted. Bob Cratchit regards the Christmas pudding served at his family's Christmas dinner "as the greatest success achieved by Mrs Cratchit since their marriage" (*Christmas Books* 52). He knows it is her efforts that count. In *Great Expectations*, anxious that her Christmas morning preparations should be unimpeded by male incomprehension, Mrs. Joe unceremoniously sends her husband and her brother Pip off to church (*Great Expectations* 18–19).

Between the later middle ages and Dickens's day, the mood of Christmas celebrations gradually moved into harmony with the kind understanding we see in these texts. The mood generated by the male rituals and frolics of the great hall became less prominent. A mood generated by the interests of women began to prevail – interests, that is to say, in narratives of domestic life, in intimate relationships, in memories of old times, in hopes for and anxieties about the future, in affections and sorrows and consolations. The narrative of the first Christmas, needless to say, offers as good a validation of such interests as you can get.

All of this, it should be clear, was only one manifestation of a more fundamental shift in sensibility, making itself felt in a variety of ways over several centuries. It is not too difficult to see how the development of this new mood for Christmas foreshadows developments in the tastes of the reading public, documented in Ian Watt's classic study, *The Rise of the Novel*. Before the novel, Watt points out, most literary forms "had reflected the general tendency of their cultures to make conformity to traditional practice the major test of truth." The novel challenged this by making "truth to individual experience" the main criterion (Watt 13). One of the factors precipitating this change, Watt argues, was the growth in the number of women readers (Watt 45–49).

He does not suggest, of course, that the novel evolved simply to meet the demands of the feminine sensibility, any more than I am suggesting that Christmas changed simply because women got more of a say in it. There were women, doubtless, just as interested as their menfolk in what could be gained from networking in the great hall, and men just as moved as their womenfolk by recollections and anticipations around the family fireside. It was more a case of a shift in customs opening up Christmas, making it an occasion emotionally more inclusive in mood, enlarging it with sentiments women are more prone to champion.

The change also signaled a shift in the distribution of power between classes. Communal Christmas celebrations, in the master's great hall, had affirmed the feudal social order, with its more-or-less stable hierarchies. The new celebrations around the family fireside were consistent with an impatience with hierarchy, and an eagerness for change. They were suited, that is to say, to the aspirations of the bourgeoisie, growing in numbers and confidence thanks to the very historical developments reshaping Christmas. Some see an affirmation of middle-class hegemony in the Victorians' championing of the family Christmas in preference to any other model (Waters ch. 3). This, to my mind, cannot be substantiated, but it certainly proclaimed an end to patrician hegemony.

Above all, the change in festive customs enabled Christmas to acquire a new role in a new kind of sensibility coming into being. Narrative was beginning to be privileged instead of ritual. Ritual persisted, of course, and continued to affirm permanence. Imperatives urging forms of observation persisted. But something new was being unleashed. Sequential time was edging out cyclical time. A keener sense of history was coming into being. Christmas would eventually come to be understood as a celebration, not of something perpetually recurrent, but of something which had happened "In the bleak mid-winter,/Long ago" (Bradley 154–57). The recurrence of the festival, year after year, was becoming a marker of progress in numberless private narratives – narratives of growth and decay, narratives of success and failure, narratives, not least, of personal redemption. For literature, this opened the way for a development as momentous as the evolution of Greek tragedy out of the dithyrambic chorus, or the emancipation of medieval religious drama from the confines of the liturgy. The festival was relocating itself in the landscape of the bourgeois sensibility. Christmas was being offered up as a subject for bourgeois texts – above all, for that great triumph of the bourgeois sensibility, prose fiction.

Towards the end of the sixteenth century, Protestant fundamentalists, or Puritans as they came to be called, began to look on Christmas festivities with a new hostility. The measures their triumphant successors took against the festivities, during the Civil War and the Interregnum, are popularly blamed for a long-term decline in enthusiasm for Christmas. But Christmas was already changing, as we have seen. Puritan measures were less effective, and the decline less dramatic, than is often supposed. The Restoration of the monarchy in 1660 deprived the Puritans of power, and their remorselessly disobliging iconoclasm gradually mutated into something more accommodating, or at any rate less confrontational. Doctrines espoused by the Puritans, in the long run, only helped to relocate Christmas in the new kind of sensibility emerging. They offered a rationale for the switch from communal to domestic festivities. They further eroded the apparatus of feudal customs and assumptions underpinning traditional Christmas practices.

Christmas tradition had for centuries permitted, among other relaxations, the consumption of beer, cider, and wine in generous quantities, dressing-up and disguise, tricks and games, and a deliberate overthrow of decorum. There was plenty here for austere and pious Puritans to take offense at.

Before there were any Puritans, though, things had gotten out of hand from time to time. From the later middle ages through to the eighteenth century, evidence shows, Christmas revelry was prone to degenerate into mob disorder. This provided a pretext both for the disapproval of the godly, and the disdain of the respectable. Mumming had caused problems from an early date. Thieves took advantage of the custom, adopted mummers' disguises, gained access to houses, and stole property.   In 1418, the Corporation of London had forbidden mummings. Bristol had abolished them in 1487. Henry VII decreed mummers should wear no masks. In 1511 Parliament made it illegal for them to enter houses (Kightly 172–73; Pimlott 26).

Christmas boxes had caused problems from around the same date. In 1419 the City Corporation had banned servants from demanding Christmas boxes because, in doing so, they had taken to menacing mayors, sheriffs, officers, and other less exalted personages (Huelin 164).

Nor are prohibitions that postdate the emergence of Puritanism necessarily attributable to pious prejudice alone. In 1572, soon after the term *Puritan* began first to be used, York's ancient procession of Yule and his wife was banned by the diocese because it "led to enormities and distracted people from coming to church" (Pimlott 38). The ban may have been the work of killjoys, but the charge is not intrinsically unbelievable.

Much the same may be said of some other institutional festivities to which objections were made. By the 1620s, the Christmas revels of the Inns of Court were evidently degenerating. Students had wrested control of them from the benchers, and the old courtly traditions were giving way to dicing, gambling, and heavy drinking. Towards the end of James I's reign, despairing no doubt of recovering their ancient dignity, Lincoln's Inn discontinued its revels (Prest 105, 205).

Puritans, of course, did not object only to overindulgence and disorderly conduct. Ancient misgivings and contemporary prejudices were activated. The Puritans disliked the pagan antecedents of

Christmas. They found no warrant in Scripture for its celebration. And they deplored any use of the papist term "mass." Christmas keeping, declared the pamphleteer William Prynne, derived "from the Pagan Saturnalia, from whence Popery hath borrowed and transmitted it unto us at the second hand."

> When our Saviour was borne into the world at first, we hear of no feasting, drinking, healthing, roaring, carding, dicing, Stage-playes, Mummeries, Masques or heathenish Christmas pastimes; alas these precise puritanicall Angels, Saints and shepheards (as some I feare account them) knew no such pompous pagan Christmas Courtships or solennities, which the Divell and his accursed instruments have since appropriated to his most blessed Nativitie. (Prynne 768)

This kind of theological correctness became sufficiently endemic to attract the attention of satirists. A 1646 pamphlet, entitled *The Arraignment, Conviction, and Imprisoning of Christmas*, solemnly declared that Christian stomachs "must be fed with sound doctrine," not with "good brawne and Christmas pie, roast-beef and plum-porridge" (Dawson 209).

The evident relish with which Puritans demonized the customs and values of those with whom they disagreed is unedifying, but proscription was not all they had to offer. One strand of the complex fabric of Puritanism was, in effect, a repudiation of feudalism − a repudiation of authority sanctioned by feudal principles, of customs affirming the feudal social order. Puritans questioned norms sanctioned by tradition alone, demanded explicit, unambiguous, scriptural authority, and applauded moral or devotional insights gained in the course of personal spiritual odysseys. It was not through works, through public observation of precepts, that justification was earned, they believed, but through faith, acquired by individuals in private narratives of salvation. The alteration of sensibility this marked has been seen as a proximate cause in the rise of the novel. It had an effect on Christmas customs too.

As it happens, one of the earlier effects of Puritanism had little to do with the quelling of disorder or overindulgence. Puritans were suspicious of the custom of carol-singing, even when sedately conducted. Carols were ousted from church once again. Defended by traditional Anglicans and royalists, they remained popular outside the church walls. In 1619 Launcelot Andrewes, Bishop of Winchester, noted how Christmas was a day celebrated "as well as at home with Carolls, as in the Church with Anthemes." A 1631 account of domestic Christmas customs mentions "the evergreen ivie trimming and adorning the portals . . . and the usual carols, to observe antiquitie, cheerefully sounding." On the very eve of the Interregnum, carols had their champion. Countering Puritan doctrines in the spirit of Archbishop Laud, in 1648 a royalist clergyman, Thomas Warmstry, published a *Vindication of the Solemnity of the Nativity of Christ*, arguing among other things that "Christmasse Kariles, if they be such as are fit for the time, and of holy and sober composures, and used with Christian sobriety and purity, are not unlawfull, and may be profitable, if they be sung with grace in the heart." But Puritans looked on carols as one of the relics of paganism. The Scottish Kirk, indeed, was ready to interpret carol-singing as a sign of witchcraft. Unsurprisingly, the Long Parliament did not heed Warmstry's advice. Carols were one of the Christmas customs it banned (Bradley xii–xiii).

From the start of the Civil War, the Puritans began to exercise real political power, and a concerted campaign was mounted against the traditional customs. Despite protest not stopping short of riot, between 1642 and 1654 a series of private initiatives, acts of Parliament, and administrative orders banned all secular celebration of the festival and all Christmas services in church. Christmas Day was declared a working day, with Parliament setting an example by sitting on 25 December. The preparation of Christmas pies was made a punishable offence, and feasting banned. The decoration of houses was forbidden, and in 1647, porters adorning the house of the lord mayor of London, no less, were arrested (Hutton, *Merry England* 209–11; Dawson 207–10).

The subsequent history of Christmas becomes more intelligible as we contemplate this singling out of the lord mayor's establishment. Open celebration of the festival by those in prominent positions was guaranteed to alienate the Puritan authorities, easy to spot, easy to suppress, and risky for those who wished to maintain their place in society. Dignitaries, aristocrats, landlords, leaders of great institutions had little choice but to comply.   As a result, a tradition already in decline was dealt a heavy blow.

But it was harder to know what humbler folk did in the privacy of their own homes with their own families, harder to exercise control over the remotest corners of the kingdom, harder to bring to heel those with little to lose.   "The Christmas customs and Festivities could not be abolished by the harsh measures of the republicans," Sandys justly observes, "though banished from high places . . . " (xl).   Communal Christmas customs sponsored by the elite dwindled, but modest domestic ones may even have thrived.   Evidence about festivities the authorities failed to suppress suggests they were, for the most part, private and modest.   Christmas became ever more centered around the family hearth.   Communal customs would be revived after the Restoration, to be sure, but those which survived for more than a few decades were ones which could be pursued without the patronage of the elite.

The Puritans, in fact, should not be blamed for doing more damage than they did.   The bans they imposed during the 1640s and 1650s were actively resisted, and nowhere near uniformly effective.   Pamphlets such as John Taylor's *Complaint of Christmas* (1646) indignantly suggest the festival was scarcely observed at all by the mid 1640s.   Public evidence of its celebration had undoubtedly diminished, but we should not overlook the effects of polemic zeal, or the fact that other testimony tells a different story – and even Taylor acknowledges the anger of tradesmen, apprentices, and servants who stood to lose from the neglect of old customs.

Many of these were falling out of fashion anyway, and beginning no longer to suit a changing way of life.   The revels of the Inns of Court, for instance, degenerated before Puritans were politically capable of imposing bans, and their discontinuance seems to have been accepted with little protest.

The way of life of the elite was changing, at least as much as anyone else's.   By the start of the seventeenth century, there was a widespread repudiation of their ancient duties by many of those who had traditionally sponsored Christmas revelry in the countryside for the majority of the population.   For many years, fewer and fewer landlords had been keeping open house at Christmas. Now fewer were at home to keep it. Puritan prohibitions only forbade what many had given up anyway.

During James I's reign, a debate developed about a noticeable migration of the aristocracy and gentry to London during the winter months, from October onwards. The king denounced those "swarms of gentry who, through the instigation of their wives and to new-model and fashion their daughters . . . did neglect their country hospitality and cumber the city, a general nuisance to the kingdom." Doubtless James was right to impute much of it to frivolity, but the increasing centralization of power and wealth lay behind it, too. The wealthy and influential had business to conduct in London. Charles I ordered landowners back to their estates from time to time, and in 1632 about a quarter of the peerage, a sixth of the baronets and knights, and 130 untitled gentlemen were hauled before Star Chamber for defying such an order (Inwood 206–07). Assuming all were caught who should have been, that is still an extraordinary number. The majority of landlords, of course, were still to be found on their estates at Christmas time, but it is not hard to imagine the effect upon them of their most powerful, prosperous, and fashionable neighbors being away in London during the festival, indifferent to their ancient role in it.

This annual migration to the capital excited popular criticism, as well as regal. In his 1622 "Christmas Carol," George Wither observes how some landlords were spending money at Christmas time, not on hospitality in the country, but

> On lust and pride at London.
> There the roisters they do play,
> Drab and dice their land away,
> Which may be ours another day;
> And therefore let's be merry.

Wither was probably unduly severe about the behavior of landlords, but changes were undoubtedly taking place in the routines of upper-class life, implying even greater changes in the relations between classes. These were the root cause of changes in the celebration of Christmas. The Puritan assault upon the festival did little more than accelerate the process.

Puritan measures against observances in church, to be sure, were largely effective while they were in force. That is something else easy to spot and control. Anglicans and royalists argued in support of Christmas services. Edward Fisher's *Feast of Feasts* (1644) declared Christmas to be as legitimate as any other Christian festival. But by 1656, there was a general recognition that appeal to Scripture was fruitless, and the Puritans would accept no other. Their case, in this respect at least, was unanswerable. The only possible validation of the Christmas liturgy was tradition, and tradition was now frowned upon. Eventually the conservatives desisted. From 1652 to 1655, the diarist John Evelyn was unable to find a church in London open on Christmas Day. In 1656 he took holy communion in a priest's home (Evelyn 3: 185), and in 1657 he attended a service at Exeter Chapel, but "The Chapell was surrounded with souldiers: All the communicants and assembly surpriz'd & kept Prisoners by them." Evelyn was asked

> why, contrarie to an Ordinance made that none should any longer observe the superstitious time of the *Nativity* (so esteem'd by them), I durst offend, & particularly be at *Common prayers*, which they told me was but the *Masse* in *English*, & particularly pray for Charles stuard, for which we had no Scripture. I told them we did not pray for Cha: Steward but for all *Christian Kings, Princes, & Governors.* The(y) replied, in so doing we praied for the K. of *Spaine* too, who was their Enemie & a papist, with other frivolous & insnaring questions, with much threatning, & finding no colour to detaine me longer, with much pitty for my Ignorance, they dismiss'd me. (3: 204)

Even in such a case, it seems, lack of legal instruments or of will limited the authorities' response to ineffectual finger-wagging, more embarrassing than threatening. And only three years later the traditions of the Anglican church were restored along with the monarchy.

No Puritan victory was ever secured over secular Christmas customs practised by humbler and more obscure members of society. Thanks to absenteeism among employees, *The True Informer* – a newspaper which supported the parliamentary cause – failed to appear at Christmas in

1645, "the temper and disposition of the vulgar," it sourly notes, "being wholly taken up with recreation." In 1646, apprentices rioted in Bury-St-Edmunds against shops staying open on Christmas Day. In 1647, in Canterbury, a mob vandalized shops open on 25 December. Father Christmas, in *The Vindication of Christmas* (1653), rejoices in his warm reception by Devon farmers, and drily observes, " . . . welcome, or not welcome, I am come" (Hutton, *Merry England* 209–11; Sandys xl-xli).

Tracts were published justifying the feast by reminding readers of the charity, fellowship, and jollity associated with it. The citizens of London were plainly less than thoroughly persuaded by Puritan strictures. In 1650, 1656, and 1657, it is recorded, most shops in the city were shut on Christmas Day. In 1652 the widespread feasting and singing of carols was commented upon. In 1654, the Venetian ambassador reported festivities lasting almost a week.

The same year, provincial ministers, evidently Puritan in their sympathies, complained of parishioners clinging to "customary and promiscuous communions" at Christmas, while royalists boasted of churches being "excellently adorned with rosemary and bays." Mumming was put down in the Lancashire parish of Woodplumpton in 1648, but remained unsuppressed in Calne, Wiltshire, as late as 1655. Celebrations in Devon and Cornwall, John Taylor reported in 1652, continued unabated, with card-playing, carol-singing, dancing, drinking, and the playing of traditional games, such as "Hotcockles, Shoeing The Wild Mare and the like harmless sports" (Hutton, *Merry England* 215–16).

Looking back after the Restoration, a contemporary versifier commented:

> The high-shoe lords of Cromwell's making
> Were not for dainties – roasting, baking;
> The chiefest food they found most good in
> Was rusty bacon and bag-pudding;
> Plum-broth was popish, and mince-pie –
> O that was flat idolatry. (Pimlott 46[6])

It is by no means an unfair summary of the Puritan assault on Christmas customs, but the bantering tone is a sign of how ineffectual that assault had been on the practices of the majority, and how easily its effects were shaken off. That is not to say it had no effect at all, but the effect it did have was not so much to diminish Christmas festivities as to encourage change in them.

George Wither's poem, "A Christmas Carol" was among the last robust affirmations of the old Christmas traditions before the Civil War. Plodding though his verse is, as an historical document the poem is valuable because it painstakingly enumerates customs practiced.   It extols sociability, hospitality, merriness, charity, and the deliberate confounding of rank.   It rejoices in plenty, feasting, drinking, music, singing, dancing, folly, tricks, games, Christmas pies, Yule logs, decorations of greenery, personal adornment, wassailing, Christmas boxes, and mumming, Christmas is "our joyful'st feast," he declares:

> Though some churls at our mirth repine,
> Round your foreheads garlands twine,
> Drown sorrow in a cup of wine,
> And let us all be merry.

Those are words he published in 1622.   Very soon afterwards Wither became a Puritan convert, and devoted the rest of his writing career to religious and political causes.   In the English Civil War, he served on the parliamentary side.

Henry Vaughan was an entirely different kind of writer – much better to begin with, but an Anglo-Catholic visionary too, and a royalist. By profession a physician, Vaughan, it is believed, served as a surgeon with the royalist army.   Yet his poem "The True Christmas" (1678) is perhaps the most powerful lament to be published, after the Restoration, for Puritan austerity:

> So, stick up *ivy* and the *bays*,
> And then restore the *heathen* ways.
> Green will remind you of the spring,
> Though this great day denies the thing;
> And mortifies the Earth, and all
> But your wild *revels*, and loose *hall*.
> Could you wear *flowers*, and *roses* strow

Blushing upon your breasts' *warm snow*,
That very *dress* your lightness will
Rebuke, and wither at the ill.
The brightness of this day we owe
Not unto *music, masque*, nor *show*:
Nor gallant *furniture*, nor *plate*,
But to the *manger's* mean estate.
His *life* while here, as well as *birth*,
Was but a check to *pomp* and *mirth*;
And all man's *greatness* you may see
Condemned by his *humility*.
Then leave your open *house* and *noise*,
To welcome him with *holy joys*,
And the poor *shepherds'* watchfulness;
Whom *light* and *hymns* from Heaven did bless.
What you *abound* with cast abroad
To those that *want*, and ease your load.
Who empties thus will bring more in;
But riot is both loss and sin.
Dress finely what comes not in sight,
And then you keep your *Christmas* right!
(Vaughan 374)

This is vastly more persuasive than either Prynne's insolent pamphleteering or Wither's unreformed jollity. The poem begins by testily echoing the old normative texts, prescribing Christmas rituals. The imperative mood predominates throughout. But ironic prescription is succeeded by earnest, and the feudal call for communal ritual mutates into something more familiar to modern ears. The Nativity myth is now read as an invitation, not to sociability, but to inward contemplation. The narrative foregrounded is the private narrative of personal redemption. The poem, in fact, dramatically enacts emergence from a medieval mindset into a self-consciously modern one.

A lover of old Christmas customs could support the Puritan cause, then, a royalist and an Anglican denounce them as heathenish. This is not what the popular understanding of the history of Christmas leads us to expect. Stereotypes are being violated here. What surer indication could there be that to blame change in the celebration of the festival chiefly on Puritan antagonism is to offer an inadequate explanation?

Social change, rather, and a related shift in sensibility, were at the root of ritual change. Puritan antagonism accelerated change, and confirmed the shift in sensibility. But even without the indignities it suffered at Puritan hands in the 1640s and 1650s, it seems reasonable to suppose, Christmas would have become more private and domestic. Most of the population remained devoted to the festival, and enthusiastic about it, but they gradually settled for celebrating it differently, more intimately, at home, and in gatherings they themselves organized. Such a development was both practical, and suited to the emerging temper of the age. It would be many years, though, before it had much of an impact on literary culture.

Dickens understood what had happened, and was the first great writer to make a point of reflecting it. He made little of the Puritans' role in modifying Christmas festivities. In *A Child's History of England*, he judges the Puritans with notable restraint and evenhandedness. Written in a simple style for its young readers, the book is nevertheless emphatic in the Whiggish verdicts it reaches. The author's distaste for the Puritans of Elizabeth I's reign is plain enough. In his view they were, "for the most part an uncomfortable people, who thought it highly meritorious to dress in a hideous manner, talk through their noses, and oppose all harmless enjoyments" (289). But Dickens's Radical sympathies persuaded him to extol members of the Long Parliament as "spirited and determined men" (325), and to forbear mentioning religious affairs at all under Oliver Cromwell (345–60).

Not the least of Dickens's achievements, indeed, in the transformation of Christmas he effected, was reaching an accommodation with the kind of attitude expressed in "The True Christmas." He was second to none in his support for traditional merrymaking, and all the rituals of the season, but for him the festival was more important for the place it could assume within private narratives. For the individual, in his vision of the festival, the coming round of Christmas each year marked growth or decay, success or failure in enterprises human beings give their hearts to. The festival was a time for inward contemplation, self-discovery, and personal redemption.

Dickens, in fact, met and countered at least some of the Puritans' objections to Christmas. He had none to overcome in himself, though, as we shall see. He had been reared among those affected neither by Puritan prejudice against the festival, nor by any other – among a class, that is to say, whose members, along with the bulk of the population, had never ceased enthusiastically to celebrate Christmas.

THE ENGLISH CHRISTMAS, 1660 TO 1840

On 29 May 1660, Charles II entered London amid wild rejoicing. He had landed at Dover four days earlier, and ridden to the capital along roads lined with well-wishers, many weeping unashamedly. At Blackheath he had been greeted with a morris dance, and then escorted in triumph to Whitehall by the lord mayor, at the head of a procession of 120,000 people. Thanks to widespread consent, the monarchy was restored.

The Restoration had been preceded by defiant taunting of the faltering Commonwealth authorities. Across the country on May Day, four weeks earlier, there had been a rash of maypoles – forbidden for nearly twenty years – and some incautious Puritan objectors had been roughly handled.

During the months that followed, however, a spirited rearguard action was fought in defence of Puritan practices. In July, a Presbyterian minister, Thomas Hall, published a tract, *Funebriae Florae*, denouncing the maypoles that had reappeared two months earlier, and warning against the temptations that Christmas would bring. He repeated and elaborated Prynne's arguments about the pagan origins of the festival. Prynne, indeed, was a member of the transitional Convention Parliament (1660–1661), one of the block of unreconstructed Puritans who, Restoration notwithstanding, attempted to perpetuate the Puritan social order.

The attempt was unsuccessful, it should be said. The ban on Christmas services was lifted immediately. At Christmas 1660, in cathedrals especially, members of the restored Anglican hierarchy celebrated the feast punctiliously. And then, in May 1661, after a meeting between the Cavalier Parliament and the Convocation of the Church of England, the traditional liturgy was re-established. As a result, by the end of 1662 the old calendar of the Church year was being followed, and traditional customs were being lawfully practised. (Hutton, *Merry England* 223–25; Pimlott 61).

To many it must have seemed as if Christmas was being restored to what it once had been. The putting back of clocks, however, has no effect on the passage of time. The festival would be rehabilitated, certainly, but, as with the monarchy, too much had changed for there to be a return to the status quo ante. Society had changed and was continuing to change. The same was true of habits and attitudes. The old Christmas was irrecoverable. A new kind would have to evolve. For the majority of the population, Christmas never ceased to be the most popular festival of the year, but where it was celebrated, how it was celebrated, and by whom it was celebrated most vigorously, would all change. Some customs would die out. Some would become more popular. Some new ones would be developed. But still the festival would flourish.

We cannot clearly see that this was so, however, unless we carefully sift such evidence as there is. It is not always easy to distinguish the real from the ideal in sources produced between 1660 and 1840. Among them, we can find rejoicing at the revival of customs which were in fact dying out, lamentation at the decline of customs which we can deduce to have been in good health, and indifference to customs which were soon to prove popular. Literary texts still admired today are particularly unhelpful, and often misleading. Between the Restoration and the beginning of the nineteenth century, talented writers grew less and less interested in Christmas as a subject. After the first decade or so of the eighteenth century, published works of any merit tended to reflect the embarrassment felt by the metropolitan elite at Christmas. That was a response, though, that the majority of the population never shared.

Magazine articles, letters, diaries, household records, and other informal sources often provide more reliable testimony than literary texts – no less oblique, perhaps, but usually less prejudiced. At the end of 1785, for instance, Edward Phelips, the squire of Montacute in Somerset, made a note of the fact that "in the course of the Xmas Holidays I began Digging the foundation of the New West Front."[1] Typically, this tells us nothing of what the holidays were devoted to, apart from digging, but at least it shows they were observed, and it needs no deciphering.

Much of the source material is confusing because attitudes towards Christmas were varied, and in a state of flux. I have shown how Puritan attitudes towards the festival during the Interregnum had less of an effect upon it than is often supposed. Their effect after the Restoration was even smaller and, over the years, diminished perceptibly. Even so, Puritan disapproval persisted for a generation or two, and had to be reckoned with. If it did nothing else, it provided a precedent for indifference towards Christmas.

As we have seen, Puritans did not just capitulate and vanish in 1660. On the contrary, they survived and flourished, some unreconstructed, some adapting by mutation. At odds with the established Church, unreconstructed Puritans would henceforth be known as Dissenters or Nonconformists. They continued to speak out on religious, moral, and political matters. The spiritual independence they claimed appealed to many members of the ever-more-confident middle classes. And for the more zealous among them, Christmas remained a heathen and papist festival. Many dissenting shopkeepers persisted in opening for business on Christmas Day. Early in the next century the *Spectator* character, Hezekiah Thrift, would denounce the beadles and officers of the Royal Exchange for indolence, and for having "the impudence at Christmas to ask for their box" (*Spectator* 4: 106). His name alone would have told readers he was a Dissenter.

The objections of Dissenters gradually grew more muted, however. They did not speak with one voice, and rivalry diminished their influence. Sects dissented from other sects as frequently and as intemperately as they did from the established Church. Presbyterians and Quakers, for instance, shunned the festival for generations. A few still do. But Methodists, evolving in the eighteenth century, rejoiced in it. Over the years, moreover, tolerance grew among Dissenting congregations. Their pronouncements became less and less abrasive. Some withdrew into redoubts of doctrinal purity, but ceased to demand everyone else join them there. Others relented. Another *Spectator* character, Sir Roger de Coverley, would commend the 1711 Act of Occasional Conformity, and find evidence of its beneficial effect in the way a "rigid Dissenter," dining with him on Christmas Day that year, "had been observed to eat very plentifully of his Plumb-porridge" (*Spectator* 2: 303).

By the early nineteenth century, in England at any rate, only antiquarians, and members of a few isolated sects, would remember the old Puritan objections to Christmas. By then, indeed, some Dissenters were attending Anglican Christmas services, to assert their right to do so, a gesture which would have appalled their Puritan predecessors.[2] Scruples about precisely how to celebrate persisted, but public antipathy towards any celebration whatsoever had become rare.

A change in Anglican attitudes was more lasting and influential than residual Puritan disapproval. It was a change not simply to be explained by the popularity of Calvinist doctrines among erstwhile Puritans who had rejoined the main stream of the established Church. In the 1630s and 1640s, Archbishop Laud's doctrines had seemed the antithesis of Puritanism, yet he had chosen to fight Puritans on their own ground. He bequeathed to posterity an example of sober and conscientious inquiry into ritual tradition, not to be identified with Puritan theological correctness, but addressing the same theological problems. We saw in the last chapter how, in the spirit of Laud, Thomas Warmstry had defended Christmas customs, and recommended the singing of carols, so long as they were "used with Christian sobriety and purity" (see p. 46 above). Written after the Restoration, Henry Vaughan's "The True Christmas," also quoted in chapter 2, exemplifies the same spirit, if with a different emphasis (see pp. 51–52 above). Vaughan exhorts Christians to repudiate the old ways of celebrating the birth of Christ:

> Then leave your open *house* and *noise*,
> To welcome him with *holy joys* . . . .

Warmstry and Vaughan captured a growing mood. Restraint, the tempering of mirth with piety, became an increasingly popular theme among thoughtful Anglicans after the Restoration, as they contemplated Christmas. On Christmas Day 1662, Samuel Pepys heard George Morley, bishop of Winchester, preach in the Chapel Royal, Westminster. Morley extolled Christmas joy and hospitality, but deplored "the common jollity of the court," and reproached courtiers for "their excess in playes and gaming." "Upon which it was worth observing," Pepys notes, "how far they are come from taking the Reprehensions of a bishop seriously, that they all laugh in chapel when he reflected on their ill actions and courses" (Pepys 3: 293).

The scorn of courtiers notwithstanding, Morley's admonition continued to reverberate. On Christmas Day 1704, the sermon of the popular preacher Offspring Blackall, at St. Dunstan's in the West in London, was devoted to *The Lawfulness and the Right Manner of Keeping Christmas and Other Festivals*. "This is the time, the time of the whole year, for good Eating and Drinking," he grants, but regrets that "our thoughts are commonly taken up and our time so much employed in these things, that we have no mind to, or no leisure for anything that is good" (Blackall 4–5). Clerical laxity during the eighteenth century was to become notorious, but this conscientious spirit was kept alive, and did much to animate the evangelical movement late in the century.

The absorption of some Puritan doctrines by the Anglican clergy, it is clear, and the carefully argued repudiation of others, yielded scruples which were translated into action, which persisted, and which, for many, changed the mood of Christmas celebrations. It was not only dissenting congregations, for instance, which eschewed Christmas greenery; not a few Anglican churches remained undecorated.[3] And carols were once again agonized over. It was in the established Church, now, that anxiety about their secular content spread, and mistrust of carols prevailed. For most of the eighteenth century, only one was officially encouraged in Church of England Christmas services – Nahum Tate's "While shepherds watched" (written around 1698), which reassuringly follows St. Luke's narrative (Bradley xiii).

From 1660 onwards, in fact, the impulse towards license and excess that characterized Restoration manners and morals was challenged. If the Commonwealth experience had wearied people of killjoy injunction, it had also made them wary of any sentiment too emphatic or extreme. As the era of self-conscious reaction gave way, as political developments in Europe and domestic events like the Glorious Revolution of 1688 vindicated compromise, many leaders of opinion and taste would begin to deplore "enthusiasm," as they disapprovingly called it. They recommended restraint, moderation, balance, reason. The frame of mind that characterized the restoration of the old order favored extravagant merrymaking at Christmas, but it was not a frame of mind which would endure into the Augustan age, and it would soon lose influence.

We should not be surprised, then, to find some old customs revived in a way that was patchy and temporary. It was possible once more openly to enjoy "good brawne and Christmas pie, roast-beef and plum-porridge"; there is no doubt about that. Alms distribution to the poor was resumed (Huelin 168–69). Christmas persisted as one of the three customary annual holidays for London apprentices (Pimlott 61). But the grand Christmas gestures of the great, despite strong emotional attachment to them, were never to recover their old confident glory. Hospitality on a magnificent scale, of the kind that had once characterized the festival, was becoming ever rarer. Puritan bans had weakened adherence to old habits, and others were beginning to prevail.

Many at the time, it should be said, believed quite otherwise, and boasted about the recovery of the old order. A late seventeenth-century ballad claimed that landowners were once again celebrating Christmas with open house:

> All travellers as they do pass on the way
> At gentlemen's halls are invited to stay.

But evidence suggests that, although there may have been some short-lived exceptions, this was not generally the case. Sentimental claims of this kind were made from time to time for many years, evidently based more on wishful thinking than on actual practice (Hutton, *Merry England* 243).

In the years following the Restoration, to be sure, there were examples of traditional hospitality being resumed – if not the custom of open house. At the royal court, every effort was made to reverse change and restore the old Christmas. Charles II once again hosted balls and parties during the festive season, making a special feature of Twelfth Night, now always celebrated on 6 January. But even here some change was tolerated, not to say welcomed. Masques, for instance, deemed old-fashioned, were discontinued, and gambling took on greater prominence

(Hutton, *Merry England* 241). The old courtly rituals gave way to something exposed, even by the third Christmas of the Restoration, to criticism such as the bishop of Winchester's.

Venerable institutions like the Oxford and Cambridge colleges, which, for unavoidable reasons, preserved a communal life centered on the great hall, resumed their revels. At least two Oxford colleges, Merton and St. John's, were electing Lords of Misrule as late as the 1690s, and festivities of one kind or another persisted for many years.

In 1773, for instance, the Rev. James Woodforde was Sub-Warden of New College, Oxford. Christmas Day customs he records in his diary include attendance at chapel, followed by a "very handsome dinner of my ordering" for the senior fellows. They ate cod and sole in oyster sauce, roast sirloin, pea soup, orange pudding, wild duck, forequarter of lamb, salad and mince pies, with plum cake to follow. Toasts were exchanged in an elaborate ceremony during the dinner:

> We had a grace cup before the second course brought by the Butler to the Steward of the Hall who was Mr. Adams a Senior Fellow, who got out of his place and came to my chair and there drank to me out of it, wishing me a merry Xmas. I then took it of him and drank wishing him the same, and then it went round, three standing up all the time. From the high Table the grace Cup goes to the Batchelors and Scholars. (Woodforde 86)

At Queen's College, the Boar's Head Gaudy was celebrated, as it had been since the middle ages, as indeed it is today. The head was carried in procession into the hall on a silver salver, followed by the choristers singing the Boar's Head Carol (Selander).

Notwithstanding the degeneration of their revels before the Civil War, the Inns of Court also seem to have revived the custom of appointing a Lord of Misrule, and to have persisted in it well into the eighteenth century (Dawson 218). Both the university colleges and the Inns of Court, however, eventually dropped this practice, in favour of more decorous celebrations. In institutions less wedded to tradition, like the court, there was evidently insufficient will even to revive the custom, or too much anxiety about the confounding of rank.

Immediately after the Restoration, some country landlords strove once again to play a central role among their neighbors at Christmas time. Sir Justinian Isham entertained the poor, local laborers, and the "better class inhabitants," in two Northamptonshire villages. Sir John Reresby fed his tenants, the local Yorkshire gentry, the local clergy, and tradesmen, all on different days during the Christmas season (Hutton, *Merry England* 243). Others were more halfhearted. Pepys tells with relish a story about his erstwhile employer, the public servant and financial advisor Sir George Downing. Sir George sought to create a good impression at Christmas 1666, by inviting poor neighbors to his country mansion, "but did give them nothing but beef, porridge, pudding, and pork, and nothing said all dinner, but only his mother would say, 'It's good broth, son.' He would answer, 'Yes, it is good broth' . . . ." Sir George's guests accepted his invitation, in Pepys's judgment, "not out of love or esteem . . . , but to eat his victuals, knowing him to be a niggardly fellow; and with this he is jeered now all over the country" (Pepys 8: 85). None of these landowners, note, kept open house. They invited specific guests on specific occasions.

But they were following ancient custom by spending Christmas on their estates rather than in London. And in this, at any rate, they were not quite alone. One metropolitan observer, around 1730, noted that "several of the Gentry are gone down to their respective Seats in the Country, in order to keep their *Christmas* in the old way, and entertain their Tenants and Trades-folks as their Ancestors used to do" (*Round about our Coal Fire* 6).

Some, doubtless, spent Christmas in the country, because they could not afford to do otherwise. Others had reasons for avoiding London. There were Catholics, for instance, like the Tempests of Broughton Hall, near Skipton, who rarely visited the capital before the Catholic Emancipation Act of 1829. At Broughton Hall, family and servants cherished their own customs, and began Christmas every year by attending midnight mass together in the family chapel.[4] Still others returned to the country because they loved to do so. The Digby family, for instance, always kept Christmas at Sherborne Castle.

Household accounts, however, suggest that, during the eighteenth century, it became the custom for key staff at Sherborne not to work on Christmas Day, and for the family to make little of it. No longer did landlord, servants, and dependants spend the feast together in communal revelry. The Digbys did, to be sure, invite neighbors and relations to dinner on 26 and 27 December.[5]   But this scarcely amounted to communal revelry.   To keep Christmas in the country, too much after the old manner, was tantamount to declaring yourself at best resolutely old-fashioned, at worst ignorantly unfashionable and devoid of metropolitan clout.

Ever fewer landlords, in fact, were to be found entertaining in the country at Christmas time, in however subdued a manner. Early Stuart London had attracted members of the aristocracy and gentry during the winter months. Late Stuart and Hanoverian London attracted even more of them. The city once again became the center for both serious affairs and frivolous pleasures. From 1689, Parliament sat annually, normally from November to May.   Most of the peerage, and around 500 gentlemen, needed to be in town for its sittings. Others, with interests in the law, business, the arts, or fashion, found it convenient or agreeable to emulate. Wives and children, doubtless, clamoured to accompany the menfolk. Soho, St. James's, and Mayfair were developed as fashionable quarters for the town houses of landowners, occupied by them and their families during the Season (Inwood 251–52). The attraction of London at Christmas is indicated in a 1670 ballad, "The Old and Young Courtier":

> With a new fashion, when Christmas is drawing on,
> On a new journey to London straight we all must begone,
> And leave none to keep house, but our new porter John,
> Who relieves the poor with a thump on the back with a stone.
> (Dawson 217)

The scansion may be elusive, but the information is plain enough.

By the beginning of the eighteenth century, it must have been apparent that open house in the squire's great hall at Christmas was a thing of the past, dying out if not quite dead. One prominent piece of evidence at first sight seems to contradict that, but not on closer inspection.   Joseph Addison's account of Sir Roger de Coverley's Christmas was published in the *Spectator* of 8 January 1712. Readers are told that

> Sir Roger, after the laudable Custom of his Ancestors, always
> keeps open House at *Christmas*. I learned from him, that he had

killed eight fat Hogs for the Season, that he had dealt about his
Chines very liberally among his Neighbours, and that in
particular he had sent a string of Hog-puddings with a pack of
cards to every poor Family in the Parish. I have often thought,
says Sir ROGER, it happens very well that *Christmas* should fall
out in the Middle of Winter. It is the most dead, uncomfortable
Time of the Year, when the poor people would suffer very much
from their Poverty and Cold, if they had not good Cheer, warm
Fires, and *Christmas* Gambols to support them. I love to rejoyce
their poor Hearts at this Season, and to see the whole Village
merry in my great Hall. (*Spectator* 2: 303).

On the face of it this seems a declaration that change was being
resisted. But it is fiction, and the "good old Knight" was, from the
outset, designed as a self-evident anachronism. Readers' attention
would have been captured by the oddity of his conduct. "He is a
Gentleman that is very singular in his Behaviour," they had been told
when first introduced to him on 2 March 1711, "but his Singularities
proceed from his good Sense, and are Contradictions to the Manners of
the World, only as he thinks the World is in the wrong" (*Spectator* 1: 6).
Sir Roger was created, not to reflect contemporary behavior, but to
critique it. The description of his Christmas was published, it is worth
noting, not just before the festival, as Dickens's Christmas books and
stories were, but two weeks after it. The intention was to provide
readers, not with a model to imitate, but with a contrast to reproach their
own recent festivities. There was an ever-widening gap between
precept and practice. By around 1730, this would be openly
acknowledged. It was only "in former Times," we are told, that "every
one in the Country where a Gentleman resided, possess'd at least a Day
of Pleasure in the *Christmas* Holy days" (*Round about our Coal Fire*
2–3).
  Sir Roger would have been seen as old-fashioned, not least in his still
maintaining a great hall as such, in which to keep Christmas. The great
hall was not merely an indispensable architectural space for celebrations
in the old manner. It was an affirmation of the social order of which
such celebrations were an expression, the social order for which there is
no better term than feudal – hierarchical, but aspiring to harmonious
integration. The great hall was one of the places where all the

intricacies of such a society were on show, and tested. Now, however, the gradual decline of the hall into a mere entrance lobby was under way.

As early as the sixteenth century, builders of country mansions had begun to construct halls smaller than formerly, plainly of less significance than once they had been in the life of a household. Now, new mansions no longer featured a great hall at all. Many old halls, meanwhile, were being divided up, or adapted to new functions. The fashion for this had been launched even before the Interregnum. At the little manor-house of Westwood, in Wiltshire, some time between 1616 and 1642, John Farewell split his great hall into lower and upper halves. The lower became a spacious but low-ceilinged entrance lobby, the upper a handsome great parlour (Sutton 18–22). In 1650, Edmund Prideaux shortened the magnificent great hall at Forde Abbey, Dorset, built by its last abbot. Prideaux's reconstruction could scarcely have been more eloquent. He partitioned off the dais where once the high table had stood, and in its place constructed a private family dining room (*Forde Abbey* 8). At Powderham Castle in Devon, Sir William Courtenay partitioned his great hall into two compartments, installing an elegant new staircase in one, and converting the other into a family parlour. This work was completed by 1736 (*Powderham Castle* 8, 13).

In some grander country houses, to be sure, entrance halls big in size continued to be in favor. As late as 1756, the architect Isaac Ware recommended they should be "large and noble," so that they could be used for dining in summer, and for receptions "at public feasts." But there was a touch of nostalgia even in this. Offering hospitality to the whole neighborhood, at whatever time of year, was passing out of fashion. Instead, the gentry and aristocracy concentrated on entertaining country neighbors of equal or near equal rank. And for this they demanded what exiled royalist grandees had grown used to on the Continent during the Interregnum: a series of elegant saloons running into each other, comfortably removed from the hall and front entrance. Even the most modest mansion now featured a separate dining room and drawing room, each adapted to its purpose and distinct from the other. The hall had long since ceased to function as a common living room for the entire household, into which the greater part of the surrounding community might be invited (Girouard 88, 126, 136, 194). Social change was making the great hall redundant, and its disappearance was in turn accelerating social change.

In London there were no local communities towards which country landowners might feel obligations, but even if they had wanted to recreate traditional Christmas celebrations there, few had suitable accommodation in which to do so. The old palaces of the nobility on the Strand and elsewhere had become alienated, and been allowed to decay. After the Restoration, only a few grandees commissioned splendid new mansions in town, like Burlington House or Clarendon House. Most aristocrats and gentlemen settled for bourgeois accommodation writ large: relatively spacious terraced houses, that is to say. Isaac Ware owned that the hall in a gentleman's town house need be only a vestibule. Horace Walpole remarked in 1743 on the way the nobility in London had "contracted themselves to live in coops of a dining room, a dark back room with one eye in a corner, and a closet." Some offered lavish Christmas hospitality in such accommodation, but only to the selected friends and relations who could be fitted into it (Girouard 136; Inwood 253; Dawson 232).

These developments in architectural style and social habit were signs of radical economic and demographic change, rendering the traditional Christmas in the "hall," under the eye of the "master," ever more archaic. Nothing is easier than overestimating the coherence of the old manorial communities, but it can scarcely be disputed that, during the late seventeenth century, urbanization, developments in agricultural technology, and rural impoverishment were loosening the tie between the great house and its hinterland. Landlords were once again beginning to enclose common land. New methods of agriculture required less labor. The surplus rural population was drifting to the towns. Agricultural workers who remained in the countryside became poorer. Inevitably, the gulf between the great house and the cottage deepened. During the following century it would deepen further, as more and more estates were bought up by men with little knowledge of country traditions, and little interest in maintaining them, who had prospered in commerce and industry.

Relations within the great house were changing, too. How, can be illustrated by changes detectable in the use of the word *family*. The Latin word *familia* had been used primarily to designate the servants and

slaves of a household. Before 1660, the English word was understood
to mean everyone under the same roof: parents, children, servants –
servants' dependants even. The entire retinue of a monarch or a
nobleman was his family, the entire household of a gentleman or
member of the bourgeoisie. *Family* in the modern sense – parents and
their children but not those living under the same roof unrelated by
blood – can not be dated earlier than 1667. Pepys, in the 1660s,
included his servants when he spoke of his family, but the usage would
soon become archaic (although servants themselves, and the
linguistically conservative, would continue to use it in the old sense well
into the nineteenth century). A new distinction was being made,
reflecting the growing separation of employers and employed in the
great house.

Noblemen and gentlemen were now distanced, socially, from all but
a few of their country neighbors, and were choosing to pass the better
part of their lives with their relations only, in private rooms where
servants came only to perform duties. The upper-class sensibility was
rearranging itself around the family instead of the community, just as the
bourgeois sensibility had already done. For most members of the upper
classes now, the thought of communal festivities – of being cheek by
jowl with servants, tenants, and dependants throughout the Christmas
season – was becoming unenticing.

Changes such as these finally put an end to communal Christmas
festivities under the patronage of the squire. It should not be supposed,
though, that only former recipients of patrician hospitality felt the loss.
Members of the patrician classes themselves, so the evidence suggests,
were made uneasy by what had happened, however much it was their
choice. A splendid meal shared with all one's closest relations was no
once-a-year rarity for the rich and the leisured. For them, Christmas
celebrations in the new style held fewer attractions than they did for
poorer folk. But presiding once a year over the revels of an entire
community was an irreplaceable experience, unwelcome demands for
affability notwithstanding. The upper classes had lost a role at
Christmas time. It was a role few coveted any longer, but with it went a
dignity some seem to have regretted. Vague expectations lingered about
the responsibilities of the nobility and gentry during the festival. Few
wanted to meet all of those expectations. Fewer still wanted to be

stigmatized for disappointing them.

During the eighteenth century, strategies evolved for coping with this unease.   Puritan hostility to Christmas provided a precedent, the Anglican emphasis on restraint a pretext, but minds were made up by a change in manners. Elegance, urbanity, civility – none of these were easy to reconcile with robust merrymaking. Laughter now became the fashionable response to what were seen as archaic customs and vulgar revels. Transgressive behaviour, of which there was certainly some, was made a justification for disdaining the festival. By the closing decades of the century, there was a barely suppressed wish among members of the upper classes that Christmas, as a social occasion at any rate, might be forgotten about entirely, and a manifest instinct to treat it as no more than a painful annual embarrassment.

The growth of this attitude can be traced. In his *Trivia* of 1716, John Gay declares Christmas "the joyous period of the year" (Gay 75). After that date, for the rest of the century, such unequivocal appreciation became rare. What is implicit in the account of Sir Roger de Coverley's Christmas became explicit. Making much of Christmas ceased to be fashionable.

As a Catholic, Pope stood aside from English fretting about the celebration of Christmas, but he was ever alert to fashionable posturing, and ever ready with irony. He saw the way attitudes were changing. Writing to another Catholic, John Caryll, at Christmas in 1717, the year after the publication of Gay's *Trivia*, he declared:

> I am strongly inclined to think that there are at this very day at Grinstead, certain antique charities and obsolete devotions yet in being: that a thing call'd Christian cheerfulness, ([not] incompatible with Christmass pies and plum-broth) whereof frequent is the mention in old sermons and almanacs, is really kept alive and in practice at the said place: That feeding the hungry and giving alms to the poor, do yet make a part of good housekeeping in a latitude not more remote from London than forty miles; and lastly that prayers and roast beef, do actually make some folk as happy, as a whore and a bottle. (Pope 1: 457)

Horace Walpole was unquestionably one of the patrician classes. He was a member of parliament, and an inheritor of the culture of the Whig grandee. In violation of conventional taste, however, he was a lover of all things medieval. He made his home, Strawberry Hill near Twickenham, into "a little Gothic castle," and his *Castle of Otranto* (1764) is generally regarded as the first Gothic novel. Few eighteenth-century figures, you might think, were more likely to appreciate the old-fashioned festival, but Walpole was evidently in two minds about it. In a letter he wrote to Sir Horace Mann from Strawberry Hill, on 26 December 1748, there is a mixture of defiance and apology. "Here am I come down to what you call keep my Christmas!" he tells him. "Indeed it is not in all the forms; I have stuck no laurel and holly in my windows, I eat not turkey and chine, I have no tenants to invite, I have not brought a single soul with me" (Walpole 16). As a keen antiquarian Walpole was well aware of customs endorsed by ancient practice, but he was unable sufficiently to free himself from fashion, to practice many of them himself.

Less reflective minds were unafflicted with such perplexities. For the wealthy authoress and society hostess, Elizabeth Montagu, Christmas in 1774 was just dreary. In her circle, many families went down to their estates briefly at Christmas time, but returned to London for the New Year, for festivities in the royal drawing room. "When our Maccoroni [sic] Beaux and Coterie dames go into the Country to pass the Christmas Holydays I have no great opinion of the festivity and joy of the party," she wrote. "Its [sic] for the young." Many of those who go to their "drery [sic] mansions," she foretold, "will not laugh till they return to town."[6]

She spoke for members of the *ton*, as it was known. Their preoccupation with politics, gossip, and sexual intrigue left them little time or energy for traditional festivities. Families that made up the *ton* might spend Christmas in their own country mansions, in the mansions of friends, in London, or abroad, but they were reluctant to entertain the same circle of neighbors and dependants, in the same house, year after year.[7]

An account of a "Christmas-Day Entertainment," published in 1778, expresses what had become the fashionable attitude, by then, towards any Christmas festivities incorporating the old traditions. Readers are told of a gathering in the house of a country squire. "A great chine of bacon and an overgrown two years old turkey" mark the season, plus a little music, badly performed. The chief diversion is malicious gossip. Only once is there any indication of joy, and even that is mischievous. One old lady declares plum porridge an inappropriate dish at Christmas, on the curious grounds of its provoking lust. The young ladies, however, dispute this: "Why, it is a festival time, in which we not only ought to be very merry ourselves, but assist in making all others about us so" (Lovefun 48–61).

Fashionable attitudes began to change again as the eighteenth century gave way to the nineteenth, but for several decades a largely unvoiced indifference towards the festival lingered on among the aristocracy, gentry, and upper-middle classes who, so the evidence suggests, barely noticed its annual passing. Between 1790 and 1835, we note, as its date came around each year, *The Times* forbore even to mention Christmas (Hutton, *Stations of the Sun* 112).

Fiction, however, probably offers a better balanced representation of this neglect than any accumulation of factual data can. An episode of Jane Austen's *Emma*, published in 1816, indicates just how cool sentiments towards the festival had become among the prosperous and the leisured. Characters in the novel are invited to a Christmas Eve dinner at a country mansion. What the narrative excludes is as significant as what it includes. No mention is made of any Christmas custom save visiting friends. What the dinner guests eat is unrevealed – no mention is made of festive fare. All but one of them behave precisely as they do at other times, conversing politely and speculating on the meaning of what others say or do.

Emma's father, Mr. Woodhouse, a valetudinarian, is indignant at being asked to spend an evening away from home in December, Christmas or not. "A man," he says, "must have a very good opinion of himself when he asks people to leave their own fireside, and encounter such a day as this, for the sake of coming to see him. He must think himself a most agreeable fellow; I could not do such a thing."

Only the young vicar of Highbury, Mr. Elton, notable for imperfect manners and conceit, alludes in any way to the festival:

> " . . . This is quite the season indeed for friendly meetings. At Christmas every body invites their friends about them, and people think little of even the worst weather. I was snowed up at a friend's house once for a week. Nothing could be pleasanter. I

went for only one night, and could not get away till that very day
se'nnight." (ch. 13)

We cannot miss, behind the sententiousness, his indifference to Mr.
Woodhouse's apprehensions, and his appetite for self-gratification.
These undermine our confidence in his judgment, and make us see the
bare mention of Christmas as a solecism.

Emma herself wakes up on Christmas morning rejoicing, but only
because thick snow stops her attending divine service conducted by Mr.
Elton, who had made an unwelcome proposal of marriage to her after
the dinner party (ch. 14).   Thanks perhaps to the influence of
evangelicalism, overt distaste for Christmas is no longer evident, but no
one could call this merrymaking.

Merrymaking belonged to the past, many felt – to the master's great hall,
and to communities of a kind that no longer existed.   Christmas was
inevitably no more than a shadow of its former self – a social occasion
barely distinguishable from others, however much of an event it might
be in the Church calendar.   Notions such as this, however, took no
account of plebeian devotion to the festival. Broadly speaking, for most
of the   period between 1660 and 1840, the lower people were in the
social hierarchy, the more likely they were to celebrate Christmas
vigorously.

In the years following the Restoration, the poorer classes celebrated
the festival openly, with little inhibition, and regardless of patronage.
"The Shrop-shire Wakes" is a broadside ballad, printed in London some
time between 1672 and 1696.[8] We cannot read it as a direct expression
of the tastes of the poor. It was, rather, something the printer thought
could be sold to the poor. Even so, it suggests there was an appetite for
revelry at Christmas time, not stopping short of riotous behaviour. The
ballad tells of country people celebrating the festival by feasting,
drinking, dancing, kissing, and playing games, on the village green and
in a tavern. That sounds innocent enough, but the mood of the piece is
indicated in the refrain:

> Then high to Christmas once a year
> Where we have Cakes, both ale and beer,

> And to our christmas feast there comes,
> Young men and Maids, to shake their bums.

The story ends with drunkenness, violence, destruction of property, and the departure of the men from the tavern without paying. Yet these are "Delightful Sports," the preamble insists. Such behaviour was evidently no mere fiction. William Hone records a 1731 denunciation of servants and tradesmen dining all too well at an alehouse, and dancing at a "threepenny hop," on the proceeds of their Christmas boxes (Hone 1: 1645–46).

Plebeian excess offered a pretext to those who wished to disparage Christmas, yet plebeian lack of inhibition could also excite something like envy, even among those who shuddered at vulgarity. Eighteenth-century poems about Christmas, written for more affluent readers, are rare. One such rarity, however, was first published around 1730.[9] It plainly owes something to ballads like "The Shrop-shire Wakes," but it is much more carefully crafted and, importantly, it features no transgressive behaviour. Its anonymous author, I submit, hit upon a perfect solution for containing mixed feelings about the festival, among those who did not identify with plebeian revellers:

> O you merry, merry souls,
> Christmas is a-coming;
> We shall have flowing bowls,
> Dancing, piping, drumming.
>
> Delicate minced pies
> To feast every virgin,
> Capon and goose likewise,
> Brawn and a dish of sturgeon.
>
> Then, for your Christmas box,
> Sweet plum cakes and money,
> Delicate holland smocks,
> Kisses sweet as honey.
>
> Hey for the Christmas ball,
> Where we shall be jolly;

Jigging short and tall,
Kate, Dick, Ralph and Molly.

Then to the hop we'll go,
Where we'll jig and caper;
Maidens all-a-row;
Will shall play the scraper:

Hodge shall dance with Prue,
Keeping time with kisses;
We'll have a jovial crew
Of sweet smirking misses.

The verse form, the milieu evoked, the bumpkin names, the voice the poet adopts, all make this a version of pastoral. Few literary genres convey meaning in as complex a fashion as pastoral, but the sentiments this example is intended to provoke are plain enough. "This is what simple people do at Christmas time," the reader is invited to reflect. "It is good they do it, and in doing it they express a humanity we can all recognize. Manners and dignity stop gentlefolk like us from joining in, but we can observe wistfully and applaud, even while wincing at some of their antics." It is scarcely a good poem, but mixed feelings about Christmas are neatly balanced in it.

It was mixed feelings such as these that stopped the patrician classes neglecting Christmas utterly. They were embarrassed by festive revelry, but unable to disown it entirely, and well aware that poorer folk were never going to do so. Surprisingly often, even if grudgingly, they recognized a duty to support plebeian revels.

They did not want reminders of this duty. William King's 1708 poem, "The Art of Cookery," urged those "careful of [their] Fame" at Christmas time, to make sure "the old Tenant's Table" be properly furnished with a boar's head, sack and spiced wine, the wassail bowl, plum porridge, turkey and a joint of meat (King 2: 47–49). In 1754, the *London Magazine* advised readers not to forget that "Christmas is looked upon as a festival in the most literal sense, and held sacred to good eating and drinking" (Pimlott 65).

There is evidence, too, that such advice was heeded. Between 1767 and 1773, at Stanway House in Gloucestershire, for instance, tenants were entertained to an audit dinner just before Christmas each year. Contemporary attitudes are reflected, though, in the fact that the landowner, a judge, would rarely have been able to return from London to host it.[10]

Whatever the patrician classes felt about Christmas, it is clear that their patronage, freely or grudgingly given, continued to sustain it. The end of communal revelry notwithstanding, in many a manor house festivities were still organized. In his 1819 sketch "Christmas Eve," Washington Irving tells how his fictional Squire Bracebridge "permitted, and even encouraged" Christmas revelry in the servants' hall. Evidence suggests this was not just eccentricity recorded or imagined by a writer on the look-out for quaintness.

The servants' hall evolved as a result of the change in relations between classes, largely responsible for the transformation of Christmas festivities. The first servants' hall constructed in England was probably the one at Colehill, in Berkshire, designed by Roger Pratt in about 1650, not long after the degeneration of the communal Christmas in the great hall first began to be remarked upon. To preserve a symmetrical plan, Pratt put the house's main staircase into the great hall, making it unsuitable for dining. Another hall in the basement was provided for servants' meals. By the end of the seventeenth century such an arrangement had become standard. The lives of masters and servants were diverging in the country house, and the servants' hall confirmed this (Girouard 123, 136).

Its evolution, however, made it possible for landowners to preserve a vestige of the old-fashioned communal revelry. They could lay on festivities there, at least for their own servants, without giving up any of their own private space, or becoming more involved themselves than they wanted to. In many great country houses to this day Christmas parties are organized for servants, their dependants, and sometimes for tenants too.

It is a tradition which presents problems to the historian. The custom is an ancient one. In some cases such festivities may have directly succeeded the ending of open house in the great hall, in others they may be due to a nineteenth-century revival. But in most, no one knows how ancient the origins are. At Broughton Hall there was an annual Christmas ball for servants in the servants' hall until 1933. At Lyme

Park, Disley, servants were presented with joints of beef on Christmas Eve, and entertained at a servants' ball on New Year's Eve, not in the servants' hall in this case, but in the entrance hall.[11]   John Fryer-Spedding of Mirehouse, Keswick, remembers Christmas parties in the servants' hall as late as the 1950s.[12]   When these customs began it is impossible to say.

There is some evidence, however, enabling us to trace the tradition at least as far back as the end of the eighteenth century. Later editions of Brand's *Popular Antiquities* (see pp. 86–87 below) describe festivities, organized for his servants on Christmas Eve 1795, in the house of "Sir — Holt, Bart," of Aston, Birmingham. Such festivities are declared to be an annual event (250).

The archives of Petworth House, in Sussex, show clearly that, for nearly two decades during the early nineteenth century, Christmas festivities in the servants' hall were more pronounced than they were in the Wyndham family's own more splendid rooms. Between 1819 and 1837, when Petworth was the home of the third Earl of Egremont, housekeeping records show no unusual gatherings in the grand reception rooms during the Christmas season. Ten to twenty family members and friends were fed each day, as they were throughout the year. But every year, on at least two occasions during the season, the number of people fed in the servants' hall at least doubled: always on 25 December, and always on one or two other dates as well. At a servants' ball on 18 December 1834, no fewer than 500 were fed in the servants' hall. These figures cannot be explained by unusual numbers of guests in the house, bringing their own servants with them.[13]

At Renishaw Hall, in the 1820s and 1830s, there was often a servants' dance on the evening of New Year's Day rather than the more normal New Year's Eve, because, as Mrs. Swinton explains, "my parents did not approve of the old custom of dancing the New Year in" (Sitwell 8).   Whatever their masters and mistresses did, it seems, domestic servants in the country were often encouraged to celebrate vigorously during the Christmas season.

Nor was charity for the poor forgotten by landlords. At Renishaw, Sir George and Lady Sitwell distributed beef among the elderly of the parish. Their daughter remembered "a little roomful at the butcher's, arranged with ticketed joints and pieces of meat" (Sitwell 6).   At

Sherborne Castle, new-minted pennies were distributed to local children and to the elderly on Christmas morning. When this tradition originated is unknown, but records of it date back as far as 1828.

Nor was it only landowners who recognized a duty towards their neighbors at Christmas time. Thanks chiefly to their habit of keeping diaries, the generosity of clergymen is among the best documented. From them, too, we learn what they observed of their parishioners' festivities. Some Restoration clergy, like the rector of Clayworth in Nottinghamshire, had feasted their parishioners at Christmas time (Hutton, *Merry England* 242). Woodforde's diary indicates that similar traditions were still being followed a hundred years later. A choir from Castle Cary entertained the household at Woodforde's Somerset parsonage on Christmas Eve in both 1768 and 1769, and was suitably rewarded for its pains. By 1776 Woodforde was a country parson in Norfolk. His entry for Christmas Day that year notes the gift of a hindquarter of lamb from his upholsterer, and a dinner in the parsonage to which he entertained old people of the parish, each of whom received a shilling from him after church (Woodforde 54, 64, 128–29).

The diaries of two Somerset parsons early in the next century document contrasting attitudes towards their parishioners' merriment. Twice on Christmas Day during the 1820s, the melancholic John Skinner was provoked into complaining about being awakened earlier than suited him, by bells "announcing the joyous day." "Half the parish at least will be drunk," he grumbled in 1823. And in 1827, he piously reflected that his parishioners "had better retire within themselves, and commune with their hearts, and be still" (Skinner 256, 305). Bad temper apart, this is an echo of Henry Vaughan.

William Holland was usually more generous, though he could be provoked. His parishioners, too, were in the habit of waking him on Christmas morning, with carols. In 1801, he complained that "The Singers at the window tuned forth a most dismal ditty, half drunk too and with the most wretched voices" (Holland 61). More often than not, though, he rewarded them with money, even when, as in 1809, they awakened him at three in the morning (189). And he was conscientious about his obligations, distributing food to the needy on Christmas Eve – "boiling pease" (53) or wheat at Corn Law prices (290) – and providing hospitality on Christmas Day. In 1800 he organized a Christmas dinner for the Sunday School, as well as entertaining some of his poorer neighbors in his kitchen: "I think that there were no less thirty nine [sic] that dined at my expense" (54). In 1807 he fed twelve poor neighbors in his kitchen, "where they had Port, Beef and Plum Pudding and as good strong beer after dinner as ever was drunk" (161). Echoing Morley and Blackall, Christmas, he observed in 1804, "is the day of joy and Enjoyment in a decent way" (102).

Country dwellers of lower rank, too, made provision for their less fortunate neighbors at Christmas time. A tradition was still being followed in Devon in 1816, entitling laborers to claim seasonal food and drink from farmers whose corn they had reaped in the autumn (Hutton, *Merry England* 243).

In towns and cities, by the beginning of the nineteenth century, such charity was less readily available to the poor. There were, after all, few such establishments as Petworth and Renishaw in urban settings. But if domestic servants in town could not expect elaborate festivities to be organized specially for them, public servants did their best to secure Christmas privileges from their middle-class clients. In the late eighteenth and early nineteenth century, lamplighters, bellmen, beadles and others employed in public duties, mindful of Boxing Day, circulated printed verses to householders (Huelin 170). In 1807, a lamplighter of Shoe Lane, London, wished his clients Christmas joy and plenty, but asked them not to be forgetful:

> Then while we face every blust'ring storm and wind,
> O Keep the industrious lamp-man in your mind,
> And while you've peace and plenty thus in view,
> Be kind, and then we shall partake it too.
> In gratitude we then shall loudly sing,
> Health crown our master, and Long Live the King!

In 1810, a London bellman distributed lines to "All my Worthy Masters and Mistresses in the Ward of Coleman Street Within and Without the Walls." He reminded them that

> Constant as Christmas in the annual round,
> Your votive Bellman at his post is found

> Anxious his Friends with heartfelt joy to meet,
> And at this jocund Season all to greet.

William Sandys reports that even the dustmen and scavengers of the era distributed "printed applications for their Christmas-boxes" (Sandys xcvi).

Such applications were not always welcomed, it should be said. There are early nineteenth-century texts which foreshadow *A Christmas Carol*, in representing poorer people asking for Christmas perquisites, and richer people granting them only grudgingly, if at all. One broadside published between 1819 and 1830 features a watchman asking for a Christmas gratuity, and a client reminding him that, no thanks to the watchman, his house has been burgled: "For which Mr. Watchman you ought to be well flogged round the square. However, there's half-a-crown for you and mind you take better care for the future."[14]

But few poorer people were deterred by such reproof. Puritan prejudice was lost in the past. The patronage of the squire could be dispensed with. Disdain for the festival could be left to the fashionable. Christmas was the jocund season. For the majority, nothing was going to change that.

The duration of the festivities, however, could be changed. For most people, between 1790 and 1840 the Christmas holiday diminished in length, thanks largely to the demands of industrialization. Not everyone was affected; the process of change was slow and uneven; but the trend was unmistakable.

William Holland's parish clerk took a week off for Christmas in 1806, plus "Old Christmas Day" at the beginning of January.[15] Sheffield cutlers kept their four to eight days well into the nineteenth century. Devon and Somerset lace-makers continued to have a week off work. Some northern miners were given two weeks. Most of these, of course, were unpaid holidays, and as such a mixed blessing, but they were holidays nonetheless.

An observer in the 1820s, however, exclaimed at the way "Christmas day only or at most a day or two are kept by people in general." In 1797 the Customs and Excise Office closed between 21 December and 6

January. By 1838 it was closing on Christmas Day only. In 1818, Charles Lamb complained that the same was already true of India House, where he was employed as a clerk. The 1833 Factory Act set a minimum standard by making Christmas Day and Good Friday the only mandatory public holidays. Philanthropists and supporters of the anti-Poor Law movement remarked indignantly on the fact that, in poorhouses and houses of correction, the festival was scarcely observed at all (Holland 137, Hutton, *Stations of the Sun* 112; Pimlott 77–78, 81; Hone 1: 1623).

The curtailing of festivities, however, had no effect on their intensity, among those determined to keep Christmas, and free to do so. Poorer people had nothing to gain and much to lose by not keeping it. The proliferation of goose clubs in towns and cities shows they did keep it. These clubs ensured appropriate provisions for Christmas dinner in the homes of working men. Weekly payments were made at taverns, for geese supplied by the tavern-keeper and distributed by lot on Christmas Eve. There were also clubs to ensure provision of plum pudding, cake, and coal. Such clubs were operating before 1837, when Victoria came to the throne, and flourished thereafter (Pimlott 79; Cantacuzino 127).

Dickens recognized how important Christmas was to the less affluent. We cannot be sure what period during his life Forster was alluding to, but in his biography of the author, he speaks of accompanying Dickens "for several consecutive years" every Christmas Eve,

> to see the marketings for Christmas down the road from Aldgate to Bow; and he had a surprising fondness for wandering about in poor neighbourhoods on Christmas-day, past the areas of shabby genteel houses in Somers or Kentish Towns, and watching the dinners preparing or coming in. (Forster bk. 11, ch. 3)

Stave 3 of *A Christmas Carol* famously describes the Christmas preparations of the poor in a way that seems to be based on such observation (*Christmas Books* 47). But that was not the first time it had been hinted at in his works. In the third part of *Master Humphrey's Clock*, published on 18 April 1840, Master Humphrey speaks of "the little tokens of festivity and rejoicing, of which the streets and houses present so many" on Christmas Day; of the working man carrying his baby "in its gaudy hat and feathers," and of his wife in "her gay clothes"; of "the bright fires that cast their warm reflection on the windows as I passed"; and of "the sociality and kind-fellowship that everywhere prevailed" (*Master Humphrey* 59). Dickens was evidently making such excursions into poor neighborhoods before 1840, Forster or no Forster. It can be assumed he was faithfully reporting Christmas customs of the London poor, and of the lower-middle classes.

The chief effect of the shortening of the holiday, among the majority of the population, was to place special emphasis on the family Christmas dinner. Less time was left for other, communal activities. The domestic Christmas that I spoke of in the last chapter, with women playing a key role in it, became central to what people understood by the festival (see pp. 41–42 above).

Although there is little reliable source material for many decades during the period, there is some evidence to show how such private Christmas celebrations developed between 1660 and 1840. In the diary of Samuel Pepys (1633–1703), we can see arrangements made by a member of the professional classes during the 1660s.[16] We can see, too, Pepys's surprise, from time to time, at the unfamiliar shape he found his festivities taking. The form in which they are recorded – a diary – is in itself significant. The old understanding of Christmas had affirmed permanence. The festival had been represented in texts which documented the unchanging. Now a new understanding was evolving. Change had become at least as interesting as permanence. His chief motivation in writing the diary was manifestly Pepys's fascination with change in himself, in his circumstances, and in the world at large. The way was opening for Christmas to be represented in narrative texts. The indicative mood was superseding the imperative.

While he was writing his diary, between January 1660 and May 1669, Pepys was the seventeenth-century equivalent of a civil servant, living and working in London. He was the son of a tailor, but he was also a Cambridge graduate and, in his cousin Edward Montagu, from 1660 the first earl of Sandwich, he had a patron. Without the earl's patronage, Pepys's career, for all his talent, would not have been the success it was. He was largely dependent on office for his fortune. It was during the period covered by the diary that he grew rich. His home, at the Navy Office in Seething Lane, comfortable to begin with, became elegant and even luxurious thanks to his efforts. His success as a naval administrator kept him in the company of the great. But Pepys's roots were in the urban middle class. He aspired to eminence, but did not take the customs and values of the eminent for granted.

The diary documents bourgeois Christmas customs more distinctly than any earlier source. Christmas Day for Pepys and his wife – a childless couple – was a quiet interval in the working year, spent chiefly at home. They entertained only on a very modest scale. They were not entertained themselves by a patron, despite the quasi-feudal relationship Pepys had with Lord and Lady Sandwich. The diary, in fact, does not always record how they marked the day, probably because there was sometimes little of note to record. Usually, it seems, Pepys attended church at least once, with or without his wife, and ate a better dinner than usual at home with her, normally featuring one or more of the traditional dishes. Sometimes they entertained a friend or relation, but they never received more than two guests. What remained of the day after dinner would normally be devoted to conversation, books, or music. On 31 December 1663, Pepys and his wife dined in style on turkey and mince pie, but he reflected on the way they had "kept our Christmas together all alone almost – having not once been out" (Pepys 4: 438).

The family servants seem to have been only marginally involved in the Christmas Day celebrations. Mrs. Pepys was up till four in the morning on Christmas Day 1666, "seeing her maids make mince-pies." Her husband dined on the pies and roast beef, went out to go to the theater, found none open, returned home, and spent the rest of the day rearranging his library. The maids who cooked the pies probably contrived their own festivities, but they were not involved in their employers' (Pepys 7: 420–21). On Christmas Day 1667, Pepys, his wife, and the small servant-girl they kept, were "alone at dinner – a good Christmas dinner" (Pepys 8: 589). Whether that means the servant-girl shared it, or just served it, is not clear.

Doubtless because of the king's example, Twelfth Night seems to have been a more sociable occasion for Pepys than Christmas Day, although not to begin with. There is no sign of his having recognized it at all until 6 January 1663, when he attended a performance of Shakespeare's *Twelfth Night*, which he declared to be "but a silly play

and not relating at all to the name or day" (Pepys 4: 6). On Twelfth
Night 1665, he provided a Twelfth Cake for his household, played the
viol for them, and went to bed leaving his wife and servants "at their
sports" until morning (Pepys 6: 5). In 1666 he attended "a great dinner"
at Greenwich on Twelfth Night, and discovered a clove in his piece of
Twelfth Cake – the mark of the knave – but secreted it in a neighbor's.
Back home he found his wife, servants, and guests dancing to a fiddler,
and left them to choose a king and a queen, once again preferring bed
(Pepys 7: 5–6).[17] Although his Christmas festivities did not involve all
the household for the entire season in the old grand fashion, Pepys
evidently felt bound to provide one occasion the servants could enjoy. It
is worth noting that his wife, who often quarrelled with the servants,
nonetheless exerted herself to this end more than he did.   The
importance of the role of women in the festivities was beginning to be
recognized.

Unsurprisingly, while the fashionable were turning their backs on the
festival, few texts were produced documenting the sort of domestic
Christmas celebrations Pepys describes. By the end of the eighteenth
century, however, we find evidence for them reappearing. *Christmas*,
by Romaine Joseph Thorn, was published in 1795. Thorn was a Bristol
poet who seems to have taken much the sort of pleasure William
Cowper did, in the trivia of provincial middle-class life. His poem is
untouched by the usual eighteenth-century ambivalence towards the
festival.   It extols familiar phenomena: carols, waits, games, plum
puddings, mince pies, barons of beef, Christmas bells and Christmas
boxes. It speaks of excited schoolboys, and of guests crowding into the
farmer's hall. It commends relief of want. And it confirms what we
find in Pepys's diary. The locus of Christmas is the family home, and
women are playing a key role in it. "In *country towns*, Britannia's
Housewives, blithe," we are told, hurl themselves into a frenzy of
cleaning at the approach of the "Convivial Season":

> Well pleas'd, their store of fam'ly *plate* they take,
> From *cupboard* lock'd, where, haply, it hath stood
> A period long, by all the household train
> Untouch'd, unseen; but, now, is burnish'd up
> (To dignify th'approaching festive hours,
> And gaily entertain expected friends) .... (Thorn 8)

Thorn wrote within the Augustan tradition, but contemplated things the Augustans had overlooked. "Country towns" were his subject, not the metropolis. "Housewives" people his verse, not conspicuously leisured ladies. Attention is switched from the patrician classes to the comfortably-off provincial middle classes. And they had no qualms about celebrating Christmas.

No mention is made in the poem of the landowner's great hall. It is not even the object of nostalgia. A source published thirty years later indicates how completely it had vanished from middle-class thinking about Christmas. In January 1825, the *New Monthly Magazine* published an essay about a village Christmas. Festivities in the big house are deemed remarkable by the essayist, not because they are the fount of Christmas joy for the whole village but because, rank notwithstanding, they are identical to everyone else's:

> At the manorhouse it is pretty much the same as elsewhere. Girls, although they be ladies, are kissed under the mistletoe. If any family among us happen to have hit upon an exquisite brewing, they send some of it round about, the squire's house included; and he does the same by the rest. (Dawson 252)

The middle-class perspective on Christmas is now considered worthy of respect. The landowner features now only as an object of mild curiosity.

Even among the poorer classes, it seems, the focus of Christmas celebrations was becoming the family home, and the family Christmas feast. Before Dickens directed attention to festivities among the working classes and lower-middle classes, sources documenting such matters were rare. Broadsides, however, devised at least to appeal to the poor, offer some data. One, entitled "Christmas," and printed in Norwich some time between 1780 and 1830, shows how central to the festival the family reunion had become:

> 'Tis next we see, 'midst homely glee,
>   Grand-dames, Aunts, and Cousins,
> Surround the board with dainties stored,
>   both old and young by dozens;
> Who wisely chat o'er this and that,

bad business and bad weather,
And how at last, its dangers past,
they've crept again together.[18]

Whatever the fashionable thought, it is clear that, during the early decades of the nineteenth century, in private homes across the nation, Christmas was thriving.

Late in the eighteenth century, moreover, an attitude towards Christmas had begun to take shape, recommending it once again to the fashionable. This occasioned confusion, it should be said, and still does. The way the attitude is more often than not expressed encourages the supposition that Christmas was in danger of extinction. It is to this that we can attribute the obdurate notion that the festival needed rescuing in the nineteenth century: either by Dickens alone, or by Dickens in concert with others.

A variety of eighteenth-century sources, as we have seen, indicate that Christmas was changing, and was being neglected by some. But few before 1800 suggest it was in danger of being forgotten entirely. It was not. It was popular. That is why we need to concentrate now, less on evidence about what it was people were doing, more on evidence about what it was they were thinking. Only thus can we gain a clear picture of what was really happening. We need to understand how nostalgia, in some quarters, yielded lamentation at the decline of the festival, how sympathy with plebeian culture, in others, yielded appreciation of its vitality.

The earliest signs of a change in attitude are to be found in an alteration in the religious temper of the age, encouraging devotional affirmation of the feast. From the 1780s the evangelical movement became widely influential among all classes, both inside and outside the Church of England. It perpetuated many of the doctrines of the Puritans, but there were important differences. Attention was switched from questions of hierarchy and ritual to the need for individual salvation, reached through emotional and imaginative comprehension of Christ's sacrifice. By de-emphasizing ritual, the evangelicals made it less problematic. Austerity satisfied them: prohibition was unnecessary.

Mrs. Swinton's memoirs recall Christmas in the 1820s and 1830s as celebrated by a landowning Anglican family, living in a predominantly Anglican community, but all clearly under the influence of evangelical doctrines. At Eckington church, services were "simple and primitive like the congregation"; "there were no musical prayers nor intoning of any kind." But at Renishaw Hall, Lady Sitwell saw to it that Christmas was duly marked, however austerely:

> we kept Christmas as a really religious festival, though a very joyous one, and went to church in the morning and afternoon. My mother would not allow any dancing on Christmas night, nor did she approve even of games.
>
> When Christmas Day, with its two church services, was over, the choir, together with several village musicians and a few friends as audience, came again and sang hymns and anthems and played other sacred music in the hall.

Sedate though that may sound, the company, the evergreen decorations in the hall, the blazing fire, and the happy children remained among Mrs. Swinton's fondest memories of her childhood. Secular revelry, moreover, accommodated to the evangelical conscience, was permitted on other days during the season (Sitwell 5–8).

The high-church Oxford Movement, in contrast, launched some decades later, rejoiced in elaborate ritual. In 1827, one of its principal founders, John Keble, published *The Christian Year*, a collection of poems celebrating all the feasts of the Church in turn. "Christmas Day" seeks to impress on priests ("shepherds") the importance of Christ's nativity:

> Still, as the day comes round
> For Thee to be reveal'd,
> By wakeful shepherds Thou art found,
> Abiding in the field.
> All through the wintry heaven and chill night air,
> In music and in light Thou dawnest on their prayer. (Keble 25)

It is the priest's duty, that is to say, to be aware of Christmas, and to worship in appropriate fashion at the right time. The mention of music is more than incidental. Music was important to the Oxford Movement, which would eventually be responsible for the reintegration of carols into the Anglican liturgy (Bradley xvi–xvii). During the 1830s, under the leadership of Keble, John Henry Newman, and Edward Pusey, the movement attracted many followers.

Both evangelicalism and the Oxford Movement can be seen as essentially Romantic in nature, the one stressing imagination, intensity, and emotion, the other the value of ancient tradition. The rehabilitation of Christmas among elite groups, in fact, plainly had much to do with that unfathomably complex revolution in thought and feeling we call Romanticism.

It has been argued that the Industrial Revolution damaged and diminished Christmas festivities. "The genius of the present age requires work and not play," observed Sandys in 1833, and to this he attributed a decline he detected – wrongly I believe – in the observance of Christmas during the early decades of the nineteenth century (Sandys l). Industrialization and urbanization, in fact, prompted many with inquiring minds to study ancient customs, preferably rural, which seemed to signify a more humane way of life than could be found in the expanding towns and cities. Old Christmas customs were among those studied. Their contemplation, it was felt, offered an understanding of what had been lost.

The study of such customs was initiated by the work of eighteenth-century antiquarians, investigating, classifying, and cataloguing in the encyclopaedic fashion encouraged by the Augustan mind-set. Two stand out. John Brand's *Observations on Popular Antiquities* was first published in 1777. Joseph Strutt's *Sports and Pastimes of the People of England*, his last completed book, was published just after the turn of the century in 1801. Both catalogue Christmas customs, including many rare and discontinued ones; both proved popular, each going through several editions during the nineteenth century, most of them large and expensive. Strutt, certainly, manifests a Romantic nostalgia for the kind of ceremony recoverable from medieval and Tudor texts. "England was then 'Merry England,'" he mournfully declares (xxxii). Brand and Strutt had an enormous influence on writers of the Romantic era. They are alluded to and echoed repeatedly, and they made Christmas a fit subject for literature once more. Their work had the effect of encouraging the abandonment of disdain or indifference towards the festival, in favor of lively inquiry. But they also promoted pessimism about its future, out of proportion to discoverable facts.

Admirers of Brand and Strutt, among the first generation or two of Romantic writers, looked wistfully back to medieval and Tudor discourse on Christmas, but transformed advice they found there on how to celebrate, into lamentation at the festival no longer being celebrated as advised. More than anything else, they lamented the end of revelry in the great hall under the patronage of the master. Either they ignored the private celebrations that had replaced such revelry; or they were unaware of such celebrations; or they felt such celebrations were no substitute for what had been lost. Whatever it was they knew or felt, many early Romantics chose to absorb regret at the decay of old Christmas traditions into fashionable Romantic pessimism. It was a seductive attitude to strike, but it does not seem to have been warranted.

As it happens, we can often detect an awareness of contradictory fact lurking behind fashionable pessimism. At first sight, one much quoted text, by a writer prominent among the Romantics, flatly denies any such awareness. Robert Southey was evidently thinking of Brand and Strutt, or of notions they popularized, when he wrote what seems to be an unusually explicit declaration that Christmas was decayed beyond recovery. His *Letters from England* was published in 1807. One of the letters states that mince pies on Christmas Day and Twelfth cakes on Twelfth Night are all that survive of Christmas customs in England.

> All persons say how differently this season was observed in their fathers' days, and speak of old ceremonies and old festivities as things which are obsolete. The cause is obvious. In large towns the population is continually shifting; a new settler neither continues the customs of his own province in a place where they would be strange, nor adopts those which he finds, because they are strange to him, and thus all local differences are wearing out. In the country, estates are purchased by new men, by the manufacturing and mercantile aristocracy who have no family customs to keep up, and by planters from the West Indies, and adventurers from the East who have no feeling connected with times and seasons which they have so long ceased to observe.
> (*Letters from England* 362)

The error most commentators make in interpreting these words is to assume they can be understood as Southey's own.   They cannot. Somewhere behind *Letters from England* stands Goldsmith's *Citizen of the World* (1762). The book is an exercise in ventriloquism. Much of it can be read as straightforward travel writing, to be sure, but there are warnings to the reader not always to trust the judgment of Espriella, the young Spaniard purportedly the writer of these letters.   There are moments when his freedom from English prejudice has to be balanced against a proneness to misunderstanding, yielding comedy. Elsewhere, Espriella observes that books in England are bought only by those who do not read them:

> I have heard of one gentleman who gave a bookseller the dimensions of his shelves, to fit up his library; and of another, who, giving orders for the same kind of furniture, just mentioned that he must have Pope, Shakespeare and Milton, "And hark 'ye," he added, "if either of those fellows should publish any thing new, be sure to let me have it, for I choose to have all their works." (349)

The description of the English Christmas provokes a similar uncertainty in the reader. Eight years earlier, in "The Old Mansion House," Southey had lamented its decline less indirectly. An old countryman, in the poem, speaks wistfully of his former mistress's "Christmas kitchen" and "Christmas cask." "But I shall never see such days again," he says sadly (*Poems, 1799*). In 1807, however, the form of *Letters from England* allowed Southey to luxuriate in a fashionable attitude without having to take responsibility for it.

Walter Scott's antiquarian interests would have familiarized him with Brand's work.   Both of them were students of Thomas Tusser, for instance. And Strutt exerted a direct influence on Scott. After Strutt's death in 1802, Scott undertook the task of completing his unfinished romance, *Queenhoo Hall*. In a preface to the third edition of *Waverley*, Scott acknowledged how this task inspired his own ambitions as a writer of fiction, and expressed admiration for the learning that had enabled Strutt to compose a tale so meticulously illustrating fifteenth-century customs (*Waverley* 10–11).

It is no surprise, then, to find a vigorous defence of old Christmas traditions, echoing Strutt, in *Marmion*, published in 1808. "We'll keep our Christmas merry still," Scott defiantly declares, and he enumerates the festive customs of the baron's hall. If the festival has degenerated, he suggests, then much has been lost:

> England was merry England, when
> Old Christmas brought his sports again.
> 'Twas Christmas broached the mightiest ale;
> 'Twas Christmas told the merriest tale;
> A Christmas gambol oft could cheer
> The poor man's heart through half the year.

In a poem set in 1513, elegiac words on the baronial Christmas are not inappropriate. But Scott knew that not all had been lost. Something remained, even in Scotland:

> Still linger in our northern clime,
> Some remnants of the good old time. (Introduction to
> Canto 6)

Scott's words license pessimism about the decline of Christmas, but do not ignore contemporary practice.

Traces of the old Christmas "still linger," Scott told his readers. This word *still*, and a cluster of other words similar in function, feature prominently in early-nineteenth-century texts touching on Christmas, and affected to a greater or lesser extent by Romanticism. "In many parts of the kingdom, especially in the northern and western parts, this festival is still kept up with spirit among the middling and lower classes," declares Sandys, "though its influence is on the wane even with them" (Sandys 1). Again and again we encounter the notion of the festival "lingering." Vestiges of the old festival are "still" to be found, such texts repeatedly declare. Make the most of them. Soon they will all be gone. Traces of ancient customs are plotted on a downward curve. Evergreen Christmas decorations were once again being noticed, for instance, but as echoes of a bygone age, doomed to fade away. In 1829, one observer declared that "'Christmassing,' as we call it, the decorating our churches, houses and market-meats with evergreens, is yet retained among us."[19] And in 1830, the author of an East Anglian dialect dictionary spoke of "the evergreens with which our churches and houses are still decorated at the season of *Christmas*" (Forby 1: 63–64). Carols too were thought of as a relic of the past. In London, Sandys mournfully notes, "a solitary itinerant may be occasionally heard in the streets croaking out 'God rest you merry gentlemen, . . . ' to an ancient and simple tune" (Sandys cxxv).

Paradoxically, all this wistfulness about the last lingering traces of Christmas are signs of what we can in hindsight see to be an unmistakable revival of interest in the festival, among those who made their voices heard. The curve was in fact upward.

Some observers undoubtedly misinterpreted what they saw, but faithful reporting merged imperceptibly with attitudinizing. The Romantic pessimist could lay claim to perspicacity in detecting the last echoes of a nobler age, to bravado in defying inexorable historic processes. Christmas was cast in the role of the old Cumberland beggar or the leech-gatherer. But while Wordsworth's poems really were about what was passing and soon to be lost, Christmas did not belong in that category.

There were Romantic writers, though, not so much given to attitudinizing, as eager to make it their theme. One of Scott's keenest disciples was the American writer Washington Irving, who lived in England between 1815 and 1820, and visited Scott at Abbotsford in 1817. Under the pseudonym of Geoffrey Crayon, Gent., Irving wrote five short pieces on the English Christmas, publishing them in his *Sketchbook* (1819–1820).[20] These are complex works. Irving weaves a fantasy in them, in which contradictory affirmations vie with each other. Old Christmas traditions, we find ourselves being invited to suppose, are in a flourishing condition. They are not flourishing, we are equally invited to suppose, and need to be revived. And there are strong hints, to complete the picture, that any attempt at reviving them is laughable, that it invites trouble. Irving's avoidance of unqualified nostalgia was probably a feature that endeared him Dickens.

Bewildering though these sketches may be, as a guide to what contemporary English men and women were actually doing at Christmas time, they are clearly not despondent about the festival. Few American writers of the Romantic era were pessimists. Irving viewed the past more as a storehouse cheerfully to be raided, than as a crumbling legacy sorrowfully to be conserved. The *History of New York*, which he had published in 1809 under the penname of Diedrich Knickerbocker, pokes fun at antiquarian pedantry. In the Christmas sketches, awe at the European heritage struggles with a similar playfulness. Full of admiration for Scott, Irving could not help but assume something of his elegiac tone, but the Romantic melancholy he permits himself is counterbalanced by native irreverence. Customs such as those that mark Christmas, he declares,

> are daily growing more and more faint, being gradually worn away by time, but still more obliterated by modern fashion. They resemble those picturesque morsels of Gothic architecture which we see crumbling in various parts of the country, partly dilapidated by the waste of ages, and partly lost in the additions and alterations of latter days.

He is showing he can do Romantic melancholy, but then there is a deftly handled change of gear:

> Poetry, however, clings with cherishing fondness about the rural game and holiday revel, from which it has derived so many of its themes, – as the ivy winds its rich foliage about the Gothic arch and mouldering tower, gratefully repaying their support by clasping together their tottering remains, and, as it were, embalming them in verdure. (*Old Christmas* 1–3)

Poetry (in its broadest sense) certainly inspires a key character in the Christmas sketches, the squire of Bracebridge Hall. He is said to be "a strenuous advocate for the revival of the old rural games and holiday observances," and to be "deeply read in the writers, ancient and modern, who have treated on the subject" (44). But this has landed him in trouble. "A few years before," we are told, the squire

> had kept open house during the holidays in the old style. The country people, however, did not understand how to play their parts in the scene of hospitality; many uncouth circumstances occurred; the manor was overrun by all the vagrants of the country, and more beggars drawn into the neighbourhood in one week than the parish officers could get rid of in a year. Since

> then, he had contented himself with inviting the decent part of
> the neighbouring peasantry to call at the Hall on Christmas Day,
> and distributing beef, and bread, and ale, among the poor, that
> they might make merry in their own dwellings. (110)

Irving was in fact prophetic. His drollery would soon be replicated
in events. During the 1830s and 1840s, architectural fashion led to the
construction of Neo-Gothic great halls in many country houses, old and
new, for landowners who wanted to provide "old English hospitality"
(Thornton 220). At Powderham Castle, barely a hundred years after his
great grandfather had dispensed with the authentic medieval hall, the
tenth earl of Devon commissioned a brand new dining hall. Completed
by the eleventh earl, it is medieval in both style and structure, complete
with screen and minstrels' gallery (*Powderham Castle* 2–3). To what
extent landowners realized the intention of providing traditional
hospitality in such halls, it is hard to say.[21]

Irving's good sense and debunking instincts stopped him suggesting
indiscriminate hospitality would work in the nineteenth century. He
allows the squire's nostalgic impulses some success, though, in the
servants' hall, where,

> a great deal of revelry was permitted, and even encouraged, by
> the squire, throughout the twelve days of Christmas, provided
> every thing was done conformably to ancient usage. Here were
> kept up the old games of hoodman blind, shoe the wild mare, hot
> cockles, steal the white loaf, bob apple, and snap dragon: the
> Yule clog and Christmas candles were regularly burnt, and the
> misletoe, with its white berries, hung up, to the imminent peril of
> all the pretty housemaids. (*Old Christmas* 52–53)

There is comedy in the spectacle of the squire checking that only the
right games are being played – presumably with a copy of Brand or
Strutt to hand – but something actual filters through as well. Gifts of
festive fare to the poor and revelry in the servants' hall were, as we have
seen, contemporary Christmas practices not at all uncommon.

Irving's Christmas sketches afforded English readers, Dickens among
them, a sample of attitudes towards the festival out of phase with those
with which they were familiar. Christmas practices in the United States,

early in the nineteenth century, were as varied as they were in England, but the variation had more to do with region and community than with class.[22]

In most of New England, stern Puritan regulation was only just beginning to give way. In 1659, Calvinist legislators in Massachusetts had decreed a five-shilling fine for those caught observing "any such day as Christmas or the like, either by forbearing of labour, feasting, or any such way." In Connecticut, reading the Book of Common Prayer had been forbidden, together with making mince pies, playing card games, and performing on musical instruments. In 1749, a Swedish visitor to Philadelphia had noted that Quakers did not celebrate Christmas at all. Presbyterians could not bring themselves to approve of it, but grudgingly held Christmas services to stop members defecting to Anglicanism.

In the South, however, things had always been different. The first states to make Christmas a legal holiday were Alabama in 1836, Louisiana and Arkansas in 1838. Virginian planters strove to perpetuate the old English revels. There were balls and fox hunts. Homes and churches were decorated with greenery. Carols were sung. Celebrations continued until Twelfth Night and later.

While Puritan pastors continued to preach against Christmas merrymaking, different traditions evolved in different regions, shaped by memories more of homeland custom than of bygone religious or social dissension. The Anglicans of Williamsburg garnished their window frames with holly. German settlers decorated their homes in German style, with wreaths and candles. And the Moravians of Bethlehem, Pennsylvania, were decorating trees – growing trees, outdoors – as early as the first decade of the nineteenth century.

American society had long been predominantly plebeian and bourgeois. Few looked to a squire in a big house for Christmas revelry, or mourned the fact that he was no longer providing it. The bourgeois Christmas, celebrated in the modest family home, was established with as little fuss as it was in England, but it was recognized as the norm a decade or two earlier in the United States, and Americans were quicker to accept unfamiliar customs. The Christmas tree, not popularized in Britain until the 1840s, was to be found in American homes, Harriet Martineau records, as early as 1832 (Gewertz). St. Gregory had called

Christmas the "festival of festivals," the editor of *Parley's Magazine* informed his young readers in January 1838. "It is consecrated in the Romish church," he continued; "but almost all persons observe it now" (6: 12). Untruthfulness on this point would not have impressed the American children he was addressing.

Customs relating to Santa Claus, introduced to the American colonies by Dutch immigrants, had died out, but Irving had reminded readers of them in his *History of New York*. The immigrants, he declared, had not allowed the feast of St. Nicholas to pass by, "without making presents, hanging the stocking in the chimney, and complying with all its other ceremonies" (*History of New York* 2: 308). A revised edition of 1812 had included a description of St. Nicholas flying in a magic wagon.

Irving was not the only American writer to dwell upon such matters early in the century. This magical element was popularized in 1823, with the publication of that Christmas icon, the "Account of a Visit from St Nicholas":

> 'Twas the night before Christmas, when all thro' the house,
> Not a creature was stirring, not even a mouse; . . . .

Readers will be familiar with the poem, but perhaps need to be reminded of its date of publication. And it may have been composed a good deal earlier than 1823. The supposition used to be that it was written by Clement Clarke Moore, just before it was published. Don Foster – not always to be relied upon, admittedly – now suggests that it was written by Major Henry Livingston Jr., in either 1807 or 1808. The poem certainly shaped the figure of Santa Claus for subsequent generations, and wedded magic and fantasy with Christmas. Readers are told, remember, of "a miniature sleigh, and eight tiny rein-deer." St Nicholas, "dress'd all in fur," comes down the chimney, fills all the stockings, and departs exclaiming, "Happy Christmas to all, and to all a good night."[23] The poem is devoid of anything like an Arnoldian touchstone, but the imaginative liberties taken with the subject seem to me distinctly American. The author was not anxious about conformity to ancient precedents, or what he might have been showing about his social background.

And this poem, remember, was published when Dickens was eleven, written possibly before he was even born.

Irving awarded poetry the task of preserving old customs. He might well have been prescribing for John Clare, whose *Shepherd's Calendar* was published in 1827. In this we find an attitude towards Christmas quite different from the conventional Romantic one, and reliable testimony about actual practices, too. Clare's stanzas for December refute any notion of Christmas being widely neglected at that date. They are unambiguous about the distribution of rejoicing:

> Christmass is come and every hearth
> Makes room to give him welcome now
> Een want will dry its tears in mirth
> And crown him wi a holly bough
> Tho tramping neath a winters sky
> Oer snow track paths and ryhmey stiles
> The husewife sets her spining bye
> And bids him welcome wi her smiles
>
> Each house is swept the day before
> And windows stuck wi evergreens
> The snow is beesomd from the door
> And comfort crowns the cottage scenes
> Gilt holly wi its thorny pricks
> And yew and box wi berrys small
> These deck the unusd candlesticks
> And pictures hanging by the wall
>
> Neighbours resume their annual cheer
> Wishing wi smiles and spirits high
> Glad christmass and a happy year
> To every morning passer bye
> Milkmaids their christmass journeys go
> Accompanyd wi favourd swain
> And childern pace the crumping snow
> To taste their grannys cake again

"Every hearth," Clare insists, welcomes Christmas. "Each house" is swept. "Annual cheer" is resumed. And a familiar catalogue follows: kisses beneath the mistletoe, waits, Christmas bells, morris dancers, mumming plays, wassail singers, carols, Christmas boxes, yule logs, children's gifts, stories round the fireside. Smooth Augustan periods, detectable even through Clare's demotic vocabulary and orthography, plus the ingrained habit of generalizing, cast a sheen of idealization over all, but there is no reason to believe he was not recording faithfully. There is reason, indeed, to suppose that this son of a laborer was recording customs casually overlooked by writers less familiar with plebeian ways. Such writers found Christmas practices to admire in a golden past, but it was observation that supplied the data of writers from humbler backgrounds.

A question is posed, of course, by Clare's title alone – *The Shepherd's Calendar*. He saw himself as a poet of rural life. Was he writing only of country practices? Although his setting is plainly rural in this instance, it was not his intention, it seems, to contrast country practices with urban ones. He does express anxiety about the decay of Christmas, but he attributes it to class rather than to urbanization. Clare was too conscious a writer entirely to ignore the patrician attitude to Christmas, or the Romantic alternative. Absorbing them into these stanzas, he pinpoints a distinction rarely made explicit, but real for all that. Plebeian appetite for merrymaking is contrasted with patrician indifference. Romantic melancholy is invoked to foretell a victory for the latter:

> Old customs O I love the sound
> However simple they may be
> What ere wi time has sanction found
> Is welcome and is dear to me
> Pride grows above simplicity
> And spurns it from her haughty mind
> And soon the poets song will be
> The only refuge they can find (Clare 124–26)

He was wrong about this, of course, but wrong in good company.

The Romantic attitude to Christmas in fact persisted well into the 1830s. Nor was it restricted to literary texts. As late as 1838, Dickens's friend, the painter Daniel Maclise, exhibited an enormous canvas at the Royal Academy, entitled "Merry Christmas in the Baron's Hall." It depicts a Jacobean grandee, feasting with his immediate family, amid a throng of servants and tenants who are playing games, singing carols, and observing as many old Christmas customs as could be crowded in. Maclise wrote a defiant poem about his painting for *Fraser's Magazine*, lamenting the passing of such merrymaking, but declaring it recoverable:

> If those were barbarous ages then,
> Let us be barbarous again. (Croquis 643)

Satire even more forthright than Irving's had proved incapable of dislodging such sentiment. In *Crochet Castle* (1831), Thomas Love Peacock shows nineteenth-century ladies and gentlemen celebrating Christmas at Chainmail Hall, "after the fashion of the twelfth century." "An excellent dinner, though, peradventure, grotesquely served," is anticipated by the guests, plus "an old harper," "old songs and marches," "old hospitality; old wine; old ale; all the images of old England; an old butler." "You will sit on old chairs," they are told,

> round an old table, by the light of old lamps, suspended from pointed arches, which, Mr. Chainmail says, first came into use in the twelfth century, with old armour on the pillars and old banners in the roof. (ch. 17)

As a remedy for the social unrest of the age, Mr. Chainmail can recommend nothing more efficacious than contemplation of the twelfth century, "its manners and habits, its community of kind feelings between master and man" (ch. 18). Peacock, in short, derides the Romantic vision of Christmas as nostalgic fantasy.

Yet pessimism about the festival's future was widespread. There can be no doubt about that. Clare, a working-class lover of Christmas, saw all around him celebrating it, but still believed it was passing into history. Sandys believed the same. He was a lawyer, an antiquary, a musicologist, and a meticulous observer, who loved Christmas no less than Clare. How can we be certain they were wrong? How can we confidently assert that Christmas was thriving?

Prediction cannot have been easy, of course. Christmas had changed and was continuing to do so. People were celebrating in different ways, some less vigorously than in earlier times, others less visibly. Customs were changing, as they usually do, slowly and unevenly. Fashion endorsed pessimism.

Statistically significant data is too scanty to show how misconceived the pessimism was. Nevertheless, there are clear signs that Christmas was flourishing during the early nineteenth century. They are to be found, above all, in the development of festive customs. Key Christmas practices were perceptibly growing in popularity, especially after 1800. They were attracting attention. Old ones were being changed to suit the times, flagging ones were being revived, and new ones were being developed.

Carols were an ancient custom. With their old robustness, they endured yet another shift in fashion during the eighteenth and early nineteenth centuries. Their prohibition had come to an end with the Restoration, when a book of *New Carolls for this Merry Time of Christmas* had been optimistically published. The Church hierarchy, however, had become suspicious of them. This did not stop congregations singing them in churches remote from supervision. In *The Vicar of Wakefield*, written between 1761 and 1762, Oliver Goldsmith emphasizes the inaccessibility of a northern parish by declaring that the parishioners "kept up the Christmas carol" (ch. 4). Christmas services seem to have featured carols for most of the century in the west country, too, where they often took the place of Psalms.

But surprisingly, given their earlier attitudes, it was Dissenters who revived interest in carols, which they now began to look upon favorably, prompted as much by a love of music and an eagerness to attract converts, as by thoughts of doctrine. During the eighteenth century, musical skills were more carefully cultivated in the chapel than in the church. One Archbishop of Canterbury in the 1760s declared, "Something must be done to put our psalmody on a better footing; the Sectarists gain a multitude of followers by their better singing" (Scholes 631).

In *Paradise Lost* (1667), Milton, always a music-lover, had spoken with evident approval of "a choir of squadroned angels" singing "his carol" at the birth of Christ (12.366–67). He foreshadowed the attitude of Nonconformist congregations in the following century. Methodists, among others, saw how they could attract converts, particularly working-class ones, by taking pains with sacred music, and by accommodating Christmas rejoicing in religious worship. In a way that would doubtless have shocked their Puritan predecessors, Dissenters took to singing carols in their chapels at Christmas time.

They did more than just sing. They collected the broadsides on which jobbing printers all over the country, generation after generation, had preserved the memory of old carols. From these they learned "The Holly and the Ivy," "The First Nowell" and "A Virgin Most Pure." Others Dissenters composed new carols. Charles Wesley wrote "Hark, How all the Welkin Rings" as early as 1739. It was later transformed by other hands into "Hark, the Herald Angels Sing."

The preservation of ancient carols was a cause taken up in the early nineteenth century by antiquarians and musicologists such as Sandys, most of them convinced they were rescuing a half-forgotten folk music from oblivion. Like Sandys, William Hone was pessimistic about the survival of carols. In 1825, he remarked on the way they had begun "to be spoken of as not belonging to this century," and regretted "that collectors have almost overlooked carols as a class of popular poetry."

Some of the more ancient, to be sure, were no longer being sung, but Hone himself testifies that more than ninety broadside carols were being published annually, and Sandys accepts this to be the case (Hone 1: 1599–1603; Sandys cxxv, cxxxi). Records show that a brisk market in such sheets persisted at least until the 1860s, when they were superseded by more durable forms of publication. The Bodleian Library Broadside Ballads collection contains two to three hundred sheets of carols, published between the 1770s and the 1860s, and these, it should be noted, are only the ones chance has preserved. Buyers of such sheets usually got the words of more than one carol, sometimes as many as nine. They were rarely supplied with the music. This suggests there was a lively choral tradition. Key singers were evidently able to remember and teach tunes, but needed inexpensive reminders of words.

Thoughts of oblivion for the carol, clearly, were premature. The interest taken in it by Hone and by Sandys, whose collection was published in 1833, was in fact anticipated by Davies Gilbert, who published the first modern collection of traditional carols in 1822, likewise supposing them on the verge of extinction. There was a healthy tradition, you might say, of lamenting the demise of the carol, unjustified by events. Interest, in fact, continued to flourish. Sandys's collection was followed in 1836 by Thomas Wright's *Songs and Carols*, transcribed from a Sloane manuscript in the British Museum.

And carols continued to be popular as Christmas entertainment among ordinary people. Doubtless in recognition of this, new ones were being composed. Most of those in *The Christmas Box* (1825), and in J. W. Parker's *Christmas Carols* (1831), are forgotten today, but they are nevertheless a tribute to the vitality of the form. In the west country, certainly up until the end of the eighteenth century, it had been the custom in homes on Christmas Eve to hand around hot cakes and cider or beer early in the evening, and to sing carols late into the night. William Holland's diary, as we have seen, shows how, in Somerset, awakening neighbors with carol-singing on Christmas morning persisted into the nineteenth century. Mrs. Swinton remembered "the sweet strains of 'Christians, awake!' and 'Hark! the herald angels sing,'" sung by villagers outside Renishaw Hall in Derbyshire, at midnight on Christmas Eve in the 1820s and 1830s (Bradley xiii–xvi; Sandys cxxvi–cxxviii; Dearmer et al. x–xii; Sitwell 6).

Other kinds of Christmas music were adapted to changing circumstances. The waits were among the few providers of popular entertainment the Commonwealth authorities had not sought to suppress, and there are records of companies being paid for performances as late as 1833, but by 1773 the term "waits" was being used principally for amateur singers and musicians who went in groups from house to house, specifically during the Christmas season. Waits, carol singers, and wassailers were in fact substantially conflated. Distinctions between them became a matter only of minor differences in local custom and terminology (Scholes 1103; Crewdson 138; Bradley xiv).

In the last chapter I described how mumming plays began to enjoy a revival, or perhaps a rebirth, during the eighteenth century. By the reign of Queen Anne, performances of mumming plays in a tradition that stretched from the middle ages through to the Restoration were rare, and confined to remote areas of the country. A quarter of a century later, however, mumming plays began to reappear, and they evidently flourished from about 1780. Whether the plays of this revival were in any way similar to the plays of the earlier tradition is an unanswered question (Palmer and Lloyd 104; Hutton, *Merry England* 8).

For historians of drama and folklore this is frustrating, but not for historians of Christmas. Whether an ancient dramatic form was being revived or a substantially new one invented, it is clear that effort, imagination, and enthusiasm were being expended on maintaining and developing a Christmas tradition. Mumming plays, wrote Strutt in 1801, "have ceased . . . of late years to attract the notice of the opulent" (202). Perhaps so, but some of the opulent evidently found mumming plays forced upon their attention. During Christmas week in the 1820s and 1830s, Mrs. Swinton recalls, many groups of mummers used to perform at Renishaw Hall.

> They were attired in shirts and trousers profusely ornamented with gay ribbands, with shoulder knots, cross belts and stripes, and wore plumed caps, sashes and tin swords. Chanting some old ballad about St George, they paced up and down, pretending to strike and wound each other. They were accompanied by a fool, sometimes in diced costume with a cap and bells hung all over him, who made grimaces and shook his money-box under the windows, soliciting alms, or rather beer money. We did not encourage them on Christmas Day, but as many as ten or twelve parties sometimes appeared between morning and evening on the other days of the Christmas week . . . . (Sitwell 7)

It was not the opulent who were responsible for the revival of mumming. The writers or transcribers of the scripts performed were not eminent authors. The producers of the chapbooks by which scripts were distributed were not leading publishers. The villagers who acted the plays were members of no elite. But all of them agreed with the sentiment voiced by Father Christmas, with minor variations, in mumming plays performed all over the country:

> Here comes I old Father Christmas welcome or welcome not;
> I hope old Father Christmas will never be forgot. (Tiddy 144)

The earliest records of Christmas show, not just mumming plays, but a variety of different kinds of dramatic performance as a staple of festive entertainment. As grandees and great institutions left off commissioning such performances, the professional theater, as well as the amateur, seems to have responded to the lack, and in towns and cities theater-going became a Christmas custom. In 1838, the *Memoirs of Joseph Grimaldi* were published, edited and introduced by Dickens. In the introductory chapter, Dickens speaks of memories of pantomimes, often starring Grimaldi, that he saw as a child during the teens and twenties of the century, and of his persistent delight in the genre:

> Each successive Boxing-day finds us in the same state of high excitement and expectation. On that eventful day when new pantomimes are played for the first time at the two great theatres, and at twenty or thirty little ones, we still gloat as formerly upon the bills which set forth tempting descriptions of the scenery in staring red and black letters, and still fall upon our knees, with other men and boys, upon the pavement by shop-doors, to read them down to the very last line. Nay, we still peruse with all eagerness and avidity the exclusive accounts of the coming wonders in the theatrical newspapers of the Sunday before, and still believe them as we did before twenty years' experience had shown us that they are always wrong. (*Grimaldi* 10–11)

Nor is this the only occasion during the 1830s on which Dickens alludes to the long-standing popularity of the Christmas pantomime. In *Pickwick Papers* (1836–37), we are told that the Fat Boy "made the most horrible and hideous face that was ever seen out of a Christmas pantomime" (*Pickwick Papers* 745). Miss Snevellicci's father, it is said in *Nicholas Nickleby* (1838–39), had been an actor "ever since he had first played the ten-year-old imps in the Christmas pantomimes" (*Nicholas Nickleby* 358).

William Hone, too, confirms the popularity of the Christmas pantomime in the early nineteenth century. He relates how busy the Covent Garden and Drury Lane Theaters were in January 1826, and how, in the oyster shops afterwards, the new pantomimes were eagerly discussed (Hone 2: 57-60).

Pantomimes and harlequinades had been common at Christmas time on the London stage from the early eighteenth century. Only rarely had they been the main feature of the evening's entertainment, though, and they were performed at other times of the year too. Their popularity at Christmas was boosted at the beginning of the new century by the comic and acrobatic genius of the clown whose memoirs Dickens edited. Grimaldi's Covent Garden appearance at Christmas 1806, in *Harlequin and Mother Goose; or, the Golden Egg*, launched a tradition which quickly became popular. A poem in *The New Monthly Magazine* of January 1825 tells how, during the Christmas season, "the tricks of Grimaldi were sure to be seen" by middle-class Londoners.

The use of mistletoe in a variety of customs at Christmas seems to have proliferated during the early decades of the nineteenth century, as a result of a few scattered references planted in the eighteenth. In AD 77, Pliny the Elder had declared mistletoe a plant held sacred by the druids but, despite widespread belief to the contrary, there is no evidence of its having played a part in the mediaeval or Tudor Christmas (Pliny 16: 95; Hutton, *Merry England* 6). Robert Herrick alludes to mistletoe, simply as greenery for Christmas decorations, in the early seventeenth century.[24] Gay's *Trivia* shows that it was being used for the same purpose early in the eighteenth century (Gay 75). In his *Medallic History of Carausius* (1757–59), William Stukeley suggests that the Druids foresaw the coming of the Christian Messiah. Their winter-solstice ceremonies, involving mistletoe, were simply perpetuated by Christians, he argues (Stukeley 2: 163–64). The suggestion is fanciful, to say the least, but it evidently caught the public imagination. Dickens is not alone in speaking of mistletoe as a "magic" or "mystic" plant (see pp. 133–34 below). Brand mentions the tradition of kissing beneath the mistletoe late in the eighteenth century (Brand 281). Beyond these sources, little significant documentation of mistletoe customs at Christmas is to be found before 1800.

By the early nineteenth century, however, it was widely believed that kissing beneath the mistletoe was an ancient custom. "The mistletoe is still hung up in farm-houses and kitchens at Christmas," wrote Washington Irving in 1819, following Brand; "and the young men have the privilege of kissing the girls under it, plucking each time a berry from the bush. When the berries are all plucked the privilege ceases" (*Old Christmas* 161).

On balance, Christmas customs associated with mistletoe seem more likely to have been of ancient origin, than simply to have been invented, but the sheer lack of evidence in medieval and Tudor sources, and its scarcity before 1800, suggest the customs were far from universal. Originally, they may well have been obscure and localized, but they evidently spread swiftly. The popularity of one, to be sure, was pretty well guaranteed, once it became familiar. Getting to kiss whomever you wanted, without reproach, at the trouble only of a little deft manoeuvring, was a powerful recommendation. Even so, mistletoe customs could scarcely have spread as they did without a widespread sense of Christmas as a special time, and a general enthusiasm for promoting the festivities.

The tradition of telling ghost stories around the fireside at Christmas, so important to Dickens, is better documented, but the custom seems to have spread throughout society only after 1800.[25]

Good storytellers can exploit gloom and flickering firelight, so it is scarcely surprising ghost stories are associated with winter nights. "A sad tale's best for winter," says Shakespeare's Mamillius; "I have one/Of sprites and goblins" (*A Winter's Tale* II.i). But in *Hamlet*, Marcellus firmly dissociates Christmas and ghosts:

> Some say that ever 'gainst that season comes
> Wherein our Saviour's birth is celebrated,
> This bird of dawning singeth all night long,
> And then they say no spirit dare stir abroad . . . .
> (*Hamlet* I.i)

Some might feel, I suppose, that this would make Christmas nights the best time of all for telling stories about ghosts. By the early eighteenth century, however, the telling of such stories at any time met with disapproval, and was deemed a diversion unfit for gentlefolk. In the *Spectator* of 14 March 1711, Mr. Spectator describes young girls, neighbors of his landlady, telling each other "dreadful Stories of Ghosts as pale as Ashes that had stood at the Feet of a Bed, or walked over a Church-yard by Moonlight." "Were I a Father," he sternly observes, "I should take a particular Care to preserve my Children from these little Horrors of Imagination, which they are apt to contract when they are young, and are not able to shake off when they are in Years" (*Spectator* 1: 38–39).

The first publication firmly linking ghost stories with Christmas appeared *circa* 1730. *Round about our Coal Fire* is a curious Grub-Street production, subtitled "Christmas Entertainments." The anonymous author, however, was evidently less interested in the festival than in apparitions, witches, ghosts, fairies, and the like. Several stories of the supernatural, now well-known, are recorded for the first time in the book, and its contents evidently seized the public imagination. Other editions followed: one in 1740, another in 1796, more during the nineteenth century. But despite his evident fascination with the subject, the author claims only to be recording "one of the great Amusements, when the Countryfolks begin to repose themselves" (12). Fielding too, in 1749, supposed the telling of ghost stories at Christmas to be only a country tradition. His narrator describes Tom Jones at midnight – blood-stained, bandaged, brandishing a sword, and carrying a candle: "I believe a more dreadful apparition was never raised in a church-yard, nor in the imagination of any good people met in a winter evening over a Christmas fire in Somersetshire" (*Tom Jones*, bk. 7, ch. 14).

The fashion for Gothic fiction made the ghost story more widely acceptable (Clery passim), and may well in effect have licensed a wider telling of such stories at Christmas time. After 1800, references to the custom become more numerous, and indicate settings socially more diverse. "On Christmas eve a Christmas tale" is appropriate entertainment, Scott declares in *Marmion* (1808). He foresees the reproach of his friend Richard Heber, the book collector:

> "What! leave the lofty Latian strain,
> Her stately prose, her verse's charms,
> To hear the clash of rusty arms;
> In fairy Land or Limbo lost.
> To jostle conjuror and ghost,
> Goblin and witch!" (Introduction to Canto 6)

There is no indication, however, that Scott felt such a reproach should be heeded.

Shelley is reported to have terrified listeners by reading a translation of Gottfried August Bürger's ghostly ballad "Lenore," one Christmas Eve, probably during the teens of the nineteenth century (Dowden 2: 123). Irving, a lover of ghost stories as well as of Christmas, unites the two in "The Christmas Dinner."   Thomas K. Hervey's *Book of Christmas*, of 1835, confirms the custom of telling ghost stories was well established at that date. At Christmas time, he relates,

> we have formed a portion of happy groups, when some thrilling story has sent a chain of sympathetic feeling through hearts that shall beat in unison no more; – and tales of the grave and its tenants have sent a paleness into cheeks, that the grave itself hath since made paler still. (142)

Written probably in 1837 or 1838, "The Epic," Tennyson's frame for his "Morte d'Arthur," features a group of friends around a Christmas Eve fire, lamenting "How all the old honour had from Christmas gone." "The poet Everard Hall," is persuaded to read aloud a fragment of an epic he has written.   It is of course the "Morte d'Arthur" – the marvellous story of Arthur's dying hours, and of his passage in a barge "To the island-valley of Avilion." After the reading, the narrator goes to bed, where he dreams, "Arthur is come again: he cannot die," and wakes to hear "The clear church-bells ring in the Christmas-morn" (Tennyson 582–98).

By the second half of the 1830s, evidently, telling stories of the supernatural around the fireside was a Christmas custom widely practiced and accepted.

As the nineteenth century unfolded, kinds of literature more formal than the oral ghost story, appealing especially to middle-class tastes, began to be a feature of the Christmas season. Simon Eliot has shown how, during the 1840s and 1850s, the number of titles published each autumn gradually overtook the number published during the spring, previously the publishing trade's peak period (*Aspects of the Victorian Book*). He attributes this to the growth of public interest in Christmas, but it was the result of a surge in interest, not of publishers awakening for the first time to a marketing opportunity. During the 1820s and 1830s, they were evidently adjusting their lists with Christmas in mind. Thackeray wrote a review essay for *Fraser's Magazine* entitled "Our Batch of Novels for Christmas 1837." None of the books he discusses is about Christmas, but they were plainly published when they were to entice Christmas buyers.

That was the case, too, with annuals (as yearbooks were known).[26]

The publisher Rudolph Ackermann issued *Forget-Me-Not,* the first British literary annual, in 1823. By 1831 more than sixty handsomely produced "keepsakes" were being published each year, principally for the Christmas trade, evidently a brisk one. A *Comic Annual* by Thomas Hood was published every Christmas from 1830 to 1842 (Prickett 44–45).[27]

There were books devoted to the subject of Christmas, too. Traditional customs are extolled in W. H. Harrison's *The Humourist: a Companion for the Christmas Fireside* (1830). T. K. Hervey's *Book of Christmas,* of 1835, popularizes the findings of Brand and Strutt. *Peter Parley's Tales about Christmas* of 1838, by either George Mogridge or Thomas Tegg, blends description of traditional Christmas customs with fiction.

Among popular writers on the subject, the one perhaps most likely to have influenced Dickens was William Hone (1780–1842). Like Dickens at a later date, Hone had finished his formal education early, known financial hardship, toiled in solicitors' offices as a boy, supported radical causes, and produced periodicals all but single-handedly. Hone greatly admired Dickens. At his request, George Cruikshank took Dickens to see Hone on his deathbed, and together they attended his funeral. "He was not a common man," Dickens said in a letter to the Royal Literary Fund, seeking support for Hone's widow (*Letters* 3: 366). The inventory Dickens and his wife compiled in 1844, of the contents of their house, shows his library contained, by that date, the edition of Strutt's *Sports and Pastimes* Hone had edited in 1838, and an edition of the same date of Hone's *Every-Day Book* (*Letters* 4: 716).

The latter was a typical Hone project. He was strongly attracted to the periodical form. *The Every-Day Book* (1825–27), *The Table Book* (1827–28), and *The Year Book* (1830–31) were all short-lived, idiosyncratic periodicals. In each, Hone's interest in Christmas is manifest. He made room for Romantic lamentation at traditions lost, but, in addition to collecting historical data about the subject, he published information about contemporary Christmas practices among all classes of people, and expressed his own fascination with the festival in competent and lively verse and essays. In visiting him on his deathbed at the end of 1842, the year before he wrote and published *A Christmas Carol,* Dickens might almost have been picking up a baton

Hone was passing on.

There was a revival of interest in Christmas, then, during the early years of the nineteenth century. The festival was no longer celebrated as it once had been, and it was not misleading to say so. The Romantic notion of the festival's being doomed to extinction, however, was no more accurate as a reflection of contemporary practice, than it was as a prediction of future practice. It was a tortuous expression, rather, of renewed interest in the festival. Until 1843, coolness towards Christmas festivities continued to be normal in London society, and among followers of metropolitan fashion. Coolness in such quarters, moreover, can license coolness elsewhere. Fashion filters downwards. But a ground swell was beginning to make itself felt. Attitudes were shifting, new opinions were being formed. Publishing strategies attest to a new enthusiasm among the book-buying public. The appetite for Christmas revelry, moreover, had never diminished among the majority of the population. And now the taste of the majority was beginning to be heeded.

One thing, though, was still lacking. The festival was not yielding literature commensurate with its significance in national life. The literary elite had yet to warm again to the festival, and to escape fixation upon customs of long ago. Pleasure taken in Christmas by working people, and by the resolutely old-fashioned, was finding expression chiefly in slight texts, by writers middling at best. An opportunity existed for mating the cultural richness of Christmas with literature worthy of it. That was where Dickens came in.

DICKENS AND CHRISTMAS, 1812 TO 1842

Before he wrote *A Christmas Carol* in 1843, Dickens made experiments with the topic of Christmas. He saw that it offered material particularly suited to his talents. He sensed that it connected with impulses that gave shape to his sensibility. But the topic was so complex, his response to it was so undirected, and his craft was so embryonic, that he was unable immediately to find satisfactory ways of engaging with it. It was not a topic he chose to concentrate upon. He just returned to it from time to time, to see what else he might do with it. It was not until 1843 that he was able firmly to link it with the great themes he sought to address, and to place it at the center of his art.

Christmas was always more than its customs to Dickens, however – in important ways, more even than the revelation of divine goodness he devoutly believed it to be. From the beginning of his career, it offered him an opportunity to explore conduct, emotion, memory, redemption, and a host of related themes, but he fumbled for the means to accommodate all this. At times, unwisely, he resisted what his imagination prompted. At times he submitted to it, but all too briefly. The literary techniques he had mastered were out of phase with what he sought to convey.

By the start of the 1840s, however, the place Christmas occupied in his sensibility, and the means at his command to represent it, were becoming adjusted. He was ready to create a masterpiece that would not only delight generations of readers: *A Christmas Carol* would change the kind of writer he was.

Dickens adored Christmas from early childhood onwards. He was born in 1812. The popular understanding, today, of the English Christmas as it was between 1812 and 1843, is mistaken. That is not altogether surprising, as we have seen. A seductive hypothesis is to blame, and evidence can be found which at least seems to substantiate it. Dickens scholars, though, have been among those seduced. That is surprising. They fail to reconcile the hypothesis with Dickens's own words.[1]

From the beginning of his career, texts he wrote about Christmas speak of the customs they describe as if they were both ancient and popular. Most of them were ancient, and all of them were popular, but let us for the moment suppose this not to have been the case. In order to reconcile what we read in his books with the notion that Dickens launched the modern Christmas, we should have to entertain one of two propositions: either that he persistently deluded himself; or that he created a fiction not only sustained but audaciously transparent. Neither proposition features much in the literature of the subject. What we find instead is a determination to ignore what Dickens says, or to explain it away. Acknowledge that he was faithfully describing popular customs, some of which had been practiced for centuries, and there is nothing left to reconcile. On the contrary, things fall briskly into place. The way opens for a clearer understanding of what he wrote about the festival, and why he wrote it.

Texts Dickens wrote about Christmas, both before and after 1843, show that he knew its customs well. His intimate knowledge of them becomes more intelligible the more we study his family and the circumstances of his early years. He was exposed to abundant discourse on the traditions of Christmas, of course, but he had first-hand experience of them, too. He was demonstrably celebrating the festival vigorously as a young adult, before 1843. Evidence encourages us to suppose that such celebrations had been familiar to him from early childhood. A few clues, however slight, suggest that Christmas merrymaking had been normal in his family for generations.

For two generations at least, and almost certainly for more, his family, on the paternal side at any rate, had been among those least affected by fashionable indifference towards Christmas, and most given to celebrating it heartily. His paternal grandfather, William Dickens, had been an upper servant – steward or butler – at Crewe Hall in Cheshire, home of John Crewe.[2] His grandmother, Elizabeth Dickens, had risen to be housekeeper there. William Dickens had died in 1785, two months after the birth of Dickens's father, John, but Elizabeth lived on until 1824 – when Charles, her grandson, was twelve – continuing to perform her duties as housekeeper for many years, despite having been widowed with two infant sons. John Dickens had lived at Crewe Hall until he was nineteen years old when, thanks to the influence of Mr. Crewe, a clerkship had been found for him at the Navy Pay Office in London, and with it entry to the lower middle classes.

Influence was something John Crewe had plenty of. He was without question one of the powerful and fashionable. For thirty-four years he was a Whig member of parliament for Cheshire. In 1806 he was elevated to the peerage. He was one of the coterie of Whig politicians who supported the Prince of Wales. His wife Frances, a renowned beauty, cultivated friendships with politicians like Fox, Burke, and Canning, with artists and writers like Sir Joshua Reynolds and Richard Brinsley Sheridan. These, and the Prince of Wales, were among the guests who accepted the Crewes' hospitality.

The Crewes spent much of the year living and entertaining in London. They were members of the *ton*. But unlike some other members, John Crewe was no absentee landlord. He and his wife also entertained at Crewe Hall, especially at Christmas time.[3] Evidence suggests they revered the festival no more than other members of their class, but they contrived nevertheless to "wile away the dreary hours"[4] with games, and with amateur theatricals, a particular passion of Frances Crewe, who was mistress of the Hall from 1766 until her death in 1818 – during all of John Dickens's life there, that is to say, and for most of the time his mother was housekeeper.

The Hall was one of those country mansions, it seems, where the festivities of servants were not forgotten at Christmas time. Family members, guests, and servants were all involved in the theatricals. "The plays," it is related, "were ably conducted by the gamekeeper, Thomas Fawcett, a brother of the celebrated actor of 'genteel comedy'.[5] He and his wife were themselves no mean actors, and took a part in the performances" (Hinchliffe 307–08).

Given what we now know of servants' Christmas festivities in great country houses at this time, it seems reasonable to assume that, at Crewe Hall, more was permitted than this source indicates. It may be that it was only Mr. and Mrs. Fawcett who actually took part in the theatricals, but it is hard not to suppose this the tip of an iceberg. And even if we avoid making too much of the plays as evidence, some things can be said. Dickens's grandparents had been servants in a country house where effort and imagination were expended on Christmas activities, from which servants and their families were not, on principle, excluded. Dickens's father had spent the first nineteen years of his life in the same house. Dickens's propensity to put on plays at Christmas time was something two previous generations of his family would have been familiar with. To say no more, this is information which diminishes the list of Christmas traditions it might be tempting to suppose Dickens invented or revived.

Dickens's father, John Dickens, it is clear, was never a man to neglect the festival. By the beginning of 1839 his son was famous. *Pickwick Papers* (1836–37) and *Oliver Twist* (1837–38) had been spectacularly successful. *Nicholas Nickleby* (1838–39) was proving no less so. The prosperity Dickens enjoyed as a result of this success was evidently something his father felt he could exploit: he incurred debts and importuned for loans on the strength of it. Nor was it the first time he had behaved in this way. Exasperated beyond endurance, Dickens caught a coach to Exeter in March 1839, rented and furnished a cottage for his parents in nearby Alphington, returned to London, and dispatched them to Devon forthwith – in disgrace. There they were to stay, together with Dickens's youngest brother, Augustus, until October 1842.

But a series of letters John Dickens wrote to George Franklin, a young friend in Exeter, shows that the three of them returned to London each Christmas for protracted visits, inevitably at some cost to Dickens himself (Parker, "John Dickens to George Franklin"). Disgrace notwithstanding, Christmas had imperatives of its own, which neither Dickens nor his father felt able to ignore. Dickens's writings on Christmas more than once foreground the family reunion, during which differences are overlooked or forgotten. His parents' annual return to London, during these years, suggests he was as good as his word.

John Dickens made the most of these annual trips. In one letter written in January 1840 he told Franklin he would be returning to Devon "in about a fortnight." In fact, he was able to prolong his visit until the second half of March. After barely nine months in disgrace in the country, he and Dickens's mother contrived three months' holiday in and around London, thanks to Christmas. Dickens's son Walter was born on 8 February 1841, providing an additional excuse for the elder Mrs. Dickens's presence in London that winter, but it was probably not until 21 February that she and her husband returned to Devon.

John Dickens was punctilious about Christmas etiquette, regularly sending seasonal greetings to Franklin and his family. "Pray make my best regards to your Father and all the family," he says in one letter, "and wishing them & you a merry Christmas & a happy new year." In another he hopes "that you may enjoy now & always, a happy Christmas & merriness – & new year & years."

Merriness was certainly on the agenda for his own Christmas program in London, evidently a crowded one, as was his son's. In a letter of 27 January 1840, he declares, "We have been very quiet since Christmas." But Christmas itself had been far from quiet in the Dickens household. His servants, Dickens reflected on 3 January, had "been up very late indeed for a great many nights," and a turkey of "astonishing capabilities" sent by Bradbury and Evans, printers of Dickens's novels, had been made good use of (*Letters* 2: 1). Even towards the end of January John Dickens was contemplating "two or three little out breaks this week, such as Theatres &c."

Unsurprisingly, the theater seems to have figured prominently in his idea of Christmas festivities. In a letter written just before Christmas in 1841, he describes a visit he had paid to the Tower of London with Augustus. "This is the only 'light' I have yet seen," he declares,

> as we are so much engaged in other ways[;] the next for me will be the re-opening of "Drury" on Monday. Augustus has a Box at the Adelphi tomorrow to see Barnaby Rudge which is very well dramatised there[,] Yates playing the parts of both "Sir John Chester" & ["]Miggs".[6]

The festivities alluded to in these letters were at Christmas in 1839, 1840, and 1841: before the supposed watershed of 1843, that is to say. It was *A Christmas Carol*, more than anything else, which persuaded the fashionable to resume Christmas merrymaking, but in Dickens's own milieu no resumption was called for. The merrymaking had never been discontinued.

There is persuasive testimony, indeed, that Dickens's parents had taken pains with Christmas festivities from his earliest childhood. "A Christmas Tree" was the first of the short Christmas pieces he wrote after he gave up the attempt to publish a Christmas book each year (*Christmas Stories* 3–18). It originally appeared in the 1850 Christmas number of *Household Words*, the weekly periodical Dickens had launched in March that year. In chapter 6, I shall be considering it as a literary text. Here I want to delve into it for autobiographical data alone.

That is no straightforward exercise, it should be said. Though Dickens himself never declared it fiction,[7] the narrative voice of "A Christmas Tree" cannot be precisely identified with his own. To say no more, it calls up memories of travelling home from school for Christmas. Dickens had attended none but day schools. Boarding school was an experience he reserved for imaginary selves such as David Copperfield (*David Copperfield* chs. 5–7, 14–18).[8] But most of the early childhood memories described in "A Christmas Tree" are best accounted for by supposing them Dickens's own. Memories of past Christmases occupy a key place in his vision of the festival. It would be odd to suppose that there were none precious to him personally, or that he never used them in his writings. I shall offer below some additional reasons for supposing he was doing so in "A Christmas Tree" (see pp. 142–43). Let me just say here that no observation, even of his own children, could have supplied him with inwardness such as we find in this text. There is certainly nothing like it in literature he might have read.

The piece opens with contemplation of children clustered admiringly about "that pretty German toy, a Christmas Tree" (*Christmas Stories* 3). This inspires the narrator to recollect his own childhood experiences of Christmas. He remembers gifts of toys especially:[9]

> the Tumbler with his hands in his pockets, who wouldn't lie
> down, but whenever he was put upon the floor, persisted in
> rolling his fat body about, until he rolled himself still, and
> brought those lobster eyes of his to bear upon me – when I
> affected to laugh very much, but in my heart of hearts was
> extremely doubtful of him. Close beside him is that infernal
> snuff-box, out of which there sprang a demoniacal Counsellor in
> a black gown, with an obnoxious head of hair, and a red cloth
> mouth, wide open, who was not to be endured on any terms, but

could not be put away either; for he used suddenly, in a highly
magnified state, to fly out of Mammoth Snuff-boxes in dreams,
when least expected. Nor is the frog with cobbler's wax on his
tail, far off; for there was no knowing where he wouldn't jump;
and when he flew over the candle, and came upon one's hand
with that spotted back – red on a green ground – he was horrible.
The cardboard lady in a blue-silk skirt, who was stood up
against the candlestick to dance, and whom I see on the same
branch, was milder, and was beautiful; but I can't say as much
for the larger cardboard man, who used to be hung against the
wall and pulled by a string; there was a sinister expression in
that nose of his; and when he got his legs round his neck (which
he very often did), he was ghastly, and not a creature to be alone
with. (4–5)

Gifts of books inspire memories just as powerful:

Thin books, in themselves, at first, but many of them, and with
deliciously smooth covers of bright red or green. What fat black
letters to begin with! "A was an archer, and shot at a frog." Of
course he was. He was an apple-pie also, and there he is! He
was a good many things in his time, was A, and so were most of
his friends, except X, who had so little versatility, that I never
knew him to get beyond Xerxes or Xantippe – like Y, who was
always confined to a Yacht or a Yew Tree; and Z condemned for
ever to be a Zebra or a Zany. (7)

Thoughts of the *Arabian Nights*, always fondly recollected by
Dickens, restimulate the kind of engagement with a text few but
children experience:

Oh, now all common things become uncommon and
enchanted to me. All lamps are wonderful; all rings are
talismans. Common flower-pots are full of treasure, with a little
earth scattered on the top; trees are for Ali Baba to hide in;
beef-steaks are to throw down into the Valley of Diamonds, that
the precious stones may stick to them, and be carried by the
eagles to their nests, whence the traders, with loud cries, will
scare them. Tarts are made, according to the recipe of the
Vizier's son of Bussorah, who turned pastrycook after he was set

down in his drawers at the gate of Damascus; cobblers are all Mustaphas, and in the habit of sewing up people cut into four pieces, to whom they are taken blind-fold. Any iron ring let into stone is the entrance to a cave which only waits for the magician, and the little fire, and the necromancy, that will make the earth shake. (8–9)

The insight into the way Christmas gifts are absorbed into a child's imaginative world suggests these are Dickens's own memories, thinly fictionalized if at all. Occam's razor alone urges such a conclusion. "A Christmas Tree" prompts us to suppose Dickens's parents celebrated Christmas during his childhood without inhibition, sought to make it memorable for their children, and succeeded beyond expectation with at least one of them – succeeded indeed in placing memory at the center of his understanding of the festival. Such an emphasis on merrymaking is what we would look for in his father, certainly – lower-middle-class, mindful of boyhood Christmases spent among servants in a great country house, and every bit as convivial as Mr. Micawber, who was modelled upon him.

A general point to be made about the piece, at any rate, cannot be disputed. Those who wish to believe next to no one celebrated Christmas with enthusiasm in the early nineteenth century, before 1843, should scrutinize "A Christmas Tree" carefully. They need to explain how readers in 1850 might have been persuaded to accept memories of early childhood enchantment at the festival, recalled by an adult narrator looking back over "many years" (10). Delusions about the nineteenth-century Christmas can be dispelled by taking more than one passage Dickens wrote about it, and doing a little simple arithmetic.

As a young adult, there can be no doubt, Dickens upheld family tradition, and strove, in turn, to make Christmas memorable for those he shared it with. His Christmas festivities are better documented from 1843 onwards, certainly, and may indeed have been intensified from that date. "Such dinings, such dancings, such conjurings, such blindmans-buffings, such theatre-goings, such kissings-out of old years and kissings-in of new ones," he told Cornelius Felton in January 1844, "never took place in these parts before" (*Letters* 4: 2–3). But it is the degree of rejoicing he is speaking of, not rejoicing as such. He seems to be thoroughly familiar, we cannot help noting, with the kinds of rejoicing enumerated. And we know that he was, with several of them.

There was keen interest, inevitably, in what the author of *A Christmas Carol* did during the festival, and a forgivable readiness on the part of that author to supply detail. From 1843, Dickens became more self-conscious about his Christmas activities. But his daughter Mamie, five years old by Christmas that year, later insisted, "Christmas was always a time which, in our home, was looked forward to with eagerness and delight, and to my father it was a time dearer than any other part of the year."

> In our childish days my father used to take us, every twenty-fourth day of December, to a toy shop in Holborn, where we were allowed to select our Christmas presents, and also any that we wished to give to our little companions. Although I believe we were often an hour or more in the shop before our several tastes were satisfied, he never showed the least impatience, was always interested, and as desirous as we, that we should choose exactly what we liked best. As we grew older, present giving was confined to our several birthdays, and this annual visit to the Holborn toy shop ceased. (*My Father as I Recall Him* 25–26)

An adult's memory of early childhood is not always to be relied upon, but it is likely Mamie Dickens would have remembered whether or not the family Christmas celebrations of 1843 were unprecedented.

And we know there were precedents. We know, for instance, that Dickens hosted a charades party on Christmas Eve 1840, closely followed by a second on 4 January, with dancing as well as charades (*Letters* 2: 172-73, 179). In his circle, Christmas was evidently a sufficient occasion for his friend Charles Smithson, in 1841, to send a gigantic Christmas pie from Yorkshire, home of such fare, and for justice to be done to it. Smithson was wished "very many happy Christmases, and New Years" for his generosity (*Letters* 2: 448-49).

Dickens's eldest child, Charley, was born on 6 January 1837. A year later, his parents organized a small party, with a cake and forfeits, in honor both of Charley's birthday and of Twelfth Night (*Letters* 1: 630). John Forster and Daniel Maclise, the painter, were among the adults invited to a somewhat larger gathering on 6 January 1841 (*Letters* 2:

179-80). By 6 January 1842, Dickens had already left London, with his wife, on his first visit to North America, and was not present at Charley's birthday party that year. In subsequent years, however, Twelfth Night became a special day in the family calendar. The Twelfth Night party of 1843 – the last night of Christmas 1842, that is to say – featured a Twelfth Cake and other refreshments, dancing, a magic lantern show, and, for the first time, Dickens's own conjuring act. He dazzled his infant audience, plus not a few of the adults, with a series of baffling tricks, transforming a box of bran, for instance, into a live guinea pig, and producing a piping-hot plum pudding out of an empty saucepan (Ackroyd 392–93).

Such customs were maintained in later years. Two years later, the family was living in Genoa at Christmas time. Their festivities lasted from Christmas Eve to Twelfth Night. The Twelfth Cake on that occasion weighed ninety pounds, no less, and had been dispatched to Genoa by Dickens's philanthropist friend, Angela Burdett Coutts (*Letters* 4: 242). Captain Marryat was among the guests on Twelfth Night at the family home in Devonshire Terrace in 1846. He reported "lots of fun," "convivial songs," "speeches," a "ball and capital supper" (*Letters* 4: 466n2). Mamie Dickens remembered, among other details, how she and her sister Katey had taught their father the polka for the Twelfth Night party of 1849 (*My Father as I Recall Him* 27–28).

From 1852, Dickens began to organize dramatic performances for the Twelfth Night party, with his children playing key parts. That year there was a performance of the burlesque, *Guy Fawkes*. The following year, the play was *William Tell* (*Letters* 7: 53, 232n). And in 1854 he adapted Fielding's *Tom Thumb*, for domestic performance, staging it with his four-year-old son Henry Fielding Dickens (named after the author) in the title role. Dickens himself played the ghost, and Thackeray, among the audience, is reported to have fallen off his chair with laughter (MacKenzie 261).

Even after Dickens separated from his wife in 1858, he continued to organize ambitious Christmas gatherings in his Kentish country home at Gad's Hill (MacKenzie 336; Fitzgerald, "Christmas at Gadshill" passim), and on Boxing Day 1866 he threw open his cricket field there, for a day of competitive sports, which over 2,000 local people attended (MacKenzie 350–51).

But these festivities were only a continuation of the family tradition he had inherited as a young husband and father from his parents. Clearly, neither they nor he had ever been deterred by the fashionable indifference towards Christmas cultivated during the eighteenth century. During the 1830s and early 1840s, as we have seen, Romantic attitudes were tempering such indifference, but Dickens knew that open rejoicing during the festival, and demonstrations of emotion in conjunction with it, had long been interpreted as signs of low social standing. In *Barnaby Rudge*, set in the 1770s and 1780s but addressed to readers in 1841, Mr. Chester, who insists on his patrician status, is reluctant even to discuss emotional attachments with his son. "I believe you know," he says, "how very much I dislike what are called family affairs, which are only fit for plebeian Christmas days, and have no manner of business with people of our condition" (*Barnaby Rudge* 120). The disdain expressed at "plebeian Christmas days" had not been forgotten in 1841. Indeed, it was the overcoming of such disdain, I suggest, that prompted Thackeray and Jane Carlyle to marvel at the impact of *A Christmas Carol* (see p. 17 above).

Dickens, clearly, had always withstood such disdain. In *Pickwick Papers*, for those who can spot it, there is a moment during which the low esteem attached to Christmas customs is shown to have special personal resonance for him. Advising his son on the composition of a valentine, the coachdriver, Tony Weller, observes "Poetry's unnat'ral; no man ever talked poetry 'cept a beadle on boxin' day, or Warren's blackin', or Rowland's oil, or some of them low fellows . . . " (*Pickwick Papers* 443). Dickens had been humiliated by his employment as a child at Warren's Blacking Warehouse (Parker, *The Doughty Street Novels* 18–58). The association – in the mind of a coachdriver – of Boxing Day customs, Warren's advertising jingles, and low social status suggests a moment of private defiance on Dickens's part – an impulse at once to acknowledge and to face down prejudice against what was significant in his life. He evidently brought a similar attitude to practical Christmas merrymaking. And texts about Christmas that he wrote before 1843 invite us to applaud such an attitude.

On 27 December 1835, an essay entitled "Christmas Festivities"

appeared in *Bell's Weekly Messenger.* The author was declared to be
"Tibbs." Two months later, however, the piece reappeared in the first
series of *Sketches by Boz*, where it was renamed "A Christmas Dinner."
It was Dickens's first work devoted to the subject of Christmas.

To anyone familiar with his later works on the subject, the first
paragraph of "A Christmas Dinner" is astonishing – in more ways than
one. Its opening words alone encapsulate the theme of *A Christmas
Carol*:

> Christmas time! That man must be a misanthrope indeed, in
> whose breast something like a jovial feeling is not roused – in
> whose mind some pleasant associations are not awakened – by
> the recurrence of Christmas. (*Sketches by Boz* 220)

The sketch is not about the repudiation of Christmas rejoicing. Quite
the contrary. But, in the moment that he embarked upon the subject,
Dickens glimpsed the narrative possibilities of such repudiation.
Repudiation, indeed, was a state of mind which would take on a central
importance for him, and to which he would bend his art. To open with
it was, however momentarily, to sound potential depths of character and
plot. These, his first published words on Christmas, are in effect a
memorandum upon tasks yet to be undertaken.[10]

For the time being, however, Dickens sought only to recommend
jovial feeling and pleasant associations. "A Christmas Dinner" confirms
the historical and biographical evidence we have been reviewing.
Tortuous readings of the piece, to be sure, make it possible to deny this.
Anything more straightforward compels us to recognize that, as a young
man typical of the class into which he had been born, Dickens loved
Christmas, had always done so, expected his readers would do so too,
and was ready to denounce anyone who did not. Christmas Day is
declared "the merriest of the three hundred and sixty-five" (220). This
was not Dickens writing in the days of his fame – a Dickens who might
have told his readers what to think, and have them think it, true or not.
This was a journalist of just twenty-three, whose success depended on
an ability to offer readers something to which they could eagerly assent.
And what he offered them was Christmas Day as "the merriest of the
three hundred and sixty-five." He was clearly expecting them to be in
agreement, not puzzled.

The subject of the sketch is Christmas as it was celebrated in the mid-1830s by the majority of the population, which Dickens chose to represent in this instance by a middle-class family of a kind he was familiar with – a family with plebeian roots, unashamed of homely customs, lower-middle-class in its habits, however comfortably off. It is a subject that vindicates the full title he gave the book in which the piece is collected: *Sketches by Boz/Illustrative of Every-day Life and Every-day People*.

By 1835 Christmas was a fashionable topic for writers and, in publishing the sketch, the young Dickens was inevitably negotiating a place for himself within a tradition of Christmas writing. More specifically, he was declaring himself a follower of Washington Irving. In a letter of 21 April 1841, Dickens told Irving he had copies of all his books, and had loved them since childhood (*Letters* 2: 267–68). When he changed the title of his sketch to "A Christmas Dinner," for the more durable form of publication, he was proclaiming himself a member of Irving's school. "The Christmas Dinner" is a name Irving gave to one of his own Christmas sketches. The change, moreover, harmonizes gracefully with the tribute to Irving's *Sketchbook* paid in Dickens's choice of title for the entire collection.

But if Dickens was acknowledging a debt to Irving, he was not slavishly imitating him. "A Christmas Dinner" owes more to the literature of sentiment – to Addison, Sterne, and Mackenzie – and to contemporary melodrama, than it does to any text specifically devoted to the subject of Christmas. Irving influenced Dickens in more ways than one, but it was the fact he had written about Christmas which was important in this case, not the manner in which he had done so. Irving's Christmas sketches are fantastical in a way "A Christmas Dinner" is not. A genuine interest in actual practices only occasionally filters through delight in the antics of Squire Bracebridge, held up for contemplation precisely because he is patrician, eccentric, and unrepresentative. Irving was fantasizing about what might happen if the gentry tried to put into practice Romantic notions about Christmas. Documentation of what humbler people actually did during the festival is only incidentally to be found in the Christmas sketches. Work like Hone's, of course (see pp. 107–108 above), had pioneered faithful reporting of the bourgeois and plebeian Christmas. The example this kind of writing set for Dickens is acknowledged in the full title of the *Sketches.* Hone's manner, though, influenced Dickens no more than Irving's.

The notion that Dickens might have been trying to illustrate everyday life and everyday people in "A Christmas Dinner," however, is one that has been resisted. The sketch squarely contradicts popular notions about the history of Christmas and Dickens's role in it; so much so that elaborate readings have been contrived to explain this away. Ruth Glancy is a Dickens scholar of real substance and achievement, but her entry on Christmas in the *Oxford Reader's Companion to Dickens* advises readers that "the well-to-do Londoners of 'A Christmas Dinner' are an old middle-class family rather than the *nouveau riche* class that Dickens frequently satirizes in *Sketches by Boz*" (Schlicke 95). She is upholding the notion of Christmas merriment in the 1830s as the exception rather than the rule, as something kept up by those of higher rank in defiance of mass indifference. Now, though, we can see things differently. During that decade, an "old middle-class family" in London would have been among the minority least likely to celebrate with any conviction.

A few details of the story, admittedly, might be taken to license a reading such as Glancy's. Members of the household upon which the sketch focuses are comfortably off. Some of the family described are deemed positively wealthy. Their annual gathering assembles both rich and poor, we are told. One member, Margaret, has married a poor man without the consent of the family matriarch, "and poverty not being a sufficiently weighty punishment for her offence, has been discarded by her friends, and debarred the society of her dearest relatives" (*Sketches by Boz* 223). Dynastic ambitions are evidently nourished. None of this, though, is irreconcilable with nouvelle richesse.

Numerous small clues, in fact, indicate the family has the same social standing as the Pickwickians in *Pickwick Papers.* Members are among successful new recruits to the middle classes, promoted to them by the Industrial Revolution and the Napoleonic wars – probably no more than a generation or two into middle-class life, that is to say, prosperous, ambitious, eager to acquire superior styles, but for all that still comfortable with older, humbler ways, still appreciative of comforts earlier generations had never known. They belong to a class Dickens would have become acquainted with in his parents' circle, and through his work as a journalist.[11]

One small clue we notice, for instance, is that domestic work is not left entirely to servants, as it would be in a grander household. Family members are intimately involved in preparations for the Christmas party. Grandpapa, we are told, "always WILL toddle down, all the way to Newgate-market, to buy the turkey." Grandmamma by no means scorns the kitchen, recruits all the children to stone the plums, and

> insists, regularly every year, on uncle George coming down into the kitchen, taking off his coat, and stirring the pudding for half an hour or so, which uncle George good-humouredly does, to the vociferous delight of the children and servants. (221)

On Christmas morning, most of the family go to church, "leaving aunt George at home dusting decanters and filling casters, and uncle George carrying bottles into the dining-parlour, and calling for corkscrews, and getting into everybody's way" (222). "Dining-parlour" alone suggests domestic arrangements less formal than those of the upper-middle classes. There are none but female servants for uncle George to get in the way of, moreover. Grandmamma has "purchased a beautiful new cap with pink ribbons for each of the servants" (221). There is no butler, valet, footman, or groom to be offended by this.

The narrative indicates that family members are self-conscious about formal clothing. Grandmamma's "high cap, and slate-coloured silk gown," Grandpapa's "beautifully plaited shirt-frill, and white neckerchief" (222) are not things taken for granted, by those who have known nothing but prosperity and the style that goes with it. Relations arrive by hired hackney-coach, not in their own carriages. Small children sit down to dinner, not in a nursery, but with the adults. Comic songs are sung. No one sings comic songs during the Christmas episode of *Emma* (see pp. 70–71 above). I could go on.

But perhaps the single most persuasive clue is the emphasis on emotion in the sketch, and on the way it guides behaviour. What people feel at Christmas is given at least as much attention as what they do. Writers such as Addison, Sterne, and Mackenzie supplied Dickens with models for the display of ennobling emotion. Contemporary melodrama emboldened him to spring surprises with unexpected emotion. Both traditions were underpinned by theories of moral sentiment articulated by such writers as the Earl of Shaftesbury and Adam Smith.[12] Dickens, too, rooted morality in sentiment, but he would eventually develop a more complex understanding of the connection than we can find in any of the precedents he looked to.

Hesitantly, "A Christmas Dinner" begins to explore, not only the moral promptings of feeling, but also its complexities and contradictions. Such emotional untidiness at Christmas time, we should however remember, could still be read as a social indicator. Do not forget Mr. Chester's words: "What are called family affairs are only fit for plebeian Christmas days." Perturbations of this kind, many felt, were not for polite society. It took *A Christmas Carol* to change the manners of the metropolitan elite at Christmas time. However fashionable sentiment might have been in the 1830s, the emotions on show in "A Christmas Dinner" were a sign of plebeian roots, Dickens's own, and those of the family featured in the sketch.

Dickens still lacked sureness, though, in his handling of untidy emotions. They evidently unsettled him. To begin with, the narrator urges suppression of painful memories, in the interest of rejoicing. Later, we are given an example of remembered emotion correcting moral judgment, but it is only pleasurable emotion that is remembered. What the narrative formally tells us, indeed, suggests it is only such emotion that can be remembered profitably. This early work reveals Dickens's incipient interest in conflict of mind: in disaffection, repudiation, denial, repression; but it reveals it more by manifesting such conflict and letting it stand, than by scrutinizing it. Dickens would eventually launch a tradition of texts composed for Christmas, in which memory – of pain as well as of pleasure – is used to achieve mental balance and moral soundness. In such texts memory becomes an instrument of redemption, the trigger of recognition – of what Aristotle calls anagnorisis (Aristotle ch. 11). But that was some way off yet. He had first more thoroughly to explore his own feelings about the festival.

One thing, though, is clear. He was attempting something new. He could have contented himself just with recycling accounts of the old Christmas customs documented by antiquarians and Romantics but, even at this stage in his career, he chose a different strategy. An interest in such matters would come to him, but for now he chose not to dwell on the ancient customs of a community – forgotten, persisted in, or revived. It was the much more problematic past of the individual and of the family that seized his attention. The family Christmas offered him a territory to be searched for ways in which, for each of us, the past lives in the present and informs the future, ways in which old emotion is restimulated and has to be accommodated.

On this occasion, however, he explored with little deliberation, more instinctively than consciously. The struggle of contrary impulses within him led him into an atrocious lapse of judgment and taste – a revealing one, though, and one to which I shall come. He was only twenty-three, we should remember, and he evidently learned from this mistake.

The way emotion is handled in "A Christmas Dinner" owes much to its form. For this, and for many of the other *Sketches by Boz*, Dickens chose to adopt a form developed by eighteenth-century essayists. The sketch occupies an indeterminate zone between sagacious (or would-be sagacious) general observation and particularized fiction, between essay and short story. Sometimes the narrative voice addresses the reader directly, informing, advising, encouraging, and exhorting, sometimes it just tells a tale. General recommendation is substantiated by particular instance – normally in that order.

The principal transition between the narrator's general observations and particularized fiction is made with some skill, a quarter of the way through the sketch. There has been discussion of the kind of things people do at Christmas, and of family parties. "The Christmas family-party that we mean," the narrator tells us,

> is not a mere assemblage of relations, got up at a week or two's notice, originating this year, having no family precedent in the last, and not likely to be repeated in the next. No. It is an annual gathering of all the accessible members of the family, young or old, rich or poor; and all the children look forward to it, for two months beforehand, in a fever of anticipation.

On the brink of the particular this may be, but it is still general observation. The next words, however, with a self-conscious audacity the reader is invited to admire, immerse us in the particular. "Formerly," we are told, the party

> was held at grandpapa's; but grandpapa getting old, and

> grandmamma getting old too, and rather infirm, they have given
> up house-keeping, and domesticated themselves with uncle
> George; so, the party always takes place at uncle George's
> house . . . . (221)

This, though, is only the most distinct transition. The sketch is characterized by repeated adjustments of focus, between sentiment uttered by the narrative voice and economically particularized incident. *Mutatis mutandis*, it was a technique Dickens would adapt for his novels. In this embryonic form it facilitates a mood of peculiar emotional intimacy between narrator and reader. "I know what you are talking about," the reader is encouraged inwardly to murmur from time to time. "There is no need to spell out more detail."

To begin with, however, Dickens's instincts took him deeper into the turbulence of emotional life than he was prepared to go, and he took fright at the plunge. We can see his judgment faltering. Advice intended to be sagacious becomes obnoxious. Yet we can also see how he learned by his temerity.

The first paragraph of the sketch provides an extraordinary moment, at once familiar and grating, for readers accustomed to Dickens's better-known Christmas works. "There are people who will tell you that Christmas is not to them what it used to be," the narrator says,

> that each succeeding Christmas has found some cherished hope,
> or happy prospect, of the year before, dimmed or passed away;
> that the present only serves to remind them of reduced
> circumstances and straitened incomes – of the feasts they once
> bestowed on hollow friends, and of the cold looks that meet
> them now, in adversity and misfortune. Never heed such dismal
> reminiscences. There are few men who have lived long enough
> in the world, who cannot call up such thoughts any day in the
> year. Then do not select the merriest of the three hundred and
> sixty-five for your doleful recollections, but draw your chair
> nearer the blazing fire – fill the glass and send round the song –
> and if your room be smaller than it was a dozen years ago, or if
> your glass be filled with reeking punch, instead of sparkling
> wine, put a good face on the matter, and empty it off-hand, and
> fill another, and troll off the old ditty you used to sing, and thank
> God it's no worse. Look on the merry faces of your children (if

you have any) as they sit round the fire. One little seat may be empty; one slight form that gladdened the father's heart, and roused the mother's pride to look upon, may not be there. Dwell not upon the past; think not that one short year ago, the fair child now resolving into dust, sat before you, with the bloom of health upon its cheek, and the gaiety of infancy in its joyous eye. Reflect upon your present blessings – of which every man has many – not on your past misfortunes, of which all men have some. Fill your glass again, with a merry face and contented heart. Our life on it, but your Christmas shall be merry, and your new year a happy one! (220)

This declares a preference for ritual – doing the right thing in the right way at the right time – over narrative. The customs of the season are more important, it insists, than private memories the season might provoke. "Dwell not upon the past," however, is an injunction readers familar with *A Christmas Carol* will find strange. And it gets worse. "Never mind that it is Christmas and your child is dead," the narrator in effect says. "Have another glass of gin and hot water." So much for the Tiny Tims of 1835. There are strong feelings and generous sentiments at work in the passage, there is no doubt about that, but they lead to tactlessness awesome in magnitude, and entirely self-defeating. Only a twenty-three-year-old, maturing unevenly, could be tempted to suppose a sorrowing parent might be comforted with the words, "think not that one short year ago, the fair child now resolving into dust, sat before you, with the bloom of health upon its cheek, and the gaiety of infancy in its joyous eye."

But the chemistry of the passage is remarkable. Instinctively – barely consciously – Dickens uses the tension he senses between ritual and narrative, the polarity the form imposes between general recommendation and particular experience, to generate, almost despite himself, a representation of a very complex state of mind. When we look carefully at this passage, we can discover ingredients he would soon be blending much more skilfully into his unique and compelling Christmas vision. There is the happy family gathering around the Christmas fireside. There is comparison of past and present. There is tenderhearted dwelling – by the narrator at any rate – upon an occasion of grief. And it is this combination which gives the opening of the sketch its strange, brooding power.

Dickens's vision of Christmas is characterized by a feature, which critics rarely spell out.[13] It is important plainly to state it here: in his imagination, Christmas was closely associated with the death of loved ones, especially of children. Nothing could more powerfully promote the singularities of narrative over the periodicities of ritual. It is an association which called upon him to reconcile contradictions, and to understand emotional complexities, moreover, in a way the tame formulae of the literature of sentiment scarcely allowed. The understanding of personality Dickens would develop – and which, thanks to his interest in Christmas, he fumbles with in this passage – was centered upon the human need to accommodate memories of trouble and sorrow, as well as of joy.

Premature death, and infant mortality in particular, were things all too common in the early nineteenth century. Mourning at Christmas time was something few families could have been spared. Dickens had a better memory, moreover, and a keener sensibility than was found in most families, a sensibility capable of courageous and surprising syntheses. His insistent association of Christmas and death, particularly the death of children, may well have been rooted in his own childhood experiences.

Two of his siblings had died when he was a child. Alfred Allen Dickens had died in Portsmouth, aged seven months, on 6 September 1814, when Charles was two and a half. Harriet Ellen Dickens had died, aged three, some time during 1822, when Charles was ten.[14] It is likely that he had sensed, at Christmas in 1814 and 1822, how his parents were trying to master their grief for the sake of the other children. Some such experience, at any rate, doubtless restimulated by later bereavements, seems permanently to have marked his apprehension of Christmas.

But this mark is what makes it more than a protracted encomium of plum pudding and holly. What started as idiosyncratic association, half rejected, he would eventually recognise as lucky inspiration. An awkward mixture would be converted into thrilling dissonance. He would achieve wholeness in texts he wrote about Christmas, by compelling the changeless and the changing to vitalize each other. Against the rhythm of the annual festival, transcending the vicissitudes of life, he would set contingent narratives of life and death, love and grief, joy and sorrow, success and failure, preserved in the memory of merrymakers.   He would capitalize upon the shift from ritual to narrative, encouraged by changes in the way Christmas was celebrated. Little wonder that, for all the lack of tact, the flash of intensity we detect in this initial paragraph makes it stand out from the rest of "A Christmas Dinner."

On this occasion, to be sure, Dickens fails to accommodate remembrance of bereavement and grief in a way he was later to do. A young man's appetite for merriment prevails. It traps the narrator into recommending the rejection of memory. It is this failure that is so grating. With deep feeling, the reader is urged to shun deep feeling. Grievers are urged to forget, but what it is they should forget is indicated in uncompromisingly memorable terms. The phrase "in denial" springs to mind.

But it is difficult not to suppose Dickens's error here taught him a lesson. The power of the passage lies in its contradictions. Tensions between wanting to remember and not wanting to, wanting to rejoice and not wanting to, may not be acknowledged, but the reader can certainly sense them. The components of Dickens's Christmas vision are being assembled, if not put into full working order.   Failure notwithstanding, we can see something new and authentically Dickensian coming into being. Though he scarcely realizes it, Dickens is working towards seeing the annual coming-round of the festival as an occasion for the resolution of emotional contradictions, essential to mental balance, essential ultimately to moral understanding. It was this vision that would change the way people think and feel about Christmas.

Dickens manages tamer and safer emotions more skilfully in "A Christmas Dinner," but to less powerful effect. For this, he employs a reassuring convention of melodrama which permits recognition of only limited emotional complexity, and no proper resolution of contradictions. Many of the effects of melodrama are, in effect, based on a theory of emotional latency. Only one emotion can dominate the behavior of an individual at any given time, we are encouraged to believe, but a latent emotion may replace it. A formulaic eruption of memory, triggered by circumstances, can yield a formulaic change of heart.

"Poor aunt Margaret," in the sketch, puts in an unexpected appearance at the family party. Grandmamma "draws herself up, rather stiff and stately," at the thought of receiving the miscreant once again.

> But Christmas has come round, and the unkind feelings that have struggled against better dispositions during the year, have melted away before its genial influence, like half-formed ice beneath the morning sun. It is not difficult in a moment of angry feeling for a parent to denounce a disobedient child; but, to banish her at a period of general good-will and hilarity, from the hearth, round which she has sat on so many anniversaries of the same day, expanding by slow degrees from infancy to girlhood, and then bursting, almost imperceptibly, into a woman, is widely different. The air of conscious rectitude, and cold forgiveness, which the old lady has assumed, sits ill upon her; and when the poor girl is led in by her sister, pale in looks and broken in hope – not from poverty, for that she could bear, but from the consciousness of undeserved neglect, and unmerited unkindness – it is easy to see how much of it is assumed. A momentary pause succeeds; the girl breaks suddenly from her sister and throws herself, sobbing, on her mother's neck. The father steps hastily forward, and takes her husband's hand. Friends crowd round to offer their hearty congratulations, and happiness and harmony again prevail. (223)

Double-blind testing might not yield many predictions that the writer of this was to be acclaimed a great novelist within months. To say no more, he still has to learn to avoid phrases like "bursting, almost imperceptibly." And the sudden conversion we witness is not merely formulaic. It is stagey – literally so. A few years later, Dickens was to lampoon melodramatic contrivance such as this in *Nicholas Nickleby*. Nicholas tells an actor about a part he is adapting for him. Overcome with remorse at his crimes, and preparing to shoot himself, the character the actor is to play hears a clock strike ten.

> "You pause," said Nicholas; "you recollect to have heard a clock strike ten in your infancy. The pistol falls from your hand – you are overcome – you burst into tears, and become a virtuous and exemplary character for ever afterwards."
> (*Nicholas Nickleby* 277)

Staginess notwithstanding, "A Christmas Dinner" is stylishly put together. Reaching the end, only a grudging reader could withhold assent from the narrator's neatly turned peroration:

> And thus the evening passes, in a strain of rational good-will and cheerfulness, doing more to awaken the sympathies of every member of the party in behalf of his neighbour, and to perpetuate their good feeling during the ensuing year, than half the homilies that have ever been written, by half the Divines that have ever lived. (*Sketches by Boz* 224)

Yet nothing else in the sketch matches in intensity that strange, self-defeating advice against memory of loss and bereavement in the first paragraph. However inadvertently, Dickens confronts life and death there. He confronts the need to accommodate such fundamentals in the human heart, the need to adjust conduct in recognition of them. He shows more assurance in writing of lesser matters – of family ambitions, family disputes – but, almost despite himself, perceives greater possibilities.

Dickens's search for a way to engage his art with Christmas began with a find, then, little better than accidental, and anxiously resisted, but he was too much of an artist not to recognize, if only instinctively, the potential of what he had stumbled upon. Within a year, he would be conducting another experiment with the topic of Christmas.

Within that year, the promising young journalist became a best-selling novelist. The first monthly part of *Pickwick Papers* was issued in March 1836. By June the novel was proving a publishing phenomenon. There are plenty of indications why in the tenth part. Issued in December 1836, it includes two chapters (28 and 29) devoted to Christmas festivities. These show Dickens trying out different perspectives upon the festival, but still inexorably drawn towards the perception that had come to him unwittingly in the first paragraph of "A Christmas Dinner."

The design of *Pickwick* did not, in fact, accommodate it to the unique response to Christmas that was taking shape in Dickens's

imagination, if not in his consciousness.   In the book, he displays a
mastery of his craft and a confidence, not to be found in the *Sketches*,
but there is still an awkwardness about the Christmas chapters.   He
offers no tactless advice this time, but he fails to integrate what he feels
with what the book calls for.

It calls, primarily, for the close observation of manners.   Doubtless
that is why an awareness of ancient and popular Christmas customs can
be accommodated in these chapters.   "Christmas was close at hand," the
narrator tells readers,

> in all his bluff and hearty honesty; it was the season of
> hospitality, merriment, and open-heartedness; the old year was
> preparing, like an ancient philosopher, to call his friends around
> him, and amidst the sound of feasting and revelry to pass gently
> and calmly away. (*Pickwick Papers* 365)

There is a hint here of Christmas as a marker of time and change, but
much more distinctive is the echo of the medieval call for everyone to
be sociable, hospitable, and merry. Dickens saw an opportunity to dilate
upon Christmas rituals.

In the months that elapsed between "A Christmas Dinner" and part
10 of *Pickwick*, he must have been reading, re-reading, or at least
thinking about texts that document old Christmas customs.   The very
title of chapter 28 ironically alludes to the Romantic view of such
matters:

> A good-humoured Christmas Chapter, containing an Account of
> a Wedding, and some other Sports beside: which, although in
> their way even as good Customs as Marriage itself, are not quite
> so religiously kept up, in these degenerate Times.[15] (366)

Dickens had read Irving's Christmas sketches as a child.   By 1844 he
would own copies of Hone's *Every-Day Book* and Strutt's *Sports and
Pastimes*. Both were editions published in 1838 (see p. 107 above), but
that does not mean he was unaware, in 1836, of the contents of earlier
editions.

The Christmas chapters of *Pickwick*, at any rate, repeatedly allude to just the traditions such sources document. Mention is made of "the sprigs of holly with red berries" in the window of an inn (369), and of garnishing food with "a bit o' Christmas" (376). The food, we are told, includes mince pies and a Christmas pie (376), the drink a wassail bowl (384). Christmas games are played – blindman's buff, snapdragon, and forfeits (384–85). Christmas songs and carols are sung (385–86, 388). A ghost story is told (387–97).

It would be a mistake, though, to suppose Dickens knew of such traditions only from books. His attention may have been drawn to them by books. Books may have persuaded him to give them more prominence than perhaps experience warranted. But it is hard to avoid the conclusion that Dickens had learned of them at firsthand too.

The celebrations we witness in the novel take place in the Kentish farmhouse of Mr. Pickwick's friend Mr. Wardle, located by Dickens not far from his childhood home in Chatham, near Rochester, where the family had lived when his father was a pay clerk at Chatham dockyard. The setting selected this time is not the home of an urban, middle-class family, but a center for a big, diverse, old-fashioned, rural community – home and workplace both. It is the sort of location where, so evidence suggests, ancient traditions of communal merrymaking did in fact survive. The festivities of rich farmers are alluded to in *Christmas*, by Romaine Joseph Thorn (see pp. 82–83 above). And a broadside ballad by "Laura Maria," published in London in 1800, anticipates with some precision what we find in *Pickwick*:

> The *Farmer's* kitchin [sic] long had been
> Of annual sports the busy scene;
> The wood fire blaz'd, the chimney wide,
> Presented seats on either side:
> Long rows of wooden *trenchers*, clean,
> Bedeck'd with *holly-boughs* were seen;
> The shining tankard's foamy ale
> Gave *spirits* to the *goblin* tale,
> While many a rosy cheek grew pale.
>
> It happen'd that, some sport to show,
> The ceiling held – a MISTLETOE:
> A magic bough, and well design'd

> To prove the coyest maiden *kind*:
> A magic bough, which DRUIDS old
> In sacred mysteries enroll'd;
> And which, or gossip FAME's a liar,
> *Still* warms the soul with vivid fire . . . .[16]

In *Pickwick*, festivities begin in the great kitchen of the farmhouse, "in which the family were by this time assembled, according to annual custom on Christmas eve, observed by old Wardle's forefathers from time immemorial." Brand, Irving, and writers such as "Laura Maria," had all made much of kissing under the mistletoe. Dickens was not to be outdone:

> From the centre of the ceiling of this kitchen, old Wardle had just suspended, with his own hands, a huge branch of mistletoe, and this same branch of mistletoe instantaneously gave rise to a scene of general and delightful struggling and confusion; in the midst of which, Mr. Pickwick, with a gallantry that would have done honour to a descendant of Lady Tollimglower herself, took the old lady by the hand, led her beneath the mystic branch, and saluted her in all courtesy and decorum. The old lady submitted to this piece of practical politeness with all the dignity which befitted so important and serious a solemnity, but the younger ladies, not being so thoroughly imbued with a superstitious veneration for the custom: or imagining that the value of the salute is very much enhanced if it cost a little trouble to obtain it: screamed and struggled, and ran into corners, and threatened and remonstrated, and did everything but leave the room, until some of the less adventurous gentlemen were on the point of desisting, when they all at once found it useless to resist any longer, and submitted to be kissed with good grace. (382)

Uninterrupted traditions, revered customs – what Dickens is suggesting seems plain enough.

This is neither wishful thinking against what could be observed at the time, nor a description of pious revival. No writer of his era was less inclined than Dickens towards the revival of old customs out of piety. For the author of *The Mudfog Papers* (1837–38), for the chronicler of Sir Joseph Bowley's New Year dinner in *The Chimes* (*Christmas Books*

145–52), nostalgic reenactment was something not to extol, but to ridicule. And we are now in a position to see that observation could have supplied him with much data about festive customs. In town and country, the majority of the population was keeping up Christmas: working people, certainly; lower-middle-class people, certainly; and many others too, including some great landowners. Squires were feasting their servants, clergymen their poor parishioners. The Pickwickian Christmas is set in the year 1827. The coincidence is arbitrary, but it does seem worth remarking that 1827 was the year John Clare's *Shepherd's Calendar* appeared, with stanzas for December insisting that Christmas was welcomed round "every hearth." There is bookish influence on the Christmas chapters of *Pickwick*, we can be confident, but there is no need to suppose they owe their very existence to books.

Dickens was eagerly contributing to a growing discourse on old Christmas customs. He was not trying to rescue a festival all but defunct. He was responding to a surge of interest in it. His aim was to spread knowledge of festive customs among those eager to learn, to recommend customs which may have been rare, localized or half-forgotten, to preserve abundance and diversity and, above all, to counter an indifference which, for all that it was not widespread, was fashionable. He knew that neglect of Christmas, in some circles, met with no opprobrium, and that offended him. The first words he had published on the topic were a denunciation of the misanthrope, "in whose breast something like a jovial feeling is not roused – in whose mind some pleasant associations are not awakened – by the recurrence of Christmas." It is a sentiment echoed in chapter 29 of *Pickwick*, when the goblin reproaches the sexton for digging a grave on Christmas Eve, "when all other men are merry" (392). Dickens writes as a man who knows he has the majority of his readers with him.

He makes sure that conscious effort to maintain festive tradition is commended. Mr. Pickwick's servant, Sam Weller, asks Mr. Wardle's servant, Emma, if it is true "your family has games in the kitchen" on Christmas Eve.

"Yes, Mr. Weller," replied Emma; "we always have on

Christmas eve. Master wouldn't neglect to keep it up on any account."

"Your master's a wery pretty notion of keepin' anythin' up, my dear," said Mr. Weller; "I never see such a sensible sort of man as he is, or such a reg'lar gen'l'm'n." (380–81)

Sam and Emma's interest in the maintenance of such a tradition is to be expected. Servants had everything to gain by it. We may be inclined, though, to wonder whether such a figure as Mr. Wardle would have shared their interest. He is introduced as a "stout old gentleman," who keeps his own barouche. His home, Manor Farm, Dingley Dell, is not a farm producing food for a separate manor but a manor in its own right, which his family has occupied for generations. At least one titled member of the gentry – Lady Tollimglower – has been among the family's acquaintance. But Mr. Wardle is also a working farmer. His home is repeatedly called "the farm." Farmers among his guests discuss the merits of his land.

There are moments when the text seems to suggest Mr. Wardle is a small squire. He is called "the hearty old landlord," for instance. There are others when it seems to suggest he is a substantial yeoman farmer. "If any of the old English yeomen had turned into fairies when they died," we are told, the best sitting room of the farmhouse "was just the place in which they would have held their revels." The ambiguity can in fact be explained quite simply. Landlords, freehold farmers, and large tenant farmers had done well during the Napoleonic Wars, and had been protected by the Corn Laws since. Small squires and rich farmers were converging (Parker, *The Doughty Street Novels* 100–101). Sam Weller perceives Mr. Wardle as a "reg'lar gen'l'm'n." Members of his class were widely so perceived. But the master of Manor Farm was clearly no member of the metropolitan elite, nor was he among those members of the country gentry most likely to follow its fashions. If anyone could, it would be rich farmers such as Mr. Wardle who, in the early decades of the nineteenth century, could declare,

"Everybody sits down with us on Christmas eve, as you see them now – servants and all; and here we wait, until the clock strikes twelve, to usher Christmas in, and beguile the time with forfeits and old stories." (384–85)

We can believe that Mr. Wardle's family would have been as little infected by fashionable disdain for Christmas as the urban, middle-class family of "A Christmas Dinner." But we can see, too, how likely it was to have been less distanced from older, communal traditions of merrymaking.   We do not know whether Dickens had ever been acquainted with anyone like Mr. Wardle, but Percy Fitzgerald, who was friendly with Dickens from 1858, maintained that the Christmas scenes at Manor Farm, "were reminiscences of early experiences."   Dickens was "clearly thinking of his old Rochester times" (Fitzgerald, "Dickens in his Books" 703). It seems likely, at any rate, that he perceived an affinity between the attitude of Mr. Wardle's class towards Christmas, and the attitude of the class from which he had himself risen.

Documentation of Christmas customs was something encouraged by the kind of book *Pickwick* is.   It gave Dickens an opportunity to promote practices he cared for.   In the Christmas chapters, though, he was still reaching out instinctively, beyond manners, towards a different and more challenging kind of subject matter.   Readers familiar with "A Christmas Dinner" are unsurprised to hear a solemn note being struck in chapter 28.   However inappropriately, Dickens was continuing to cultivate the understanding of the festival that, almost despite himself, he had chanced upon a year earlier. The hearts of Mr. Pickwick and his friends were gladdened by the season, we are told.

> And numerous indeed are the hearts to which Christmas brings a brief season of happiness and enjoyment. How many families, whose members have been dispersed and scattered far and wide, in the restless struggles of life, are then reunited, and meet once again in that happy state of companionship and mutual good-will, which is a source of such pure and unalloyed delight, and one so incompatible with the cares and sorrows of the world, that the religious belief of the most civilised nations, and the rude traditions of the roughest savages, alike number it among the first joys of a future condition of existence, provided for the blest and happy! How many old recollections, and how many dormant sympathies, does Christmas time awaken!
>
> We write these words now, many miles distant from the spot at which, year after year, we met on that day, a merry and joyous circle. Many of the hearts that throbbed so gaily then, have

ceased to beat; many of the looks that shone so brightly then, have ceased to glow; the hands we grasped have grown cold; the eyes we sought have hid their lustre in the grave; and yet the old house, the room, the merry voices and smiling faces, the jest, the laugh, the most minute and trivial circumstances connected with those happy meetings, crowd upon our mind at each recurrence of the season, as if the last assemblage had been but yesterday! Happy, happy Christmas, that can win us back to the delusion of our childish days; that can recall to the old man the pleasures of his youth; that can transport the sailor and the traveller, thousands of miles away, back to his own fire-side and his quiet home! (366–67)

This is curiously out of place, it has to be said. It stands out as an oddity in a novel dwelling so intently upon the ridiculous. An unfamiliar voice interrupts the narrative – certainly not the voice we hear at the beginning of the novel, of the deluded editor, thrilled by the Pickwick Club's papers, and in awe of the "gigantic brain of Pickwick" (4). A feature of the novel, admittedly, is the sentimental education of that editor, in parallel with that of Mr. Pickwick himself, but the change here is too abrupt. The sentiments expressed, moreover, have nothing to do with the tale being told. Mr. Wardle's Pickwickian guests are thoroughly deracinated and show no sign they are thinking of absent loved ones. Only Mr. Winkle acknowledges any relation at all, a father whom he disobeys and with whom he has to be reconciled. The chronology of the novel, such as it is, suggests the Pickwickians have known Mr. Wardle for not much more than a year, his family for only seven months. All of them meet together for the first time in mid-May 1827, when Mr. Wardle reminds the Pickwickians that he "spent some ev'nins at your club last winter" (55). The friends being reunited, then, can scarcely be supposed old ones.

Pickwick Papers is an extraordinary novel, but it is a novel of little more than immediate experience. In it we see Mr. Pickwick changing and growing, to be sure, yet the events chronicled take no more than two years. Emotion, of which there is plenty, is provoked only by what happens during this period. Character is marked and intelligible, but none of its roots are exposed. Relationships unfold within the same short time scheme. And there is nothing wrong with this. It works triumphantly. What we see in this passage, however, is a capricious experiment with a more penetrating and expansive kind of narrative, brought on by thoughts of Christmas. Partly inspired by the literature of sentiment, but working towards something altogether more distinctive, Dickens is reaching out towards a fiction in which identity is deeply layered, in which the past matters, in which even the dead play a part. Unlike the narrator of "A Christmas Dinner," the narrator of *Pickwick*, far from forgetting bereavement at Christmas time, makes a point of remembering it, and evidently feels more whole through doing so. But he is forgetting the job in hand.

Not until *A Christmas Carol* would Dickens successfully construct a fiction of the kind he looks towards here. It would be constructed, thanks not least to the feelings Christmas aroused in Dickens. It would be constructed with Christmas at the heart of it. In *Pickwick*, however, his subject matter was behavior, motivated no more than need be. This was consonant with the illustration of old customs, but not with an exploration of the memories and feelings Christmas brings. In the passage we have been looking at, he has the teller of his tale insert such an exploration by force, regardless of the tale. Dickens was refining his craft, certainly, but in the wrong book for it.

Yet for all its being out of place, the passage builds up to a moment of great power. Gone are the clumsiness and tactlessness of "A Christmas Dinner." This time Dickens organizes the components of his Christmas vision into a fine synthesis. The first paragraph is a little preachy, perhaps – and not even right. Not all religions promise happy reunion with loved ones after death. But there is no finer writing in *Pickwick* than we find in the second paragraph. No jarring note distracts us this time. The injunction, "Dwell not upon the past" has a place no longer in what is said. Quite the contrary. Repression is discouraged, memory extolled. Christmas brings happiness, it is suggested, not only by reuniting the living with each other, but also by reuniting the living with the dead, and by recalling memories of lost happiness, lost loved ones, in a way that diminishes rather than revives pain. Dickens brings to the passage a new mastery of tone, new assurance. Distance and proximity, vitality and dissolution, past and present, are balanced with an exactness that yields a kind of heartfelt calm. Emotional contradictions are resolved. Only by such means, the passage urges, can what is true be steadily seen, what is precious be steadily valued. It encapsulates what was to remain, for the rest of his life, the core of Dickens's thinking about Christmas, and marks a key stage in his search for a fulfilling understanding of the festival.

But because the passage is a digression, this cannot be made a moment of recognition. We seem to be on the brink of a declaration, to be sure, that the narrator has achieved some kind of transfiguration, some kind of redemption, but it is never uttered. *Pickwick*, after all, is not about its narrator.

Chapter 29 of *Pickwick Papers* is devoted to a ghost story, told by Mr. Wardle on Christmas Eve. Such a story, like some of the other interpolated tales in the novel, offered Dickens, among other things, an opportunity to see what he could do with a more extended chronology. He took it, if a little uncertainly.

During the late eighteenth and the early nineteenth century, two ghost-story traditions were pulling in opposite directions. There was a Romantic tradition which sought to suspend disbelief in ghosts, and revive something comparable to medieval and Renaissance credulity. This is expressed in stories by Walpole, Lewis, Maturin, and Hogg, and accounts for the continuing popularity of older works like *Round about our Coal Fire* (see p. 105 above). And there was an Enlightenment tradition which sought to couple the *frisson* provoked by ghost stories with rational explanation. This is expressed in Mrs. Radcliffe's novels, and formulated in the subtitle of an anthology, *Ghost Stories*, published by Ackermann in 1823. The stories, it declared, were "Collected with a Particular View to Counteract the Vulgar Belief in Ghost and Apparitions, and to Promote a Rational Estimate of the Nature of Phenomena commonly considered as Supernatural."

But the most successful ghost stories of the era playfully resist containment within either tradition, and constitute a third. Burns's verse narrative, "Tam O'Shanter" (1791), allows readers to wonder what Tam's apparitions owe to ale and "usquebae." Irving's "Legend of

Sleepy Hollow" (1820) stops just short of declaring Brom Bones and a pumpkin responsible for Ichabod Crane's visitation. Readers are left teasingly suspended between natural and supernatural explanations. At the hand of such writers, ghost stories resolve into comedy. Comically evoked terrors are used to expose character, to investigate human weakness, perversity, and eccentricity.

Such temporization suited Dickens, too. Common sense made him sceptical about ghosts, Forster suggests (bk. 11, ch. 3), but he was reluctant to forego the opportunities that belief, however provisional, opened up to his imagination.

"The Story of the Goblins who stole a Sexton" is about Gabriel Grub, who hates Christmas, until the ministrations of goblins reform him. In it, Dickens follows the tradition of Burns and Irving. Gabriel's sobriety, like Tam's, is in question. He has frequent recourse to a wicker bottle. But Dickens develops the tradition. High-spirited comedy modulates into something more solemn.

The story is plainly a prototype for A Christmas Carol,[17] but is decidedly inferior to the production model. Unlike Scrooge's, Gabriel Grub's misanthropy is unexplained and motiveless. Dickens forgoes the opportunity to explore the conflicts of mind that produce such perversity. Unlike the ghosts of A Christmas Carol, the goblins have no clearly defined mission, no dignity. To change their victim, they rely as much upon physical torment as upon affecting visions. This scarcely inspires awe. And because the visions granted Gabriel are so stereotypical, they sink into mawkishness. None of them is keyed into Gabriel's own previous experience, in the way that makes the visions shown to Scrooge so overwhelming.

But the story has merits, too, that are more than just promising. Gabriel is perverse, and perversity is a sign, if not much more than that, of the kind of conflict of mind that would come to fascinate Dickens. Gabriel's perversity, moreover, is made convincing and interesting. For the first time in his career, in this story, Dickens creates a character consciously rejecting Christmas rejoicing, and that is an oddity which seizes the reader's attention. Like Scrooge – and like many of Dickens's great villains to come in different circumstances – Gabriel has clearly made an existential choice. He makes himself perfectly comfortable within his misanthropy, keeping it up with dedication, ingenuity, and a morbid wit the narrative cunningly feigns to endorse. On his way to dig a grave, late on Christmas Eve, he is offended by the spectacle of excited children. "Gabriel smiled grimly," however, "and clutched the handle of his spade with a firmer grasp, as he thought of measles, scarlet-fever, thrush, hooping-cough, and a good many other sources of consolation besides" (388). Finishing work on the grave, he chants a jaundiced little ditty, "Brave lodging for one . . . ," and amuses himself with a joke: "A coffin at Christmas! A Christmas Box. Ho! ho! ho!" (389). The reader is admitted into Gabriel's mind, allowed to share his uncouth pleasures, and persuaded that, for want of better, they are indeed pleasures of a kind.

Compared with the ghosts of the *Carol*, the goblins who reform Gabriel are unimpressive, but close students of Dickens's Christmas writings – and readers of this book – may notice something familiar about them. In shaping them, Dickens doubtless used bookish models his era made available to him. His description of the Goblin king's appearance, and Hablot Knight Browne's etching too, may owe something to an illustration by George Cruikshank, for an 1823 translation of the Grimms' story of Rumplestiltskin (Edgar Taylor 139–41). The blend of spiteful caprice and moral indignation, in the goblins' treatment of Gabriel, echoes a thousand traditional fairy stories.

But Gabriel's response to the goblins is characteristically Dickensian. The sexton tries to appear at ease, and to placate his tormentors with good manners. We have already seen grotesque creatures associated with Christmas, who inspire fear, but are greeted with feigned nonchalance. The goblins have much in common with the toys Dickens was to feature fourteen years later in "A Christmas Tree" (see pp. 114–143 above), and reinforce my contention that such toys were indeed among his own childhood memories.

Like the cardboard man operated with a string, the King of the Goblins has "very pliable legs," which he can flourish above his head, in his case prior to administering kicks (*Pickwick Papers* 395). Like "the Tumbler with his hands in his pockets," he has a remarkable capacity for abandoning and recovering his balance. At one point, the narrative declares, he stood upon his head, or rather upon the very point of his sugar-loaf hat, on the narrow edge of the tomb-stone: whence he threw a somerset with extraordinary agility, right to the sexton's feet, at which he planted himself in the attitude in which tailors generally sit upon the shopboard. (392)

Like the "demoniacal Counsellor in a black gown," the subordinate goblins spring into sight nightmarishly. And, given to unnerving jumping like "the frog with cobbler's wax on his tail," they delight in leaping over tombstones "with the utmost marvellous dexterity" (392–93).

Just like the toys, the goblins are "horrible," "not to be endured on any terms," not creatures "to be alone with." But they provoke in Gabriel a strategy of concealment, comparable to that remembered by the narrator of "A Christmas Tree," who recalls how, as a child, he "affected to laugh very much" at the tumbler, "but in my heart of hearts was extremely doubtful of him." Gabriel affects to be impressed by the chief goblin's flourishing of his legs, but is "half dead with fright." "Very curious, and very pretty," he politely observes, "but I think I'll go back and finish my work, sir, if you please" (392).

To see the memories described in "A Christmas Tree" in this way, underpinning the goblins of Gabriel Grub's story, is to gain an insight into the powers of absorption and synthesis that characterized Dickens's imagination, but it also shows us Dickens missing an opportunity at this stage in his career. Memories of toys given him at Christmas time, during early childhood, stayed with him, along with memories of the mixture of laughter and apprehension some of them had provoked. They formed a pattern that became imprinted. At twenty-four, writing a story designed to make readers laugh, but also to make them appreciate disquiet, Dickens recycled those memories, remodelling the toys as goblins, dividing laughter and apprehension, now, between the reader and Gabriel. At thirty-one, he added substance to the figure of Scrooge, by recycling the memories again, and giving Scrooge desperate little jokes to crack, to lighten his terror of the ghosts. And finally, at the age of thirty-eight, he went back to the source, and confronted the memories undisguised, in "A Christmas Tree."[18] In the story of Gabriel Grub, however, although he used early memories to shape it, he did not exploit early memories as a theme, as he was later so powerfully to do.

Nevertheless, the story does show us Dickens advancing his exploration of the theme of Christmas, by finding a new way to develop the association between Christmas, death, love, and memory. Now, a moral dimension is added. Gabriel's reform is signaled both by a new respect for Christmas, and by his turning from making coarse jokes about death to seeing it as something sanctified by love, against which the value of life must be measured in the memories of the living.

In their cavern beneath the earth, the goblins inflict physical pain upon Gabriel, but force him also to see his fellow creatures more clearly, and against a longer time-scale. One vision they show him is of a poor family, first seen in its modest dwelling, greeting the weary father's homecoming with joy.

> But a change came upon the view, almost imperceptibly. The scene was altered to a small bedroom, where the fairest and youngest child lay dying; the roses had fled from his cheek, and the light from his eye; and even as the sexton looked upon him, with an interest he had never felt or known before, he died. His young brothers and sisters crowded round his little bed and seized his tiny hand, so cold and heavy; but they shrunk back from its touch and looked with awe on his infant face; for calm and tranquil as it was, and sleeping in rest and peace as the beautiful child seemed to be, they saw that he was dead, and they knew that he was an angel looking down upon and blessing them from a bright and happy Heaven.

Other children die. The parents grow old, "but content and cheerfulness sat on every face and beamed in every eye as they crowded round the fireside, and told and listened to old stories of earlier and bygone days." Finally the father dies, shortly followed by his wife.

> The few who yet survived them knelt by their tomb and watered the green turf which covered it with their tears, then rose and turned away, sadly and mournfully, but not with bitter cries or despairing lamentations, for they knew that they should one day meet again; and once more they mixed with the busy world, and their content and cheerfulness were restored. (394)

It is difficult not to believe that the intensity of this has to do with Dickens's own memories of the death of siblings. "They saw that he was dead, and they knew that he was an angel looking down upon and blessing them from a bright and happy Heaven": this is an observation that reflects words such as sorrowing parents use to comfort bewildered little brothers and sisters. Many of today's readers will find such passages mawkish. We cannot help feeling that Dickens offers here a vision too closely wedded to a questionable and infantile theology. Infantile or not, it was a theology he subscribed to throughout his life, and it seems to me no more questionable than any other, but it can, to be sure, get in the way of an appreciation of what Dickens was working towards. Even within the ghost-story framework, rewards in heaven coexist uneasily with the kind of cause and effect we look for in fiction. Though he never abandoned the notion of dead children becoming angels, by the time he wrote *A Christmas Carol* Dickens had learned that, for literary purposes, foregrounding such a notion was less effective than dwelling on the complex and tender feelings aroused by the death of a loved one.

A foretaste of this more robust technique is afforded, momentarily, by the restrained disclosure of Gabriel's response to what he sees. He looks upon the dying child, "with an interest he had never felt or known before." Nothing more plainly prefigures the sentimental education of Scrooge (*Christmas Books* 52).

In chapter 28 of *Pickwick*, Dickens had digressed from his narrative to extol memories of sorrow and grief, seen as positively therapeutic. Now he begins to make them the hinge of narrative. Members of the poor family live with their past. They neither repress memory nor allow it to overwhelm them with distress. They are full of "content and cheerfulness" as they listen to "old stories of earlier and bygone days" (*Pickwick Papers* 394).

Narrative opportunities are missed, to be sure. Gabriel is made to contemplate such matters at Christmas time, but the tribulations and consolations of the poor family, and of people in other visions shown to Gabriel, are unrelated to Christmas. Gabriel's hatred of Christmas, moreover, is no more than a symptom of his moral defects. There is no suggestion that participation in festive rejoicing teaches moral understanding.   Dickens fails to exploit the potential of Christmas memories as a trigger for recognition and redemption.   He was not to do so before *A Christmas Carol*, but he was learning.

How swiftly, we can see in a couple of odd details.   After his experience with the goblins, Gabriel resolves not to return home, but to "seek his bread elsewhere."   Fellow townspeople find his lantern, his spade, and his wicker bottle in the churchyard, but not the sexton himself.   "It was speedily determined," the narrative declares, "that he had been carried away by the goblins."   Alert readers notice a failure of coherence here.   Dickens has forgotten that the townspeople know nothing of the goblins.[19]   Only Gabriel has seen them, and even he, it is suggested, might not have done so but for the wicker bottle.   Closure is reached, moreover, with Gabriel's reformation.   What, then, can have been Dickens's reason for this clumsy extension?

It makes room, it has to be said, for a joke about human gullibility. "There were not wanting some very credible witnesses," we are told, "who had distinctly seen him whisked through the air on the back of a chestnut horse blind in one eye, with the hind-quarters of a lion, and the tail of a bear."

Another detail, though, is more a sign of the direction Dickens's imagination was taking.   After ten years, we learn, Gabriel reappears in the town, "a ragged, contented, rheumatic old man" (396–97).   Dickens was unwilling, I suggest, to stop at the events of a single night.   Here again we see how he was working towards stories in which time mattered, in which memories of the past shape the present for an individual.   Clumsy though the extension is, it converts a story about a man changed, into one about a man grateful and happy over the years for a change wrought upon him.   It converts a story of reform into a story of redemption.   Dickens was learning the kind of story he needed to construct if his fiction was to become an adequate vehicle for his feelings about Christmas, if he was to use those feelings to enrich his fiction.

One more detail of the story of Gabriel Grub calls for comment.   It is an interpolated tale.   Such tales are inserted into novels, not least because of the narrative opportunities they provide.   A story told by a character or read from a document that the narrator describes, is not a story for which the narrator can be held responsible. Formally speaking, it is simply something he draws attention to, not something he endorses. Because of that, interpolated tales can be used to vary and enrich the design of a novel. They can provide a contrast with the main narrative, for which the narrator takes full responsibility. They can differ in content, in style, and in demands made upon readers' credulity. They can expose the main narrative to keener scrutiny, and invite keener appreciation of it, by acknowledging different kinds of understanding, and by distinguishing the sort readers can simply allow themselves to enjoy, from the sort they are invited to share.

But if an interpolated tale can enhance appreciation of what is believable in the main narrative, the main narrative, simply by being believable, can licence every kind of fancy and implausibility in an interpolated tale. It can provide a reassuring frame, within which wonders can be contemplated without doubt or anxiety. Dickens would need the equivalent of such a frame for the story of ghosts he was to tell in *A Christmas Carol*. In writing the story of Gabriel Grub, he was conducting an experiment in the packaging of a ghost story.

Master Humphrey's Clock was a weekly journal Dickens produced between April 1840 and December 1841. Chapman and Hall were the publishers but, like the editors of the eighteenth-century periodicals he was imitating, Dickens had complete control – except, of course, over his readership. He would have preferred, like those editors, to have filled each issue with miscellaneous short pieces – some by contributors other than himself – but the readership he had by then created looked to him for novels, and fell away when he failed to provide them. As a result, for most of its duration, the journal was devoted to serialization: first of *The Old Curiosity Shop*, then of *Barnaby Rudge*. In the circumstances, Dickens found it not worth his while to use other contributors for the material interspersed with the novels.

This varies greatly in quality. Some of the best pieces are those Dickens uses to build up the characters of his chief narrator, Master Humphrey, and of Master Humphrey's friends – imaginary subordinate contributors in lieu of real ones. Because in such pieces there is no overriding narrative objective with which character has to be integrated, Dickens was able to experiment with techniques of character construction more freely than ever before. What he learned from these experiments would help in the composition of *A Christmas Carol*.

Christmas, and what he might do with it, we can see, were intermittently on his mind while he was writing this miscellaneous material. At moments he seems almost to have been rehearsing for the *Carol*, conducting tests both with the idea of the festival itself, and with adjacent topics. We have already seen the description in *Master Humphrey* of festive rejoicing in working-class districts of London, prefiguring a key passage in Stave Three of the *Carol* (*Master Humphrey* 59; *Christmas Books* 47–48). Other features of the *Carol* are prefigured too. In a pair of striking passages, Dickens has Master Humphrey imaginatively conjure up ghosts and visions in his narrative. These helped to shape, among other things, the deeper, more layered sense of personal identity Dickens was reaching out for, as does his coupling of Christmas and memory in another passage. All of this would be echoed in the *Carol*.

In part 3 of the periodical, published on 18 April 1840, the old, malformed, and reclusive Master Humphrey finds himself alone by his fireside, appreciating the midnight hour, "when long buried thoughts favoured by the gloom and silence steal from their graves and haunt the scenes of faded happiness and hope." He finds himself inclining towards support for the "popular faith in ghosts":

> For who can wonder that man should feel a vague belief in tales of disembodied spirits wandering those places which they once dearly affected, when he himself, scarcely less separated from his old world than they, is for ever lingering upon past emotions and by-gone times, and hovering, the ghost of his former self, about the places and people that warmed his heart of old? It is thus that at this quiet hour I haunt the house where I was born, the rooms I used to tread, the scenes of my infancy, my boyhood, and my youth; it is thus that I prowl around my buried treasure (though not of gold or silver), and mourn my loss; it is thus that I revisit the ashes of extinguished fires, and take my silent stand at old bedsides. (*Master Humphrey* 58)

Prose of this quality is more often than not a sign that Dickens was learning, and memorizing lessons for the future.   Using Master Humphrey as a mouthpiece, he is speculating about the use of ghosts in fiction for more than Grand Guignol effects, exploring the use of memory in the construction of character, and consenting to the resolution of emotional contradictions that he had shied away from in "A Christmas Dinner," but would triumphantly affirm in the *Carol*. With much less overt fuss than hitherto – without any of the Gothic apparatus, for instance, that he had used in the story of Gabriel Grub – Dickens achieves an extraordinary emotional plenitude here, a tender joy in the recollection of sorrow – nothing less than gratitude for sorrow, proportionate to the loss that was its occasion.   There is a heartfelt sobriety about the writing, achieved not least through the deftness and restraint with which the shaping metaphor is developed.   It would be hard to find a passage more distinctly marking the beginning of a major switch in his art: a switch away from the sketching-in of inner life as a justification for behavior, to an intense focus upon inner life as the source of behavior.

Within a page or two of this passage, we find Master Humphrey speculating about introspection and memory specifically at Christmas time. He tells of his first encounter with someone who was to become a close friend – the deaf gentleman, whom he discovers sitting alone in a tavern on Christmas Day:

> His mind was wandering among old Christmas Days, I thought. Many of them sprung up together, not with a long gap between each, but in unbroken succession like days of the week. It was a great change to find himself for the first time (I quite settled that it *was* the first) in an empty silent room with no soul to care for. I could not help following him in imagination through crowds of pleasant faces, and then coming back to that dull place with its bough of mistletoe sickening in the gas, and sprigs of holly parched up already by a Simoom of roast and boiled. (60–61)

The deaf gentleman, in Master Humphrey's estimation, is doing precisely what the narrator of "A Christmas Dinner" had urged readers not to do. He is comparing his circumstances now, and on previous

Christmas days. But this earns him sympathy and respect, not reproach. Memory now is privileged. We are called upon to share Master Humphrey's vision of man as, preeminently, a remembering creature. Human beings, we begin to see, are to be understood and valued and loved because, at their most dignified, they endure what time brings, and live with the knowledge of what it takes away. It is a lesson Scrooge has to be taught in *A Christmas Carol*.

But it is in the penultimate part of *Master Humphrey's Clock*, published on 27 November 1841, that we find the most complex and powerful foreshadowing of the *Carol*. Dickens draws together what he has been exploring in these passages, what he has been exploring in earlier experiments, and adds something new. Alone again by his fireside, Master Humphrey contemplates not what has been, but what has never been. "When everything is in a ruddy genial glow," he tells readers, "and there are voices in the crackling flame, and smiles in its flashing light, other smiles and other voices congregate around me, invading, with their pleasant harmony, the silence of the time."

> For then a knot of youthful creatures gather round my fireside, and the room re-echoes to their merry voices. My solitary chair no longer holds its ample place before the fire, but is wheeled into a smaller corner, to leave more room for the broad circle formed about the cheerful hearth. I have sons, and daughters, and grandchildren, and we are assembled on some occasion of rejoicing common to us all. It is a birthday, perhaps, or perhaps it may be Christmas time: but be it what it may, there is rare holyday among us, we are full of glee.
>
> In the chimney-corner, opposite myself, sits one who has grown old beside me. She is changed, of course; much changed; and yet I recognise the girl even in that gray hair and wrinkled brow. Glancing from the laughing child who half hides in her ample skirts, and half peeps out, – and from her to the little matron of twelve years old, who sits so womanly and so demure at no great distance from me, – and from her again, to a fair girl in the full bloom of early womanhood, the centre of the group: who has glanced more than once towards the opening door, and by whom the children, whispering and tittering among themselves, *will* leave a vacant chair, although she bids them

not, – I see her image thrice repeated, and feel how long it is
before one form and set of features wholly pass away, if ever,
from among the living. While I am dwelling upon this, and
tracing out the gradual change from infancy to youth, from
youth to perfect growth, from that to age; and thinking, with an
old man's pride, that she is comely yet, I feel a slight thin hand
upon my arm, and, looking down, see seated at my feet a
crippled boy – a gentle, patient child – whose aspect I know
well. He rests upon a little crutch – I know it, too – and leaning
on it as he climbs my footstool, whispers in my ear, "I am hardly
one of these, dear grandfather, although I love them dearly.
They are very kind to me, but you will be kinder still, I know."

Master Humphrey understands the gift imagination is bringing to
him.

I have my hand upon his neck, and stoop to kiss him: when
my clock strikes, my chair is in its old spot, and I am alone.
What if I be? What if this fireside be tenantless, save for the
presence of one weak old man! From my house-top I can look
upon a hundred homes, in every one of which these social
companies are matters of reality. In my daily walks I pass a
thousand men whose cares are all forgotten, whose labours are
made light, whose dull routine of work from day to day is
cheered and brightened by their glimpses of domestic joy at
home. Amid the struggles of this struggling town what cheerful
sacrifices are made; what toil endured with readiness; what
patience shown, and fortitude displayed for the mere sake of
home and its affections! Let me thank Heaven that I can people
my fireside with shadows such as these; with shadows of bright
objects that exist in crowds about me: and let me say, "I am
alone no more." (141–42)

The mixture of ingredients is one with which we shall become
familiar, for all their being assembled in different ways. Christmas is
evoked or, in this case, "some occasion of rejoicing common to us all" –
"perhaps it may be Christmas time." A solitary sits by his fire after
nightfall: in this case, a solitary through misfortune; in Scrooge's case, a
solitary thanks to his own transgressions; in the case of Redlaw,

protagonist of *The Haunted Man* (1848), a solitary because of the transgressions of others. And to this solitary there come ghosts or visions which may agitate, admonish, or sooth, but which ultimately teach and heal. They show what is precious and remains so, what is precious and must be lost, what can stay precious despite loss. They show this to the man whose personal experience has not taught him it, to the man who has never understood it, and to the man who has forgotten it. Without the insight bestowed by such teaching and healing, the reader is made to feel, no one can be whole.

In this passage we see Dickens moving towards an understanding of Christmas as a time for private contemplation, such as Henry Vaughan had voiced:

> Dress finely what comes not in sight,
> And then you keep your *Christmas* right!

The festival is more than its customs, its rituals. It is a time for introspection, emotional openness, and revaluation.

The crippled boy shows us something else. In 1835 Dickens had tried – without success – to fend off thoughts of the death of loved ones at Christmas time. In 1836, he had contrived an elaborate Gothic apparatus to turn Gabriel Grub's mind to such thoughts. Now he was ready to explore the subject intimately. Now he was ready for Tiny Tim.

It was a good time to be ready with material for a story about Christmas. It was the beginning of the 1840s, a decade during which the festival would once again become fashionable at every level of society, a decade during which Christmas customs and attitudes to Christmas would evolve rapidly.

The example set by Queen Victoria and her consort, Prince Albert, helped make enthusiasm for the festival acceptable throughout society.[20] For the queen, Christmas was a "most dear happy time." George IV's consort, Caroline of Brunswick, had familiarized the court with Christmas trees early in the century, and they had been a central feature of the festival for the young princess. In her journal entry for Christmas Eve 1832, the thirteen-year-old Victoria excitedly describes the two trees at Kensington Palace, "hung with lights and sugar ornaments," and surrounded with gifts. Prince Albert brought with him to England, from his native Coburg, an affection for this and for other German customs. After their marriage, in 1840, the queen took care to see that he was made to feel at home through the practice of such customs.

But she did not care only for the pleasures of Christmas. Its duties exercised her as well. At Christmas in 1836, when she was seventeen, she had persuaded her mother to send food, blankets, and fuel to a group of gypsies camped nearby. She was "safe and happy at home in that cold night and today when it snowed so," Victoria reflected, but she was sad to think how, at the same time, "our poor gypsy friends should perish and shiver from want." After she succeeded to the throne in 1837, she kept up the tradition of royal New Year bounty in Windsor, distributing beef, potatoes, plum puddings, bread, coal, blankets, and scarlet cloaks, to the poor of the town.

The royal example popularized the Christmas tree in England during the 1840s. *The Illustrated London News* for 1 January 1848 speaks of sideboards at Windsor having been "surmounted with stately 'Christmas Trees', glittering with pendant bonbons," and it provides an illustration of the scene. Three years later, Dickens wrote of a Christmas tree without the tell-tale quotation marks. The first references to Christmas crackers date from 1841. The first commercially produced Christmas cards went on sale in 1843. Hand-made cards had been sent before this, but in 1843 Henry Cole (later Sir Henry) commissioned 1,000 cards, lithographed and hand-coloured, from the illustrator John Calcott Horsley. In the form of a triptych, the card shows three generations of a family in the central panel, enjoying their Christmas dinner, while the side panels show want being relieved.

In 1840 and 1841, Dickens was drawing threads together. In 1843 he would work on them with all the concentrated intensity he was capable of. By Christmas that year, he would produce something that would influence public attitudes much more than any of these trifles, something of extraordinary complexity and richness. Although he was as yet unaware of it, his imagination was shaping itself to produce a great work. The way was being prepared for the composition of *A Christmas Carol.*

1843 : *A CHRISTMAS CAROL*

When *A Christmas Carol* went on sale, just before Christmas in 1843, readers must have seen Dickens was up to something he had not tried before. It would not have taken them long, though, to work out what it was. The title and the timing of publication would have been powerful clues, but so would some unexpected features of the volume. As a text the *Carol* was much shorter than any of his previous books, in physical dimensions it was much smaller, and in finish it was much more handsome. Potential buyers were evidently to be tempted by something bijou.

There is no question of this having been anything but deliberate. Dickens had lavished attention on the production of the book. He had taken charge of the design himself, sidelining his publishers, Chapman and Hall, and busying himself over all the details. The little book was bound in a salmon brown cover, embossed with a gilded design. The edges of the pages were gilded too, the endpapers were colored, and the title page was color-printed. There were eight illustrations by John Leech: four etchings tinted by hand, and four monochrome wood engravings. Such a combination of refinements was unusual in a book of the 1840s.

Various explanations have been offered for the pains Dickens took over design. The fineness of finish, suggests one, was proportionate to his understanding of the *Carol* as a major step in his writing career (Ackroyd 407–13). It was a major step, and Dickens may well have been influenced by sensing it to be such, but surely not decisively. It is much easier for us to make this kind of judgment in hindsight than it would have been for him in 1843, busy writing, and far from sure about what he might do in the future.

Another popular explanation has to do with his urgent need to make money. Dickens agreed with Chapman and Hall to take only a commission on sales of the *Carol*, after deductions for production costs. He saw this as a way of maximizing his profit (Patten 26–27). The finish he insisted upon was a special lure for buyers, to be sure, but there was more to it than that. By 1843 Dickens knew where his talents lay, and what his books were bought for. We do him an injustice if we suppose he was trying to tempt buyers with finish as an end in itself. He was always eager to maximize sales, but was passionate about his craft, too. The physical appearance of his previous books was something to which he had given attention; never to the same extent, though. Why the difference now?

A simple explanation is in fact readily available. Dickens planned the finish of the *Carol* to suit a sense of occasion he knew his readers would share with him. He was producing a Christmas book for the Christmas market. Shoppers in that market knew, up to a point, what it was they wanted. Dickens was ready to supply it – plus a great deal else besides.

He understood how important Christmas was to the book-buying public. The surge of publications after 1843, geared to Christmas, can be traced ultimately to the influence of the *Carol* itself, but the Christmas book market was already healthy enough (see pp. 106–07 above). Dickens recognized this, and sought to exploit it. His hopes of tempting buyers with the *Carol* were based, not only upon confidence in his own talents, but also upon an assessment of that market. He saw that, for the book to succeed, it would have to offer potential buyers, among other things, something of the elegant finish they had grown used to in Christmas publications. Otherwise, his talents, great as he knew them to be, would be competing at a disadvantage.

Dickens gave the term "Christmas book" its modern meaning. It was popularized by the publication, in 1852, of a collected edition of all five of his longer Christmas tales under just that title – *Christmas Books*. But, as we have seen, for twenty years prior to 1843 there had been a special market for books in England at Christmas time, a market dominated by annuals.[1] Ackermann's *Forget-Me-Not, a Christmas and New Year's Present*, had first appeared in 1823. It survived until 1847. *The Keepsake*, originally published by Hurst, Chance, and Company, had been launched in 1828, and survived until 1857.[2] There were numerous imitators: in 1831, as many as sixty-two annuals appeared (Booth 4–6). Most, if not all, were designed to exploit the Christmas season. Although they gave employment chiefly to minor talents, authors as celebrated as Wordsworth, Scott, Moore, and Southey were among those persuaded to contribute. They were noted, moreover, for fine design and unsparing use of high-quality materials. Standards of printing were high. Morocco or watered-silk binding was usual, as was gilding, both of covers and page edges. Many were illustrated with steel engravings of works by artists as noted as Turner and Lawrence. And they were vigorously advertised.

That alone would doubtless have made Dickens mindful of them, but he had access to an insider's view as well. Between 1841 and 1849, *The Keepsake* was edited by his friend Lady Blessington. In 1852 – after he had stopped publishing a yearly Christmas book – he would briefly become a contributor, with his story "To be Read at Dusk."

George Eliot, in the 1870s, remembered how popular the annuals had been. One of Rosamond Vincy's suitors, in *Middlemarch* (1871–72), gives her what we can assume to be the 1831 *Keepsake*:

> He had brought the last "Keepsake," the gorgeous watered-silk publication which marked modern progress at that time; and he considered himself very fortunate that he could be the first to look over it with her, dwelling on the ladies and gentlemen with shiny copper-plate cheeks and copper-plate smiles, and pointing to comic verses as capital and sentimental stories as interesting. Rosamond was gracious, and Mr. Ned was satisfied that he had the very best thing in art and literature as a medium for "paying addresses" – the very thing to please a nice girl. (*Middlemarch* bk. 1, ch. 27)

This is evidence enough of the reputation among book buyers the annuals had established for themselves.

Dickens's plan, it appears, was to undercut them with a rival product. *The Keepsake* retailed at thirteen shillings for the octavo version, at two pounds, twelve shillings, and sixpence for the royal octavo version. It was a publication targeted at more prosperous buyers. *A Christmas Carol*, in contrast, went on sale at five shillings a copy.[3] By offering a comparable finish, but at a lower price, and with Dickens's name on the cover, he and his publishers could hope, not only to gain access to a market hitherto dominated by annuals, but also to expand that market. Their hopes were realised. The *Carol* was the most successful book to be published that Christmas season. In the six days between publication day and Christmas Eve, some six thousand copies were sold (*Letters* 3: 615–16).

Another explanation of the book's popularity may be found in the way it dwells on Christmas itself. The annuals, for the most part, only exploited the occasion of Christmas. In the *Carol*, Dickens made it his subject. It is a deliberate celebration of the most popular English festival. In writing it as he did, and publishing it when he did, Dickens was not just joining in the annual merrymaking. He was in effect insisting upon the centrality of Christmas in national life, reminding the nation of established traditions and of values the festival affirmed, and suggesting new values it might yet affirm.

The book's continuing success, doubtless, owes something to this. The public's eager response persisted. Buoyant sales continued well into the new year. By March the *Carol* was into its sixth edition.

Sales soared as they did, not least because people were made to feel better for having read it. Writing in *Fraser's Magazine* in February 1844, Thackeray declared it impossible to publish a hostile review: "who can listen to objections regarding such a book as this? It seems to me a national benefit, and to every man or woman who reads it a personal benefit" (*Works* 13: 58).[4] Readers were clearly ready to hear what the *Carol* says.

It says something – unequivocally – about Christmas rejoicing. Christmas rejoicing, we can safely assume, was nothing new to most of its readers – not even to those who intensified their merrymaking in response to the book, raising it from the low level to which, for a minority, fashion had reduced it. We have seen plenty of evidence for this already, but detail after detail of the *Carol* confirms it. Let us consider just a few of them. After that, I can have done with the question of whether Christmas was popular in the early nineteenth century until I ask, in my final chapter, why it is modern readers have been encouraged to suppose it was not.

An open-minded reading of *A Christmas Carol* should prompt the same question, page after page, from readers coached in modern responses to the book: if Dickens's contemporaries knew little of Christmas customs, and cared less, why were they not puzzled by what he had written? Why, on the contrary, were they so pleased by it? What is wrong with Ebenezer Scrooge, the *Carol* suggests, is demonstrated in the way he does not rejoice at Christmas as others do. The correction of what is wrong with him is demonstrated in his learning to rejoice, if anything more heartily than most. If few readers rejoiced much themselves, why would they have been persuaded by this? Why indeed would they not have been insulted by it?

We find broad generalizations about Christmas behavior in the book. In a key passage, Scrooge's nephew thinks of it as

> " ... a good time: a kind, forgiving, charitable, pleasant time: the only time I know of, in the long calendar of the year, when men and women seem by one consent to open their shut-up hearts freely, and to think of people below them as if they really were fellow-passengers to the grave, and not another race of creatures bound on other journeys." (*Christmas Books* 10)

Some contemporary readers, like some modern ones, would doubtless have detected idealization in this, or at least have insisted there were exceptions to the rule – Scrooge himself, to begin with, of course – but what sense could they have made of the book, and what sense can we make of it, if this is seen to be a radically untruthful representation of the way most people behaved and felt at Christmas time before 1843?

There are particularized descriptions of Christmas customs in the book:

> The brightness of the shops where holly sprigs and berries crackled in the lamp-heat of the windows, made pale faces ruddy as they passed. Poulterers' and grocers' trades became a splendid joke: a glorious pageant, with which it was next to impossible to believe that such dull principles as bargain and sale had anything to do. The Lord Mayor, in the stronghold of the mighty Mansion House, gave orders to his fifty cooks and butlers to keep Christmas as a Lord Mayor's household should; and even the little tailor, whom he had fined five shillings on the previous Monday for being drunk and blood-thirsty in the streets, stirred up to-morrow's pudding in his garret, while his lean wife and the

baby sallied out to buy the beef. (13)

Either the shops made a glorious spectacle, or they did not. Either most Londoners, from the lord mayor down to the poorest citizen, celebrated to the best of their ability, or they did not. And if they did not, why would contemporary readers have trusted this?

There are descriptions in the book of people rejoicing at Christmas, undeterred by difficult circumstances:

> Again the Ghost sped on, above the black and heaving sea –
> on, on – until, being far away, as he told Scrooge, from any
> shore, they lighted on a ship. They stood beside the helmsman at
> the wheel, the look-out in the bow, the officers who had the
> watch; dark, ghostly figures in their several stations; but every
> man among them hummed a Christmas tune, or had a Christmas
> thought, or spoke below his breath to his companion of some
> bygone Christmas Day, with homeward hopes belonging to it.
> And every man on board, waking or sleeping, good or bad, had
> had a kinder word for another on that day than on any day in the
> year; and had shared to some extent in its festivities; and had
> remembered those he cared for at a distance, and had known that
> they delighted to remember him. (56)

Would readers have been moved by the book, had they supposed this not just a selective or exaggerated representation of contemporary behavior, but an utter misrepresentation?

We can answer all these questions simply enough. *A Christmas Carol* would have made sense and proved acceptable in 1843, primarily to readers who habitually rejoiced and made merry at Christmas time. To them we may add readers who did not do so, or did scarcely at all, but who recognised that in this they were unlike their neighbors. Anyone else – if there was anyone else – would have been likely to find the book alien and barely intelligible. To see it as a fresh start in English ritual life, in other words, is not only to ignore the historical evidence. It is to misread the book itself. Misreadings have prevailed for many years, of course, not least because the context in which the *Carol* was published has been so misrepresented.

Let us be clear, then. Few of the original readers of *A Christmas*

Carol would have found the customs described in it unfamiliar. What would have been unfamiliar to them was their being described, lovingly and in such detail, by a writer of Dickens's stature. Dickens was decisively relegating to their proper, subordinate place the antiquarian and Romantic whimsies about Christmas with which reputable writers had entertained themselves for so long. He was contemplating behavior and customs which only writers as quirky as Clare and Hone had been ready to document, but with a talent and perspicacity neither Clare nor Hone had ever been able to match. Without apology, he was extolling the plebeian and bourgeois Christmas, celebrated at that time around the family fireside by most English men, women, and children. There is nothing oblique about the way he tackles the subject. It is not slipped in, this time, subordinate to something else. *A Christmas Carol* is an astonishingly complex book, with many shades of meaning, but it is absurd to deny what above all else it is: a book for Christmas and about Christmas, addressed to readers for whom Christmas mattered.

As a publishing venture, then, the *Carol* emerged from a matrix of well established traditions, and it dwelt upon things with which readers were familiar. But that is far from saying that Dickens was simply seizing a marketing opportunity, or that there was nothing new about the book. To speak of it just as a publishing venture is to say little about the *Carol*. And among everything familiar, contemporary readers would have found much to astonish them. Dickens displays an extraordinary and courageous inventiveness in the book. The tame formula of the annuals – the patchwork of verses and stories George Eliot remembered – was abandoned in favour of a single, compelling tale about Christmas itself, a tale of miraculous happenings at Christmas time. It is a tale, moreover, unmistakeably designed to disturb readers as much as to comfort them. The book was much smaller than most annuals, offered nothing of the diversity annuals did, but provided instead an intense reading experience, a challenge to the imagination, such as only Dickens could issue.

This challenge, although little diminished for today's readers by the passage of time, was substantially provoked by the historic moment that called the book into being. For eight years Dickens had been seeking a way of engaging his art with Christmas. He sensed it to be a topic ideally suited to his talents. He had discovered features of the topic he could develop in ways special to himself. But he lacked a purpose sufficiently large and worthy to which he could marry it. Now he discovered such a purpose. Dickens realized he could relate his love of Christmas to the indignation he felt at a spectacle of preventable suffering.

He wrote the *Carol* as a text for the 1840s, a decade dominated by the issue of poverty. During it, few in Britain could have been unaware of how widespread and persistent poverty was. Christmas was traditionally a time to be mindful of the poor, and to relieve their suffering. Nor had this been forgotten by Dickens's generation. Witness the charitable impulses of the young Victoria, as princess and queen, or the design of Henry Cole's first Christmas card (see p. 153 above). The same Christmas that saw the publication of the *Carol*, saw the *Pictorial Times* urging its readers "to think of the poor – of the poor who, without their aid, can have no enjoyment."[5] It was a timely reminder, in the 1840s.

But for Dickens, the realization that he could link Christmas with the great issue of poverty was momentous. It was precisely the link he needed to forge. It transformed what had been a marginal preoccupation for him – a little self-indulgent, perhaps, an excuse for introspection – into something at the center of his art, something capable of yielding profound insights, both about personal identity and about society at large. Concern for the well-being of the entire community was added to concern for individual emotional and moral health. The two were made one, and Dickens's reach as an artist was greatly extended. The demand for introspection persisted, but without a trace of self-indulgence. Introspection, he began to see, was a way of tapping the deepest resources of the imagination in order, among other things, to affirm the individual's membership of the larger community.

An awareness of the conditions in which the poor lived – and, if they were lucky, worked – had been a feature of Dickens's art from the beginning of his career. In *Oliver Twist*, for instance, he had impugned the 1834 Poor Law Amendment Act. The act sought to minimize costs to ratepayers by centering poor relief upon workhouses, on the grounds that, when this caused hardship, it would be "hardship to which the good of society requires the applicant to submit" (Checkland 376). But now, because of what was unfolding around him, Dickens found himself impelled to confront the problem of poverty more systematically.

During the early nineteenth century, mass migration from rural areas to industrial towns and cities exposed ever greater numbers to the vicissitudes of the trade cycle, and to hardship resulting from fluctuating food prices. A bank crisis in 1837, plus the bad harvest of that and the following year, had led to a shortage of capital during the years preceding 1840, to lay-offs, and to high bread prices. The effects of this combination of events would be felt for more than a decade. Another crisis in 1847, preceded by two bad harvests, would reinforce the recession (Wood 103–04). Not for nothing did the 1840s become known as the "hungry forties." It was a decade marked by unemployment, famine, and the scandal of barely tolerable living and working conditions for vast numbers of the nation's poorest. Inevitably, it was marked by popular discontent too.

The depth of demoralization these developments yielded in many communities can be illustrated with just one piece of evidence from one town, dating from the year before the *Carol* was published. The economy of Hinckley, near Birmingham, was dominated by hosiery knitting, but trade had been declining since the end of the Napoleonic wars in 1815. In June 1842, posters were pasted up around the town, displaying this text:

> No Work. No Bread. No Hope. A meeting of the inhabitants of Hinckley will be held near the Holy Well on Tuesday evening, June 28, 1842 at seven o'clock to consider and to adopt such resolutions as are required by the present times, in which the Hosier has little Trade and no Profit; the Landlord no rent; the Shop-keeper no Custom; the Stockinger neither Bread nor Hope; and in which the heavy Poor-Rates are involving the Householder and the neighbouring Farmer in one Common Ruin.

Eventually, action such as this led to the setting up of a parliamentary commission to consider the framework knitters' predicament, and the commissioner began to take evidence for his report – but not until two years later in 1844 (Beavin).

Faced by unprecedented problems, without tried solutions, governments acted slowly, hesitantly, and all too often reluctantly. Fashionable doctrines were used to impede prompt and decisive action. Influential voices denounced the very principle of government intervention in economic matters, and were heeded. An attentive audience was to be found among politicians, industrialists, merchants, financiers, landowners, and ratepayers.

One of the fashionable doctrines was utilitarianism. Utilitarians understood morality as a process for achieving the greatest happiness for the greatest number. It is hard to gainsay the principle, but it could be used to justify pitiless subservience to statistics. The version of utilitarianism developed by John Stuart Mill (1806–73) underpinned some of the most far-reaching reforms of the nineteenth century, but the system of poor relief proposed by the movement's founder, Jeremy Bentham (1748–1832), was capable of ungenerous interpretation. It could be used (in J. K. Galbraith's formula) to get the poor off the conscience of the rich. Bentham recommended a network of "industry houses," managed by a National Charity Company, distanced from the government, and operating on commercial principles. Relief would be directed towards the industrious and frugal poor, not towards the indolent and dissolute, whose ways it would only encourage (Bentham 124–208). Many found these views soothing. They undoubtedly influenced the framers of the 1834 Poor Law Amendment Act. Bentham himself did not live to see their effect upon the miseries of the 1840s.

Selective interpretation affected the influence of another writer spared that spectacle. Robert Malthus (1766–1834) held that poverty is inevitable, because population increases in a geometrical ratio, subsistence only in an arithmetical ratio. Catastrophe is averted, he believed, through the limitation of population growth, either by the "positive" checks of famine, disease, and war, or by the "preventative" check of prudence (Malthus passim). He acknowledged the value of the preventative check in early writings, and emphasized it as he grew older. Even so, his recommendations make few concessions to humanity, and were eagerly echoed at a later date by less dispassionate voices. Poverty, he made it possible to argue, was the fault of the poor, and of their unrestrained fecundity. The rich could not be held responsible for it. Parish relief for children should be abolished. The hardship thus caused would reduce population growth, and poverty with it.

Against such a background of ideas, it is not surprising that legislation to ease the lives of the poorest in the community was slow in coming. One focus of popular anger was the Corn Laws. When the end of the Napoleonic wars and renewed access to foreign markets had triggered a collapse in cereal prices, a new act had been passed to perpetuate wartime protectionism. The interests of British landowners and farmers were guarded by prohibitive conditions on the import of cheap cereals. Bread prices were thus kept artificially high, and the poor suffered. An Anti-Corn Law League had been founded in 1839. A Free Trade Hall had been built in Manchester in 1840, to house anti-Corn Law meetings. But the Corn Laws were not repealed until 1846.

Another grievance was the long hours demanded of industrial workers, and the conditions in which too many were required to work. The need to regulate work in factories and mines was highlighted by a House of Lords select committee report of 1842, but legislation was introduced only very gradually, despite the activities of the Ten Hours Movement, which sought to reduce working hours. Factory Acts had been passed in 1819 and 1833, limiting the employment of children in mills. Another was passed in 1844, limiting the working hours of women too, and imposing safety precautions against dangerous machinery. A Ten Hours Act was actually passed in 1847, but poor drafting made it easy to evade. It was in fact 1874 before the ten-hour working day was successfully enforced.

If government met the material needs of the working population slowly and grudgingly, it met their less material needs scarcely at all. Not until 1870 was the first Education Act passed, ensuring every child in England and Wales an elementary education. From 1833, to be sure, an obligation – not always honored – had been laid upon employers, to provide education for working children. And grants had been made to church-run organizations for the establishment of schools. Other voluntary bodies had set up schools as well, but provision was inevitably thin and patchy.

Provision for self-improvement was no better. Some towns and cities opened public libraries towards the end of the 1840s, and a Public Libraries Act of 1851 authorized councils to levy a rate to fund such instruction could look only to scattered mechanics' institutes, polytechnic institutes, and athenaeums, all voluntarily funded. It was clear that any aspiration working people had, beyond brute needs, was likely to be met more through the operation of benevolence and luck, than as a result of responsibility accepted by the established authorities.

It was hard, then, for the working classes in the early 1840s, not to feel neglected by governments, and by the prosperous classes that elected them. Little wonder that it was the heyday of Chartism.

The chief aim of the Chartists was the extension of the franchise to working men, to give them some influence over the conditions in which they and their families lived and labored. The "People's Charter," presented to Parliament by their representatives in 1839, was supported by a petition with 1,280,000 signatures. It demanded manhood suffrage, equal electoral districts, voting by ballot, annual parliaments, the abolition of property qualifications for candidates, and salaries for elected members to live upon. Parliament rejected the petition by 235 votes to 46. This led to the formation of a National Charter Association in 1840, and a second petition in 1842, supported this time by 3,317,702 signatories. It was again dismissed, by 287 votes to 49.

Unsurprisingly, these flinty rebuffs provoked boycotts, strikes, riots, and arrests. In 1842 there was a wave of strikes throughout the industrial midlands and north, and in Scotland too. Industry in the north was brought to a halt by the "plug riots," so called because rioters pulled plugs from boilers, to immobilize machinery.

For the rest of the decade, Chartists debated ways of achieving their ends. There were some who advocated violence. The European revolutions of 1848 inspired a final petition. Chartist leaders boasted of 5,706,000 signatures, but there were in fact fewer than 2,000,000, many of those faked. Needless to say, the petition was again rejected by Parliament. Chartism lingered on for another decade, a spent force, but the discontent it had given voice to would eventually have to be addressed.

The suffering of the working classes was naturally the subject of investigation, polemic, and vigorous debate during the 1840s. Poets wrote about it. Elizabeth Barrett's "Cry of the Children" was published in 1842, Thomas Hood's "Song of the Shirt" in 1843. There were novelists who made it their theme. Mrs. Trollope's *Michael Armstrong:*

in 1842, Thomas Hood's "Song of the Shirt" in 1843. There were novelists who made it their theme. Mrs. Trollope's *Michael Armstrong: The Factory Boy* was published in 1840, Mrs. Gaskell's *Mary Barton* in 1848.

Edwin Chadwick (1800–90) was a civil servant who treated the subject more discursively. He was a disciple of Bentham, and one of the architects of the 1834 Poor Law Amendment Act, but he sought earnestly and indefatigably to improve the conditions in which the poor lived and worked. He made his name with a report published in 1842, about the sanitary condition of housing for the working classes, to which this was the chief conclusion:

> That the various forms of epidemic, endemic, and other disease caused, or aggravated, or propagated chiefly amongst the labouring classes by atmospheric impurities produced by decomposing animal and vegetable substances, by damp and filth, and close and overcrowded dwellings prevail amongst the population in every part of the kingdom whether dwelling in separate houses, in rural villages, in small towns, in the larger towns – as they have been found to prevail in the lowest districts of the metropolis. (Chadwick 369)

It was a conclusion based on exhaustive statistical studies, and accompanied by practical proposals for remedies.

Although German, Friedrich Engels (1820–95) spent most of his adult life in Manchester, working for the family textile business. In 1845 he published his *Condition of the Working Class in England*. In it, he contrasts the comfortable lives of the Manchester bourgeoisie with those of mill workers and their families, and declares the interests of the two groups to be "diametrically opposed" (Engels 13). Not only does he compare the physical conditions in which they lived and worked; he argues that discontent is the inevitable result of factory employment:

> There is no better means of inducing stupefaction than a period of factory-work, and if the operatives have, nevertheless, not only rescued their intelligence, but cultivated and sharpened it more than other working-men, they have found this possible only in rebellion against their fate and against the bourgeoisie, the sole subject on which under all circumstances they can think

> and feel while at work. Or, if this indignation against the
> bourgeoisie does not become the supreme passion of the
> working-man, the inevitable consequence is drunkenness and all
> that is generally called demoralization. (269)

The intimations of alienation and threat here foreshadow the theories
Engels was to assist Marx in shaping.

Suffering and discontent, then, were widespread among the poor in
the 1840s. Among the more prosperous, responses were varied. Many
were bewildered by the novelty and magnitude of the problems to be
solved. Some sought to deny that anything could be done, or that they
should be called upon to do it. Others were indignant at this repudiation
of responsibility, and at the scale of suffering permitted. A number
spoke out.

Dickens was one of that number. The hungry forties triggered in him a
complex set of responses, distressing for him, but of enormous benefit to
his art. His fascination with Christmas was caught up in the process. It
offered him a means for organizing those responses.

The way he reacted to the problems of the decade displays that
mixture of selfless passion and private anxiety which is the best most of
us can bring to current affairs. What is noteworthy, though, is the way
stimulation of private anxiety characteristically diverted his energy away
from the worthy campaigning to which he was given, into the
composition of literary texts. His polemical fiction did not always lead
the way for reforming movements, but it gave them more sharply
defined objectives than any amount of investigating, lobbying, and
speechifying on his part might have done.

His experiences during 1843 concentrated his mind upon problems
that characterized the decade. It was a year of mixed fortune for him. It
began well, and it closed with rapturous panegyrics for *A Christmas
Carol*. In February, when he turned thirty-one, he had few reasons for
anxiety or self-doubt. He was a successful and acclaimed author. He
had completed five novels: *Pickwick Papers* (1836–37), *Oliver Twist*
(1837–38), *Nicholas Nickleby* (1838–39), *The Old Curiosity Shop*
(1840–41) and *Barnaby Rudge* (1841). All had sold in huge numbers by

contemporary standards. *The Old Curiosity Shop* had peaked at as many as 100,000 copies per weekly part. *Sketches by Boz* (1836), and the travel book, *American Notes* (1842), had both sold well, too.

But by March 1843 it was becoming apparent that sales of the novel Dickens had launched in January were unlikely to be on the scale of his previous serials. Monthly parts of *Martin Chuzzlewit* (1843–44) were attracting as few as 20,000 buyers, a fifth of those who had flocked to buy the *Curiosity Shop* at its zenith. The reading public was less receptive than it had been with previous novels, and the recession was hitting book sales generally. Because of this, Chapman and Hall spoke of invoking a clause in their contract with Dickens, to reduce his income by fifty pounds a month (Patten 133–37). He became alarmed and angry.

Any reduction in income would be a serious matter for him. He was by now the father of four children, and his wife, Catherine, fell pregnant with a fifth during 1843. He had grown used to the rewards of success – comfort, stylishness, generous hospitality, travel. He was responsible for the lease of a house in the fashionable Regent's Park district of London, a house of "'undeniable' situation, and excessive splendour" (*Letters* 1: 598). Inevitably, there was a numerous retinue of servants to pay for. To help with the children, moreover, his wife's younger sister, Georgina Hogarth, had become a member of his household – welcome, indispensable even, but not without cost. His father was continuing to be expensively troublesome (Ackroyd 395). And to cap it all, Dickens was getting into debt himself.[6]

He began to have thoughts of a period of retrenchment in some inexpensive French or Italian resort – thoughts which were to crystalize into a coherent plan he put into effect the following year (*Letters* 3: 472–73 and 587–88). The *Carol* was another expedient. He wrote it during the autumn, and got it onto the market – all in less than two months – spurred by imaginative engagement with his subject, certainly, but by anxiety about money, too. He anticipated earning £1,000 or more from it (*Letters* 3: 461, 585; Forster bk. 4, ch. 1). When Chapman and Hall's first payment to him amounted to no more than £230, plaudits and runaway sales notwithstanding, he would be deeply disappointed and furiously indignant (*Letters* 4: 42–43).

There is nothing to suggest Dickens ever supposed his problems with money were of the same order as those of the poor. Even so, as 1843 unfolded, ever more worried about money himself, he immersed himself ever more deeply in the issue of poverty, and denounced indifference towards it ever more vehemently. He made speeches about poverty and health (*Speeches* 40–43). He wrote letters about poverty and crime (*Letters* 3: 436–37 and nn; 570). But one aspect of the larger problem exercised him more than any other – poverty and education. As the year wore on, he focused more and more closely upon the threat to the social fabric he saw in the combination of want and ignorance, a combination he would feature, briefly and – for most readers – puzzlingly, in the *Carol*. The book, in fact, barely glances at the problem of poverty and education, but it was a topic that would take Dickens into the deepest recesses of his imagination, where he would find old pain, old anxieties, that he could use to make the *Carol* what it is.

Early in the year, a member of the Children's Employment Commission sent him a preview of a report to be published at the end of February. Dickens was dismayed by its contents, but in replying to the sender, Thomas Southwood Smith, he wondered whether it was the right time to prescribe hours of work, as the report recommended:

> Want is so general, distress so great, and Poverty so rampant – it is, in a word, so hard for the Millions to live by any means – that I scarcely know how we can step between them, and one weekly farthing. (*Letters* 3: 436–37).

A month later, however, on 6 March, he told Smith he was planning a pamphlet: "An appeal to the People of England, on behalf of the Poor Man's Child" (*Letters* 3: 459). Four days after that, he announced that he had rethought his strategy, and did not now propose to publish until the end of the year. Smith would nevertheless be pleased with the result, he believed:

> you will certainly feel that a Sledge hammer has come down with twenty times the force – twenty thousand times the force – I could exert by following out my first idea. Even so recently as when I wrote to you the other day, I had not contemplated the means I shall now, please God, use. But they have been

suggested to me, and I have girded myself for their seizure – as
you shall see in due time. (*Letters* 3: 461)

This may well mark Dickens's realization that he could effectively
unite his deep feelings for Christmas with the no less deep indignation
he felt at the poverty he saw around him. His imagination was evidently
at work, and was urging something more intricate than a straightforward
appeal. The decision about the timing of publication could be a sign that
Christmas was entering the picture. Certainly, his confidence in the
impact of what he was planning suggests he was proposing to tap
sources to which his imagination naturally turned, sources of great
power for him. It is clear, at any rate, that the connection between the
festival and Dickens's indignation at widespread poverty had to be made
at some time, and nothing points to another date. The pamphlet he
spoke of was never written, of course. It would not be needed. The
Carol would do its work, and more.

Soon Dickens would be thinking, not just about poor children, but
about their education, too. A letter from Joseph Soul, secretary of the
Orphan Working School, which offered vocational training to needy
children in London, prompted a short reply from Dickens on 26 May.
He apologized for not having visited the school, but it was evidently on
his mind. He was to become one of its governors the following year
(*Letters* 3: 497 and n5).

On 16 September Dickens wrote to Macvey Napier, editor of the
Edinburgh Review, offering him another piece destined to remain
unwritten, on the Ragged Schools for slum children, and schools in jails
(*Letters* 3: 565). A misunderstanding about deadlines seems to have put
an end to this scheme. Dickens had not abandoned it by the time he
wrote again to Napier on 24 October, but by then he had started work on
the *Carol*, which would have overshadowed and diminished any such
paper (*Letters* 3: 585–86).

His proposal to Napier grew out of a personal involvement with the
Ragged Schools movement. This stimulated feelings always among the
sharpest spurs to his invention. On 12 September he had initiated a
correspondence with Samuel R. Starey, treasurer of the Field Lane
Ragged School, set up amid the slums of London's Saffron Hill. Acting
for Angela Burdett Coutts, who was helping with funding, he inspected

the school and, in an emotional letter to her, expressed consternation at
the condition of the children:

> I have seldom seen, in all the strange and dreadful things I have
> seen in London and elsewhere, anything so shocking as the dire
> neglect of soul and body exhibited in these children. And
> although I know; and am as sure as it is possible for one to be of
> anything which has not happened; that in the prodigious misery
> and ignorance of the swarming masses of mankind in England,
> the seeds of its certain ruin are sown, I never saw the Truth so
> staring out in hopeless characters, as it does from the walls of
> this place. The children in the Jails are almost as common sights
> to me as my own; but these are worse, for they have not arrived
> there yet, but are as plainly and certainly travelling there, as they
> are to their Graves. (*Letters* 3: 562)

The pessimism is hyperbolic. In a failure properly to care for and
direct children, Dickens is foreseeing a fearful destiny. Pragmatically,
he acted as if the fate he foresaw were far from inevitable. He was
doing his best to ameliorate the effects of poverty and neglect. He was
working hard, making sound practical recommendations – to Miss
Coutts about funding, to Starey about the organization of the school
(*Letters* 3: 564, 574). But the dire vision that came to him momentarily
overrode all practical considerations.

On 5 October, in contrast, he found himself contemplating an
institution which excited in him nothing but admiration and hope. That
was when he presided over a *soirée* of the Manchester Athenaeum. In a
speech to its assembled patrons, he took comfort from the thought that,
in Manchester,

> while her factories re-echo with clanking of stupendous engines
> and the whirl and rattle of machinery, the immortal mechanism
> of God's own hand, the mind, is not forgotten in the din and
> uproar, but is lodged and tended in a palace of its own.
> (*Speeches* 45–46)

He had no doubts about what hard-won learning conferred:

the first unpurchasable blessing earned by every man who makes an effort to improve himself in such a place as the Athenaeum is self-respect [*hear*] – an inward dignity of character which once acquired and righteously maintained, nothing, no, not the hardest drudgery, nor the direst poverty, can vanquish. [*Applause.*] Though he should find it hard for a season even to keep the wolf of hunger from his door, let him but once have chased the dragon of ignorance from his hearth, and self-respect and hope are left him. [*Applause.*] (48)

This time it is the optimism that is hyperbolic. Dickens does not see the possibility Engels saw, of knowledge only angering and alienating factory workers. He has utter confidence in the beneficence of what the Athenaeum offered. The strong feelings he betrays, I suggest, had as much to do with remembered distress at help denied him in the past, when he had needed it, as with observation in the present.

For admirers of his books, in fact, it is the erratic judgment and disproportionate emotion that are most of interest in these passages. Something was being stirred up, it is clear, beyond a selfless concern for the welfare of the dispossessed. Troubled times led Dickens valiantly to combat poverty as best he could. His own money worries made him prone to the reawakening of private anxieties, led him to dwell particularly on a problem which had a special resonance for him, and guided his imagination to matters that vitalized it. This is evidenced in the way we can detect a quite distinct narrative struggling to emerge from behind his discourse on education for the poor. Sober reviews of fact, steady practical recommendations, praise and blame, are disrupted by intimations of doom and redemption, scarcely helpful in the shaping of policy, but the very stuff of fiction. We can detect Dickens developing as an artist here.

Details of *A Christmas Carol*, it is often remarked, can be related to a formative episode in Dickens's childhood. The family of Bob Cratchit, Scrooge's downtrodden clerk, we notice, lives in a four-roomed house in Camden Town (*Christmas Books* 14, 49). Dickens knew about such houses. In 1822, when he was ten, his father had been transferred from Chatham dockyard to the London headquarters of the Navy Pay Office, and the family had moved into a small terraced house, scarcely more commodious than Bob's, at 16 Bayham Street, Camden Town. Already in debt, his father had been further embarrassed by the move to London. This was the beginning of a series of events which, within two years, had culminated in humiliating employment for the boy at Warren's Blacking Warehouse, and imprisonment for his father in the Marshalsea debtors' jail (Parker, *The Doughty Street Novels* 18–58). Dickens had awaited this fate, for much of the period, in a home very like the Cratchits'.

He had felt utterly neglected during his ordeal as a child laborer at Warren's. The boy Scrooge, alone at school at Christmas time, feels neglected, too. Apparently abandoned by his family, he is, however, reprieved by his sister, who comes to tell him their father has relented, and that she is to take him home – "Home, for good and all. Home, for ever and ever" (*Christmas Books* 32). Dickens's release from his drudgery at Warren's had been as abrupt and strange. His father and the manager had quarrelled, he explains in the account he wrote for Forster, and as a result he had been dismissed. "With a relief so strange that it was like oppression," he wrote of this moment, "I went home" (Forster bk. 1, ch. 2).

The Warren's episode, which these passages seem to recall, probably lasted for over a year, forging a mortifying association in Dickens's mind between poverty and educational deprivation. For more than a year before he had been set to work at the warehouse, his parents' money troubles had denied him schooling such as he had previously enjoyed. At Warren's he had felt this loss even more keenly. It was not only the uncongenial work that had grieved him, he told Forster. There was more:

> no one had compassion enough on me – a child of singular abilities, quick, eager, delicate, and soon hurt, bodily or mentally – to suggest that something might have been spared, as certainly it might have been, to place me at any common school. Our friends, I take it, were tired out. No one made any sign. My father and mother were quite satisfied. They could hardly have been more so, if I had been twenty years of age, distinguished at a grammar school, and going to Cambridge.

He had been in danger of sinking to the level of his fellow workers, he felt – boys whose lack of education and of aspirations dismayed him. He had been oppressed by

> the misery it was to my young heart to believe that, day by day, what I had learned, and thought, and delighted in, and raised my fancy and my emulation up by, was passing away from me, never to be brought back any more.

It was not only his social status that had been threatened, he felt, but the hold he had on values which affirmed it. At Warren's, he believed, he could easily have turned into "a little robber or a little vagabond" (Forster bk. 1, ch. 2.).

Memories of Warren's made the condition of the Ragged School children deeply perturbing for Dickens, and what the Athenaeum was offering to Manchester working men utterly beguiling. His release from the warehouse, and his starting school again (Forster bk. 1, ch. 3), never took from him the memory he had of slipping into mental and moral vacuity, into depravity even. For him, lack of teaching had been more than a blow to his chances in life. It had triggered an imaginative shift. He had felt the seed of corruption being sown within him. It had shown him what it was to be without dignity, humanity, or hope, and he had felt the horror of it.

In March 1843 the spectacle of child poverty had touched his imagination – perhaps even turned his mind towards Christmas – but whatever had inspired him then, in September and October restimulation of old pain provoked something more profound. Poverty continued to absorb his attention but, for imaginative purposes at any rate, the matter of formal education was shelved. His imagination was carried into deeper, darker regions. He began to ask what it is that makes an individual whole, whether formally taught or not; what it is we need to hold on to; what it is we need to learn, and think, and delight in, and raise our fancy and our emulation up by. He sought to explain what we lose through an exclusive preoccupation, imposed or chosen, with getting and spending; what we lose when there is nothing to remind us of our common humanity. He sought, in other words, to uncover the roots of human corruption and, conversely, to find what hopes there are for human redemption. He began to write.

An allusion in the letter to Napier of 24 October, is the first we find unmistakably to the *Carol* as such. Dickens tells Napier how he had

> plunged headlong into a little scheme I had held in abeyance during the interval which elapsed between my first letter and your answer; set an artist at work upon it; and put it wholly out of my powers to touch the Edinburgh subject until after Christmas is turned. (*Letters* 3: 585)

Forster dates Dickens's first thoughts of the book to the beginning of October and the Manchester Athenaeum *soirée*, but this letter confirms that it was on his mind before 16 September, when he wrote the initial letter to Napier. Probably more reliably, Forster also tells us that Dickens began work on the book soon after his return to London (Forster bk. 4, ch. 1). Whenever he first conceived it, letters Dickens wrote during November indicate that he was busy with it that month (*Letters* 3: 595, 601–02).

By the beginning of December it was finished. He wrote to his lawyer (and friend), Thomas Mitton, to whom he had evidently sent proofs. "I am extremely glad you *feel* the Carol," he told him, and exulted in "the effect of such a little *whole* as that" (*Letters* 3: 605). In a letter sent on the day of publication, 19 December, he confided to the journalist and poet, Charles Mackay, "I was very much affected by the little Book myself; in various ways, as I wrote it; and had an interest in the idea, which made me reluctant to lay it aside for a moment" (*Letters* 3: 610). In saying as much he echoes the short preface he had written for the book:

> I have endeavoured in this Ghostly little book, to raise the Ghost of an Idea, which shall not put my readers out of humour with themselves, with each other, with the season, or with me. May it haunt their houses pleasantly, and no one wish to lay it. (*Christmas Books* 5)

He thought the book capable of being felt, then, more as if it were a poem or a piece of music than a work of fiction. He thought of it as a unified whole. Above all, he thought of it as something expressing an idea.

It is not an idea scholars have been eager to explain. Unsurprisingly, perhaps. Dickens himself seemed at least as comfortable speaking of the book's effect, or of feeling it, yet he insisted there was an idea and we can scarcely ignore that. It was an idea, I submit, that grew out of his need to transcend the awkwardness detectable in "A Christmas Dinner" and in the Christmas chapters of *Pickwick*. It was something he was reaching out for in parts of *Master Humphrey*. It was something prompted by the way his imagination had developed during 1843.

The idea was for a story of redemption through memory. Thrown back by chance upon old pain, Dickens found his imagination, not constrained, but liberated by this. He found himself able dramatically to exploit precisely that doubt about the value of memory he had unthinkingly let himself express in "A Christmas Dinner." He found himself able positively to remonstrate against forgetfulness. The book explores a man's relation to his own past, his readiness or otherwise to live with it. It explores the consequences of choices he makes in the matter, upon his understanding and his conduct.

A helpful way of thinking about *A Christmas Carol* is to see it as a story about narrative. I have laid emphasis on the way changes in the celebration of Christmas can be related to a shift in interest from ritual to narrative. This is what the *Carol* above all exemplifies. To remember is to be compelled to construct a narrative out of experience. Scrooge is someone who is made to remember by ghostly visitors, and is coaxed by them into narratives from which he seeks to exclude himself, coaxed not to deny such narratives to others. In the book, stories of the past matter, and stories of the future, too. With narrative, we make connections, the book insists, and develop sympathy. To repudiate narrative is to repudiate humanity. To acknowledge it is to bestow value upon fact. To begin with, Scrooge prefers the statistic and the wisecrack to narrative – discontinuous, atomistic, unchained to value. It is only when he consents to "live in the Past, the Present, and the Future" that he can regain the humanity he has forfeited (*Christmas Books* 79).

If it is difficult to pinpoint Dickens's "idea," it is less difficult to identify ways in which he chose to convey it. One means he chose is another matter about which most scholars remain silent, but which calls out for consideration. Why did Dickens name the book *A Christmas*

Carol in Prose, and divide it into five "staves" in imitation of a carol? Was this just a piece of self-indulgent whimsy? Would he not have done better to use the conventional term, "chapter," and to call the book "A Christmas Story," "A Christmas Tale," "The Christmas Ghosts," or something of that kind?

To frame an answer we must again remember that Christmas was a popular festival, familiar to Dickens and to his readers alike. Because of that, he could evoke its various traditions by foregrounding one which, more than any other, summoned up the rest. Mournful prognostications notwithstanding, Christmas carols were well known and well liked in the early 1840s. Dickens had even written one himself. In chapter 28 of *Pickwick Papers*, an earlier piece of text with the title "A Christmas Carol" is sung by a "merry old gentleman."[7] Spring, summer, and autumn, he sings, all have their drawbacks.

> But my song I troll out, for CHRISTMAS stout,
> The hearty, the true, and the bold;
> A bumper I drain, and with might and main
> Give three cheers for this Christmas old!
> We'll usher him in with a merry din
> That shall gladden his joyous heart
> And we'll keep him up, while there's bite or sup,
> And in fellowship good, we'll part. (*Pickwick Papers*
> 385–86)

Luckily, potential buyers of the *Carol* had better examples to admire (see pp. 98–100 above). They bought and sang the dozens of broadside carol sheets published every year. They sang traditional carols from the anthologies published by Gilbert in 1822, Sandys in 1833, and Wright in 1836. They sang new carols from *The Christmas Box* (1825), and from J. W. Parker's *Christmas Carols* (1831). Some would have been Nonconformists, who sang carols in their chapels (Anglicans had yet to revive this tradition). Some would just have been been aware of old country traditions. We should not forgot that, migration notwithstanding, the population of England was still substantially rural in 1843, still exposed to rural ways.[8] Many readers, including recent migrants to urban areas, would have been familiar with the ancient carols, often unpublished, sung by country folk in their own homes, and outside the homes of their neighbors. The corpus of carols with which readers were familiar was a storehouse of Christmas myth and tradition. And it was a handle by which the whole bundle of Christmas customs could be seized.

Whatever else they might be, carols are one of the forms Christmas celebrations take. Many of them, moreover, like Dickens's own initial experiment with the form, urge yet more celebration, echoing the ancient call for sociability, hospitality, and merriness. "A Virgin Most Pure," first recorded in *New Carolls for this Merry Time of Christmas* of 1661, is among those Gilbert sought to rescue in 1822. Its refrain is typical:

> Aye, and therefore be you merry,
> Rejoice and be you merry,
> Set sorrows aside!
> Christ Jesus, our Saviour,
> Was born on this tide. (Bradley 10–13)

Many carols, too, call attention to the plight of the poor, and to the need for charity to relieve it. The wassailing carols conventionally speak on behalf of the poor. A traditional Yorkshire one, "We've Been Awhile A-Wandering," demands food and sympathy for poor, tired, and hungry singers:

> Bring us out a table
> And spread it with a cloth,
> Bring us out some mouldy cheese
> And some of your Christmas loaf;
> For it's Christmas time, when we travel far and near:
> May God bless you and send you a happy New Year.
>
> Good master and good mistress,
> While you're sitting by the fire,
> Pray think of us poor children
> That's wandered in the mire;
> For it's Christmas time, when we travel far and near:
> May God bless you and send you a happy New Year.

One variant of this was appearing in broadside form as late as 1850 (Dearmer et al. 34–35).

And of course carols constitute a great store of narrative. The Nativity story itself, needless to say, lies at the center. The variety and inventiveness of treatment brought to it make it a virtually inexhaustible resource. But in some carols the Nativity is only implicit. Many that call for Christmas rejoicing only allude to the story. Others admit different narratives. "Saint Stephen," for instance, recorded by both Sandys and Gilbert, tells the story of the first Christian martyr, remembered on 26 December (Dearmer et al. 52–53).

Carols offered a model, moreover, for a special kind of narrative. Again and again they insist upon the superabundance of the miraculous at Christmas time. Marvels proliferate in them. The central miracle of mankind's redemption, we are invited to suppose, spills over, year after year, into subordinate miracles. The Gospels themselves encourage this notion, with their heavenly choirs, guiding stars, and warning dreams. Folklore too, some of it perhaps adapted from older pagan sources, tells of beasts in the field kneeling in reverence on Christmas Eve, of bees swarming to hum a Christmas hymn, of water turning to wine.

In some carols, the marvels described are symbolic, but are integrated into narrative nevertheless. "Down in Yon Forest" was first documented in the fifteenth century. It found its way into print more than once during the nineteenth, as did a rival version to a different tune, "All Bells in Paradise." Both conjure up enigmas, only mysteriously related to the nativity. They are captivatingly eerie:

> Down in yon forest there stands a hall:
> *The bells of Paradise I heard them ring:*
> Cover'd all over with purple and pall:
> *And I love my Lord Jesus above any thing.*

The eeriness is sustained through further enigmas: "In that hall there stands a bed . . . : Cover'd all over with scarlet so red"; "Under that bed there runs a flood . . . : The one half runs water, the other runs blood"; "Over that bed the moon shines bright . . . : Denoting our Saviour was born this night" (Dearmer et al. 134, 392–93).

Other carols tell more plainly, not of symbolic marvels, but of uncanonical miracles. Recorded by Sandys, the Cherry Tree Carol is about Joseph's being made to understand the divine origin of Mary's child, by a cherry tree bowing to her and offering its fruit (Bradley 169–76). Ten years after the publication of *A Christmas Carol*, the Victorian era began to produce its own carols of this kind. J. M. Neale's *Carols for Christmastide* (1853) includes his "Good King Wenceslas," telling of a saintly and charitable king, whose footprints in the snow, at Christmas time, warm the blood of a hypothermic page (Bradley 113–17).

The title of *A Christmas Carol*, then, was no mere dainty touch on Dickens's part. It indicates an underlying structural metaphor, clearly conceived and carefully executed. The persistent implications of the metaphor do much to account for the way the book can be "felt," as Dickens claimed it could, the way it can be grasped as a whole. It justifies the compactness of the book, and its neat form. And it also validates content. It invites readers to accept a familiar combination of ingredients: a call for Christmas merrymaking; a recognition of the plight of the poor and of the need to relieve it; and, most importantly, a narrative violating the norms of conventional prose fiction with marvels, related, however obliquely, to the miracle of Christ's sacrifice.[9]

But the carol provided Dickens with a model only for his chief motifs. Something else was needed upon which to shape the development of the story. And something else was available. In determining the very structure of his book, it is clear, Dickens was attentive to more than one Christmas tradition. The subtitle he chose is *A Ghost Story of Christmas*. The book may be like a carol in important respects, but it unquestionably is a ghost story. Dickens merges a fanciful and a formal model. And, formally, he chose to locate his tale within the popular tradition of ghost stories told around the fireside on Christmas Eve.

The two models, to be sure, invite blending. The roots of the Christmas carol and of the Christmas ghost story are tangled and not wholly distinct. The many carols that dwell upon the superabundance of the miraculous at Christmas time do what all of the ghost stories do. Both traditions embody a belief in Christmas as a magical time, when spirits walk and mysteries proliferate. Both probably echo a pagan conviction that the inexplicable rebirth of the year is accompanied by other wonders, other rebirths even.   Only the ghost stories select unwelcome ones.

In Stave One of the *Carol*, Dickens dwells on such unwelcome ones. He follows the tradition of "Raw-heads and Bloody-bones," first lifted from orally transmitted folktale by *Round About our Coal Fire* (see p. 105 above).   On Christmas Eve, Scrooge is terrified by a visit from the ghost of his partner, Jacob Marley, seven years dead.   But terror is not all Dickens dwells on, it must be said.   So rich a text is the *Carol*, it is hard to say anything about it, without being aware of a need to augment, qualify, or balance what we say, with something quite different.   Stave One is also used to launch a theme: the responsibility men and women have for those less fortunate than themselves – especially at Christmas time.   And into it is woven the sparkling thread of comic invention that runs through the entire book.

We have already seen how, in the best ghost stories, terror and comedy can coexist (see pp. 140–41 above).   Dickens contrives an extraordinarily successful synaesthesis in Stave One.   Readers are made to feel Scrooge's terror, and simultaneously to laugh, without either response diminishing the other.   This is something attempted in innumerable Gothic self-parodies, in books and on screen, but rarely with such success.   Usually, the comedy contaminates and cheapens the apparatus of terror.   The ghosts of Stave One, however, are unquestionably anguished and frightening.   Perhaps we see them as such all the more readily, thanks to the comedy.   It is as if their capacity to shock is confirmed by its withstanding an alien mood.

A sceptical Scrooge puts it to Marley's ghost, in Stave One, that he is nothing but a trick of Scrooge's own digestive system: "you may be an undigested bit of beef, a blot of mustard, a crumb of cheese, a fragment of an underdone potato."

> At this, the spirit raised a frightful cry, and shook its chain with such a dismal and appalling noise, that Scrooge held on tight to his chair, to save himself from falling in a swoon.   But how much greater was his horror, when the phantom taking off the bandage round its head, as if it were too warm to wear indoors, its lower jaw dropped down upon its breast!
>
> Scrooge fell upon his knees, and clasped his hands before his face.

"Mercy!" he said. "Dreadful apparition, why do you trouble me?" (20)

The cluster of ghosts shown to Scrooge at the end of Stave One is as unnerving, although equally touched by comedy:

> The air was filled with phantoms, wandering hither and thither in restless haste, and moaning as they went. Every one of them wore chains like Marley's Ghost; some few (they might be guilty governments) were linked together; none were free. Many had been personally known to Scrooge in their lives. He had been quite familiar with one old ghost, in a white waistcoat, with a monstrous iron safe attached to its ankle, who cried piteously at being unable to assist a wretched woman with an infant, whom it saw below, upon a door-step. The misery with them all was, clearly, that they sought to interfere, for good, in human matters, and had lost the power for ever. (23–24)

The misdeeds in life of the ghosts are indicated. Their chains, in particular, provoke reflection. Marley's is composed of "cash-boxes, keys, padlocks, ledgers, deeds, and heavy purses wrought in steel" (17). But in this part of the book, intent as he was upon moral meaning, Dickens was especially concerned to generate the atmosphere of horror and menace customary in ghost stories. Moral meaning is drip-fed in symbolic detail, and openly stated in the words of Marley's ghost. "It is required of every man," the ghost, for instance, tells Scrooge,

> "that the spirit within him should walk abroad among his fellow-men, and travel far and wide; and if that spirit goes not forth in life, it is condemned to do so after death. It is doomed to wander through the world – oh, woe is me! – and witness what it cannot share, but might have shared on earth, and turned to happiness!"
>
> Again the spectre raised a cry, and shook its chain and wrung its shadowy hands. (20)

This inventive pneumatology is preparation for what is to come, but atmosphere is unaffected. The cry, the shaking of chains, the wringing of hands, seize the reader's attention.

The following three staves are different. The mood shifts. Grand

Guignol terror gives way to existential anxiety. In Stave One, horror
coexists with other elements, but in the following staves it recedes into
the background. The ghosts provoke less of a *frisson*, more of a search
for meaning. All of them alarm and dismay Scrooge, certainly. The
Ghost of Christmas Yet To Come alarms and dismays him a great deal.
All three of them acquaint Scrooge with the dead, or with intimations of
death, but none of them is the spirit of someone once living, tainted by
the grave. All are creatures of symbolism, opaque enough to confer
narrative interest, transparent enough to reward deliberation. And yet
they are solidly characterized – inexorable but benign. They belong to a
world of miracle, of divine intervention in human affairs. In this respect
they evoke the mood of the carol at least as much as that of the ghost
story. Dickens's two models are expertly blended into something
obscurely meaningful and mysteriously moving.

It is the ghosts who undertake the task of weaning Scrooge from his
addiction to a cold, atomistic perception of human behavior. They
persuade him to accept narrative, warm and connective. They teach him
that men, women, and children are creatures of time – Scrooge himself
not least. They make him understand how individuals are shaped by
joys and sorrows, capable of uniting them with, or dividing them from,
others. They show him how Christmas retrieves joys and sorrows from
the past, to let us judge what it is we are, what it is we might be.

The symbolism of the Ghost of Christmas Past, in Stave Two,
displays the delight in paradox found in so many carols. "Veiled in
flesh, the Godhead see!" is a typical carol conceit (Bradley 126).
Awakened at one o'clock on Christmas morning, Scrooge finds a ghost
at his bedside provoking similar conceptual confusion:

> It was a strange figure – like a child: yet not so like a child as
> like an old man, viewed through some supernatural medium,
> which gave him the appearance of having receded from the
> view, and being diminished to a child's proportions. Its hair,
> which hung about its neck and down its back, was white as if
> with age; and yet the face had not a wrinkle in it, and the
> tenderest bloom was on the skin. The arms were very long and
> muscular; the hands the same, as if its hold were of uncommon
> strength. Its legs and feet, most delicately formed, were, like
> those upper members, bare. It wore a tunic of the purest white,

and round its waist was bound a lustrous belt, the sheen of which was beautiful. It held a branch of fresh green holly in its hand; and, in singular contradiction of that wintry emblem, had its dress trimmed with summer flowers. But the strangest thing about it was, that from the crown of its head there sprung a bright clear jet of light, by which all this was visible; and which was doubtless the occasion of its using, in its duller moments, a great extinguisher for a cap, which it now held under its arm. (*Christmas Books* 27–28)

This powerfully suggests much that is now familiar to us in Dickens's attitude to memories of past Christmases, much that falls into place once the ghost announces its identity. What is ancient and gone from us can nevertheless remain with us, new and fresh and innocent. Memories of old joy are powerful, tenacious, and beautiful. They illuminate the present. It is perilous to deny the narratives of our lives, and at no time of the year do those narratives speak to us more distinctly than at Christmas time.

The Ghost of Christmas Past, and the effect it has upon Scrooge, owe much to the perception Dickens had Master Humphrey voice.[10] It causes Scrooge to linger upon "past emotions and by-gone times," and to hover, "the ghost of his former self, about the places and people that warmed his heart of old" (see p. 148 above). It unlocks forgotten emotions in him. "Your lip is trembling," it can characteristically observe. "And what is that upon your cheek?" (29). Thrust back into his own narrative in this way, Scrooge finds himself softening towards others, and reluctantly admitting regret at missed opportunities for kindness. "There was a boy singing a Christmas Carol at my door last night," he wistfully recalls. "I should like to have given him something: that's all" (32).

But Scrooge's re-education has only just begun. More remains to be achieved. So it is no surprise to find him, at the end of the stave, symbolically enacting the suppression of memory which has caused him to become the man he is. "Haunt me no longer!" he despairingly cries, and grapples with the ghost:

In the struggle, if that can be called a struggle in which the Ghost with no visible resistance on its own part was undisturbed

> by any effort of its adversary, Scrooge observed that its light was
> burning high and bright; and dimly connecting that with its
> influence over him, he seized the extinguisher-cap, and by a
> sudden action pressed it down upon its head.
>
> The Spirit dropped beneath it, so that the extinguisher
> covered its whole form; but though Scrooge pressed it down
> with all his force, he could not hide the light, which streamed
> from under it, in an unbroken flood upon the ground.
>
> He was conscious of being exhausted, and overcome by an
> irresistible drowsiness; and, further, of being in his own
> bedroom. He gave the cap a parting squeeze, in which his hand
> relaxed; and had barely time to reel to bed, before he sank into a
> heavy sleep. (40–41)

A heavy sleep indeed. Scrooge, we see, is reverting to an habitual state.
He prefers to be unconscious of the past, and with it his humanity.

In his person, and in the emblems with which he surrounds himself,
the Ghost of Christmas Present, in Stave Three, embodies the rituals of
Christmas that Scrooge has been rejecting, along with the more
searching perceptions they provoke. He finds the ghost in his sitting
room:

> It was his own room. There was no doubt about that. But it
> had undergone a surprising transformation. The walls and
> ceiling were so hung with living green, that it looked a perfect
> grove, from every part of which, bright gleaming berries
> glistened. The crisp leaves of holly, mistletoe, and ivy reflected
> back the light, as if so many little mirrors had been scattered
> there; and such a mighty blaze went roaring up the chimney, as
> that dull petrification of a hearth had never known in Scrooge's
> time, or Marley's, or for many and many a winter season gone.
> Heaped up on the floor, to form a kind of throne, were turkeys,
> geese, game, poultry, brawn, great joints of meat, sucking-pigs,
> long wreaths of sausages, mince-pies, plum-puddings, barrels of
> oysters, red-hot chestnuts, cherry-cheeked apples, juicy oranges,
> luscious pears, immense twelfth-cakes, and seething bowls of
> punch, that made the chamber dim with their delicious steam.
> (43)

The iconography proclaims that defiance of the year's ebb, which neither denunciation, nor prohibition, nor indifference had succeeded in eliminating from the English Christmas: the injection of color, light, warmth, and plenty into a season short of them all – a season which Scrooge, however, has shown no sign of wanting to mitigate. "It was cold, bleak, biting weather," the text has told us (8). Scrooge lives alone in "a gloomy suite of rooms, in a lowering pile of building up a yard" (14). He is content to illuminate them with a single tallow dip – "darkness is cheap, and Scrooge liked it"; content to diminish their chill with "a very low fire indeed" (16). Scrooge's Christmas Eve fare has been a "melancholy dinner in his usual melancholy tavern" (14), followed by medicinal gruel before his feeble fire (16). The ambush of comfort and abundance the ghost contrives is not just an appeal for Christmas over-indulgence. It is an invitation to joyous ritual feasting and conviviality, countering Scrooge's wish that "every idiot who goes about with 'Merry Christmas,' on his lips, should be boiled with his own pudding, and buried with a stake of holly through his heart" (10).

The ghost itself, seated upon the heaped provisions, is "a jolly Giant, glorious to see; who bore a glowing torch, in shape not unlike Plenty's horn, and held it up, high up, to shed its light on Scrooge."

> It was clothed in one simple deep green robe, or mantle, bordered with white fur. This garment hung so loosely on the figure, that its capacious breast was bare, as if disdaining to be warded or concealed by any artifice. Its feet, observable beneath the ample folds of the garment, were also bare; and on its head it wore no other covering than a holly wreath set here and there with shining icicles. Its dark brown curls were long and free; free as its genial face, its sparkling eye, its open hand, its cheery voice, its unconstrained demeanour, and its joyful air. Girded round its middle was an antique scabbard; but no sword was in it, and the ancient sheath was eaten up with rust. (43–44)

Everything about the ghost declares generosity, lack of constraint, scorn of concealment, naturalness, and joy – all qualities appropriate to the ancient call for sociability, hospitality, and merriment, all qualities which Scrooge has unlearned and needs to relearn. The empty, rusting scabbard proclaims the devotion to peace on earth hymned by the herald angels. We are told nothing of Scrooge's attitude to discord among

nations, but we have seen his attitude to discord among individuals. He
has been a man ready both to give and to take offence, a man who lets
antagonism fester, and will not take the longer view that heals it. We
have seen him toy with the honest sentiments of the portly gentlemen
collecting for charity (11–13). We have seen him deaf to his nephew's
Christmas invitation, mindful only of a contingent grudge. "Why did
you get married?" he growls (11).

But he has changed, if not yet enough. He has become more open to
persuasion. Resistance notwithstanding, the Ghost of Christmas Past
has taught him "a lesson which is working now." "To-night, if you have
aught to teach me," Scrooge tells his new visitor, "let me profit by it"
(44). The ghost complies.

Its chief role is to grant Scrooge visions of Christmas joy in the
present, contrived in defiance of the harsh, restrictive values which have
led him to deny his common humanity – contrived, indeed, in defiance
of every kind of discouragement. Scrooge is shown merrymakers
known and unknown. He is shown seasonal kindness and good will
prevailing repeatedly over hard circumstances and reasons for
discontent. The spirit sprinkles incense from his torch on the Christmas
fowls and joints of meat poor people are taking to bakers' shops to be
roasted in the oven:

> And it was a very uncommon kind of torch, for once or twice
> when there were angry words between some dinner-carriers who
> had jostled each other, he shed a few drops of water on them
> from it, and their good humour was restored directly. For they
> said, it was a shame to quarrel upon Christmas Day. And so it
> was! God love it, so it was! (47)

The great set piece of Stave Three is the Cratchit family's Christmas
dinner, a fair representation of lower-middle-class custom, we can now
see – no wishful fantasy. The Cratchits let neither poverty nor anxiety
discourage them. They are sustained by love and mutual loyalty. "They
were not a handsome family," we are told;

> they were not well dressed; their shoes were far from being
> water-proof; their clothes were scanty; and Peter [the eldest son]
> might have known, and very likely did, the inside of a

pawnbroker's. But they were happy, grateful, pleased with one another, and contented with the time . . . . (54)

Their goose was "a feathered phenomenon, to which a black swan was a matter of course: and in truth it was something very like it in that house" (50). But, "eked out by the apple-sauce and mashed potatoes, it was a sufficient dinner for the whole family; indeed, as Mrs. Cratchit said with great delight (surveying one small atom of a bone upon the dish), they hadn't ate it all at last!" (51). All the family say something about the Christmas pudding, "but nobody said or thought it was at all a small pudding for a large family. It would have been flat heresy to do so. Any Cratchit would have blushed to hint at such a thing" (52).

With some persuasion, their generosity of spirit is extended even to Scrooge. Bob proposes a toast to "the Founder of the Feast."

> "I'll drink his health for your sake and the Day's," said Mrs. Cratchit, "not for his. Long life to him! A merry Christmas and a happy new year! He'll be very merry and very happy, I have no doubt!" (53)

Bob's wish prevails, nonetheless, and the toast is drunk.

What the ghost shows Scrooge, in this episode, is the value of a seasonal conviviality, literally understood: the value of a time when it is customary for members of a family to live their lives together, to share what they have in common, to sense the continuous narrative of their joint lives and take strength from it. Suffering and discontent are not forgotten. There is no attempt at forgetfulness such as Dickens had incautiously recommended in "A Christmas Dinner." Adversity is faced with mutual support. Scrooge hears Mrs. Cratchit ask Bob how their ailing and crippled son has behaved at church.

> "As good as gold," said Bob,"and better. Somehow he gets thoughtful, sitting by himself so much, and thinks the strangest things you ever heard. He told me, coming home, that he hoped the people saw him in the church, because he was a cripple, and it might be pleasant to them to remember upon Christmas Day, who made lame beggars walk, and blind men see."
> Bob's voice was tremulous when he told them this, and

> trembled more when he said that Tiny Tim was growing strong
> and hearty. (50)

Bob is troubled, but hope sustains him, and no one dreams of robbing him of it. Impressed, Scrooge attends closely to the vision he is granted of the family, "and when they faded, and looked happier yet in the bright sprinklings of the Spirit's torch at parting, Scrooge had his eye upon them, and especially on Tiny Tim, until the last" (54). He begins, that is to say, to take an interest in their story. He warms to narrative.

Postwar literary theory, and the kind of fiction such theory favors, have made us hesitate to accept endorsement of successful family life such as we find in this episode of the *Carol*. The theories urge interrogation of the family as an institution affirming current ideological practices. Explicit or implicit, Marxist notions have become conventional.

Catherine Waters speaks of Dickens's "worship of the family" (Waters 74). Sally Ledger speaks of his "focus on domesticity as a panacea" (*Christmas Books* xxvii). Peter Ackroyd suggests that the Victorian privileging of domestic contentment, that we can detect in the *Carol*, was positively enhanced by awareness of suffering beyond the domestic fireside:

> In many Victorian homes the exterior world seems literally to be kept at bay by a whole artillery of protective forces – screened by thick curtains and by lace inner curtains, muffled by patterned wallpaper and patterned carpets, held off by settees and ottomans and what-nots, mocked by wax fruit and wax candles, its metaphorical and literal darkness banished by lamps and chandeliers and candles. The central idea is one of ferocious privacy, of shelter and segregation, and it was in *A Christmas Carol* that Dickens divined it and brought it forth to the surface. (Ackroyd 414)

The Victorian love of home and family was doubtless sometimes a cover for darker instincts, though it seems unduly severe to find such instincts in a liking for privacy, color, comfort, and light. And this remonstrance, it should be clear, in no way reflects the Cratchit home, in which the "family display of glass" consists of "two tumblers, and a custard-cup without a handle" (*Christmas Books* 52). For Dickens, it is clear, domestic contentment was an end in itself, not a means to an end. This contention, of course, will not persuade dedicated Marxists, but I have no wish to persuade them. Condemnation to perpetual sophistry is a fitting punishment for them and an apt warning to others. Looking at it against the backdrop of contemporary discourse on Christmas, we can see the episode of the Cratchit family's Christmas dinner for what it really was: a fresh depiction of Christmas as the family festival it had become – idealized perhaps, but not to the extent of glossing over life's troubles.

The final vision granted to Scrooge in Stave Three, moreover, dispels any notion that the *Carol* offers family life as a refuge from disquieting social realities. Scrooge is confronted with suffering unappeased by any kind of support, suffering mirroring what Dickens had detected at the Field Lane Ragged School, suffering such as Scrooge had declined to relieve in Stave One, Christmas notwithstanding.

He sees something disquieting protruding from beneath the spirit's robe. "Is it a foot or a claw!" he asks.

> "It might be a claw, for the flesh there is upon it," was the Spirit's sorrowful reply. "Look here."
> From the foldings of its robe, it brought two children; wretched, abject, frightful, hideous, miserable. They knelt down at its feet, and clung upon the outside of its garment.
> "Oh, Man! look here. Look, look, down here!" exclaimed the Ghost.
> They were a boy and a girl. Yellow, meagre, ragged, scowling, wolfish; but prostrate, too, in their humility. Where graceful youth should have filled their features out, and touched them with its freshest tints, a stale and shrivelled hand, like that of age, had pinched, and twisted them, and pulled them into shreds. Where angels might have sat enthroned, devils lurked, and glared out menacing. No change, no degradation, no perversion of humanity, in any grade, through all the mysteries of wonderful creation, has monsters half so horrible and dread.

The spirit explains these figures:

" . . . This boy is Ignorance. This girl is Want. Beware them both, and all of their degree, but most of all beware this boy, for on his brow I see that written which is Doom, unless the writing be erased. . . ." (62–63)

In Stave One, Scrooge had taunted the charitable gentlemen collecting money to relieve the poor. "Are there no prisons?" he had scoffed. "And the Union workhouses?" Told that many would sooner die than enter a workhouse, instead of helping he had summoned up Malthusian doctrine: "they had better do it, and decrease the surplus population" (12). The Ghost of Christmas Present has already suggested Tiny Tim might die to "decrease the surplus population" (52). Now, devastatingly, he shames Scrooge again:

"Have they no refuge or resource?" cried Scrooge.
"Are there no prisons?" said the Spirit, turning on him for the last time with his own words. "Are there no workhouses?" (63)

This vision is as unsettling as it is, the spirit's questions as humbling as they are, because the two children are at once alien and familiar, repulsive and pitiable. Dickens insinuates no sentimental solution. Without suggesting an easy alternative, in this episode he challenges the utilitarian impulse to ignore the humanity of those among the poor supposed irredeemable. It would be possible to see these children as members of "another race of creatures bound on other journeys," but Scrooge finds himself coaxed into seeing them as "fellow-passengers to the grave" (10). He cannot any longer reduce their degradation to statistical data. He begins to understand them as fellow creatures, with stories of their own, like his, capable of suffering such as he is beginning to experience. Dickens's private anxieties about ignorance are perhaps insufficiently digested and absorbed into the fable here, but it scarcely matters. With a jolt, the two children adjust Scrooge's understanding of Christmas, and the reader's, too.

Scrooge knows what his visitations are for. From the beginning of the book charitable giving, and compassion for the poor, are declared a key feature of the season. Marley's ghost had instructed Scrooge in his duties to those less fortunate than himself, and in the penalty for neglecting those duties, especially at Christmas time. But until now

Scrooge's attention has been secured chiefly by rival features of the festival – by demonstrations of joy he has forfeited. Now, however, charity and compassion cease to be undifferentiated among the cluster of seasonable impulses. They move to the center. Merrymaking, Scrooge begins to see, is a means to mental and moral health, but a new question is posed. Is such health attainable when there are those who have nothing to be merry about, those who know only the hand-to-mouth struggle, those who can glimpse no possibility of change for the better? Christmas, the text suggests, is a potent reminder of the need for charity, and of the need for more than mere charitable giving. It is a season calling on people to look. "Look," is a word the ghost reiterates, and in the 1840s, certainly, looking was tantamount to becoming aware of the need both for seasonal open-handedness, and for something more.[11]

The ghost of Stave Four is the most mysterious of Scrooge's visitors:

> The Phantom slowly, gravely, silently, approached. When it came, Scrooge bent down upon his knee; for in the very air through which this Spirit moved it seemed to scatter gloom and mystery.
>
> It was shrouded in a deep black garment, which concealed its head, its face, its form, and left nothing of it visible save one outstretched hand. But for this it would have been difficult to detach its figure from the night, and separate it from the darkness by which it was surrounded.
>
> He felt that it was tall and stately when it came beside him, and that its mysterious presence filled him with a solemn dread. He knew no more, for the Spirit neither spoke nor moved.
>
> "I am in the presence of the Ghost of Christmas Yet To Come?" said Scrooge.
>
> The Spirit answered not, but pointed onward with its hand.
> (64)

The future is difficult to discern, we understand. It cannot speak to us directly. Few find nothing to dread in it.

Now, though, Scrooge is conscious of what he has learned, is ready to learn more, and can master his dread:

> "Ghost of the Future!" he exclaimed, "I fear you more than any Spectre I have seen. But, as I know your purpose is to do

me good, and as I hope to live to be another man from what I
was, I am prepared to bear you company, and do it with a
thankful heart. . . ." (64–65)

This is an uneasy declaration, however. Stave Four is vitalized by
tension. Scrooge hopes the ghost's mission is to reform him, but there is
a threat that he is beyond reform, that the bad he has done will be
punished, the good he might do remain undone.

What the ghost shows him is death unmourned – people speaking ill
and indifferently of the dead, a corpse unattended in a bare room, a
neglected grave. Only in the instant before he reads it, does Scrooge
permit himself to understand what is confirmed of these visions by the
inscription on the stone – "EBENEZER SCROOGE" (76).

Learning from visions of this kind, he begs to be shown instead
"some tenderness connected with a death" (73). In response, the ghost
grants him a vision of the Cratchits' home in one year's time, and there
follows what is perhaps the most powerful episode in the entire book, all
the more astonishing for the reticence and indirectness with which it is
contrived. In his account of the visions granted Gabriel Grub, in
Pickwick (see pp. 144–145 above), Dickens had rehearsed what he was
to achieve here, but now he is master of his material.

> Quiet. Very quiet. The noisy little Cratchits were as still as
> statues in one corner, and sat looking up at Peter, who had a
> book before him. The mother and her daughters were engaged
> in sewing. But surely they were very quiet!
>
> "And he took a child, and set him in the midst of them."
>
> Where had Scrooge heard those words? He had not dreamed
> them. The boy must have read them out, as he and the Spirit
> crossed the threshold. Why did he not go on?
>
> The mother laid her work upon the table, and put her hand up
> to her face.
>
> "The colour hurts my eyes," she said.
>
> The colour? Ah, poor Tiny Tim!
>
> "They're better now again," said Cratchit's wife. "It makes
> them weak by candle-light; and I wouldn't show weak eyes to
> your father when he comes home, for the world. It must be near
> his time."
>
> "Past it rather," Peter answered, shutting up his book. "But I

think he's walked a little slower than he used, these few last
evenings, mother."

They were very quiet again. At last she said, and in a steady,
cheerful voice, that only faltered once:

"I have known him walk with – I have known him walk with
Tiny Tim upon his shoulder, very fast indeed."

"And so have I," cried Peter. "Often."

"And so have I!" exclaimed another. So had all.

"But he was very light to carry," she resumed, intent upon
her work, "and his father loved him so, that it was no trouble –
no trouble. And there is your father at the door!"

She hurried out to meet him; and little Bob in his comforter –
he had need of it, poor fellow – came in. His tea was ready for
him on the hob, and they all tried who should help him to it
most. Then the two young Cratchits got upon his knees and laid,
each child a little cheek, against his face, as if they said, "Don't
mind it, father. Don't be grieved!"

Bob was very cheerful with them, and spoke pleasantly to all
the family. He looked at the work upon the table, and praised
the industry and speed of Mrs. Cratchit and the girls. They
would be done long before Sunday, he said.

"Sunday! You went to-day, then, Robert?" said his wife.

"Yes, my dear," returned Bob. "I wish you could have gone.
It would have done you good to see how green a place it is. But
you'll see it often. I promised him that I would walk there on a
Sunday. My little, little child!" cried Bob. "My little child!"

He broke down all at once. He couldn't help it. If he could
have helped it, he and his child would have been farther apart
perhaps than they were.

He left the room, and went up-stairs into the room above,
which was lighted cheerfully, and hung with Christmas. There
was a chair set close beside the child, and there were signs of
some one having been there, lately. Poor Bob sat down in it, and
when he had thought a little and composed himself, he kissed the
little face. He was reconciled to what had happened, and went
down again quite happy. (73–74)

We cannot miss the structural function of this passage – the way it
offers contrasts to the lonely deathbed Scrooge resists seeing as his own,
to the neglected grave that awaits him. But this is not what is so

remarkable about it. The language used seems entirely transparent. The narrative, we are persuaded, is no more than a commentary, not even always accurate, on what we perceive independently. What is not said is at least as important as what is said. Dickens had long been master of such legerdemain for comic purposes, but employing it in a solemn context was a new venture for him.

We are never told Tiny Tim is dead, or that funeral preparations are being made. That is the point. We are just made to see it and feel it. Later we learn the vision is only of what the next Christmas might bring, not of what it must. Dickens avoids an affirmation he would later have to retract. But rarely is such a virtue made out of such a necessity. If the motif of the dead or dying child, in texts Dickens wrote about Christmas, can sometimes approach the mawkish, it is never further from it than here.

The words before us are no longer all we have to rely on, of course, at this stage in our reading of the book. The passage comes towards its end, and the Cratchit family has become familiar to us. We know Tiny Tim has been ailing, we know the little Cratchits are characteristically boisterous, and we grope for an explanation of anomalies related here. What we have already been made to imagine shapes our reading. In this respect, there is little that is unusual. But the impact of the passage is dependent on Dickens's delicacy of allusion, his readiness to understate, his readiness, even, to let the narrative err and to let us see it errs.

Peter's book is not identified by name, but the words Scrooge thinks he hears are identification enough.[12] His confusion about who uttered the words, his assumption that Peter read them aloud, and his puzzlement at Peter's stopping, all stir up apprehension.

Mrs. Cratchit's complaint about the color of her sewing reinforces that apprehension, and is quickly rendered heartbreaking by the simplest, deftest of comments: "The colour? Ah, poor Tiny Tim!" Seldom can mourning garb and its implications have been indicated so obliquely in fiction.

But perhaps the most powerful feature of the passage is to be found in the way the narrative is openly partisan:

> At last she said, and in a steady, cheerful voice, that only faltered once:

"I have known him walk with – I have known him walk with
Tiny Tim upon his shoulder, very fast indeed."

A lesser text would have told of Mrs. Cratchit trying to speak in a steady, cheerful voice, but faltering nonetheless. She, however, wants to speak steadily and cheerfully, and is proud of faltering no more than once. We see that the narrator, whose mediation is indispensable and to whom we shall come, wants to support and commend her, as he does all of the family. He discreetly urges us to accept her own estimation of the performance. But no emotional complexity is lost upon us. The very discretion is in itself moving.

A similar effect is achieved a paragraph or two later:

"But he was very light to carry," she resumed, intent upon
her work, "and his father loved him so, that it was no trouble –
no trouble.

Mrs. Cratchit wants her children to think her air of distraction has to do with her being "intent upon her work." We know better. And we know the narrator knows better.

The feat is repeated when we are told Bob was "very cheerful" with his family, when we are told he was "reconciled to what had happened, and went down again quite happy." While we applaud his resolution, we are left in no doubt of what it costs Bob to be cheerful and happy. We know that more could be said.

It is as if we see despite the narrative. Its indirectness and reticence enact the care with which the Cratchits are having to muster their thoughts and feelings, and the narrator's eagerness to abet that care. It calls on us to exercise similar care and, in doing so, makes us see what we are not told. We are distracted with no talk of a blissful afterlife now. We are overwhelmed, rather, by all the emotional complexities of grief. The power of the passage is irresistible.

In passages such as this, the theme of redemption in the *Carol* shows itself most clearly. We see the consequences of a ruinous choice being undone. The passage is a classic example of free indirect style. Readers are made to feel the narrator's perception and Scrooge's merging. The

delicacy and humanity we detect, we are made to understand, are a
delicacy and humanity Scrooge is learning.

In 1843, redemption was something entirely new to Dickens's art.
Mr. Pickwick is not redeemed. He stops being silly. Nicholas Nickleby
is not redeemed. He grows up. None of Dickens's protagonists prior to
the *Carol* is redeemed. Most of them change – they improve, they
reform – but none is made anew as Scrooge is. In discovering
redemption in the *Carol*, Dickens was accessing, for the first time, a
mode of moral and psychological understanding that is a triumph of the
western sensibility, and specific to it. It permeates western religious
thought and western ethics. It has had an incalculable influence on
literary genres born in the west – on tragedy, and on the novel in
particular. Dickens was not just accessing a Christian theme appropriate
to a Christmas book. He was joining the ranks of those who have most
distinctively shaped western culture. He was becoming, among other
things, a writer capable of tracing the redemption of Sydney Carton and
Pip. Little wonder that he could tell Mitton how the compact little *Carol*
had given him "a strong sense of the immense effect I could produce
with an entire book" (*Letters* 3: 605).

Scrooge's exposure to the vision of Tiny Tim's death shows us just
what Dickens was capable of in relating Christmas, love, and death. He
makes the festival mean more than it had meant, by turning it into a
reminder of mortality. He counterpoints ritual repetition against the
transience narrative exposes. Christmas rejoicing, he persuades us,
reminds us that we are all "fellow-passengers to the grave." We can if
we choose see the religious significance of Christmas in this, but we do
not have to.[13]

It is above all the changes in his attitude towards death that mark out
the stages of Scrooge's redemption. To begin with he is a misanthrope,
for whom death is scarcely more than a joke. But as the ghosts require
him to examine chances he has missed and is missing, many of which
death puts beyond recovery, we see him becoming susceptible to pain,
and we rejoice at the healing effect this has upon him.

Dickens's capacity to handle this theme may have been enhanced by
a reminder of the first serious bereavement of his adult life. On 6 May
1837 – after he had written the Christmas episode of *Pickwick*, but
before he had conducted the experiments that foreshadow the *Carol* in

Master Humphrey – his seventeen-year-old sister-in-law, Mary Hogarth, had suffered a seizure at his home in Doughty Street. She had died in his arms the following day.   As time passed, Dickens remembered an intimacy between them probably deeper than it had in fact been, but Mary had undoubtedly been close to him, as well as to his wife, her sister. His grief, certainly, was genuine (Parker, *The Doughty Street Novels* 69–80). On the anniversary of her death in 1843, at a time when the *Carol* was gestating in his mind, Dickens received a portrait of Mary from his mother-in-law. He wrote thanking her for it the following day, speaking of the effect Mary's death had had upon him:

> After she died, I dreamed of her every night for many months – I think for the better part of a year – sometimes as a spirit, sometimes as a living creature, never with any of the bitterness of my real sorrow, but always with a kind of quiet happiness, which became so pleasant to me that I never lay down at night without a hope of the vision coming back in one shape or other. And so it did. (*Letters* 3: 483-84)

At a crucial time, his mind was drawn back to bereavement, to mysterious, benign, nocturnal visitations, and to a sense of mortality in which sorrow and happiness are remembered, and blended, and accepted on equal terms.

It is such a sense of mortality that Scrooge has to be taught in the *Carol*. A variety of responses to death are indicated by the text. Scrooge fends many of them off, but he learns his lesson gradually, and it is completed by the vision of Tiny Tim's death.

To begin with, however, he is incapable of anything like delicacy and humanity. With its mixture of horror and comedy, Stave One has the character of an overtly literary exercise.   As such it mirrors Scrooge's own flippancy. We cannot lose sight of the story-teller enjoying himself, and playing with the ghost-story genre. We are exposed to horrors of the walking dead, but these are deliberately mismatched with the narrative mood. We can only laugh, for instance, at the way Marley's ghost removes the bandage fastening its jaws, "as if it were too warm to wear indoors" (20).

Scrooge does his best to sustain a similar mood, and even contrives to poke fun at the ghost. Trusting to disorders of his digestive system more than to his eyes, he tells it, "There's more of gravy than of grave about you, whatever you are!" His boldness is explained, to be sure:

> Scrooge was not much in the habit of cracking jokes, nor did he feel, in his heart, by any means waggish then. The truth is, that he tried to be smart, as a means of distracting his own attention, and keeping down his terror; for the spectre's voice disturbed the very marrow in his bones. (19)

But for all that he is still bold.

In Stave Two, comedy and death part company. The narrator is unobtrusive at moments when Scrooge is made aware of death. Ironies are allowed to arise out of the text without comment. The tenderer emotions of readers are provoked, rather than their laughter. Scrooge is made to remember the loving little sister, for instance, who rescues him from his Christmas abandonment at school:

> "Always a delicate creature, whom a breath might have withered," said the Ghost. "But she had a large heart!"
> "So she had," cried Scrooge. "You're right. I'll not gainsay it, Spirit. God forbid!"
> "She died a woman," said the Ghost, "and had, as I think, children."
> "One child," Scrooge returned.
> "True," said the Ghost. "Your nephew!"
> Scrooge seemed uneasy in his mind; and answered briefly, "Yes." (33)

Forgetfulness has its costs, Scrooge is learning.

In Stave Three, death is touched on as a possibility only, but it is a powerful moment, and words are now found to combat the harsh indifference Scrooge has cultivated. Watching the Cratchit family's Christmas celebrations, Scrooge becomes anxious about Tiny Tim:

> "Spirit," said Scrooge, with an interest he had never felt before, "tell me if Tiny Tim will live."
> "I see a vacant seat," replied the Ghost, "in the poor chimney-corner, and a crutch without an owner, carefully

preserved. If these shadows remain unaltered by the Future, the child will die."

"No, no," said Scrooge. "Oh, no, kind Spirit! say he will be spared."

"If these shadows remain unaltered by the Future, none other of my race," returned the Ghost, "will find him here. What then? If he be like to die, he had better do it, and decrease the surplus population."

Scrooge hung his head to hear his own words quoted by the Spirit, and was overcome with penitence and grief.

"Man," said the Ghost, "if man you be in heart, not adamant, forbear that wicked cant until you have discovered What the surplus is, and Where it is. Will you decide what men shall live, what men shall die? It may be, that in the sight of Heaven, you are more worthless and less fit to live than millions like this poor man's child. Oh God! to hear the Insect on the leaf pronouncing on the too much life among his hungry brothers in the dust!" (52–53)

It is a doctrine of sympathy and compassion, appropriate to the season the ghost represents, countering inhumane abstractions. Scrooge is called on here to acknowledge his oneness with the poor, to acknowledge that all are "fellow-passengers to the grave."

In Stave Four, we once again find death made comic, but in a sharply contrasting way – a way which generates uneasiness as much as laughter. Scrooge is shown a charwoman, a laundress, and an undertaker's man, meeting by accident at the shop of a dealer in second-hand goods. All three, in their way, have served the as yet unidentified man whose neglected corpse Scrooge has seen, and all come to sell what they have plundered after his death. The comedy is no longer applied from without by a joking narrator. It is Shakespearean in quality. Life goes on, we are made to reflect, and yields irony, regardless of individual destiny. It is the comedy of the grotesque. A shirt is amongst the booty the charwoman offers for sale:

" . . . Ah! You may look through that shirt till your eyes ache; but you won't find a hole in it, nor a threadbare place. It's the best he had, and a fine one too. They'd have wasted it, if it hadn't been for me."

"What do you call wasting of it?" asked old Joe.

"Putting it on him to be buried in, to be sure," replied the woman with a laugh. "Somebody was fool enough to do it, but I took it off again. If calico an't good enough for such a purpose, it isn't good enough for anything. It's quite as becoming to the body. He can't look uglier than he did in that one."

"This is the end of it, you see!" she moralizes. "He frightened every one away from him when he was alive, to profit us when he was dead! Ha, ha, ha!"

Scrooge views the gathering "with a detestation and disgust, which could hardly have been greater, though they had been obscene demons, marketing the corpse itself." And all the time the reader senses him fending off the question of the identity of the deceased. In vain he seeks soothing confirmation from the silent ghost: "I see, I see. The case of this unhappy man might be my own. My life tends that way, now" (70).

His vision of the death of Tiny Tim, in the same stave, is the final confrontation Scrooge needs. He is made to feel the anguish of the loss of a loved one. He is made to understand mortality, and left to consider how it can be endured.

We are prepared to accept Scrooge's redemption, and follow its achievement with interest, because we are made to admire him from the start, despite ourselves. In the opening pages, the narrative denounces him as "a squeezing, wrenching, grasping, scraping, clutching, covetous old sinner" (8), but it is clear that he engages vitally with those about him, however perversely. He is witty, nimble-minded, and mischievous. Like Gabriel Grub, he enjoys his own misanthropy. In Stave One he disobliges his nephew, the gentlemen collecting money for the poor, a young carol singer, and his clerk, but does so with a sure sense of style in each case. He wants to scandalize the charitable gentlemen, for instance, and knows how to do it. Discussing provisions for the poor, he seeks reassurance that "the Treadmill and the Poor Law are in full vigour."

"Both very busy, sir."

"Oh! I was afraid, from what you said at first, that something

had occurred to stop them in their useful course," said Scrooge.
"I'm very glad to hear it." (12)

As we have seen, not even Marley's ghost can daunt Scrooge entirely. Adversarial negotiation is habitual with him. When the ghost tells how it is doomed to wander the world, Scrooge reflects on the seven years that have elapsed since Marley's death, and remarks, "You must have been very slow about it, Jacob" (21). When the ghost tells him he will be visited by three spirits, separately, Scrooge has a counter-proposal. "Couldn't I take 'em all at once," he asks, "and have it over, Jacob?" (23). Scrooge is shrewd, and interacts with others shrewdly. In this respect he will not change, and we like him for it.

The Ghost of Christmas Past reminds Scrooge of what it is to be uncorrupted, giving readers more reasons for liking him in doing so. When he was an apprentice, for instance, he understood the power men and women have to improve the lives of those less fortunate than themselves. The ghost takes him back in time to the occasion of the Christmas ball thrown for his family, his workers, and his neighbors, by his old master Mr. Fezziwig. Scrooge listens to his younger self and a fellow apprentice praising their Mr. Fezziwig's efforts, but the ghost provocatively dismisses these as "a small matter":

> "Why! Is it not? He has spent but a few pounds of your mortal money: three or four perhaps. Is that so much that he deserves this praise?"
> "It isn't that," said Scrooge, heated by the remark, and speaking unconsciously like his former, not his latter, self. "It isn't that, Spirit. He has the power to render us happy or unhappy; to make our service light or burdensome; a pleasure or a toil. Say that his power lies in words and looks; in things so slight and insignificant that it is impossible to add and count 'em up: what then? The happiness he gives, is quite as great as if it cost a fortune." (36)

Scrooge has fallen into a trap, of course, and soon finds himself shamefacedly saying, "I should like to be able to say a word or two to my clerk just now! that's all" (37). His redemption has begun.

He needs redeeming, we learn, because of an error of judgment revealed in another vision the ghost grants Scrooge. He is made to contemplate the moment of parting from his one-time fiancée. Bereaved and dowerless, she releases him from vows she senses he regrets. Another idol has displaced her in his affection she says, "a golden one" (37). But it is not just Scrooge's hardness of heart readers are called to dwell upon. His struggle to choose, and his capacity for contrition are given equal prominence. There is irony in his fiancée's final words:

> "You may – the memory of what is past half makes me hope you will – have pain in this. A very, very brief time, and you will dismiss the recollection of it, gladly, as an unprofitable dream, from which it happened well you awoke. May you be happy in the life you have chosen."

Scrooge accuses the ghost of "torture" in showing him this (38). But worse is to come. He is shown the same fiancée, happily married and with children, being told by her husband of a passing glimpse of Scrooge in his office. It is Christmas Eve, seven years previously: "His partner lies upon the point of death, I hear," says the husband; "and there he sat alone. Quite alone in the world, I do believe." "Remove me!" Scrooge begs. "I cannot bear it" (40).

In Stave Three, we find Scrooge capable of unselfconscious spontaneity. The Ghost of Christmas Present takes him to his nephew's home, and Scrooge is lured into party games, invisibility and inaudibility notwithstanding. One round in a guessing game scarcely flatters him. To find the answer, players are told, they must think

> of an animal, a live animal, rather a disagreeable animal, a savage animal, an animal that growled and grunted sometimes, and talked sometimes, and lived in London, and walked about the streets, and wasn't made a show of, and wasn't led by anybody, and didn't live in a menagerie, and was never killed in a market, and was not a horse, or an ass, or a cow, or a bull, or a tiger, or a dog, or a pig, or a cat, or a bear.

His nephew's sister-in-law is the one to guess correctly:

> "I have found it out! I know what it is, Fred! I know what it is!"
>
> "What is it?" cried Fred.
> "It's your Uncle Scro-o-o-o-oge!" (60)

Yet Scrooge takes no offence at this, and is content to be toasted, *in absentia* and with qualifications:

> "Well! Uncle Scrooge!" they cried.
> "A Merry Christmas and a happy New Year to the old man, whatever he is!" said Scrooge's nephew. "He wouldn't take it from me, but may he have it, nevertheless. Uncle Scrooge!"
> Uncle Scrooge had imperceptibly become so gay and light of heart, that he would have pledged the unconscious company in return, and thanked them in an inaudible speech, if the Ghost had given him time. (61)

"Uncle Scrooge," the narrative deftly indicates, has become happy to think of himself as such. He is acknowledging bonds he has hitherto sought to repudiate.

As we have seen, Scrooge finally achieves what Aristotle calls anagnorisis in Stave Four (*Poetics* ch. 3). It is provoked by the contrast the Ghost of Christmas Yet To Come displays to him: on the one hand the deathbed of Tiny Tim, and the green burial plot, both sanctified by love; on the other the lonely deathbed and neglected grave that await Scrooge himself. At the end of Stave Four, he begs the spirit to tell him all is not ordained: "Why show me this, if I am past all hope?"

> For the first time the hand appeared to shake.
> "Good Spirit," he pursued, as down upon the ground he fell before it: "Your nature intercedes for me, and pities me. Assure me that I yet may change these shadows you have shown me, by an altered life!"
> The kind hand trembled.
> "I will honour Christmas in my heart, and try to keep it all the year. I will live in the Past, the Present, and the Future. The Spirits of all Three shall strive within me. I will not shut out the lessons that they teach. Oh, tell me I may sponge away the writing on this stone!"

> In his agony, he caught the spectral hand. It sought to free itself, but he was strong in his entreaty, and detained it. The Spirit, stronger yet, repulsed him.
>
> Holding up his hands in a last prayer to have his fate reversed, he saw an alteration in the Phantom's hood and dress. It shrunk, collapsed, and dwindled down into a bedpost. (78)

Scrooge has learned he can change, and change what he finds about him as a result. He can improve his own life, and the lives of those close to him. He can join with those who strive against ignorance and want. The joyous optimism that eventually prevails in Stave Five is predicated upon the possibility of learning and the capacity for change we are from the beginning tempted to suspect in Scrooge.

One thing tempting us to suspect it is the presence throughout of a counterpart to Scrooge, sharing features of temperament with him, but uncorrupted, manifestly without need of redemption, and standing as an example of what is attainable. I am speaking of the narrator, who affirms the oneness of sensitive narrative and moral understanding.

The narrator is a virtuoso performer, but the wonders of his performance are not just enjoyable in themselves. They provide a believable framework for an extraordinary story. They nudge the reader from one kind of response to Scrooge towards another. And they show us how to be at ease with what Scrooge tries to repudiate. The narrator is no bolt-on option, there to provide more fun. He is integral to the book's meaning.

The voice we hear speaking to us in the *Carol* is at once capricious and authentic. Dickens's third-person narrators are normally protean. The narrator of the *Carol* is that and more. He seamlessly blends the sensational, the comic, the heartbreaking, and the wonderful. Affirmation, admonishment, praise, and banter give way to each other with ease. We are confronted with an amalgamating sensibility, a narrative intelligence which, without restraint, probes the facts of his story for different kinds of significance. Sometimes we are invited to suppose we are witnessing a game, played to arbitrary rules. Sometimes the demand is that we look unflinchingly beyond the story, at distressing social realities. Sometimes we are caught in a web of imagination, and made to rejoice or suffer with the characters.

This complexity has much to do with the demands of the ghost story. Most ghost stories worth reading, we have seen, hover perplexingly on borders – of the supernatural and the psychological, the terrifying and the comic (see pp. 140–41 above). This tends to shift attention from the story to its telling. "What am I being asked to suppose?" the reader wonders, and looks at who is doing the asking. In the *Carol*, we are given not just a ghost story such as the subtitle promises, but an enactment: the telling of such a story beside the Christmas hearth.[14] We are given a teller who finds his equipoise in absorbing and balancing a mass of contingent, diverse, and intractable material. Contingency, diversity, and intractability are compelled into unity by technical virtuosity.

Readers of *Pickwick Papers* are required to suppose that the story of Gabriel Grub is related by Mr. Wardle on Christmas Eve at Manor Farm. It is an interpolated tale and, within its formal frame, the rules of verisimilitude are relaxed. But in chapter 29 of *Pickwick*, Dickens neglects an opportunity he was not to miss in 1843. The voice we hear is scarcely marked as Mr. Wardle's. It is almost impossible to distinguish it from that of the novel's narrator. A perfunctory attempt is made to establish a distinctive narrative voice for the tale. The events related, we are told at the beginning for instance, happened long ago – "so long, that the story must be a true one, because our great grandfathers implicitly believed in it" (*Pickwick Papers* 387). But this is soon forgotten, and any tension there might have been between tale and teller is dissipated. Broadly speaking, we can forget about the narrative voice. And we do.

The narrative voice we hear in *A Christmas Carol*, by contrast, is all-important. It will not let the reader rest. We find ourselves repeatedly called upon to adjust the way we are responding. If we use the conventional taxonomy of narrative form, we must call the book a third-person narrative. The narrator is not a character in the story of Scrooge's haunting. Scrooge, the ghosts, and all the other characters are alluded to in the third person. Yet the narrator uses the first-person singular often. He is the main character in an enactment – in the story of the telling of the story. The book is a kind of dramatic monologue, in fact, with the reader placed in the position of the narrator's interlocutor. Again and again the narrator calls attention to himself, and asserts an intimate relationship with the reader. Praising Mrs. Fezziwig's dancing at Mr. Fezziwig's ball, for example, the narrator declares, "she was worthy to be his partner in every sense of the term. If that's not high praise, tell me higher, and I'll use it" (*Christmas Books* 35). The voice we hear is at least as distinctive as that of Conrad's Marlow. Readers have little choice but to cooperate with Dickens in constructing some kind of identity for its owner.

Dickens doubtless hoped in 1843 that they would imagine a printed-word equivalent of the skilled raconteur holding attention around the Christmas fireside. Michael Slater hears in it the voice of "a jolly, kind-hearted, bachelor uncle" (Slater, "The Christmas Books," 20). A favorite uncle certainly seems about right, and one perhaps too saucy to be married, but it is the voice of an uncle as provoking as he is entertaining, ready to dare scepticism, knowing a good story can win assent regardless of credence – sometimes, indeed, because of incredulity – and knowing that he is ultimately trusted on matters of value.

This narrator is relentlessly mischievous. At one point in the story, Scrooge finds a phantom staring him in the face – "as close to it as I am now to you," the narrator notes, "and I am standing in the spirit at your elbow" (*Christmas Books* 27). The reader's delight in this is proportionate to the protest he must feel. Only in a metaphorical sense can the narrator of a book be close to its reader, and the closeness of the phantom's face to Scrooge's is not to be understood metaphorically. The narrator of *A Christmas Carol*, in fact, does as much to exasperate readers as to beguile them. He repeatedly places himself between them and the story being told, and counterpoints the narrative with intrusions. He digresses. He delights in provocatively incongruous figures of speech. He rides his own hobbyhorses and imposes his own judgments, knowing some readers will find them too emphatic, some not accept them at all. But it is all strategy – instinctive perhaps, on Dickens's part, but nonetheless precisely targeted. We grow to admire the narrator's audacity, and his obstreperous style ultimately defuses doubt. He makes the story his, and we grow more and more interested in it, not least because we grow more and more interested in him. We leave judgment to him. We obediently jump with him through hoops of doubt, reluctant credulity, and defensive levity. When his narrative seems more transparent than it often does, we are persuaded that restraint is being exercised and become solemn with him. When he affirms robustly, we grant he does not do so easily, and assent. We detect a fundamental soundness beneath the frivolity.

He makes his presence felt from the opening words of the book, in which he implicitly claims a role as mediator between mysteries to be spoken of and the reader's inclination to doubt:

> Marley was dead: to begin with. There is no doubt whatever about that. The register of his burial was signed by the clergyman, the clerk, the undertaker, and the chief mourner. Scrooge signed it: and Scrooge's name was good upon 'Change, for anything he chose to put his hand to. Old Marley was as dead as a door-nail.

He poses here as a judicious weigher of evidence, ready to be doubted, but ready to overthrow doubt. Immediately, though, he launches into the kind of word game we shall become familiar with, and we hear the teasing uncle speaking:

> Mind! I don't mean to say that I know, of my own knowledge, what there is particularly dead about a door-nail. I might have been inclined, myself, to regard a coffin-nail as the deadest piece of ironmongery in the trade. But the wisdom of our ancestors is in the simile; and my unhallowed hands shall not disturb it, or the Country's done for. You will therefore permit me to repeat, emphatically, that Marley was as dead as a door-nail. (7)

Word game not withstanding, this is effective. We now have two discouragements to doubt: evidence, and wanting to hear more of this voice.

And we do, of course. It continues to delight and scandalize us. The description of the apparition of Marley's face, where Scrooge's door knocker should be, is a piece of bravura narrative. The narrator compels our assent by listing all the reasons for withholding it:

Now, it is a fact, that there was nothing at all particular about
the knocker on the door, except that it was very large. It is also a
fact, that Scrooge had seen it night and morning during his
whole residence in that place; also that Scrooge had as little of
what is called fancy about him as any man in the City of
London, even including – which is a bold word – the
corporation, aldermen, and livery. Let it also be borne in mind
that Scrooge had not bestowed one thought on Marley, since his
last mention of his seven-years' dead partner that afternoon.
And then let any man explain to me, if he can, how it happened
that Scrooge, having his key in the lock of the door, saw in the
knocker, without its undergoing any intermediate process of
change: not a knocker, but Marley's face.

Within the rules of the game being played, his very indignation is
persuasive. If, after all this, even he cannot deny it, we find ourselves
asking, who are we to do so? And besides, we have no wish to spoil the
sport. We are further persuaded by his holding on, in the teeth of the
incredible, to everyday habits. He cannot resist a dig at City worthies –
we detect a hobbyhorse here. A little further on, the luminosity of
Marley's face provokes him into an incongruous simile of a kind we
shall soon see to be characteristic: it is "like a bad lobster in a dark
cellar," he tells us (15). He still has his feet on the ground, we feel. He
is not letting the contemplation of marvels change him.

He is in fact reassuringly incorrigible. He describes the family of
Scrooge's erstwhile fiancée in a manner which is not at all calculated to
please today's feminist readers, and which would surely have provoked a
measure of protest in thoughtful female readers in 1843. Happily
married to someone else, we are told, the former fiancée is surrounded
by children, but a beautiful grown-up daughter helps her manage them.
The daughter joins in the games of the children, who take liberties:

What would I not have given to be one of them! Though I never
could have been so rude, no, no! I wouldn't for the wealth of all
the world have crushed that braided hair, and torn it down; and
for the precious little shoe, I wouldn't have plucked it off, God
bless my soul! to save my life. As to measuring her waist in
sport, as they did, bold young brood, I couldn't have done it; I
should have expected my arm to have grown round it for a

punishment, and never come straight again. And yet I should have dearly liked, I own, to have touched her lips; to have questioned her, that she might have opened them; to have looked upon the lashes of her downcast eyes, and never raised a blush; to have let loose waves of hair, an inch of which would be a keepsake beyond price: in short, I should have liked, I do confess, to have had the lightest licence of a child, and yet been man enough to know its value. (39)

Dislike this as much as you please, it is in character. We hear the teasing uncle speaking again, scandalizing female listeners, but delighting them too, by enacting a parody of helpless male concupiscence, ultimately a tribute to female power. Many contemporary women readers, I suspect, would have found this soppy but forgivable. And that is the point of it. Ultimately, we trust this narrator, even when he relates wonders, even when he relates them teasingly, because we recognize him, understand him, and like him – not so much despite his faults as because of them. We like the way he pushes himself before us, resolutely refusing to be anything but himself. We like the way he can be, among other things, unashamedly soppy.

It is easy, of course, to become impatient with talk of the "narrative voice," to protest that it is Dickens's own we hear. But Dickens found himself in contradiction and multiplicity. He found the voices he spoke in through imagination and selection. None of them were achieved without creative effort. To understand the book as distinct from the man, it is useful to determine which Dickens we detect in it – which Dickens, to be more precise, was brought into being to tell the *Carol*. The voice we hear in it is one that enriched and enlarged his identity, not one he hid behind but, for all that, it is a masterly fictional construction.

And it was essential to the task he set himself. As we have seen, multiple strands had to be twisted together, in the *Carol*, into a single yarn. A gossipy, inquisitive, digressive, teasing, opinionated narrator was the solution to accommodating the diversity of material Dickens was assembling, and to setting the moral standard he wished to uphold.

The narrator can affirm robustly. Right at the beginning, he denounces Scrooge unequivocally:

Oh! But he was a tight-fisted hand at the grindstone, Scrooge! a squeezing, wrenching, grasping, scraping, clutching, covetous old sinner! Hard and sharp as flint, from which no steel had ever struck out generous fire; secret, and self-contained, and solitary as an oyster. The cold within him froze his old features, nipped his pointed nose, shrivelled his cheek, stiffened his gait; made his eyes red, his thin lips blue; and spoke out shrewdly in his grating voice. A frosty rime was on his head, and on his eyebrows, and his wiry chin. He carried his own low temperature always about with him; he iced his office in the dogdays; and didn't thaw it one degree at Christmas. (8)

Playful tropes warn readers not to be too hasty in judgment, perhaps, but we can be in no doubt that a formal position on Scrooge's character is being adopted.

At other times, the narrator can fade almost entirely away. After Scrooge has been startled by the apparition of Marley's face where his door knocker should be, he is a little more wary than usual in his chambers. To convey this, the narrative slips into a free indirect style, very close to inner monologue:

Sitting room, bed-room, lumber-room. All as they should be. Nobody under the table, nobody under the sofa; a small fire in the grate; spoon and basin ready; and the little saucepan of gruel (Scrooge had a cold in his head) upon the hob. Nobody under the bed; nobody in the closet; nobody in his dressing-gown, which was hanging up in a suspicious attitude against the wall. Lumber-room as usual. Old fire-guards, old shoes, two fish-baskets, washing-stand on three legs, and a poker. (16)

Equally, the narrative can be openly parodic. The description of all the bells in the house ringing together, and of the noise made by the approach of Marley's ghost, both draw on the standard repertoire of ghost stories. As much is admitted. Scrooge, the narrator tells us, recalls that "ghosts in haunted houses were described as dragging chains" (17). We are comforted by the thought that this is a ghost story conforming to the rules. The narrator is showing his mastery of those rules. We can chuckle at his skill in applying them, and enjoy just the odd bracing *frisson* amid all the comedy.

One such is to be experienced when the ghost passes through the closed door of Scrooge's room. Comedy gives way momentarily to something somberly powerful. Scrooge's frugal little fire reacts to its entrance: "Upon its coming in, the dying flame leaped up, as though it cried 'I know him! Marley's Ghost!' and fell again" (17).

The reader's attention is held by writing of extraordinary flexibility and variety throughout the book. Supremely in control, the narrator can veer from outrageous playfulness to heart-wringing reticence, from categorical denunciation to mesmeric evocation. But his role, I repeat, is not just to dazzle, to suspend disbelief in marvels by multiplying ways of accommodating them. He is at the moral center of the book. That is often the case with a third-person narrator. There are fascinating exceptions, but usually it is the job of such a narrator to embody the values which finally prevail. The narrator of the *Carol* embodies values taught by the recurrence of Christmas, which Scrooge needs to learn.

He holds out hope of closure, of Scrooge abandoning his repudiation of those values, but he is also, for the reader, the model of what Scrooge might attain to. Like Scrooge, he has to overcome, both for himself and for the reader, doubts about the marvels experienced. But in his shrewdness, in his instinct for mischief, in his ability vitally to engage with others, he both parallels Scrooge, and shows what Scrooge lacks. *A Christmas Carol* draws effectively to a close once it becomes hard to tell narrator and Scrooge apart.

This happens in Stave Five. Picking up the words of the charwoman (70), Dickens entitles his closing section "The End of It." The ironies are multiple. It is the end of the book, but it is not the dismal end to Scrooge's story the charwoman had depicted. Scrooge has accepted common mortality, the fact that there is an ending to all lives, not least his own, and this has enlarged his sympathies. But he has also seen how love mitigates such endings, makes them less than absolute in the hearts of those who remember thankfully. He renews his promise to the Ghost of Christmas Yet To Come:

"I will live in the Past, the Present, and the Future!" Scrooge repeated, as he scrambled out of bed. "The Spirits of all Three shall strive within me." (79)

The ghosts have given Scrooge a transcendent understanding, showing him what he is, what he shares with others, what he must do to recover his humanity.

And he does it, changing his moral identity, if not the salient features of his character. He remains as mischievous and manipulative as ever, but plays tricks and sets ambushes for selfless ends, not selfish ones. Finding it still only Christmas Day, despite his protracted ordeal, he sends a prize turkey, anonymously, to the Cratchits, gloating at the thought of their perplexity (80–81). Contrite, he makes a donation for the poor to one of the gentlemen whom he had refused on Christmas Eve, but cannot resist an element of staginess:

> "Mr. Scrooge?"
> "Yes," said Scrooge. "That is my name, and I fear it may not be pleasant to you. Allow me to ask your pardon. And will you have the goodness" – here Scrooge whispered in his ear.
> "Lord bless me!" cried the gentleman, as if his breath were gone. "My dear Mr. Scrooge, are you serious?" (82)

Throwing himself on the mercy of his nephew, he joins his Christmas party, but declines to be announced. Instead, he "sidled his face in, round the door."

> Dear heart alive, how his niece by marriage started! Scrooge had forgotten, for the moment, about her sitting in the corner with the footstool, or he wouldn't have done it, on any account.
> "Why bless my soul!" cried Fred, "who's that?"
> "It's I. Your uncle Scrooge. I have come to dinner. Will you let me in, Fred?"
> Let him in! It is a mercy he didn't shake his arm off. He was at home in five minutes. Nothing could be heartier. (83)

Scrooge's love of effect makes him forget the pregnancy of Fred's wife. We are scarcely surprised at that.

But his *pièce de résistance* is reserved for the following day. Bob Cratchit arrives late for work:

"Now, I'll tell you what, my friend," said Scrooge, "I am not going to stand this sort of thing any longer. And therefore," he continued, leaping from his stool, and giving Bob such a dig in the waistcoat that he staggered back into the Tank again: "and therefore I am about to raise your salary!"

Bob trembled, and got a little nearer to the ruler. He had a momentary idea of knocking Scrooge down with it, holding him, and calling to the people in the court for help and a strait-waistcoat.

"A merry Christmas, Bob!" said Scrooge, with an earnestness that could not be mistaken, as he clapped him on the back. "A merrier Christmas, Bob, my good fellow, than I have given you for many a year! I'll raise your salary, and endeavour to assist your struggling family, and we will discuss your affairs this very afternoon, over a Christmas bowl of smoking bishop, Bob!

Make up the fires, and buy another coal-scuttle before you dot another i, Bob Cratchit!" (84–85)

The combination of mischief and warmth we see in this final episode embodies an ideal of behavior the narrator, from the beginning, has placed before us.

In the words with which he takes his leave of the reader, the narrator's understanding and Scrooge's merge:

Scrooge was better than his word. He did it all, and infinitely more; and to Tiny Tim, who did NOT die, he was a second father. He became as good a friend, as good a master, and as good a man, as the good old city knew, or any other good old city, town, or borough, in the good old world. Some people laughed to see the alteration in him, but he let them laugh, and little heeded them; for he was wise enough to know that nothing ever happened on this globe, for good, at which some people did not have their fill of laughter in the outset; and knowing that such as these would be blind anyway, he thought it quite as well that they should wrinkle up their eyes in grins, as have the malady in less attractive forms. His own heart laughed: and that was quite enough for him.

He had no further intercourse with Spirits, but lived upon the Total Abstinence Principle, ever afterwards; and it was always said of him, that he knew how to keep Christmas well, if any

man alive possessed the knowledge. May that be truly said of
us, and all of us! And so, as Tiny Tim observed, God bless Us,
Every One! (85)

All the astonishing varieties of method and attitude to be found in the
narrative can now be left behind. The narrator is able robustly to affirm
once again, because that is what Scrooge himself can at last innocently
do. The ending is a triumph of the kind of simplicity that has nothing to
do with simplification. It is the simplicity of perception that follows the
resolution of complexities, the simplicity of feeling that follows the
discharge of conflicting emotions.

And here we see what it was that Dickens did for Christmas, why it was
the *Carol* was so influential. He did not revive a defunct or flagging
festival. He made a popular festival mean more. He encouraged the
rituals of Christmas that Thackeray enumerates, certainly: the
hospitality, the lighting of fires, the punch-brewing, the slaughter of
turkeys to be devoured, the roasting and basting of beef (see p. 17
above). But it was the "wonderful outpouring of Christmas good
feeling" that he was intent upon. He saw to it that such outpouring
ceased to be the mark only of "plebeian Christmas days" (see p. 119
above). He made the festival into an occasion for all – for liberating
feeling, for acknowledging its complexity, for reviewing selfhood, and
for revitalizing relationships.

He achieved all this, it should be said, not simply through moral
determination, but by refining his art, both morally and technically. In
attending to what Christmas meant to him, and letting the *Carol* emerge
from this attention, he turned himself into an author who could see more
clearly, convey more sharply, and judge more certainly.

Writing the closing chapters of *Nicholas Nickleby* in 1839, Dickens
described the last hours of Ralph Nickleby. Ralph is a cold-hearted
money-lender, once wealthy, now ruined. Alone in his house, he thinks
with horror of the son he has unwittingly persecuted, the wife who fled
his coldness. That son, whom he had supposed long dead, has in fact
only just died, protected from him by the nephew Ralph hates, Nicholas.
Thoughts such as these precede Ralph's suicide:

If he had known his child to be alive; if no deceit had been ever practised, and he had grown up, beneath his eye; he might have been a careless, indifferent, rough, harsh father – like enough – he felt that; but the thought would come that he might have been otherwise, and that his son might have been a comfort to him and they two happy together. He began to think now, that his supposed death and his wife's flight had had some share in making him the morose, hard man he was. He seemed to remember a time when he was not quite so rough and obdurate; and almost thought that he had first hated Nicholas because he was young and gallant, and perhaps like the stripling who had brought dishonour and loss of fortune on his head.

But, one tender thought, or one of natural regret, in his whirlwind passion and remorse, was as a drop of calm water in a stormy maddened sea. His hatred of Nicholas had been fed upon his own defeat, nourished on his interference with his schemes, fattened upon his old defiance and success. There were reasons for its increase; it had grown and strengthened gradually. Now, it attained a height which was sheer wild lunacy. That his, of all others, should have been the hands to rescue his miserable child; that he should have been his protector and faithful friend; that he should have shown him that love and tenderness which, from the wretched moment of his birth, he had never known; that he should have taught him to hate his own parent and execrate his very name; that he should now know and feel all this, and triumph in the recollection; was gall and madness to the usurer's heart. (*Nicholas Nickleby* 736–37)

The first novel Dickens started after completing the *Carol* was *Dombey and Son* (1846–48). He was working on *Martin Chuzzlewit* (1843–44) at the same time as the *Carol*, and finished it the following year. Two more Christmas books and a travel book, *Pictures from Italy* (1846), followed before Dickens began *Dombey*, but that was the first full-length novel he embarked upon after the *Carol*. It is no accident, I submit, that in *Dombey* we can detect an extraordinary advance in vision and technique. The novel exhibits an intensity of organization to be found in none of its predecessors.

Nowhere is this more apparent than in a passage for which the description of Ralph Nickleby's final despair clearly served as a rehearsal. Towards the end of the novel, Dickens describes the anguish of Mr. Dombey, once a proud, rich businessman, now ruined, deserted by his wife, and contemplating suicide. Alone in his house, he thinks of the daughter he has rejected in favor of the son whom no amount of love could save from an early death. He thinks in particular of his coldness towards her when she came to him for mutual comfort after the boy had died. A paragraph from the chapter in which this earlier episode is described (*Dombey and Son* 250) erupts into the text:

> "Let him remember it in that room, years to come! The rain that falls upon the roof, the wind that mourns outside the door, may have foreknowledge in their melancholy sound. Let him remember it in that room, years to come!"
>
> He did remember it. In the miserable night he thought of it; in the dreary day, the wretched dawn, the ghostly, memory-haunted twilight. He did remember it. In agony, in sorrow, in remorse, in despair! "Papa! papa! Speak to me, dear papa!" He heard the words again, and saw the face. He saw it fall upon the trembling hands, and heard the one prolonged low cry go upward.
>
> He was fallen, never to be raised up any more. For the night of his worldly ruin there was no to-morrow's sun; for the stain of his domestic shame there was no purification; nothing, thank Heaven, could bring his dead child back to life. But that which he might have made so different in all the Past – which might have made the Past itself so different, though this he hardly thought of now – that which was his own work, that which he could so easily have wrought into a blessing, and had set himself so steadily for years to form into a curse: that was the sharp grief of his soul.
>
> Oh! He did remember it! The rain that fell upon the roof, the wind that mourned outside the door that night, had had foreknowledge in their melancholy sound. He knew, now, what he had done. He knew, now, that he had called down that upon his head, which bowed it lower that the heaviest stroke of fortune. He knew, now, what it was to be rejected and deserted; now, when every loving blossom he had withered in his innocent daughter's heart was snowing down in ashes on him. (804)

The contrast between the two passages, and what they show, could scarcely be more striking.

The *Nickleby* passage reveals itself to be an improvisation. Dickens did not conceive Ralph Nickleby as a character who would come to question his own nature. He grew interested in him in the course of writing the novel, and took to suggesting depth and intricacy of character from time to time, by allowing Ralph moments of inconsistency and self-doubt. How *ad hoc* the process was shows, above all, in the incoherence of the last sentence of the first of the paragraphs I quote. Dickens loses his way here. The grammar calls upon us to suppose that it was Nicholas who was "young and gallant." But the young and gallant one is compared to "the stripling who had brought dishonour and loss of fortune on his head" – namely Nicholas. So, groping for coherence, the reader is forced to transfer the youth and gallantry to Ralph. Tense, however, does not help. Ralph was in no way young and gallant when "he had first hated Nicholas."

What we see here is an instinct to explore the development of character through time, to explore the role of choice, memory, and self-doubt in shaping identity, all baffled by lack of controlling vision, lack of planning, lack of technique. The picture the first paragraph gives us of Ralph's state of mind is fuzzy at best. It is almost possible to detect the relief when, in the second paragraph, Dickens reverts to a simpler Ralph, the snarling, implacable, unregenerate, villain of melodrama. In 1839, Dickens had reached out gingerly towards the theme of redemption, but had quickly abandoned his attempt. He had not been equipped for it.

The passage from *Dombey*, in contrast, is clearly part of an intensely ordered book. References to earlier episodes, earlier passages of text, do not merely demonstrate this: they give these paragraphs the lyrical, incantatory quality that makes them as moving as they are, and that mimics the treadmill of memory yielded by remorse, upon which moments of shameful error are repeatedly revisited. Mr. Dombey was designed as a fallible creature living in time, with hope for the future and memories of the past, who would commit errors, be reminded of them, brood upon them in anguish, and make himself eligible for the redemption finally granted him.

It was from telling the story of Ebenezer Scrooge, that Dickens learned how to construct such a character and organize every detail of a book around it. *A Christmas Carol* was not only a landmark in the history of the English ritual year. It was a landmark, too, in Dickens's career.

6

CHRISTMAS BOOKS AND STORIES,

1844 TO 1854

No one can be sure of writing a masterpiece on the strength of intentions, not even Dickens. So, early in 1844 Dickens must have been wondering whether he could repeat the triumph of *A Christmas Carol*.

He was drawn to Christmas – both as a subject, and as an occasion for publishing appropriate texts. Now, by letting himself be drawn, he had achieved unprecedented success – popular and critical if not financial. In writing the *Carol*, moreover, he had found a new direction in which to take his art, and a vehicle for conveying some of his deepest convictions. Within a couple of years he would be speaking of a "*Carol* philosophy," no less (Forster, bk. 5, ch. 1).

Despite the disappointment of his initial hopes, his commercial instincts were aroused. He had stimulated a new demand for Christmas reading, and enlarged the market for it. The *Carol* invited imitation, moreover. It created an appetite for short pieces of fiction about Christmas, featuring mysterious intervention in human affairs, apparently supernatural. Other writers would attempt to satisfy this appetite.[1] Why should he desist? Could he not achieve more success in the future with a genre he had invented – financial success, as well as popular and critical?[2] Soon he would be asked for another Christmas book. It was almost as if he was being invited to become an unofficial spokesman for Christmas. The problem was the *Carol* itself. Could he match it without repeating himself?

Dickens sensed the difficulty. He decided to meet the demand, but was wary about following a formula too closely. After 1843, every year for the next twenty-four – with two exceptions – he made it his business to supply readers with special texts to be read at Christmas time. He strove for variety, and did his best to deter comparisons too narrow or exact. Most of the texts he wrote for Christmas are, in fact, not about Christmas as such. This book, I should make clear, is concerned only with the texts about Christmas. Whatever their merit, the others, for my purposes, serve only to confirm the shift in sensibility that made Christmas seem an especially suitable occasion for narrative.

During the 1840s Dickens wrote four more Christmas books, as they came to be known – compact pieces of fiction published between their own covers: *The Chimes* (1844), *The Cricket on the Hearth* (1845), *The Battle of Life* (1846), and *The Haunted Man* (1848). Two of these call for scrutiny in this chapter. The interval of 1847, and the appearance of no more such books after 1848, are signs of the struggle it was for Dickens, towards the end of the decade, to allot time to their writing, competing for it as they did with *Dombey and Son* (1846–48) and *David Copperfield* (1849–50).

However, Dickens did not at this stage abandon his mission to supply the public with Christmas reading. In 1850, he launched *Household Words*, the first of the two weekly periodicals he was to edit until the end of his life. *All the Year Round* succeeded it in 1859. Editing duties made even greater demands on his time but, every year until 1867, he made sure the magazines offered buyers special reading for the Christmas season. It was only in 1868 that he desisted.

The weekly number of *Household Words* which appeared at Christmas in 1850 comprises a collection of pieces appropriate to the season, by several different writers, one of them Dickens himself. In succeeding years, he produced special additional Christmas numbers devoted to such material for *Household Words*, and later for *All the Year Round*. They always included at least one contribution exclusively his own. These have been collected, usually under the title *Christmas Stories*.[3] His contributions to the Christmas numbers of *Household Words* for 1850, 1851, and 1854 address the theme of Christmas itself. After that, none do, neither in *Household Words* nor in *All the Year Round*.

It was his engagement with this theme which yielded Dickens's finest achievements in texts he wrote specifically for Christmas reading, just as it was his engagement with this theme which advanced the development of his craft. It encouraged him to dwell upon memory, and the depths of personality this opened up for exploration. It enabled him to dramatize the fullness of life he detected in the observation of Christmas customs, the closeness of joy and sorrow the festival highlights, the struggle between sympathy and indifference it calls forth.

To address the theme did not guarantee Dickens success. To do so, as the years passed, was increasingly to risk repetition, and the slackness that is often its result. But his devotion to the theme, nevertheless, yielded some astonishing work.

His Christmas book for 1844 was *The Chimes*. In important respects it is plainly an imitation of the *Carol*, but Christmas as such is not featured in it, nor is the word *Christmas* uttered. The book focuses upon the New Year instead. It is a text for Christmas, we might be tempted to say, rather than about it. Since the conversion of the English to Christianity, however, the passing of the old year, the coming of the new, had been associated with the winter solstice and with Christmas.[4] Making the New Year his focus was a way for Dickens to feature the Christmas season, broadly understood, without repeating himself. It was a way, too, of once again confronting the turning point of the year and the reflection it invites. *The Chimes* is a kind of supplement to the *Carol*. It shows what his achievement in the *Carol* could inspire Dickens to.

It also shows how hard it was for him to emulate it. *The Chimes* scarcely rivals the *Carol*. The shift of focus was a handicap. The New Year is less freighted with doctrine and tradition than the festival of Christmas, narrowly defined. "Auld Lang Syne" notwithstanding, for most English people, there is less for memory to seize upon in the New Year festivities, and thus less for a writer like Dickens to exploit.

Dickens sensed the handicap, and strove to compensate for it. When we study the genesis of the book, it is difficult not to notice a process of cranking-up. He cranked up his own expectations and those of his friends, in an effort to persuade everyone, not least himself, that he was matching the *Carol*. But he was not. One outcome alone seemed to justify his hopes – *The Chimes* was the commercial success Dickens longed for. The first edition netted him £1,065/8/2 (Patten 161). But it did not win the acclaim the *Carol* had won, nor has it ever done so since, nor does it deserve to.

Because they distributed it, Chapman and Hall are named on the title page of the first edition of *The Chimes*, but, after his disappointment with the *Carol*, Dickens had made the decision to change publishers. It was Bradbury and Evans who in fact produced the book for him. In the agreement he signed with them in May 1844, Dickens promised a successor to the *Carol*. "The New Carol" was what he called it (Forster bk. 4, ch. 2; *Letters* 4: 121). Like its predecessor, the book was published just before Christmas – on 16 December – to exploit the Christmas market, and precedents set by the *Carol* were followed in its production. It was another luxurious little book, with a gilded red cover, and an engraved half-title designed by Daniel Maclise, also responsible for the splendidly elaborate frontispiece. The wood engravings in the text were designed by Richard Doyle, John Leech, and Clarkson Stanfield. The excessive production costs of the *Carol*, however, did prompt some economies. Top artists were used for the book but there were no hand-colored etchings, nor was there any color printing.

If we are to believe his letters, Dickens became as excited during the composition of *The Chimes* as he had been when writing the *Carol*. Few of his disclosures about the *Carol* are as unrestrained, however, and most of those that are were retrospective. Even Forster's account of the emotions Dickens felt when writing *The Chimes* it seems to have been pieced together largely from letters sent after the book was completed (Forster bk. 4, ch. 1).

From early 1843 Dickens had clearly hoped to achieve something outstanding with what eventually materialized as the *Carol*, but when he was actually working on it he became reticent. Few of his letters written during the autumn of the year convey more than the one to Macvey Napier, declaring he had "plunged headlong into a little scheme" (*Letters* 3: 585). A letter written early in November speaks soberly of his need to consult Forster about "a nice point in the tale" (3: 595). Only a note to Mitton, dated 25 November, is a little more revealing. In it Dickens speaks of having been "in the full passion of a roaring Christmas scene" (3: 602).

It was not until publication day that he felt ready to disclose the full range of his feelings about the book – to tell Charles Mackay, for instance, how affected he had been when writing it (see p. 176 above). It was not until two weeks later, when the *Carol* had become a publishing sensation, that he wrote to Cornelius Felton, telling him how he had "wept, and laughed, and wept again, and excited himself in a most extraordinary manner" (4: 2).

By contrast, Dickens seemed eager to declare his emotional investment in *The Chimes* from the earliest possible stage, and to encourage his friends to invest as well. He wrote it during October and early November 1844, while he was living with his family in Genoa (see p. 169 above). He kept Forster posted on progress, and sought his advice from time to time in a series of letters. Forster would have passed on news of the book to other friends. Before he began writing, Dickens complained about the difficulty of getting started (4: 199), but by mid-October he had his "steam very much up" (4: 200), and he was soon ready to indicate the depth of his involvement:

> I am in regular, ferocious excitement with the *Chimes*; get up at seven; have a cold bath before breakfast; and blaze away, wrathful and red-hot, until three o'clock or so: when I usually knock off (unless it rains) for the day.... I am fierce to finish in a spirit bearing some affinity to those of truth and mercy, and to shame the cruel and the canting. I have not forgotten my catechism. "Yes verily, and with God's help, so I will!" (4: 201)

This is confession with a vengeance. Dickens was allowing himself to suppose that, in writing *The Chimes*, he was reaffirming a commitment to the promises his Godparents had made on his behalf, that he would renounce evil, accept the Anglican confession, and keep God's commandments.

When he finished the book at the beginning of the following month, he announced the fact to Forster with a dramatic flourish:

> Third of November, 1844. Half-past two, afternoon. Thank God! I have finished the *Chimes*. This moment. I take up my pen again to-day, to say only that much; and to add that I have had what women call "a real good cry!" (4: 210)

No one could accuse him of keeping things back.

But perhaps the clearest manifestation of this cranking-up was to be observed during the brief visit Dickens made to London, after finishing *The Chimes*. His declared purpose was to oversee publication of the book (4: 208). He was in London between 30 November and 8 December. In order to accomplish the task he had set himself, and to be back with his family in Genoa by Christmas, against Forster's advice he committed himself to weeks of winter travel across Europe – by coach, by ship, and, for crossing the Alps, by sledge (4: 213–32, 238–42).

Whatever the declared purpose, there can be little doubt that his chief satisfaction during the trip was derived from the experience of reading *The Chimes* aloud to friends and like-thinkers. On 1 December he read it to the actor, W. C. Macready. "If you had seen Macready last night," he wrote the following day to his wife, " – undisguisedly sobbing, and crying on the sofa, as I read – you would have felt (as I did) what a thing it is to have Power" (4: 235). That evening he read the book to a group assembled by Forster in his chambers – Maclise, Stanfield, Thomas Carlyle, playwright Douglas Jerrold, journalists Laman Blanchard and W. J. Fox, literary scholars Alexander Dyce and William Harness. Dickens's brother Fred was there, too, and of course Forster himself. Maclise described the occasion in a letter to Catherine Dickens:

> ... there was not a dry eye in the house .... We should borrow the high language of the minor theatre and even then not do the effect justice – shrieks of laughter – there were indeed – and floods of tears as a relief to them – I do not think there ever was such a triumphant hour for Charles .... (4: 235n)

A sketch he drew of the scene, which Maclise also sent to Catherine, is even more telling. It is very deliberately posed, and each figure is labelled. Only Fred Dickens faces away from the viewer. Every other member of the audience – everyone of note, that is to say – betrays emotion, either upon his face or in the agitated hands that hide it. Dickens's own face is grave with sorrow, and mysterious rays are represented, emanating from his head, to clinch the impression of emotive power. With eager cooperation from Macready, Forster, Maclise, and others, Dickens was characterizing *The Chimes* in terms of the intense emotion which inspired it, the intense emotion which it could in turn inspire. "I am in great hopes," he told Lady Blessington, "that I shall make you cry, bitterly, with my little Book" (4: 227).

In using the term "cranking-up," I am not suggesting Dickens was painstakingly elevating something worthless. It was more usual for him to reveal the ardors and tribulations of composition to his friends than to conceal them. Elaborate self-dramatization was normally the means by which the revelation was made. Self-dramatization, indeed, seems to have been continuous with the process of literary composition for him. In reading *The Chimes* to friends, moreover, he was anticipating the public readings from his works that were to play such an important part in his later career. Intense emotion was something he frequently experienced while writing, something he expected to pass on both to readers and, later, to audiences at his readings. Think only of the death of Little Nell: of Dickens writing to Harness, "all next week I shall be laid up with a broken heart, for I must occupy myself in finishing the 'Curiosity Shop'" (2: 178); or of the letters he received from readers begging him to spare Nell (2: 153).

The transmission of emotion had always been an important feature of Dickens's art, and always would be, but it was only one feature. In dwelling upon it so intently as he prepared *The Chimes* for his readers Dickens betrayed what were to be the book's limitations. It would jerk many a tear. It would arouse many a conscience. But it would lack the *Carol*'s narrative vitality, its amplitude of reference, its psychological and moral intelligence. Depth would be sacrificed to effect. Dickens's greatest efforts would be devoted to wringing readers' hearts. *The Chimes* was never to be a tale of redemption, like the *Carol*, a fiction locating itself at the very heart of the western understanding of the human condition.

The book is subtitled *A Goblin Story of Some Bells that Rang an Old Year Out and a New Year In*. Like the *Carol*, it features a central character who is changed by supernatural intervention. Toby Veck, nicknamed "Trotty" after his gait, is a ticket porter, old and poor, whose natural kindness of heart is tainted. Newspapers and figures in authority persuade him the poor are born bad, and have no right to exist. But on New Year's Eve, spirits of the bells, in the tower of the church by which he awaits commissions, convince him otherwise. They show him grim visions of what the future might hold for those he loves. They teach him that "we must trust and hope, and neither doubt ourselves, nor the

Good in one another" (*Christmas Books* 172). Trotty eventually awakes from his visions on New Year's Day, to find hope confirmed by a joyful celebration of the marriage of his beloved daughter, Meg.

Even from this brief summary, the debt to the *Carol* is unmistakable, but, compared to the *Carol*, *The Chimes* is uncomplicated, even thin. This can be attributed in part to Dickens's abandonment of so much that Christmas carries with it. To begin with, *The Chimes* lacks the formal vitality conferred on the *Carol* by the powerful implications of its structural metaphor. The story of Scrooge repeatedly echoes motifs we find in Christmas carols, and these echoes move the reader. No precise sentiment such as we find in carols is evoked by the chiming of church bells at the New Year. The division of the *Carol* into "staves" is a reminder of what it is carols demand. The division of *The Chimes* into "quarters" is merely the application of appropriate decoration.

The Chimes is of course a tale of the supernatural, fitting for the Christmas season. Dickens called it a "goblin story," and goblin stories were among the folk tales popular at Christmas, enumerated by *Round about our Coal Fire* (see p. 105 above). But this time Dickens exploits his supernatural subject matter less subtly. The *Carol* is not just a Christmas ghost story. It is a mesmeric enactment of the telling of such a story. The doubt aroused by a ghost story, the imputation of artifice, is not just allayed: it is profitably used, thanks to the drama of its telling, thanks to what we are made to feel about the teller. The attempt to achieve something of the same kind in *The Chimes* is, by contrast, perfunctory. Dickens devoted little attention to the formal framing of his new tale.

The book opens, to be sure, in a way almost too reminiscent of the *Carol*. We are greeted by a narrator freely using first-person-singular pronouns, postulating an intimate relationship between the reader and himself.   But his open affirmation of this relationship reads uncomfortably like a memorandum – to Dickens himself of what he was seeking to recreate, to readers of the conditions under which they were invited to accept the story:

> There are not many people – and as it is desirable that a
> story-teller and a story-reader should establish a mutual
> understanding as soon as possible, I beg it to be noticed that I
> confine this observation neither to young people nor to little

people, but extend it to all conditions of people, little and big, young and old: yet growing up, or already growing down again – there are not, I say, many people who would care to sleep in a church. I don't mean at sermon-time in warm weather (when the thing has actually been done, once or twice), but in the night, and alone. A great multitude of persons will be violently astonished, I know, by this position, in the broad bold Day. But it applies to Night. It must be argued by night. And I will undertake to maintain it successfully on any gusty winter's night appointed for the purpose, with any one opponent chosen from the rest, who will meet me singly in an old churchyard, before an old church door; and will previously empower me to lock him in, if needful to his satisfaction, until morning. (93–94)

The memorandum, in fact, is not heeded for long. For a few pages this projection of a narrator busily mediating between story and reader is sustained. The fiction of intimacy is kept up. "They were old Chimes," the narrator tells the reader – "trust me." The bantering tone is kept up:

They had had their Godfathers and Godmothers, these Bells (for my own part, by the way, I would rather incur the responsibility of being Godfather to a Bell than a Boy): and had their silver mugs no doubt, besides. But Time had mowed down their sponsors, and Henry the Eighth had melted down their mugs: and they now hung, nameless and mugless, in the church tower.

The pretense of negotiation is kept up, between doubts readers might have and what the narrator wants them to believe. "Whatever Toby Veck said," he insists, "I say. And I take my stand by Toby Veck . . . "(95).

This dramatization of the narrative process itself is soon abandoned, though. More conventional third-person methods are allowed to prevail. Commentary continues to be intrusive:

The Alderman laughed, and winked; for he was a merry fellow, Alderman Cute. Oh, and a sly fellow too! A knowing fellow. Up to everything. Not to be imposed upon. Deep in the people's hearts! He knew them, Cute did. I believe you! (108)

This is resourceful and funny, but the narrator is scarcely revealing himself here. He is laying claim only to authority. There is no trace of the bafflement, questioning, doubt, and sheer mischief-making, that give such vitality to the *Carol*. There are no moments of self-exposure such as we find in the *Carol*: the narrator's groping for praise adequate to Mrs. Fezziwig (35), or his becoming sentimental about the beautiful daughter of Scrooge's erstwhile fiancée (39). Not until the peroration does the narrator of *The Chimes* once again place himself before us. Readers are invited to wonder whether Trotty's visions had been more than a dream. "Or are his joys and sorrows, and the actors in them, but a dream; himself a dream; the teller of this tale a dreamer, waking but now?" (176). This is just a reminder of the framing device, though. It comes after too long an interval. Readers have not been kept constantly aware of a narrator mediating between the wonderful and their disinclination to believe in it. The book is the poorer for it.

What in the end such differences compel us to acknowledge is that Dickens modelled *The Chimes* upon the *Carol* too closely for it to have sufficient independent vitality, but not closely enough for it replicate the *Carol*'s most affecting features. His switch of attention from Christmas to the New Year denied him opportunities. He applied lessons learned from the *Carol* about calling up emotion, but he cut the story off from the roots of myth, tradition, and religious doctrine that give such emotional depths to the *Carol*. The complex relationship we find in the *Carol*, between the telling of the story, and the kind of story it is, is an acknowledgement of those greater depths. The narrator, as it were, stands back and marvels. The narrator of *The Chimes* is too busy working up emotion. There is less for him to stand back from and marvel at.

The relative lack of depth becomes evident not least when we contrast the supernatural beings in the two books. The spirits of the bells, in *The Chimes*, are little more than narrative devices, scarcely memorable. Scrooge's ghostly visitors are unforgettable, because they are so complex and evoke so much. All of them – even Marley's ghost – are both reproachful and caring, and we warm to them because of it. They accuse Scrooge, but worry about him too. That is why they seek to change him. Take one example. To begin with, the Ghost of Christmas Yet to Come seems inexorable – silent, cowled, with only an outstretched hand visible, pointing menacingly onward. A powerful moment occurs, though, when Scrooge understands the implications of his own name upon the neglected tombstone. "Assure me," he implores, "that I yet may change these shadows you have shown me, by an altered life." A single short sentence transforms and enriches our understanding both of the ghost, and of what it is that is happening to Scrooge:

> The kind hand trembled. (78)

The *Carol*, in fact, is full of such moments. They plunge us deep into religious and folk traditions. They evoke that superabundance of the miraculous at Christmas time, of which I have spoken. They declare the intervention of a benign providence. Question the cosmology as much as you like, such moments are fraught with accumulated meaning and feeling.

Dickens drew on no such resources in constructing the spirits of the bells. They are mysterious, busy, scolding, prim, but never deeply suggestive. The text tells us Trotty was in awe of them, but they scarcely awe us.

Dickens strove to give them a substantial identity, it should be said. Even before his visions, Trotty is convinced the bells speak to him. "Toby Veck, Toby Veck, keep a good heart Toby!" he hears them say (104). A newspaper report about a desperate young woman who has killed both herself and her child confirms his loss of confidence in the poor:

> "Unnatural and cruel!" Toby cried. "Unnatural and cruel!
> None but people who were bad at heart: born bad: who had no
> business on the earth: could do such deeds. It's too true, all I've
> heard to-day; too just, too full of proof. We're Bad!" (133)

This despair draws him to the belfry, where he sees a vision of goblins intervening in human affairs:

> He saw them *in* the houses, busy at the sleepers' beds. He saw
> them soothing people in their dreams; he saw them beating them
> with knotted whips; he saw them yelling in their ears; he saw

them playing softest music on their pillows; he saw them
cheering some with the songs of birds and the perfume of
flowers; he saw them flashing awful faces on the troubled rest of
others, from enchanted mirrors which they carried in their hands.
(138–39)

But the arbitrary combination of malice and sympathy is very similar to
that displayed by the goblins in chapter 29 of *Pickwick Papers* –
conventional rather than suggestive. The goblins are what they appear
to be. There is no encouragement to look in them for anything deeper.

Trotty is reproached by the mysteriously animated bells. "The voice
of Time," the Goblin of the Great Bell tells him,

"cries to man, Advance! Time is for his advancement and
improvement; for his greater worth, his greater happiness, his
better life; his progress onward to that goal within its knowledge
and its view, and set there, in the period when Time and He
began. Ages of darkness, wickedness, and violence, have come
and gone: millions uncountable, have suffered, lived, and died:
to point the way before him. Who seeks to turn him back, or
stay him on his course, arrests a mighty engine which will strike
the meddler dead; and be the fiercer and the wilder, ever, for its
momentary check!" (141)

The bell is articulating an early Victorian conception of progress. It is a
notion inevitably thinner than the dense and ancient myths evoked in the
Carol, but to say as much is only to say Dickens was attempting less.
"Spirits, merciful and good," is what Trotty eventually calls the bells,
but they do not embody mercy and goodness as the ghosts of the *Carol*
do. Only in the child, the "Spirit of the Chimes," "innocent and radiant,"
are there hints of a similar warmth (143, 157).

The reduced impact of the spirits in *The Chimes* is commensurate
with the lower order of moral crisis they have to solve. Trotty's
conviction that the poor are bad, and have no right to exist, is more
eccentric than transgressive. It is like Mr. Pickwick's insistence upon
his learning and eminence, or Mark Tapley's conviction, in *Martin
Chuzzlewit*, that it is only creditable to be "jolly" in circumstances that
discourage it. It is less hamartia, than the stuff of comedy. No critical

moral choice yields it.   It is just arbitrary.   No depth of character underpins it.

In forsaking the powerful associations of Christmas as such, Dickens also forsook the perception of memory that came to him with thoughts of the festival, and his sense of character as something layered and intricate. Trotty is very simple. There is no suggestion of anything in his past to make him think as he does. We never doubt his goodness, moreover. We never feel he has sacrificed the fullness of life Scrooge has to recover. We just await the clearing of his moral vision. His error scarcely compares with Scrooge's. It does not consign him to moral ruin. He does not have to be redeemed, only corrected.

His conversion, in consequence, affords us mild pleasure, not joy at catastrophe averted. We find ourselves glad he has stopped being silly. We rejoice at the thought that his loved ones are escaping the fates foreseen for them, to be sure, but it is hard to believe the change in Trotty is instrumental in this. In his vision, Meg almost replicates the crime of the young woman who killed herself and her child, but we wonder how much of a difference might be made by either optimism or pessimism on Trotty's part (170–72). It is just as hard to see what difference they might make to the demoralization of Will Fern (167–69), or the degradation of his niece Lillian (154–57).

Only the fate of Richard, Meg's fiancé, seems to hinge on a choice between optimism and pessimism. Alderman Cute advises him against marriage:

> " . . . Why, she'll be an old woman before you're a middle-aged man!   And a pretty figure you'll cut then, with a draggle-tailed wife and a crowd of squalling children crying after you wherever you go!" (114)

In Trotty's vision, Richard follows the advice, condemning Meg to a life of lonely penury, himself to self-indulgence and degeneracy. When at last they do marry, it is too late to arrest his decline (162–65). But the pessimism that yields this fate is Richard's, not Trotty's.

The conversion that most interested Dickens, in fact, was plainly not Trotty Veck's. It was the conversion of prosperous contemporaries, attracted to the comfortable supposition that the poor deserve their misery. The emotion generated by the *Carol* is proportionate to the story told. *The Chimes* is more of an excuse for generating emotion proportionate to the social problem addressed. That, however, is precisely what makes it a supplement to the *Carol* worth reading. It is an exercise in *saeva indignatio*. It is another Christmas denunciation of the poverty allowed to persist during the 1840s, but more explicit. It is, in fact, a more eloquent defence of the humanity of the very poor. And it is, by the by, an answer to those who doubt Dickens's ability to see beyond middle-class horizons.

There is a satirical directness in *The Chimes*, more pronounced than we find in the *Carol*. Alderman Cute is a caricature of Sir Peter Laurie (1778–1861), the son of a Scottish farmer, who made a fortune as a contractor for the Indian Army and, in retirement, served as a magistrate.[5] Proud of the understanding he claimed from his humble origins, Laurie was nevertheless famously insensitive to those who appeared before the bench. Dickens makes Cute unsympathetic to poverty *tout court*. He lectures Trotty:

> " . . . there's a great deal of nonsense talked about Want – 'hard up,' you know: that's the phrase isn't it? ha! ha! ha! – and I intend to Put It Down. There's a certain amount of cant in vogue about Starvation, and I mean to Put It Down. That's all! Lord bless you," said the Alderman, turning to his friends again, "you may Put Down anything among this sort of people, if you only know the way to set about it." (111)

In the caustic observations of Mr. Filer, the perverse application of the principles of political economy is lampooned (see *Letters* 4: 209). His denunciation of Trotty's dinner of tripe, on the grounds of loss of weight during boiling, is if anything too preposterous (*Christmas Books* 108). With his laments for "the good old times, the grand old times, the great old times," Sir Joseph Bowley embodies self-indulgent Romanticism – the substitution of nostalgia for practical action against poverty (110, 119–25, 145–52). He is a less sharply drawn figure than the follower of Disraeli's "Young England" movement Forster persuaded Dickens to cut from his manuscript.[6]

The book urges compassion, among other ways, by exposing its contrary. As he told Forster, Dickens was eager "to shame the cruel and the canting." Alderman Cute, Mr. Filer, and Sir Joseph all treat Trotty and those he loves, not as fellow beings capable of suffering, but as specimens to substantiate doctrines they self-indulgently promote. The alderman counsels Meg, too, against marriage:

> "Perhaps your husband will die young (most likely) and leave you with a baby. Then you'll be turned out of doors, and wander up and down the streets. Now, don't wander near me, my dear, for I am resolved to Put all wandering mothers Down. All young mothers, of all sorts and kinds, it's my determination to Put Down. Don't think to plead illness as an excuse with me; or babies as an excuse with me; for all sick persons and young children (I hope you know the church-service, but I'm afraid not) I am determined to Put Down. And if you attempt, desperately, and ungratefully, and impiously, and fraudulently attempt, to drown yourself, or hang yourself, I'll have no pity on you, for I have made up my mind to Put all suicide Down! (113)

Dickens applied his powers to transmit emotion in *The Chimes*, in order to drive home the moral. Readers are made to acknowledge and to feel Trotty's humanity by liberal use of what might be called the comedy of affection, that cluster of techniques Dickens had been cultivating over the years, to render the narration of homely matters at once movingly innocent and funny. In this respect, if in few others, *The Chimes* at least equals what Dickens had achieved before. The game Meg and Trotty play, when she challenges him to identify his dinner by smell alone, compares favourably with Tom and Ruth Pinch's preparation of a meat pudding in *Martin Chuzzlewit* (565–83). It is less mawkish, more purely comic, yet just as suffused with respect and affection for the characters:

> "Ah! It's very nice," said Toby. "It an't – I suppose it an't Polonies?"
> "No, no, no!" cried Meg, delighted. "Nothing like Polonies!"
> "No," said Toby, after another sniff. "It's – it's mellower than Polonies. It's very nice. It improves every moment. It's too decided for Trotters. An't, it?'
> Meg was in an ecstasy. He could *not* have gone wider of the mark than Trotters – except Polonies.
> "Liver?" said Toby, communing with himself. "No. There's

> a mildness about it that don't answer to liver. Pettitoes? No. It an't faint enough for pettitoes. It wants the stringiness of Cock's heads. And I know it an't sausages. I'll tell you what it is. It's chitterlings!'
>
> "No, it an't!" cried Meg, in a burst of delight. "No, it an't!"
>
> "Why, what am I a thinking of!" said Toby, suddenly recovering a position as near the perpendicular as it was possible for him to assume. "I shall forget my own name next. It's tripe!" (*Christmas Books* 102–03)

You have only to read Mayhew to discover that the early Victorian poor were by no means always inarticulate. Trotty, moreover, is both literate and thoughtful. But the comedy of this passage is essentially the comedy of pastoral. At one level it works as the representation of appealing eccentricity. But we also see a simple, humble man being made to speak with the discrimination brought by his nominal betters to nominally greater matters. Judgment about delicacies of the poor is expressed in language mimicking the epicure's. The effect is one often achieved by pastoral. The ticket porter and his tastes, we are made to feel, are one with the rich man and his. False distinctions fade. Trotty – and Meg too – are humanized, whatever the reader's preconceptions. Nor does the complexity of this prevent our finding the passage funny. "There's a mildness about it that don't answer to liver. Pettitoes? No. It an't faint enough for pettitoes" – these are observations which distill the comedy of language taken to its margins, where only the figurative can signify, however quaintly.

Dickens's greatest efforts, however, were reserved not for comedy but for pathos. His chief aim was to make readers – like Lady Blessington – "cry, bitterly, with my little Book." Few but the hard-bitten are likely to dispute his success. The climax of the book is Meg's attempt, in Trotty's vision, to end her own life and the life of Lilian's baby, left to her by the dead girl. Watched by Trotty and the spirits of the bells, worn down by destitution, the death of Richard, and the loss of her home, Meg makes off through the night streets:

> "Now, turn her back!" exclaimed the old man, tearing his white hair. "My child! Meg! Turn her back! Great Father, turn her back!"

In her own scanty shawl, she wrapped the baby warm. With her fevered hands, she smoothed its limbs, composed its face, arranged its mean attire. In her wasted arms she folded it, as though she never would resign it more. And with her dry lips, kissed it in a final pang, and last long agony of Love.

Putting its tiny hand up to her neck, and holding it there, within her dress: next to her distracted heart: she set its sleeping face against her: closely, steadily, against her: and sped onward to the river.

To the rolling River, swift and dim, where Winter Night sat brooding like the last dark thoughts of many who had sought a refuge there before her. Where scattered lights upon the banks gleamed sullen, red, and dull, as torches that were burning there, to show the way to Death. Where no abode of living people casts its shadow, on the deep, impenetrable, melancholy shade.

To the River! To that portal of Eternity, her desperate footsteps tended with the swiftness of its rapid waters running to the sea. He tried to touch her as she passed him, going down to its dark level; but the wild distempered form, the fierce and terrible love, the desperation that had left all human check or hold behind, swept by him like the wind.

He followed her. She paused a moment on the brink, before the dreadful plunge. He fell down on his knees, and in a shriek addressed the figures in the Bells now hovering above them.

"I have learnt it!" cried the old man. "From the creature dearest to my heart! Oh, save her, save her!"

He could wind his fingers in her dress; could hold it! As the words escaped his lips, he felt his sense of touch return, and knew that he had detained her.

The figures looked down steadfastly upon him.

"I have learnt it!" cried the old man. "Oh, have mercy on me in this hour, if, in my love for her, so young and good, I slandered Nature in the breasts of mothers rendered desperate! Pity my presumption, wickedness, and ignorance, and save her!" (171–72)

It is a fine melodramatic set piece. Chiefly through comic devices, Dickens has won readers' affection for Meg and her father, and given us an insight into the love between them. Now, exploiting the contrivance of Trotty's vision, playing upon contrasting sentiments, drawing upon imagery of which he had a special command, and on his mastery of narrative momentum, Dickens builds up to an emotional crescendo.

Yet how inferior the episode is to the oblique disclosure of Tiny Tim's death in Stave Four of *A Christmas Carol*!   There almost everything is achieved by indirectness and restraint (see pp. 194–97 above).   Here feeling is cranked up.   Dickens's attitude towards *The Chimes* while he was writing it shows in the text itself.   Bob Cratchit's breakdown is momentary, soon overcome, and the more affecting for it. Trotty, in contrast, is impassioned to begin with, and becomes ever more so.   In the *Carol* episode, the narrator shares Scrooge's bewilderment and the reader's.   He endorses the Cratchit family's efforts to maintain their composure.   The effect is astonishingly powerful.   Here the narrator is entirely in control, insists on the response he wants, and openly seeks to intensify the reader's distress.   He succeeds in the attempt, but the result cannot compare with what is achieved through the hesitancy, understatement, and reticence dramatized in the *Carol*.

The Chimes satisfied Dickens's longing for a commercial success with a Christmas book.   And it struck a blow, more precisely aimed than the *Carol*'s, on behalf of those who were suffering most during the "hungry forties."   It ends with the narrator's New Year wishes to readers: "So may each Year be happier than the last, and not the meanest of our brethren or sisterhood debarred their rightful share, in what our Great Creator formed them to enjoy" (177).   Dickens's determination to promote this end, however, and his anxiety not to repeat himself, diminished the resources upon which he could draw, and restricted his inventiveness.   *The Chimes* replicates the form of *A Christmas Carol* but not its substance.   There is no complex central figure to be redeemed, no complex narrator showing, in his very complexity, the route to redemption.   *The Chimes* is a powerful little book, but not a great book like its predecessor.

The Cricket on the Hearth and *The Battle of Life* need scarcely detain us.   They are both books for Christmas rather than about it.   Neither alludes to the festival, or even suggests it obliquely.   Neither features any kind of supernatural apparatus.

Both contain memorable material, it should be said.   Many of

Dickens's talents are on display in them. The stories are cunningly related. The chirping cricket and the ancient battlefield are ingenious unifying images. Without Tilly Slowboy's baby-talk (*Christmas Books* 199), or Mr. Snitchey's encomium upon the legal entanglements of landed property (298–99), English literature would be the poorer. The comedy alone makes the books worth reading.

But even more than in *The Chimes*, in these books Dickens exploits his talent for arousing emotion at the expense of more substantial objectives. More than anything else, they are exercises in melodrama. Melodrama is less ill thought of than it once was, and its influence here is not all bad, but Dickens's dependence upon its templates limited what he could achieve in these texts.

Both are about truth and illusion, but the illusion is of infamy, and the truth is of virtue uncontaminated.   This inversion, and the heartwarming sentiments it gives rise to, are both typical of melodrama. John Peerybingle, in *The Cricket on the Hearth*, is led to doubt the fidelity of his young wife, but discovers she has been conspiring with young Edward Plummer only in order to secure him the hand of a sweetheart of old he is in danger of losing. In *The Battle of Life*, the father and friends of Marion Jeddler suppose she has cruelly abandoned her fiancé, Alfred Heathfield, and fear she has eloped with a lover. It transpires that she has fled innocently, so that Alfred might come to love and marry her sister Grace, whose feelings for him are deep but undisclosed.

There are other instances of innocent deception. Caleb Plummer, in *The Cricket on the Hearth*, persuades his beloved blind daughter that they live, not in a hovel, but "in an enchanted home of Caleb's furnishing, where scarcity and shabbiness were not, and trouble never entered" (215).   He persuades her that their grasping employer, Tackleton, is an eccentric benefactor. Michael Warden, in *The Battle of Life*, lets it be supposed he is the lover Marion has eloped with, but is discovered to have been a guiltless party to her self-sacrifice, and to have preserved her innocence.

Perplexities such as these can certainly hold the attention of readers, but do not confront them with the problems of value and identity that are the stuff of great fiction. Recognition of misjudgment is normally the pivot of such fiction. Recognition of innocent misunderstanding or benign trickery, however, rarely yields the personal revaluation that characterizes it. Perplexities such as these, in fact, tend to be little more than ways of complicating and prolonging a tale.

When Dickens is the teller, that is not entirely a bad thing. All the same, the mastery of melodramatic contrivance, on display in these books, seems to have been an easy option for him. It enabled him to entertain his readers at Christmas time with a minimum expenditure of effort, by writing to well-established and widely understood rules. It spared him engagement with the difficult and emotionally demanding theme of Christmas itself.

Dickens chose no such easy option for the last of his Christmas books. From the start, he conceived it as a text about Christmas – another Christmas ghost story, no less. But it is a different kind of ghost story, and a venture for Dickens into a different kind of fiction. Moral issues such as we find in the *Carol* and *The Chimes* are still featured – are still crucial indeed – but there is a shift in emphasis. *The Haunted Man* is concerned with order and disorder of the mind.

The mystery of personality had been a focus of Dickens's attention in the *Carol* – the mystery of Scrooge's corruption and redemption. But the dynamic of the *Carol* is Scrooge's convergence with the narrator, who exemplifies mental and moral balance. From the beginning, readers can spot qualities in Scrooge – his instinct for mischief and his wit – which promise such convergence. *The Haunted Man*, in contrast, requires readers to dwell much less upon the promise of redemption than upon the threat of ruin. They are invited to share an experience of morbid fixation.

Few modern readers are likely to resist. Interest in abnormal psychology was a defining characteristic of the twentieth-century sensibility, and seems not to be abating in the twenty-first. But however much Dickens felt himself to be examining psychology, he felt himself to be examining something more fundamental as well. He avoided a term we have no choice but to use, if we are to talk about the subject at all. Dickens was concerned with "spiritual health." Question the notion as much as you like; the effort of the historical imagination needed to grasp what mattered to Dickens brings rewards. *The Haunted Man* is worth understanding.

The shift in emphasis was no accident. Dickens pondered the book over many months. He first told Forster he was thinking of "a very ghostly and wild idea" for a Christmas book in August 1846 (*Letters* 4: 614). The demands *Dombey and Son* made on him frustrated his hope of producing it for Christmas 1847 (5: 155, 165–66), but this gave him yet more time for planning. A letter to Angela Burdett Coutts of August 1848 indicates he was still "thinking about something for Christmas" (5: 395). Late the following month he was able to tell Forster, "At last I am a mentally matooring of the Christmas book" (5: 414). He finally began writing it on 5 October, after thinking about it, intermittently, for more than two years (5: 419). Profuse emendations in the manuscript suggest just how abundant his ideas were by the time he came to write it.

Morbid fixation notwithstanding, *The Haunted Man* was another book intended for the Christmas market. Publication day was 19 December (5: 450n). As ever, the book's physical finish was elaborate and festive. It was adorned with the by-now-familiar gilded red cover. The half-title and frontispiece were designed by John Tenniel. Illustrations were provided by Tenniel, Stanfield, Leech, and Frank Stone. Some of the content has a festive flavor, too. There are sparkling comic episodes. An irrepressible narrator makes an appearance from time to time, offering shrewd commentary and affirming the possibility of high spirits. Readers are shown innocence, sympathy, and compassion in action.

The power of *The Haunted Man*, however, lies in Dickens's supremely assured control of mood. And the predominant mood is grim – tempered rather than balanced by alternatives, ultimately giving way, to be sure, but succeeded by thoughtfulness rather than exuberance. Compared to the *Carol* and *The Chimes*, the book ends on a subdued note. Mindful perhaps of the feeble effect of the goblins in *The Chimes*, Dickens was now turning away from imaginative profusion towards imaginative severity. There is just enough to dazzle us in *The Haunted Man* to provide a contrast, but, for most of the book, our attention is held by the protagonist, fixated upon past suffering, incapable of joy, and in flight from emotional pain. Dark, menacing imagery gives much of the text the flavor of a troubling dream. Readers are made to feel they are being drawn into private obsession, private despair.

That may sound like a good reason for not reading *The Haunted Man*, but Dickens was offering readers new rewards. The psychological perspicacity of the book is unmistakable. We are made to see into an abnormal state of mind, to find it intelligible, and to understand its perils. Dwelling exclusively upon painful memories, or repressing them, we perceive, are errors equally calamitous. But the impulse to repress them – which we are made to share – prompts thoughts of redemption, even if it does not promise it. What is repressed can cease to be so. What is dammed up can flow again.[7] One thing, at any rate, is implicitly promised: psychological cause will be followed by psychological effect. We read on to find out what the effect will be. Dickens was discovering a new kind of narrative dynamism.

He found it by looking at his own experience and recasting it. Like many a novelist, he was adept at finding incipient selves within him, different from the man his friends recognized, but scarcely less vivid. Among others, Dickens found damaged creatures there, who had not overcome obstacles he had, or who overcame them more laboriously, through struggle more protracted.

A Christmas Carol owes much to the restimulation in him of emotions related to painful childhood experiences. The same experiences inform *The Haunted Man*. During the late 1840s, Dickens was preoccupied with them. It was probably in 1847 that he committed to paper an account – for once free of fictional disguise – of his employment as a child-labourer at Warren's Blacking Warehouse, and of his father's imprisonment for debt in the Marshalsea Jail.[8] This was the account he confided to Forster, who later incorporated it into his *Life of Dickens* (Forster bk. 1, ch. 2). Dickens was unable to complete more than a fragment of undisguised autobiography – perhaps because he found needs unmet by the act of distinguishing an undisguised self from among the teeming occupants of his imagination. Early in 1849, however, he began work on *David Copperfield* – fiction, but fiction featuring one such occupant, more lightly disguised than most, and undergoing experiences modelled upon Dickens's own.

In 1848, some of the same troubling memories emerged in *The Haunted Man*. Dickens may have been additionally sensitized to early

recollections by the death, a month before he began writing, of his elder
sister Fanny, the sibling who, from childhood, had always been dearest
to him (Kaplan 238–39). The phantom that appears to the central
character of *The Haunted Man* reflects Redlaw's indignation at neglect
he had suffered during his childhood:

> "No mother's self-denying love, . . . no father's counsel, aided
> *me*. A stranger came into my father's place when I was but a
> child, and I was easily an alien from my mother's heart. My
> parents, at the best, were of that sort whose care soon ends, and
> whose duty is soon done; who cast their offspring loose, early, as
> birds do theirs; and, if they do well, claim the merit; and, if ill,
> the pity." (*Christmas Books* 393–94)

Dickens, there can be little doubt, was reconsidering the sense he too
had, of having been neglected as a child – during his time at Warren's, if
at no other (See pp. 174–75 above, and Ackroyd 553–54).

The Haunted Man, however, was no exercise undertaken simply to
purge old pain. In it, Dickens relives old distress, but lets it take his
central character far down a path he had only just ventured upon. The
match between the childhood miseries related in *The Haunted Man* and
his own, we cannot help noting, is rough at best. Dickens felt cast loose
when he was working at Warren's, but he was eventually rescued from
his drudgery, and his parents used their influence to help him towards a
career (Ackroyd 115–16, 132–33).

During the second half of the 1840s, moreover, he was evidently
revising his feelings – at least towards his father. In 1846, Dickens was
among the founders of a new morning paper, the *Daily News*, which he
briefly edited. John Dickens was put in charge of the reporters. The
appointment would scarcely have been made without Dickens – and
others too – recognizing his father's skills, energy, and administrative
competence (Johnson 1: 578 and n89). In both *The Haunted Man* and
David Copperfield, attention is drawn to the failings of a stepfather, not
of a natural father.

Dickens selected only what was useful to him from his memories,
and blended it with material from literature and fable, or just made up
plausible alternatives. Undisguised autobiography was not his *métier*,
he had discovered. Fiction was – fiction showing incipient selves of

which he was aware, enduring painful experiences, struggling with them more than Dickens himself had had to, but overcoming them all the same, and gaining from them. Dickens the writer was often wiser than Dickens the man. We do not entirely believe the latter's solemn protestation in the autobiographical fragment: "I do not write resentfully or angrily, for I know how all these things have worked together to make me what I am . . . " (Forster bk. 1, ch. 2). There are too many signs of resentment and anger elsewhere. But Dickens the writer certainly recognized the value of unhappy memories. They were a source of material for fiction, a source of strength and definition for character.

To write about them so effectively, Dickens must have experienced something like the despondency that is the subject of *The Haunted Man*, something like the pain of troubling memories that pervades the book, despite its condemnation of brooding upon old pain. In *The Haunted Man*, the acceptance of unhappy memories, and the gaining of mental and moral equipoise through such acceptance, is made a condition of redemption.

A Christmas Carol tells of a man morally ruined by the repudiation of memory, and of the understanding memory confers. Scrooge is redeemed only when, persuaded by spirits, he allows himself once again to remember, to see, and to foresee. Readers of the *Carol* understand that at some stage in the past he has made a choice – unwitting perhaps, but a choice for all that, and one for which he is culpable. *The Haunted Man* dwells upon someone making such a choice, consciously resolving to do what readers understand Scrooge already to have done. It examines the motives of a man choosing forgetfulness – more absolute than Scrooge's – and it plots the trajectory of consequences: his perception of the error he has made, his striving to undo it, and his redemption through acknowledgement of the value of memory, even when it is of pain.

The book tells of Mr. Redlaw, a lecturer in chemistry, learned, humane, conscientious, esteemed by students, but embittered by the memory of wrongs he has suffered. On Christmas Eve, neither for the first time nor for the last, he is visited by a phantom, his own double but grimmer, who grants him forgetfulness of past pain. It is a gift he will pass on, the phantom advises. Those he encounters will forget too.

The gift proves malign. Redlaw senses his humanity ebbing away with his memories, and finds himself becoming unfeeling. Others sink into discontent and discord. One person alone is unaffected by his presence – a street urchin. "No softening memory of sorrow, wrong, or trouble enters here," the phantom explains, "because this wretched mortal from his birth has been abandoned to a worse condition than the beasts, and has, within his knowledge, no one contrast, no humanising touch, to make a grain of such a memory spring up in his hardened breast" (*Christmas Books* 446). Memories of sorrow, and of wrong suffered, Redlaw begins to understand, complement memories of joy, in shaping our affections and in binding us to others.

The music of the Christmas waits dimly alerts him to his loss, and he begs the phantom to undo the harm that has been done – at least to others. The reply is enigmatic. Redlaw must await the meeting he has most been dreading, with Milly, wife of the college lodge-keeper, more loving and compassionate than anyone else of his acquaintance. But her womanly goodness resists his evil influence, counteracts it, and eventually redeems even Redlaw himself.

There is no reliance on the templates of melodrama this time. The story owes more to Gothic than to melodramatic tradition. It is more restrained and complex than all but a few books termed Gothic but, for all its severity, *The Haunted Man* is organized around a conspicuous artifice. The ghostly double is an elaborate motif straight from the repertoire of Gothic fiction.

Dickens adapts it deftly, however, to the representation of morbid introspection.[9] Characteristically, he turns its very conspicuousness to advantage. There is no demand that readers subscribe to a supernatural explanation of the story. The device, it is suggested, may equally be supposed a formal mechanism for representing Redlaw's inner struggle. Who contrived the mechanism is a question left deliberately unanswered. At the end, the narrator licenses a variety of explanations of Redlaw's story:

> Some people have said since, that he only thought what has been herein set down; others, that he read it in the fire, one winter night about the twilight time; others, that the Ghost was but the representation of his gloomy thoughts, and Milly the embodiment of his better wisdom. *I* say nothing. (470)

The very artifice of the device makes it easier for us to select a
psychological explanation.   It weds the book to no particular
psychology. No theory gets in the way. We can apply whichever one
we favor, or none at all.

Readers, however, are not required to choose between rational and
fanciful interpretations. The power of the book is commensurate with
the uncertainty it generates.   The *Carol* is a masterpiece not least
because it is no mere ghost story: it is a dramatization of the telling of a
ghost story, capitalizing on doubt. Dickens had offered readers of *The
Chimes* a similar entitlement to doubt, but in a more perfunctory
fashion. Now, he more nearly approaches the success of the *Carol*. In
The Haunted Man the problem of belief is absorbed into the narrative.
Throughout, we are teased with the possibility of different explanations
from the one ostensibly being offered.   Confronted with something
conspicuously marvellous, we find that a dialectic between competing
explanations only intensifies wonder.

The opening pages of *The Haunted Man* are a triumph of ambiguity.
The predominant mood of the book is set, and supernatural events are
foreshadowed, without any formal violation of realistic canons. A sense
of the figurative outweighing the literal unsettles the reader, it is true.
Uneasy thoughts of other-worldly things are provoked.   Imagery
conjures up all sorts of menaces. But the text permits readers to cling to
the normal and the familiar. A sense of its being possible to do so,
indeed, must figure in any adequate response.

To begin with, readers can choose to understand *haunted* to mean
only "beset with painful thoughts." "Visited by a ghost" is a meaning
that can be fended off. Redlaw is introduced as someone who simply
prompts use of the word:

> Who could have seen his hollow cheek; his sunken brilliant
> eye; his black-attired figure, indefinably grim, although
> well-knit and well-proportioned; his grizzled hair hanging, like
> tangled sea-weed, about his face, – as if he had been, through his
> whole life, a lonely mark for the chafing and beating of the great
> deep of humanity, – but might have said he looked like a
> haunted man?
> Who could have observed his manner, taciturn, thoughtful,
> gloomy, shadowed by habitual reserve, retiring always and

jocund never, with a distraught air of reverting to a bygone place
and time, or of listening to some old echoes in his mind, but
might have said it was the manner of a haunted man?

Who could have heard his voice, slow-speaking, deep, and
grave, with a natural fulness and melody in it which he seemed
to set himself against and stop, but might have said it was the
voice of a haunted man? (376)

Nothing in the passage demands *haunted* be understood other than
figuratively.   There is an echo, in its use, of Master Humphrey's
observations about belief in ghosts (see p. 148 above).   Redlaw, we
perceive, lingers upon "past emotions and by-gone times."   Our
propensity to such lingering can incline us toward the "popular faith in
ghosts" (*Master Humphrey* 58).   But it is only an inclination that is
summoned up.   The passage unsettles rather than alarms us.

Ghosts are soon introduced, but teasingly, for the purpose of fanciful
comparison only.   The narrator describes Redlaw, brooding alone in his
chamber in the old college.[10]   It is "the dead winter time":

> ... When twilight everywhere released the shadows, prisoned up
> all day, that now closed in and gathered like mustering swarms
> of ghosts.   When they stood lowering, in corners of rooms, and
> frowned out from behind half-opened doors.   When they had full
> possession of unoccupied apartments.   When they danced upon
> the floors, and walls, and ceilings of inhabited chambers, while
> the fire was low, and withdrew like ebbing waters when it
> sprang into a blaze.   When they fantastically mocked the shapes
> of household objects, making the nurse an ogress, the
> rocking-horse a monster, the wondering child, half-scared and
> half-amused, a stranger to itself, – the very tongs upon the
> hearth, a straddling giant with his arms a-kimbo, evidently
> smelling the blood of Englishmen, and wanting to grind people's
> bones to make his bread.
>
> When these shadows brought into the minds of older people,
> other thoughts, and showed them different images.   When they
> stole from their retreats, in the likenesses of forms and faces
> from the past, from the grave, from the deep, deep gulf, where
> the things that might have been, and never were, are always
> wandering. (378–80)

The mood is being set, possibilities are being foreshadowed, but through tropes, through talk of thoughts entertained, through images called up.

Readers are eventually alerted to a ghostly presence not at all figurative, though still shadowy. Hope of rational explanation, however slender, is sustained. Doubt and denial contend with affirmation in the text. William, the lodge-keeper, arrives with a dinner tray, he enters, and Redlaw's reverie is interrupted.

> Surely there had been no figure leaning on the back of his chair; no face looking over it. It is certain that no gliding footstep touched the floor, as he lifted up his head, with a start, and spoke. And yet there was no mirror in the room on whose surface his own form could have cast its shadow for a moment; and Something had passed darkly and gone! (380)

When at last the ghost manifests itself beyond dispute, it is scarcely Grand Guignol. It is, rather, at once unspectacular and profoundly disturbing, like a figure in a recurrent dream, familiar but dreaded. Redlaw is left alone again.

> As the gloom and shadow thickened behind him, in that place where it had been gathering so darkly, it took, by slow degrees, – or out of it there came, by some unreal, unsubstantial process, not to be traced by any human sense, – an awful likeness of himself!
>
> Ghastly and cold, colourless in its leaden face and hands, but with his features, and his bright eyes, and his grizzled hair, and dressed in the gloomy shadow of his dress, it came into its terrible appearance of existence, motionless, without a sound. As *he* leaned his arm upon the elbow of his chair, ruminating before the fire, *it* leaned upon the chair-back, close above him, with its appalling copy of his face looking where his face looked, and bearing the expression his face bore.
>
> This, then, was the Something that had passed and gone already. This was the dread companion of the haunted man! (391–93)

Redlaw evidently knows the phantom intimately. What passes between them is marked by a leaden absence of surprise.

It took, for some moments, no more apparent heed of him, than he of it. The Christmas Waits were playing somewhere in the distance, and, through his thoughtfulness, he seemed to listen to the music. It seemed to listen too.

At length he spoke; without moving or lifting up his face.

"Here again!" he said.

"Here again," replied the Phantom.

"I see you in the fire," said the haunted man; "I hear you in music, in the wind, in the dead stillness of the night."

The Phantom moved its head, assenting.

"Why do you come, to haunt me thus?"

"I come as I am called," replied the Ghost.

"No. Unbidden," exclaimed the Chemist.

"Unbidden be it," said the Spectre. "It is enough. I am here."

(393)

Even this difference between them is made to feel stale. We sense a debate about volition being sidestepped, through sheer weariness.

Gone are the extravagant ghosts of the *Carol*, dazzling, rich in symbolism, indefatigably caring. Gone, mercifully, are their dimmer counterparts of *The Chimes*. Astonishment gives way to despondency. The creature which haunts Redlaw is disquieting, not because it is strange and challenges interpretation, but because it is all too familiar to him, all too intelligible; and because, until the very end, it seems purely malevolent. Whether we look to a numinous or to a psychological explanation, it is plainly an embodiment of Redlaw's fixation. He has lost access to alternative perspectives. The phantom represents the memories that afflict him, his enslavement to them, his desire to be rid of them. Conjuring up the painful confusion of dream states, the text makes it easy to muddle man and phantom. Readers have to work at distinguishing between "he" and "it."

"I see you in the fire, . . . I hear you in music, in the wind, in the dead stillness of the night," is turned into a dismal litany, constantly under modification. It suggests an explanation of what Redlaw is experiencing, less palpable than the one the text is formally offering. And it marks the way memories can be at once harrowing and routine: Redlaw's memories, for instance, of his sister – dead, her heart broken by a false friend (394); memories of plans Redlaw once had – like the plan to marry a young woman, stolen from him by the false friend (395). Cruelly, the phantom repeats the litany: the memories that afflict him, Redlaw is reminded, "have been wont to show themselves in the fire, in music, in the wind, in the dead stillness of the night, in the revolving years" (397). Readers find themselves, with Redlaw, succumbing to fixation, longing for release.

They do so with special intensity, because what Dickens opposes to Redlaw's condition seems, for most of the book, frail by comparison. Against fixation he opposes elasticity. Against repudiation, he opposes affirmation. Against succumbing to wounds of the past, he opposes braving whatever life brings. But none of these, we are made half to suspect, are a match for the baleful influence of Redlaw's despondency.

And something more has to be said. We are swayed by Dickens's skill in making us doubt the possibility of redemption for Redlaw, his skill in making us fear the potency of his obsession, but the balance of our feelings is also affected by a local failure of imagination. Not everything Dickens uses to counteract the darkness gathering around Redlaw is of the same quality.

Repetition is used cumulatively to build up our sense of Redlaw's affliction. In the presentation of the Swidger family it is used for little more than stylistic ornament. It is easy enough to feel affection for William Swidger, the garrulous, amiable college lodge-keeper. We can accept his repetitious gossip about his wife and his innumerable Swidger relations. But his repetition of the phrase, "That's what I always say, sir" – plus variants – amounts to no more than an arbitrary badge of identity.

Philip Swidger, William's old father, is functionally important in *The Haunted Man*. He demonstrates how memory can heal, and he makes the connection between memory and Christmas. It is through him that we learn it is Christmas Eve. We first encounter him carrying holly with which to decorate Redlaw's room, and musing upon Christmas memories – even those arousing sadness, which he manfully accommodates. William, and the holly, prompt him to recall the time when he was a young father:

> "His mother – my son William's my youngest son – and I, have
> sat among em' all, boys and girls, little children and babies,

many a year, when the berries like these were not shining half so bright all round us, as their bright faces. Many of 'em are gone; she's gone; and my son George (our eldest, who was her pride more than all the rest!) is fallen very low: but I can see them, when I look here, alive and healthy, as they used to be in those days; and I can see him, thank God, in his innocence. It's a blessed thing to me, at eighty-seven." (*Christmas Books* 386–87).

This is moving enough, and his repetitions are in character for an old man, but it is tiresome to be told quite as often as we are that he is eighty-seven.

Milly Swidger's goodness and gentleness are effectively established through a variety of means – in the bald utterances of the urchin, for instance, who says things like, "I don't want you. I want the woman" (399). But she repeats, with variations, a formula that becomes too familiar: "O dear, here's somebody else who likes me. What shall I ever do!" (457). We are clearly expected to admire her lack of self-consciousness, but virtue unselfconscious to this extent becomes suspect.

Repetition works in the presentation of Redlaw. Fixation entails repetition. Repetition in the presentation of the Swidgers rarely amounts to more than showy literary technique.

Literary technique is fruitful, however, in Dickens's much more successful presentation of the Tetterby family. As so often, he is on surer ground when he allows comedy to prevail over sentiment. The episodes that feature the Tetterbys constitute a convincing textual enactment of mental elasticity, a convincing textual repudiation of fixation.

Members of the family delight us, partly because of Dickens's capacity to imagine character, partly because of his skill with dialogue, but also because of the mediation of an intrusive narrator in episodes that feature them. In this we see a late flowering of the technique which, elsewhere, I have called Dickens's "archness" (see Parker, *The Doughty Street Novels* 24–27). Related to mock-heroic, but not necessarily satirical, archness entails a comic disproportion between rhetorical means and narrative ends. We meet with it as soon as the family is introduced. In the small parlour behind his small newsagent's shop, the narrator tells us, Mr. Tetterby is surrounded by small children.

> Of these small fry, two had, by some strong machinery, been got into bed in a corner, where they might have reposed snugly enough in the sleep of innocence, but for a constitutional propensity to keep awake, and also to scuffle in and out of bed. The immediate occasion of these predatory dashes at the waking world, was the construction of an oyster-shell wall in a corner, by two other youths of tender age; on which fortification the two in bed made harassing descents (like those accursed Picts and Scots who beleaguer the early historical studies of most young Britons), and then withdrew to their own territory.
>
> In addition to the stir attendant on these inroads, and the retorts of the invaded, who pursued hotly, and made lunges at the bed-clothes under which the marauders took refuge, another little boy, in another little bed, contributed his mite of confusion to the family stock, by casting his boots upon the waters; in other words, by launching these and several small objects, inoffensive in themselves, though of a hard substance considered as missiles, at the disturbers of his repose, – who were not slow to return these compliments. (*Christmas Books* 402)

This same disproportion of means and ends is used for the extraordinary representation of the baby of the family, Sally.   To Johnny, the child charged with minding her, the narrator explains, the baby is "Moloch" – the Ammonite god, that is to say, to whom children were sacrificed:[11]

> It was a very Moloch of a baby, on whose insatiate altar the whole existence of this particular young brother was offered up a daily sacrifice. Its personality may be said to have consisted in its never being quiet, in any one place, for five consecutive minutes, and never going to sleep when required. "Tetterby's baby" was as well known in the neighbourhood as the postman or the pot-boy. It roved from door-step to door-step, in the arms of little Johnny Tetterby, and lagged heavily at the rear of troops of juveniles who followed the Tumblers or the Monkey, and came up, all on one side, a little too late for everything that was

attractive, from Monday morning until Saturday night. Wherever childhood congregated to play, there was little Moloch making Johnny fag and toil. Wherever Johnny desired to stay, little Moloch became fractious, and would not remain. Whenever Johnny wanted to go out, Moloch was asleep, and must be watched. Whenever Johnny wanted to stay at home, Moloch was awake, and must be taken out. Yet Johnny was verily persuaded that it was a faultless baby, without its peer in the realm of England, and was quite content to catch meek glimpses of things in general from behind its skirts, or over its limp flapping bonnet, and to go staggering about with it like a very little porter with a very large parcel, which was not directed to anybody, and could never be delivered anywhere. (402–03)

The zest of such writing, its openness to the contingent and the unlikely, makes it a foil, however intermittent, to Redlaw's fixation. It enacts a disposition to look outward and absorb, rather than look inward and reject.

Nor is such zest, such openness, restricted to the narrator. Mr. Tetterby's taste for improbable stylistic flourishes indicates a similar disposition. His habit of consulting choice cuttings from the newspapers that are his livelihood yields some arresting remarks:

> "Let anybody, I don't care who it is, get out of bed again," said Tetterby, as a general proclamation, delivered in a very soft-hearted manner, "and astonishment will be the portion of that respected contemporary!" .... "Johnny, my child, take care of your only sister, Sally; for she's the brightest gem that ever sparkled on your early brow." (406)

This proneness to snap up unconsidered trifles of discourse resembles Dickens's own. Mr. Tetterby reflects a facet of Dickens's sensibility every bit as distinctly as Redlaw does, brooding upon past sorrows.

Nor is Mr. Tetterby's language mere parroting, we soon realize. He instinctively makes use of discourse that travesties his thoughts and feelings. In doing so, he reveals them obliquely but cunningly, often in a form more soothing or acceptable to his interlocutor. Confessing her dismay at the poverty that threatens to spoil their Christmas celebrations, his wife tearfully suggests, " . . . you hate me, don't you, 'Dolphus?"

"Not quite," said Mr Tetterby, "as yet."

She presses on, however, wondering whether they were wise to have married and had children. "Do you hate me now, 'Dolphus?" she asks.

"Why no," said Mr Tetterby, "I don't find that I do, as yet."
(413)

Mr. Tetterby preserves his mental and moral health, and relates healthily to those around him, by thinking outside himself, by sampling discourse a different sort of man might utter, by imagining himself a different sort of person. In this respect, he is the contrary of Redlaw, who is locked into his own sufferings, and cannot escape from himself except by drastic and ignoble means.

It is no surprise, then, to find that, in the Tetterby family, there is recognition of the complexity of experience, of contradiction, of the need to balance and to reconcile. The Tetterbys can cope with distressful memories – even cherish them. Mrs. Tetterby reveals how she has freed herself from her dismay and misgiving:

> " . . . I felt as if there was a rush of recollection on me, all at once, that softened my hard heart, and filled it up till it was bursting. All our struggles for a livelihood, all our cares and wants since we have been married, all the times of sickness, all the hours of watching, we have ever had, by one another, or by the children, seemed to speak to me, and say that they had made us one, and that I never might have been, or could have been, or would have been, any other than the wife and mother I am. Then, the cheap enjoyments that I could have trodden on so cruelly, got to be so precious to me – Oh so priceless, and dear! – that I couldn't bear to think how much I had wronged them; and I said, and say again a hundred times, how could I ever behave so, 'Dolphus, how could I ever have the heart to do it!"
> (414)

When they are under the dire influence of Redlaw's gift, the

Tetterbys manage to preserve their outward-looking disposition, if only in their imaginative reach. Despite their sullen discontent, we detect a propensity that keeps us hopeful, if only just. Johnny loses his devotion to the baby and rebelliously asks his mother how she would like his duties: "How would you? Not at all. If you was me, you'd go for a soldier. I will, too. There an't no babies in the army" (450). Mr. and Mrs. Tetterby regard each other with contempt:

> "You had better read your paper than do nothing at all," said Mrs Tetterby.
> "What's there to read in a paper?" returned Mr Tetterby, with excessive discontent.
> "What?" said Mrs Tetterby. "Police."
> "It's nothing to me," said Tetterby. "What do I care what people do, or are done to?"
> "Suicides," suggested Mrs Tetterby.
> "No business of mine," replied her husband.
> "Births, deaths, and marriages, are those nothing to you?" said Mrs Tetterby.
> "If the births were all over for good, and all to-day; and the deaths were all to begin to come off to-morrow; I don't see why it should interest me, till I thought it was a coming to my turn," grumbled Tetterby. "As to marriages, I've done it myself. I know quite enough about *them*." (451)

Johnny can yoke domestic duties and the army fantastically together. Mr. Tetterby can rearrange human destiny to score a debating point. Discontent notwithstanding, in their very willingness imaginatively to seize and manipulate the larger world, they prove their undamaged awareness of it, and that holds out promise of their regaining a sense of how to act well in it.

The street urchin, in contrast, seems almost incapacitated from ever developing such a sense. He is an extraordinary creation – Ignorance and Want of *A Christmas Carol,* refined and transformed. The way he is at first described echoes the way they were (see pp. 191–92 above):

> A bundle of tatters, held together by a hand, in size and form almost an infant's, but in its greedy, desperate little clutch, a bad old man's. A face rounded and smoothed by some half-dozen

years, but pinched and twisted by the experiences of a life.
Bright eyes, but not youthful. Naked feet, beautiful in their
childish delicacy, – ugly in the blood and dirt that cracked upon
them. A baby savage, a young monster, a child who had never
been a child, a creature who might live to take the outward form
of man, but who, within, would live and perish a mere beast.

Unlike Ignorance and Want, however, the urchin is more than a
momentary personification. He has immense symbolic significance, but
is thoroughly integrated into the text, and relates vitally with other
characters. And he is made to do so against the grain of what,
previously, had been Dickens's usual practice. Nothing in *The Haunted
Man* more clearly illustrates his swing towards imaginative severity.
The urchin's words are as powerful as they are because they are so stark
– free of implication stylistic embellishment conveys, heavy with
implication this very freedom conveys.

Starkness cannot be established without contrast. The urchin's words
stand out against the mercurial discourse of the narrator and the
Tetterbys, against the closely focused but emotionally saturated
discourse of Redlaw and the phantom. "I'll bite, . . . if you hit me," the
boy says to Redlaw on first meeting him (399). Spotting food, his
response is straightforward and instantaneous: "Give me some of that!"
Only his instinctual impulse to be near Milly hints at something
incorruptible in him, starkness notwithstanding. "There!" he says,
having eaten the remnants of Redlaw's dinner. "Now take me to the
woman!" (401).

There are no deviations from standard English in Dickens's
representation of the urchin's speech. He is clearly a prototype for Jo,
the crossing sweeper of *Bleak House* (1852–53), but Jo is given things
to say like, "He wos wery good to me" (*Bleak House* 137). In Jo's
speech, Dickens strives to replicate the non-standard language of
London's street children. His strategy in *The Haunted Man*, though, is
at least as effective. By eschewing the implications dialect brings – of
particular place and time, for instance – Dickens was able to make the
urchin's discourse that much more elemental. As readers, we can
project whatever non-standard pronunciation we choose upon his words,
but they stand out the more starkly, because Dickens does not prompt us
to do so.

The urchin is Redlaw's conductor into the waste land of the "hungry forties":

> Redlaw looked about him; from the houses to the waste piece of ground on which the houses stood, or rather did not altogether tumble down, unfenced, undrained, unlighted, and bordered by a sluggish ditch; from that, to the sloping line of arches, part of some neighbouring viaduct or bridge with which it was surrounded, and which lessened gradually towards them, until the last but one was a mere kennel for a dog, the last a plundered little heap of bricks; from that, to the child, close to him, cowering and trembling with the cold, and limping on one little foot, while he coiled the other round his leg to warm it . . . .
>
> Looking back on his way to the house-door, Redlaw saw him trail himself upon the dust and crawl within the shelter of the smallest arch, as if he were a rat. He had no pity for the thing, but he was afraid of it; and when it looked out of its den at him, he hurried to the house as a retreat. (431–32)

Redlaw hopes his gift of forgetfulness will be a blessing to dwellers in such a milieu, but he discovers there how destructive it is to sever "the last thread" connecting even the most degraded to "the mercy of Heaven" (433–34).

The phantom finally reveals itself to be an agent of that mercy, and turns instructor. It insists Redlaw recognize what the urchin and his kind represent: "From every seed of evil in this boy, a field of ruin is grown that shall be gathered in, and garnered up, and sown again in many places in the world, until regions are overspread with wickedness enough to raise the waters of another Deluge."

> "There is not a father," said the Phantom, "by whose side in his daily or his nightly walk, these creatures pass; there is not a mother among all the ranks of loving mothers in this land; there is no one risen from the state of childhood, but shall be responsible in his or her degree for this enormity. There is not a country throughout the earth on which it would not bring a curse. There is no religion upon earth that it would not deny; there is no people upon earth it would not put to shame."

And Redlaw, the phantom points out, has chosen to become like the boy: "His thoughts have been in 'terrible companionship' with yours, because you have gone down to his unnatural level." These words stir feeling in Redlaw once again:

> The Chemist stooped upon the ground beside the boy, and, with the same kind of compassion for him that he now felt for himself, covered him as he slept, and no longer shrank from him with abhorrence or indifference. (447)

Thus it is that we are prepared for Milly's redemption of Redlaw. Milly's nature, we learn, has been softened by the loss of her only child, who was stillborn:

> "When I think of all those hopes I built upon it, and the many times I sat and pictured to myself the little smiling face upon my bosom that never lay there, and the sweet eyes turned up to mine that never opened to the light," said Milly, "I can feel a greater tenderness, I think, for all the disappointed hopes in which there is no harm. . . ." (466)

The dead child seems to speak to her, she tells her husband:

> " . . . For poor neglected children, my little child pleads as if it were alive, and had a voice I knew, with which to speak to me. When I hear of youth in suffering or shame, I think that my child might have come to that, perhaps, and that God took it from me in his mercy. Even in age and grey hair, such as father's, it is present: saying that it too might have lived to be old, long and long after you and I were gone, and to have needed the respect and love of younger people." (467)

Milly has been made stronger by suffering, and continues to draw strength from memories of it.

She has told Redlaw it is good to remember wrongs committed against us, so that we may forgive them (464). The example she sets, of fortitude and compassion, causes him at last to recover his memory, not least his memory of the forgiveness of sins Christmas brings to mind.

Redlaw fell upon his knees, with a loud cry.

"O Thou," he said, "who through the teaching of pure love, hast graciously restored me to the memory which was the memory of Christ upon the Cross, and of all the good who perished in His cause, receive my thanks, and bless her!" (467)

Nor does he stop at contrition. One change he makes to his life affects the urchin:

> . . . he laid his hand upon the boy, and, silently calling Him to witness who laid His hand on children in old time, rebuking, in the majesty of His prophetic knowledge, those who kept them from Him,[12] vowed to protect him, teach him, and reclaim him. (468)

Christian doctrine is overt here, more so than in any of Dickens's earlier Christmas writings, but it does not disrupt the book's strategy. The ending of *The Haunted Man* is powerful in the way the rest of the book is, thanks to Dickens's superb handling of mood.

Together with innumerable Swidgers, the main characters gather for Christmas dinner in the college hall. The mood is pensive rather than jubilant. Strong feelings are indicated, but with restraint. We are offered a measured contrast, deeply soothing in effect, to the naked despondency that has hitherto prevailed. Hope is held out for the urchin boy, but we are shown no improbably swift transformation:

> It was sad to see the child who had no name or lineage, watching the other children as they played, not knowing how to talk with them, or sport with them, and more strange to the ways of childhood than a rough dog. It was sad, though in a different way, to see what an instinctive knowledge the youngest children there had of his being different from all the rest, and how they made timid approaches to him with soft words and touches, and with little presents, that he might not be unhappy. But he kept by Milly, and began to love her – that was another, as she said! – and, as they all liked her dearly, they were glad of that, and when they saw him peeping at them from behind her chair, they were pleased that he was so close to it. (468)

Restrained, unemphatic, direct, the very prose is calming, after the intensity of what has gone before.

Dinner over, darkness begins to fall, but all remain in the hall, lit only by a great open fire: "the shadows once more stole out of their hiding-places, and danced about the room, showing the children marvellous shapes and faces on the walls, and gradually changing what was real and familiar there, to what was wild and magical." We are back where we started, with childish wonder at the effect of firelight in the gloom. But now we have seen how that which is wild and magical can heal. We have seen how torment may mysteriously yield redemption. The element of threat has been removed. With the children, we can quietly enjoy any fancies conjured up.

Not a few of the adults present find their eyes turning to the inscription beneath an ancient portrait. It is of a benefactor of the college who, among other bequests, left a fund, "to buy holly, for garnishing the walls and windows, come Christmas" (387):

> Deepened in its gravity by the fire-light, and gazing from the darkness of the panelled wall like life, the sedate face in the portrait, with the beard and ruff, looked down at them from under its verdant wreath of holly, as they looked up at it; and, clear and plain below, as if a voice had uttered them, were the words,

𝕷𝖔𝖗𝖉 𝕶𝖊𝖊𝖕 𝖒𝖞 𝕸𝖊𝖒𝖔𝖗𝖞 𝕲𝖗𝖊𝖊𝖓.

This entreaty closes the book (470), and sustains the heartfelt calm of its ending, by containing layer upon layer of meaning beneath a surface of folksy piety.[13]

The words express the benefactor's wish to be remembered, and hint wittily at the means he chose to ensure he would be. But the story we have now finished reading prompts us to think of more than this – to think of all of the dead it is good to remember. And the words are susceptible to another interpretation. As well as "do not forget me," they can also mean "do not let me forget." The story, we are reminded, is about keeping the faculty of memory itself "green," in order to preserve an outlook upon the world and its inhabitants, healthy morally and spiritually.

Ambiguity and association make the prayer that ends *The Haunted Man* rich in meaning, despite superficial simplicity.   One further meaning, more overt at the end of Dickens's next text about Christmas, is perhaps hinted at here.   On Christmas Day, Christians decorate their homes with holly to evoke one memory above all others.   For such readers, the inscription beneath the portrait is, not least, a reminder of the the incarnation of Christ, whose example inspires Redlaw's redemption.

If the measure is sales and reviews, *The Haunted Man* cannot be counted among Dickens's most successful Christmas books (Slater, *A Christmas Carol* xxii–xxiii).   It is, however, a work of extraordinary power and originality, a landmark in the development of Dickens's craft, a precursor of books to come.   Redlaw's struggle with pain from the past is the first in a remarkable series.   We see such a struggle in Esther Summerson's self-abnegation and need for love (*Bleak House*, 1852–53), in Louisa Gradgrind's sense of a childhood spoiled (*Hard Times*, 1854), in Arthur Clennam's branding of himself as "Nobody" (*Little Dorrit*, 1855–57), in Dr. Manette's compulsive shoe-making (*A Tale of Two Cities*, 1859), in Miss Havisham's obsession with her betrayal (*Great Expectations*, 1860–61).   Had Dickens finished *The Mystery of Edwin Drood* (1870), the divided personality of John Jasper would almost certainly have earned itself a place in the series.

One thing in particular stands out, when we place *The Haunted Man* within the chronological sequence of Dickens's works.   He was allowing his Christian faith to become more overt in what he wrote about Christmas.

There is evidence that he was becoming more devout.   A sign of this is a document he wrote in 1846 for his children, six in all by that date, aged between one and nine.   It is a simplified version of the story that can be pieced together from the New Testament.   In the Dickens household, it was read aloud to those children old enough to understand, until they were capable of reading for themselves.   Dickens gave the document no title, and did not intend it for publication, although it eventually was published in 1934 as *The Life of Our Lord,* after the death of the last of his children.

Some scholars have detected the influence in it of the Unitarianism that so attracted Dickens during the 1840s, although Dennis Walder finds this only in the moral emphasis of the text (Schlicke 334, 492; Walder 13). Christ is seen as a loved son of God (*Holiday Romance and Other Writings for Children* 441, 444, 453), as a worker of miracles (446–49, 451–53, 461–62), as a great teacher (454–60), and as a model of perfect goodness (441). The Trinity is nowhere implied. The Holy Ghost is featured as no more than "a beautiful bird like a dove" (444). And the distinction between Jesus and God is emphasized. Dickens quotes (or slightly misquotes) the Gospel of St. John: the resurrected Christ tells Mary Magdalene he is to ascend to "my Father, and your Father; and to my God, and your God" (John 21.17).

Although written for his children, *The Life of Our Lord* can be profitably understood as a review by Dickens of his own faith. In simplifying the Gospel stories, he was adjusting and reaffirming his own response to those stories. To see the book in this way helps to explain why Christian doctrines are so much more apparent in *The Haunted Man* than they are in *A Christmas Carol* or *The Chimes,* why they were to become still more apparent in two of the remaining texts we must examine.

In coupling his Christmas writings ever more closely with Christian belief, Dickens was taking risks. Religious belief poses problems both for writers of imaginative literature and for readers. Writers who subscribe to what are usually thought of as the great religions find at their disposal rich strands of myth, imagery, sentiment, and discourse, woven into the fabric of the culture they share with readers, which they can conjure, when need be, by the barest of allusions. But some readers will quibble over doctrine. Some will reject the whole package. And there is always a danger to the writer, of letting religious feeling supersede imagination.

Few habitual readers of imaginative literature, however, lack the experience of responding keenly to texts affirming religious views they do not accept. The fact is, a text can work as literature independently of the religious doctrine it affirms. It does so when it conveys what it is to be a believer – when it is about believing, that is to say, not just about belief.

Most of Dickens's Christmas writing is powerful because it is more about believing than belief. The best of it dramatizes struggle. Doubt jostles with affirmation, conflict is resolved only gradually, experience holds our attention, not faith.

In the *Carol*, Christian doctrines are barely more than implied. Tiny Tim takes comfort from the thought of his condition prompting others to "remember upon Christmas Day, who made lame beggars walk, and blind men see" (*Christmas Books* 50). Peter reads the Bible aloud (73). But these details can be understood as the expression of character or situation. Nor do we find any suggestion, in the book, of consolation, specifically Christian, in the face of death. Tiny Tim's words, "God Bless Us, Every One," are the last we read (85), but the expression is so common it registers only unfocused piety. Doctrinal implications are remote.

The closing words of *The Chimes* are less equivocal. The narrator states his hope that not even the poorest among us be "debarred their rightful share, in what our Great Creator formed us to enjoy" (177). Even so, this can be read as an afterthought. Nothing else in the book so plainly invites devotional thinking. In *The Haunted Man*, however, specifically Christian doctrines and specific passages of Scripture are invoked at the moment of climax. In the next work we must study, we find Dickens being drawn into an ever more Christian frame of reference.

Autumn was when Dickens wrote his Christmas books, but during the autumn of 1849 his time and energy were fully committed to other projects. He was deeply and passionately involved in *David Copperfield*, the first number of which had appeared in May, and he was planning the launch of *Household Words*, the first number of which would appear the following March (Forster bk. 6, ch. 4). There is no evidence to suggest he even contemplated a Christmas book in 1849. Memories of the previous few years may well have deterred him – memories of laboring with *Dombey and Son* from the summer of 1846 to the spring of 1848, memories of struggling to complete *The Battle of*

Life in 1846, and of failing to produce a Christmas book at all in 1847. He was learning to pace himself. If he had fretted at his inability to produce a Christmas book in 1847, in 1849 he seems to have been content to let imitators meet the demand.

Nor was the situation much different in 1850. Dickens did not complete *Copperfield* until 21 October (Forster bk. 6, ch. 7). It would have been too late in the year to start a Christmas book after that and, meanwhile, he was nursing *Household Words* through its first year. But if *Household Words* was part of the problem, it was also the answer. It meant he was already committed to offering his public some sort of reading matter at Christmas time. Publication would not be suspended during the festival, so why not fill the last weekly issue before 25 December with pieces appropriate to the season? There would be no need for him to write everything in it. The genre of Christmas writing he had founded had proved so popular, he would have no difficulty in recruiting eager and capable contributors.

That was the plan he adopted. The issue of 21 December 1850 was dubbed "The Christmas Number." It contained nine pieces. Readers were invited to imagine they were stories told, and reflections divulged, by friends gathered round a Christmas fireside, Among the titles were "Christmas in the Navy" by James Hannay, "A Christmas Pudding" by Charles Knight, and "Christmas Day in the Bush" by Samuel Sidney. In the writing of "Christmas in the Frozen Regions," Dickens collaborated with the navy surgeon and explorer, Robert McCormick. But the flagship piece was all his own.[14]

It is a miniature masterpiece. The narrative skill on display in "A Christmas Tree" is extraordinary. We hear a single, authentic, utterly convincing voice, but it is a voice of immense compass. The diversity of mood is astonishing. The point of view from which we are made to see shifts, combines, and recombines bewitchingly. In addition to joy at the Christmas season, we find, among other moods, tenderhearted reminiscence, fascination with the mysteries of personal growth, amusement at innocent delight in illusion, enjoyment of spookiness, sorrowful recollection of the dead, sober awareness of mortality, and intense religious piety. We are made to see as a child, and we are made to see as an adult. We are made to see as someone easily persuaded, and we are made to see as a rigorous doubter. No mood, no point of view, clashes with another. They balance and enhance each other, they merge with each other.

In *A Christmas Carol* Dickens had concerned himself with Christmas and transgression. In *The Haunted Man* he had concerned himself with Christmas and mental or spiritual disorder. Now he concerns himself with Christmas and normality. "A Christmas Tree" is about what Christmas might reaffirm for everyone who celebrates it.

In the *Carol* Dickens had fashioned a narrator believably mercurial, passing effortlessly from one mood to another. In "A Christmas Tree," the narrator characteristically sustains more than one mood at a time, and looks at things from more than one angle. We cast around for a term with which to signify this: irony, perhaps, or ambivalence. But there is no ranking, no doubting of value. All is generosity. Richness, however plodding, is probably the best term. "A Christmas Tree" affirms, includes, synthesizes. Between the plainly expressed opening and the powerfully charged ending, readers' emotions, readers' thoughts, are pulled this way and that, by the textual equivalent of a strenuous massage. It is the combination and recombination of moods and viewpoints that makes the piece so powerful. No other text more strikingly demonstrates the emotional complexity Dickens was capable of – his capacity simultaneously to love something, to laugh at it, to laugh at himself for loving it, and to express an all-embracing humanity through the very intricacy of the process. No other text, it should also be said, more strikingly demonstrates his capacity for mixing the comic and the grave to profound and thrilling effect.

Dickens's imagination seems to have been energized by the need for compression on this occasion. What he had once been able to say in a Christmas book issued between its own covers, he now had to say in a piece no longer than the average magazine article. But say it he does, packing in all the festival had come to mean to him. The emotional richness we find in the piece, readers are invited to suppose, belongs to Christmas itself. The festival is recommended as an occasion for contemplating what it is to be human and mortal: an occasion for examining what has made us, what brings us joy and sorrow, what relates us to others, what we must hold on to. To recover their humanity, Scrooge and Redlaw have to recover their memories. The narrator is the central figure in "A Christmas Tree," but his memory is intact. For him, memory exposes beginnings, sometimes only half recalled and understood, sometimes joyful, sometimes troubling, sometimes edifying, sometimes absurd, but never to be scorned. And this is an instructive process. Confident about who he is, about what passes and what endures, he finds himself able to face endings – the endings of those he loves, and ultimately his own ending too.

"A Christmas Tree" is one of the pieces that calls into question the title under which it is usually collected – *Christmas Stories*. It is more meditation than story – an essay, delivered in the first person. Yet there is a fictional element. Strictly speaking, the narrative voice cannot be supposed Dickens's own. We have seen how the narrator recollects travelling home from school at Christmas time, which Dickens never did (see p. 114 above). He also affects the mantle of solitude the Uncommercial Traveller was later to don, not really in keeping with Dickens's status as a family man (*Christmas Stories* 4). The fact is, "A Christmas Tree" is several things at once. It is an essay sharing perceptions of Christmas, it is an exercise in autobiography, and it is a work of fiction. If not all of these seem compatible, we should reflect that Dickens rarely saw deeply into his own personality except through the medium of fiction, be it ever so diaphanous.

Like the entire *Household Words* project, "A Christmas Tree" is a token of Dickens's enduring affection for the form of the eighteenth-century periodical essay, for its intimate mood, for the invitation it issues to readers to confirm shared experience. The piece can be seen as a recapitulation of "A Christmas Dinner," which was modelled upon the same template. This formal echo marks "A Christmas Tree" as the culmination of a quest Dickens had begun fifteen years earlier, a search for what it was in the festival that so met the needs of his sensibility. This was something he had dimly and imperfectly perceived in 1835, something he magically realized in 1850.

The voice of 1850 is vastly more authentic, the text we read more plainly free-standing. The difference is in part one of tone. The twenty-three-year-old author of "A Christmas Dinner" had been an apprentice, dutifully imitating, borrowing his tone from approved models. Not always convincingly, he had spoken as a man of the world. Urging readers not to brood upon reduced circumstances at Christmas time, he had instructed them in worldly wisdom: "There are few men who have lived long enough in the world, who cannot call up such thoughts any day in the year . . . " (*Sketches by Boz* 220). The thirty-eight-year-old author of "A Christmas Tree" felt no such need to look over his shoulder. His voice was entirely his own, his tone diverse, subtle, and capable of achieving the most extraordinary of effects through the lightest of touches.

"I have been looking on, this evening," the piece begins, plainly enough, "at a merry company of children assembled round that pretty German toy, a Christmas Tree." Queen Victoria made sure Christmas trees were a feature of the royal Christmas for Prince Albert's sake, but to the general public they were still a novelty. "It was brilliantly lighted by a multitude of little tapers," the narrative explains; "and everywhere sparkled and glittered with bright objects." We are given details: "there were fiddles and drums; there were tambourines, books, work-boxes, paint-boxes, sweetmeat-boxes, peep-show boxes, and all kinds of boxes; there were trinkets for the elder girls, far brighter than any grown-up gold and jewels . . . ." Some of the trinkets are transparent fictions: "there were real watches (with movable hands, at least, and an endless capacity of being wound up)." But that is no impediment to childish wonder: "as a pretty child, before me, delightedly whispered to another pretty child, her bosom friend, 'There was everything, and more'" (*Christmas Stories* 3–4).

Having contemplated a real tree and the effect it has upon children, once alone in his private quarters, the narrator is confronted with a visionary tree and the effect it has upon him:

> Straight, in the middle of the room, cramped in the freedom
> of its growth by no encircling walls or soon-reached ceiling, a
> shadowy tree arises; and, looking up into the dreamy brightness
> of its top – for I observe in this tree the singular property that it
> appears to grow downward towards the earth – I look into my
> youngest Christmas recollections! (4)

The tree discloses a whole series of visions, arranged like baubles on its branches, and, through them, the narrator – a projection of Dickens, let us agree, constructed for the purpose of this narrative – comes to an understanding of what it is that has made him.

Memories are evoked of Christmas gifts received in early childhood

– gifts of toys and books (see pp. 114–16 above).   The narrative
reconstructs for us the differing emotions inspired in children by such
gifts, and the differing degrees of readiness they show, with toys, to
accept illusion – sometimes displaced by an eagerness to inspect its
mechanisms. But we are not released from adult consciousness. There
is a balance that banishes mawkishness.   We find ourselves
remembering childish experiences, with neither sentimentality nor
condescension:

> O the wonderful Noah's Ark! It was not found seaworthy when
> put in a washing-tub, and the animals were crammed in at the
> roof, and needed to have their legs well shaken down before they
> could be got in, even there – and then, ten to one but they began
> to tumble out at the door, which was but imperfectly fastened
> with a wire latch – but what was *that* against it! Consider the
> noble fly, a size or two smaller than the elephant: the lady-bird,
> the butterfly – all triumphs of art! Consider the goose, whose
> feet were so small, and whose balance was so indifferent, that he
> usually tumbled forward, and knocked down all the animal
> creation.   Consider Noah and his family, like idiotic
> tobacco-stoppers; and how the leopard stuck to warm little
> fingers; and how the tails of the larger animals used gradually to
> resolve themselves into frayed bits of string! (8)

The passive voice and the imperative mood are just two of the means by
which Dickens frees readers from a fixed and limited viewpoint. Both
the innocence of the child and the self-consciousness of the adult are
made accessible to us. Mischievous phrase after mischievous phrase
demands a double response. "It was not found seaworthy" signals both
the gravity of the experimenting child and the jocularity of the
remembering adult.

   Mawkishness is also averted by inquiry into the terrors of childhood.
These, "A Christmas Tree" hints, open the way to the sadder
understanding of maturity. "When did that dreadful Mask first look at
me?" the narrator asks of one gift. "Who put it on, and why was I so
frightened that the sight of it is an era in my life?" Perhaps it was the
immobility, he speculates. "Perhaps that fixed and set change coming
over a real face, infused into my quickened heart some remote

suggestion and dread of the universal change that is to come on every face, and make it still?" (5). This touches upon a concern infiltrated into the text until, at the end, it becomes dominant.

The blending and balancing of mood is displayed also in memories of theater visits at Christmas time – conjured up as obliquely as everything else:

> And now, I see a wonderful row of little lights rise smoothly out of the ground, before a vast green curtain. Now, a bell rings – a magic bell, which still sounds in my ears unlike all other bells – and music plays, amidst a buzz of voices, and a fragrant smell of orange-peel and oil.

Melodramatic absurdity and low comedy, in the theatre, are seen for what they are, but nevertheless with affection. We are made to understand how such things can educate the sentiments of the young, and provide yardsticks, no less useful for being insufficiently reliable and subsequently supplanted:

> The devoted dog of Montargis avenges the death of his master, foully murdered in the Forest of Bondy; and a humorous Peasant with a red nose and a very little hat, whom I take from this hour forth to my bosom as a friend (I think he was a Waiter or an Hostler at a village Inn, but many years have passed since he and I have met), remarks that the sassigassity of that dog is indeed surprising; and evermore this jocular conceit will live in my remembrance fresh and unfading, overtopping all possible jokes, unto the end of time. Or now, I learn with bitter tears how poor Jane Shore, dressed all in white, and with her brown hair hanging down, went starving through the streets; or how George Barnwell killed the worthiest uncle that ever man had, and was afterwards so sorry for it that he ought to have been let off.[15]
> (10)

Language close to cliché, and the artlessness of this, prompt condescension, but the present tense and the effective enactment of a child's responses prompt a counterbalancing shame at our readiness to condescend. We are required to see and think as the child, to see and think as the remembering adult, and to synthesize the two processes.

Thoughts of stories such as these are succeeded by thoughts of
stories told in song by the Christmas waits:

> What images do I associate with the Christmas music as I see
> them set forth on the Christmas Tree? Known before all the
> others, keeping far apart from all the others, they gather round
> my little bed. An angel, speaking to a group of shepherds in a
> field; some travellers, with eyes uplifted, following a star; a baby
> in a manger; a child in a spacious temple, talking with grave
> men; a solemn figure, with a mild and beautiful face, raising a
> dead girl by the hand; again, near a city gate, calling back the
> son of a widow, on his bier, to life; a crowd of people looking
> through the opened roof of a chamber where he sits, and letting
> down a sick person on a bed, with ropes; the same, in a tempest,
> walking on the water to a ship; again, on a sea-shore, teaching a
> great multitude; again, with a child upon his knee, and other
> children round; again, restoring sight to the blind, speech to the
> dumb, hearing to the deaf, health to the sick, strength to the
> lame, knowledge to the ignorant; again, dying upon a Cross,
> watched by armed soldiers, a thick darkness coming on, the
> earth beginning to shake, and only one voice heard. "Forgive
> them, for they know not what they do!" (11)

The style is powerful, precisely because it does not particularize or
assign significance. Fragments of narrative are jumbled together almost
as a child might gather them, and in a language not far removed from a
child's.[16]   The sequence is moving because, although it seems to
progress towards something momentous, nothing is explained. It is left
to the adult reader to make sense of it all. And in doing so, we enact the
process of dawning understanding, the process of growing up and
absorbing such stories, without sacrificing the immediacy they first had
for us.

Thoughts of childhood lead to thoughts of schooling, and it is here
that Dickens inserts the fiction of the return home from boarding school
at Christmas time. He inserts it because of its metaphorical value:

> If I no more come home at Christmas time, there will be girls
> and boys (thank Heaven!) while the World lasts; and they do!
> Yonder they dance and play upon the branches of my Tree, God

bless them, merrily, and my heart dances and plays too!
And I *do* come home at Christmas. We all do, or we all should. We all come home, or ought to come home, for a short holiday – the longer, the better – from the great boarding-school, where we are for ever working at our arithmetical slates, to take, and give a rest. (12)

Dickens is conjuring up both mortality and origins, a combination of great power. Thackeray would achieve something similar, five years later in *The Newcomes*, in his description of the death of Colonel Newcome. The Colonel's last word is "Adsum!" "It was the word we used at school, when names were called; and lo, he, whose heart was as that of a little child, had answered to his name, and stood in the presence of The Master" (Thackeray, *Works* 3: 774). But Dickens conceals his art better. His tropes are as powerful as they are, because they seem so spontaneous, because they are made to grow, apparently without effort, out of the narrative. The fate of humankind could scarcely be more unassumingly touched upon: "If I no more come home at Christmas time . . . ." Comfort in the succession of generations weighs but lightly on the image of girls and boys ever coming home and playing. And few but Dickens would dare to relax a mood with the comic bathos we find in those words, "the great boarding-school, where we are for ever working at our arithmetical slates."

Towards the end of "A Christmas Tree," there is a long section devoted to ghost stories told around the Christmas fireside – stories, we see, which have helped to build up the narrator's sense of what Christmas is, and helped, more fundamentally, to shape his imagination. The complexity of mood and of point of view in this section is remarkable indeed. We are made to enjoy being taken in by such stories, we are made to enjoy scoffing at them, and we are made to acknowledge the ineluctable solemnity of their subject matter – death, its cruelty, its sadness, its mystery. These stories form a prelude to the mood of piety in which death, and the possibility of resurrection, are finally contemplated.

Amusement, it has to be said, predominates in our response to this section, thanks in part to the way Dickens deliberately overworks conventions of discourse. The first story, about the ghost of a beautiful young housekeeper, who killed herself after being betrayed by her master, is told in the first person plural and the present tense. This has the effect of making the narrative more immediate and, to begin with, poses no difficulty. It suggests the narrator is imagining himself a member of a festive group: "we drive up to a great house"; "we are telling Winter Stories" (12). It also amounts to an invitation: the reader too can imagine himself a member of the group. But this use of *we* becomes ever more strained and odd as the voice of a teller of an old tale begins to overlay that of the narrator: "We are a middle-aged nobleman, and we make a generous supper with our host and hostess and their guests . . . ." Reader resistance sets in as the convention is reduced to absurdity. "Our tongue cleaves to the roof of our mouth," we are told, "and we can't speak." " . . . it's all true," we are told; "and we said so, before we died (we are dead now) to many responsible people." A double vision is imposed on us. We accept and reject simultaneously. Fondness for such tales clashes with derision, and the use of *we*, at once inviting and repelling, mirrors the clash. The effect is deeply comic.

But, comedy notwithstanding, images of mortality linger: the stags refusing to drink from the pond in which the housekeeper drowned herself; that absurd but still arresting declaration, "we are dead now."

The narrator pokes fun at the limited repertoire of ghost stories:

> There is no end to the old houses, with resounding galleries, and dismal state-bed-chambers, and haunted wings shut up for many years, through which we may ramble, with an agreeable creeping up our back, and encounter any number of Ghosts, but (it is worthy of remark perhaps) reducible to a very few general types and classes; for, Ghosts have little originality, and "walk" in a beaten track. (13–14)

This is not as dismissive as it seems, though. More overworked conventions of discourse string together a catalogue of such stories, which we can understand either as a list of absurdities, or as cumulative substantiation. "Thus, it comes to pass," we read, "that a certain room in a certain old hall . . . has certain planks in the floor from which the blood *will not* be taken out." "Thus, in such another house there is a haunted door . . . ." "Or thus, it came to pass how Lady Mary went to pay a visit to a large wild house in the Scottish Highlands . . . " (14–15). A series of examples are introduced by the conjunction *or*. "Or, a friend of somebody's, whom most of us know, when he was a young man at college, had a particular friend . . . ." "Or, there was the daughter of the first occupier of the picturesque Elizabethan house, so famous in our neighbourhood." "Or, the uncle of my brother's wife was riding home on horseback, one mellow evening at sunset . . . " (15–16).

The repetition of *thus*, and of *or*, enacts a ploddingly systematic mode of judgment, no protection against gullibility, we see. It licenses our laughter at the all-too-familiar ghost-story motifs paraded before us. And yet, despite the laughter, there are moments of indisputable pathos. There is the beautiful seventeen-year-old girl, in the days of Elizabeth I, with a disturbing tale to tell her father:

> " . . . I met myself in the broad walk, and I was pale and gathering withered flowers, and I turned my head, and held them up!" And, that night, she died; and a picture of her story was begun, though never finished, and they say it is somewhere in the house to this day, with its face to the wall. (16)

Or there is the story of a boy killed by a cruel guardian, the sight of whose ghost was death to living boys:

> On the occasion of each child being taken ill, he came home in a heat, twelve hours before, and said, Oh, Mamma, he had been playing under a particular oak-tree, in a certain meadow, with a strange boy – a pretty, forlorn-looking boy, who was very timid, and made signs! From fatal experience, the parents came to know that this was the Orphan Boy, and that the course of that child whom he chose for his little playmate was surely run. (17)

However absurd and predictable these stories are, however much their conventions are picked out for mockery, they turn the reader's mind to death and bereavement.

So it is that readers reach the closing paragraphs of "A Christmas Tree," prepared for something solemn, but in a state of pleasurable emotional fatigue. They have been made to laugh, to shed tears, and to shiver, often all at the same time. They have explored beginnings and contemplated endings. Their hearts and minds have been vigorously exercised. They are vulnerable and suggestible.

Now it is that, with consummate skill and tremendous impact, Dickens brings to the fore a concern that the text has hitherto only glanced at, or veiled in comedy:

> A moment's pause, O vanishing tree, of which the lower boughs are dark to me as yet, and let me look once more! I know there are blank spaces on thy branches, where eyes that I have loved, have shone and smiled; from which they are departed.

The dead have played their part in making us what we are, and must be remembered too. But Christmas brings comfort for their loss, to the believer, certainly. High on the tree the narrator sees "the raiser of the dead girl, and the Widow's son." And now we understand. It is not just in pursuit of literary virtuosity that we have been made to see both as an adult and as a child. "If Age be hiding for me in the unseen portion of thy downward growth," the narrator asks of the tree, "O may I, with a grey head, turn a child's heart to that figure yet, and a child's trustfulness and confidence!" To see and understand as a child, we are urged, is a spiritual necessity. The narrative complexity of "A Christmas Tree" is vindicated.

In the last paragraph, delicate allusion and a sense of the magical combine to amalgamate contingent festive custom and fundamental religious doctrine with a grace that entails no sacrifice of power:

> Now, the tree is decorated with bright merriment, and song, and dance, and cheerfulness. And they are welcome. Innocent and welcome be they ever held, beneath the branches of the Christmas Tree, which cast no gloomy shadow! But, as it sinks into the ground, I hear a whisper going through the leaves. "This, in commemoration of the law of love and kindness, mercy and compassion. This, in remembrance of Me!" (18)

With unorthodox boldness, Dickens echoes the words of St. Luke's Gospel used to justify the sacrament of holy communion (22.19). But "A Christmas Tree" is about such fusion. Into it is packed everything which Christmas summons up, that goes into the making of an individual sensibility, from the lightest of childish fancies, to the deepest of adult convictions. That is why reading it amounts to such a profound emotional experience. It is about redemption, not just for the transgressor, not just for the disordered of mind, but for anyone prepared to celebrate Christmas. It is as powerful for the generous-minded unbeliever as it is for the devout, because Dickens places the final devotional affirmation in a setting of struggle to understand life's mysteries that anyone can respond to.

"A Christmas Tree" completes Dickens's exploration of the topic of Christmas. It was an exploration which had taught him much about what it is to be human, and how this might be expressed in his art. It was an exploration which had turned him into a writer capable of writing *Dombey and Son* and the great novels which follow it. Now there was an ever greater risk that he would repeat himself. He continued to write about the festival, but with diminishing frequency. Nothing remained for him to discover.

In December 1851, he issued the first "Extra Number for Christmas" of *Household Words.* Christmas itself is once again the theme. Most of the titles Dickens commissioned for it begin with the words, "What Christmas is . . . ." Harriet Martineau, for instance, contributed a piece called "What Christmas is in Country Places."   Theodore Buckley contributed "What Christmas is if you Outgrow it."   After he had assembled all contributions he had asked for, Dickens decided there was something lacking in the number. To supply it, he composed "a tender fancy that shall hit a great many people" (*Letters* 6: 509). The title he gave it is "What Christmas is, as we Grow Older."

This may be read as a summary of what Dickens had discovered through writing about Christmas, a statement of the understanding of Christmas which he had been constructing, and which he saw that readers were accepting. It is a skillful piece of writing, and there are deeply moving moments in it, but it is not powerful in the way the *Carol* is, *The Haunted Man* is, or "A Christmas Tree" is. It is powerful as an expression of religious conviction and of admirable sentiments, but it lacks the complexity of the great Christmas writings. It is not powerful as literature, that is to say. No sense of discovery is conveyed to readers. There is no struggle for redemption, little reconciliation of disparate points of view. Much depends upon the reader's acceptance of the religious doctrines it embodies.   There is a narrator – about as identifiable with Dickens himself as the narrator of "A Christmas Tree" is.   What he has to say is interesting and moving, but it is much less intricate and subtle than what we have become used to.   "A tender fancy" the piece may be, but it is deficient in the kind of inner drama that gives Dickens's best writing its vitality.

The narrator openly recommends the uninhibited emotional inclusiveness we have seen Dickens learning to appreciate from his study of Christmas.   "Welcome, everything!" readers are advised. "Welcome, alike what has been, and what never was, and what we hope may be, to your shelter underneath the holly, to your places round the Christmas fire, where what is sits open-hearted!"   "On this day," the narrator declares, "we shut out Nothing!" (*Christmas Stories* 21-22).

Unfulfilled dreams are to be welcomed, if for no more than the jolt they occasion when remembered: "What!   Did that Christmas never really come when we and the priceless pearl who was our young choice were received, after the happiest of totally impossible marriages, by the two united families previously at daggers-drawn on our account?"   And "do we really know, now, that we should probably have been miserable if we had won and worn the pearl, and that we are better without her?"

Unfulfilled dreams of fame rank with unfulfilled dreams of love (distinguishing the narrator for us from Dickens himself, who was famous):

> "That Christmas when we had recently achieved so much fame; when we had been carried in triumph somewhere, for doing something great and good; when we had won an honored and ennobled name, and arrived and were received at home in a shower of tears of joy; is it possible that *that* Christmas has not come yet?" (20).

Remembering our dreams makes us see how succeeding generations will be sustained by similar dreams: "we see how, when our graves are old, other hopes than ours are young, other hearts than ours are moved; how other ways are smoothed; how other happiness blooms, ripens, and decays – no, not decays, for other homes and other bands of children, not yet in being nor for ages yet to be, arise, and bloom and ripen to the end of all!" (21)

But the piece is at its most intense when Dickens turns to remembrance of the dead. This had more than usual resonance for him at the end of 1851. He was still grieving over the loss of his father, who had died in March, and of his baby daughter, Dora, who had died two weeks later. Grief at these losses, moreover, evidently made him mindful of others. It took little to remind him of the sudden death, in 1837, of his wife's younger sister, Mary Hogarth (see pp. 198–99 above). His sister, Fanny, moreover, had died only three years previously, in 1848 (see pp. 242–43 above). Family sadness at that loss had been deepened by the death, only four months later, of her crippled and sickly son, Henry. All of these losses, and more, are obliquely alluded to in "What Christmas is, as we Grow Older."

The narrator's determination to shut out "nothing" on Christmas Day is challenged by a "low voice": "Not the shadow of a vast City where the withered leaves are lying deep? . . . Not the shadow that darkens the whole globe? Not the shadow of the City of the Dead?" The reply is resolute:

> Not even that. Of all days in the year, we will turn our faces towards that City upon Christmas Day, and from its silent hosts bring those we loved, among us. City of the Dead, in the blessed name wherein we are gathered together at this time, and in the Presence that is here among us according to the promise, we will receive, and not dismiss, thy people who are dear to us!

The strange combination of rejoicing and mourning is compelling.

But we are soon being asked to accept very specific and questionable doctrines:

> Yes. We can look upon these children angels that alight, so solemnly, so beautifully among the living children by the fire, and can bear to think how they departed from us. Entertaining angels unawares, as the Patriarchs did, the playful children are unconscious of their guests; but we can see them – can see a radiant arm around one favourite neck, as if there were a tempting of that child away. Among the celestial figures there is one, a poor misshapen boy on earth, of a glorious beauty now, of whom his dying mother said it grieved her much to leave him here, alone, for so many years as it was likely would elapse

before he came to her – being such a little child. But he went
quickly, and was laid upon her breast, and in her hand she leads
him. (22)

Too much weight is being placed here upon the belief that when
children die they are turned into angels, have their physical
imperfections corrected, are reunited with those they love, and are
permitted to revisit the living in a spirit of loving kindness. We perceive
the narrator's deep need to believe all this. That is what makes the
intensity moving, and one of the things that makes passage as acceptable
as it is. The thought of how wonderful it would be if it were all true is
another that probably helps unbelievers overcome their reservations.
But there is a loss, here, of the tensions and complexities which make
"A Christmas Tree" so compelling. "What Christmas is, as we Grow
Older" is not as well constructed to withstand unbelief. It is more
exposed to the observation, "But none of this is true!"

The piece shows us, to be sure, how Dickens had moved on from the
self-defeating sentiment of "A Christmas Dinner": "Dwell not upon the
past; think not that one short year ago, the fair child now resolving into
dust, sat before you . . ." (*Sketches by Boz* 220). There is something
bracingly inclusive, as well as touching, in the determination expressed
in 1851: "Lost friend, lost child, lost parent, sister, brother, husband,
wife, we will not so discard you! You shall hold your cherished places
in our Christmas hearts, and by our Christmas fires; and in the season of
immortal hope, and on the birthday of immortal mercy, we will shut out
Nothing!" (*Christmas Stories* 23). But the inclusion is not dramatically
established in the piece itself. The close student of Dickens can see it as
a culmination of his long quest. The reader just of this piece is likely to
find in it too much affirmation, not enough enactment.

In "What Christmas is, as we Grow Older," Dickens defines "the
Christmas spirit" as "the spirit of active usefulness, perseverance,
cheerful discharge of duty, kindness, and forbearance" (21). These,
certainly, are the human qualities all of his Christmas writings, up to this
point, had sought to promote. But when we think of what he had
discovered through exploring the topic of Christmas, it amounts to a
remarkably tame summary. Dickens had in fact exhausted the vein. By
the early 1850s he was almost incapable of writing anything

uninteresting, but the great dramas that thoughts of Christmas had opened up for him were played out. Little was left for him but pious affirmation. Interesting pious affirmation, but pious affirmation for all that.

In 1854, Dickens changed his way of organizing the additional Christmas number of *Household Words*. Hitherto, readers had been invited to suppose only that they were being told stories around a Christmas fireside. Now Dickens devised a more inventive framework for the stories included. It was an overarching fiction of a kind which would characterize the special Christmas numbers right up until 1867.

The 1854 Christmas number was given a title of its own: "The Seven Poor Travellers." In inspiration, this was connected with Dickens's reawakening interest in the city of Rochester, haunt of the happiest period of his childhood, before his father's transfer from Chatham dockyard to the London headquarters of the Navy Pay Office. By 1854, Dickens was beginning to think of the city as more than a place to be treasured in memory only. The development of railways during the 1840s made day trips between London and Kent feasible. Dickens was visiting Rochester more often. Within two years he would acquire a home – Gad's Hill Place – just outside Rochester (Johnson 2: 869–70). This he would eventually make his main dwelling.

In Rochester High Street there stands to this day a sixteenth-century establishment named Watts's Charity after its founder. In 1947, the funds of the charity were diverted to meet twentieth-century needs, but an inscription on the street front still proclaims its original function. It offered "Lodging, Entertainment, and Four-pence each," to "Six poor Travellers" every night. This was Dickens's cue.

The unnamed principal narrator of the 1854 Christmas number finds himself in Rochester on Christmas Eve, discovers Watts's Charity, and resolves to give a Christmas Eve supper to the six poor travellers, making himself the seventh. After supper, they sit around the fire and tell stories. The principal narrator's introduction gives way to the story he tells himself. Both were written by Dickens. Six other stories follow, one for each traveller. Dickens primed the pump for three of them, but otherwise they were the work of George Augustus Sala,

Adelaide Anne Proctor, Wilkie Collins, and Eliza Lynn. Finally, the principal narrator – Dickens again – resumes. He tells of joining the poor travellers for coffee on Christmas morning, of their parting, and of his journey back to London, to celebrate with his own family.

It is a neatly crafted piece, ironic and relaxed in mood. For students of Dickens's Christmas writings, the relaxation is surprising. Comparing it to its predecessors, we cannot but detect a steep dip in intensity. The principal narrator prefigures the eponymous Uncommercial Traveller of the 1860s. He presents himself as an idle, sauntering fellow, observing and judging keenly. But he is reticent. We learn little of his circumstances, beyond the fact that he is "as poor as I hope to be" (*Christmas Stories* 55), and that he has a home in London with a bright fire and "brighter faces around it" (83). The only other information he offers is that he is related to the hero of the story he tells, one Richard Doubledick.

A few satirical darts are hurled in the course of the framing narrative. The narrator remarks, for instance, on the resemblance between the "odd little porches" of the minor canon's houses, near the cathedral, and old-fashioned pulpits. He fantasizes about one of the canons emerging to deliver "a little Christmas discourse about the poor Scholars of Rochester" (81). The allusion is to a scandal which had recently been exposed by the headmaster of Rochester Grammar School. The cathedral chapter, it seems, was misdirecting funds earmarked for the school (see Collins, "Dickens and the Whiston Case").

But the main emphasis of the story is upon the traditional Christmas virtues. The narrator sets an example. He is sociable, hospitable, and merry. The carrying of the feast down the High Street, from the narrator's inn where it is prepared, to the parlour of Watts's Charity, is described in loving and comic detail:

> As we passed along the High Street, Comet-like, we left a long tail of fragrance behind us which caused the public to stop, sniffing in wonder. We had previously left at the corner of the inn-yard a wall-eyed young man connected with the Fly department, and well accustomed to the sound of a railway whistle which Ben [the waiter] always carries in his pocket: whose instructions were, so soon as he should hear the whistle blown, to dash into the kitchen, seize the hot plum-pudding and

mince-pies, and speed with them to Watts's Charity, where they would be received (he was further instructed) by the sauce-female, who would be provided with brandy in a blue state of combustion.

The narrator delights in the quality and reception of this feast:

I never saw a finer turkey, finer beef, or greater prodigality of sauce and gravy; and my Travellers did wonderful justice to everything set before them. It made my heart rejoice to observe how their wind-and-frost hardened faces softened in the clatter of plates and knives and forks, and mellowed in the fire and supper heat. (63)

The surprising thing about all this, though, is how calm and impersonal it is, relatively speaking. Attention is switched back from narrative to ritual. Christmas customs are once again the focus. Private narratives are barely touched upon. The narrator reveals little of himself. He entertains strangers, whom he has never seen before, and will never see again (83). Old times play no part in the framing narrative. Readers are given no sense of change in relationships, change in human identity. Neither the narrator nor anyone else achieves the kind of redemption we witness in the *Carol* or *The Haunted Man*. There is no sense of Christmas as a key to understanding human destiny, such as we find in "A Christmas Tree."

The piece is a frame for seven private narratives, of course, but none of these has to do with Christmas. None features Christmas as a trigger for discovery. There is plenty of plangent emotion in them, to be sure. Dickens's own, "The Story of Richard Doubledick," is one of friendship, love, redemption, and forgiveness, extended over many years. But Christmas is not featured in it. Friendship, love, redemption, and forgiveness, on the other hand, are not featured in the framing narrative, which does dwell upon Christmas.

With "A Christmas Tree," I have argued, Dickens completed his exploration of the theme of Christmas – his exploration of what Christmas meant to him, what it might mean to anyone. After 1850, there was nothing left for him to discover in the subject. He could repeat himself. He could craft variations, some in their way powerful, on what it was he had come to recognize in it, but he could not break new ground or recover the excitement of doing so.

The framing narrative of "The Seven Poor Travellers," however, seems deliberately to hold back from the kind of passionate involvement with the theme that enabled Dickens to create his greatest works about Christmas. From the early 1850s, there were reasons for him to hold back. I shall explain what they were in the next chapter.

THE REMNANTS OF THE FEAST

After 1854, Christmas numbers of *Household Words* were devoted to stories for Christmas rather than stories about it. Dissension with the publishers, Bradbury and Evans, led to the winding up of the journal in 1859. It was succeeded by *All the Year Round*, but Christmas numbers followed the same pattern, until the last in 1867.

Many contributors were writers obscure in their own day, but some are still remembered today. They include Elizabeth Gaskell, Harriet Martineau, George Augustus Sala, Adelaide Anne Procter, Eliza Lynn Linton, Harriet Parr, Percy Fitzgerald, and Wilkie Collins. Together with Dickens they produced numbers that were were enormously popular. Some sold close to 300,000 copies (Forster bk. 8, ch. 5; Patten 301). That is scarcely surprising. They include such delights as "Mrs. Lirriper's Lodgings" and "Mrs. Lirriper's Legacy," Christmas numbers of *All the Year Round* in 1863 and 1864 respectively, featuring a shrewd but kind-hearted lodging-house keeper telling tales of her own life. Despite the disappearance of Christmas itself, the *"Carol* philosophy" was still in evidence. Stories by Dickens – and stories by some of his collaborators – certainly show the danger of suppressing emotion. They extol memory and forgiveness. They affirm the possibility of redemption.

But eventually, despite huge sales and critical recognition, Dickens began to find the process of assembling such collaborative fictions irksome. In 1868 he made the decision to discontinue publishing Christmas numbers. After 1867, he would write no more stories either for or about Christmas.

I have suggested that with the publication of "A Christmas Tree" in 1850 Dickens completed his exploration of the theme of Christmas. There was nothing new left for him to say about the subject. It is a thought which prompts speculation. Do we see the dwindling of a once powerful impulse in the absence of Christmas itself from Christmas stories he wrote after 1854, from the Christmas numbers he edited after 1854? Do we see yet further dwindling in his final discontinuation of Christmas numbers? Was he perhaps losing interest in Christmas? Was he aghast, even, at a monster he had created?

There was one obvious reason for a loss of enthusiasm in Dickens. The genre of Christmas writing that he had invented was proliferating, and beyond his control. He could no longer expect readers to see the Christmas numbers and their contents as unique in kind. Each year more and more inferior imitations were being published – Christmas books, Christmas stories, Christmas issues of periodicals. "Regularly as the year draws to a close," wrote E. S. Dallas in *The Times* of 5 December 1866, "we are inundated with a peculiar class of books which are supposed to be appropriate to the goodwill and joviality of the season. Most of these publications are quickly forgotten; and, indeed, are so full of display that they deserve no better fate."

Dallas exempted *All the Year Round* from his general censure, though. Its Christmas numbers were "the best of all, the liveliest, the longest-lived, and the most successful."[1]   They outshone the competition. But Dickens himself took little comfort from this.

It was not disenchantment with Christmas itself that motivated him, though. He stopped publishing Christmas numbers, it is clear, because of the disproportion he perceived between the work entailed and the result achieved. "I have invented so many of these Christmas Nos.," he told his sub-editor W. H. Wills in July 1868, "and they are so profoundly unsatisfactory after all with the introduced stories and their want of cohesion or originality, that I fear I am sick of the thing" (*Letters* 12: 159).

He was not sick of Christmas, however. Far from it. The traditions he personally observed, the parties he threw, right up to Christmas 1869 – his last – refute any such contention (see pp. 116–18 above). But, quite apart from his having gained all that he could from exploring the theme of Christmas, developments in his personal life during the 1850s made it advisable for him to withdraw from the role he had taken on as unofficial spokesman for the festival.

It is his marriage I have in mind. Dickens had married Catherine

Hogarth in 1836. After several years of discontent, he separated from her in 1858. For most of the twenty-two years, so the evidence suggests, it was a happy marriage, but it is difficult not to feel there was always something precarious about it. While it throve, certainly, it seems to have been sustained by love, but also by strength of will on his part, docile consent on hers. The process of estrangement, when it came, was painful for both of them, but the procedure for formalizing their parting was so mishandled by Dickens that his reputation was imperilled. He was famous. His fame and his success went hand in hand. A vast public was likely to take an interest in the events of his private life. The appearance of shabby behavior was something he could ill afford.

In 1830, at the age of eighteen, some years before he became famous, he had fallen in love with a young woman named Maria Beadnell.[2] She had tolerated his advances, but not his alone. He had endured her caprices until the relationship foundered unhappily in 1833. The following year he began to frequent the home of George Hogarth, a journalist colleague, his senior in age and professional standing. It was Hogarth's eldest daughter that he married in 1836.[3]

Dickens's attitude to Catherine, and to their marriage, seems substantially to have been shaped by an anxiety to avoid the unpredictability and lack of control he had endured during his previous experiment in love. He strove to mold Catherine into an ideal wife, their marriage into an ideal union. For both, he constructed mental models in advance, and to preserve those models he mustered all his resources of imagination and willpower.

There were dangers in this, clearly. Could he sustain his conflation of the ideal with the real? Much depended on Catherine's not changing – or not changing beyond certain limits. Much depended on his not changing his mind. Too much, as it proved, depended on these conditions. Events altered Catherine, as they do almost everyone. In 1851, soon after the birth of her ninth child, she succumbed to a nervous illness. No diagnosis of this has survived, but we know the treatment chosen. Dickens sent her to Malvern, for a water cure, and spent time there himself, to be with her. Her condition can scarcely have been improved, though, by the death of her baby, Dora, in London, while she was still in Malvern. It seems reasonable to suppose these events affected her permanently.

It was soon after this that Dickens began to show signs of dissatisfaction, focusing by degrees ever more precisely on his marriage. By 1854 he was telling Forster of the sense he sometimes had, "as of one happiness I have missed in life, and one friend and companion I have never made" (Forster, bk. 8, ch. 2).

Looks may have been part of the problem. Unsurprisingly, after bearing ten children – the last in 1852 – Catherine had changed in appearance, let alone character. She had been admired for her beauty, but in 1853 one observer described her as "a great fat lady – florid with arms thick as the leg of a Life Guard's man and as red as a beef sausage" (Schlicke 155). Dickens's fiction, particularly his early fiction, is full of pretty little women, wives or wives-to-be. Now there was no longer a pretty little woman in his ideal marriage, which he had constructed with the same kind of imaginative effort he put into his fiction. "The old days – the old days!" he lamented to Forster in 1856. "Shall I ever, I wonder, get the frame of mind back as it used to be then? Something of it perhaps – but never quite as it used to be. I find that the skeleton in my domestic closet is becoming a pretty big one" (Forster bk. 8. ch. 2).

To begin with, at any rate, there was nothing calculating in his change of heart. It took him by surprise, and was as much a blow to his sense of identity as it was to Catherine's contentment. When he looked into the mirror, he told Wilkie Collins in 1857, "my blankness is inconceivable – indescribable – my misery, amazing" (*Letters* 8: 423).

It was in that year, however, that he became acquainted with an attractive seventeen-year-old actress, Ellen Ternan.[4] Increasingly, after this, his reflections on his marriage seem a shade too pat. Soon he was telling Forster, "Poor Catherine and I are not made for each other, and there is no help for it. It is not only that she makes me uneasy and unhappy, but that I make her so too and much more so. She is exactly what you know, in the way of being amiable and complying; but we are strangely ill-assorted for the bond there is between us" (*Letters* 8: 430). Not long after the formal separation, for reasons unknown, Dickens declined to see Catherine any more, and evidently transferred his attentions entirely to Ellen. She acquired a series of homes, almost certainly with his assistance. There is evidence that he set up a trust fund for her (Ackroyd 994). They probably became lovers.

These are events which would have made it hard for Dickens, from the early 1850s onwards, to think of Christmas as he had previously. To put it no more strongly, he was in conflict with himself. In his own mind, and in the public's, he had established Christmas as the time above all for family joy, a time for reviewing moral identity, a time for reconciliation, recovery of past happiness, forgiveness, and redemption. And he had established himself, decked out in various disguises, as the festival's spokesman. The events of his life, however, were making him and other members of his family miserable. They were eroding his sense of identity, moral and otherwise, and making him doubt the possibility of reconciliation. At times, he saw happiness as something irrecoverable, forgiveness as something irrelevant. Redemption must have seemed the remotest of goals. His role as spokesman for Christmas was clearly being undermined. Little wonder that the framing narrative for the 1854 Christmas number of *Household Words* draws back from the contemplation of family and old times during the Christmas season.

It may have been guilt that kept Dickens from addressing the theme of Christmas after 1854 – guilt however deeply suppressed. He did not find it easy to admit wrong-doing, but late in life, there is evidence to suggest, he came near to apologizing for some of his actions. In the last conversation he had with his daughter Kate, it is reported, he regretted his "domestic mistake relative to Ellen Ternan" (Parker and Slater 7). He also expressed the wish, we are told, that he had been "a better father – a better man" (Storey 132–34).

From the date of the formal separation, however, he had a reason to avoid the theme of Christmas, whether or not he felt guilty. That reason was prudence.

No one, frankly, could call the manner in which he conducted the process of separation discreet or clean. With her usual docility, Catherine consented to his publishing an announcement about their parting. This appeared in *The Times* and other papers on 7 June 1858, in *Household Words* on 12 June. It reveals Dickens's indignation about rumours being circulated, but the nub of it is in this statement:

> Some domestic trouble of mine of long-standing, on which I will make no further remark than that it claims to be respected, as being of a sacredly private nature, has lately been brought to an arrangement, which involves no anger or ill-will of any kind, and the whole origin, progress and surrounding circumstances of which have been, throughout, within the knowledge of my children. It is amicably composed, and its details have now but to be forgotten by those concerned in it.

Announcements in the national press are an odd way to preserve respect for something of "a sacredly private nature," an odd way to promote merciful forgetfulness, but worse was to follow.

On 16 August, the *New York Tribune* published a letter about the separation that Dickens had sent to Arthur Smith, manager of the public readings he was by then giving. He had not wanted it released to the press, Dickens declared, but did not blame Smith for its appearance. Whatever the truth may be, whoever the intended readers were, the letter seems designed to damage Catherine's dignity. The initiative behind the separation was hers, it suggests, and Dickens had resisted for the children's sake. Allusion is made to the role of her sister, Georgina, in the Dickens household: "In the manly consideration toward Mrs. Dickens which I owe to my wife, I will merely remark of her that the peculiarity of her character has thrown all the children on some one else." Dickens also speaks of "a mental disorder under which [Catherine] sometimes labours" (*Letters* 8: 740–41). Nothing is even indirectly said of Ellen Ternan. The letter was published in England in the autumn, and excited not a little comment (Ackroyd 817–20).

Dickens might have been able to square writing about Christmas in the old way with his own conscience, after all this. He might even have told himself he could justify the kind of narrative voice with which we have become familiar – a voice claiming the right to rejoice in family affections at Christmas time, and to moralize about the values Christmas highlights. But he must surely have sensed that, in the circumstance, his continuing to write in this way would have startled some readers. He had always delighted in the adoration of the public. It was something he craved even more now, appearing as he did before it, reading his own works. Discretion about Christmas, and all that he had made it suggest, must have seemed advisable.

Paradoxically, though, the public readings enabled him partially to evade the need for discretion. To his great satisfaction, he found he was able to perform works about Christmas long accepted by the public, without provoking uncomfortable questions. He had begun giving public readings in 1853, for charity. They proved enormously successful and, eventually, enormously profitable. From the start, his version of *A Christmas Carol* had been a favorite, both with Dickens himself and with audiences. Mindful, doubtless, of the sensation caused in Forster's chambers in 1844 (see p. 226 above), he also put together a version of *The Chimes*, first performed as part of the series of readings for profit he embarked upon in the spring of 1858. Several of the Christmas stories were turned into readings too, for subsequent series, none, though, dwelling upon the theme of Christmas itself. The *Carol*, however, remained a general favorite throughout Dickens's long and lucrative public-reading career. It was the main item in his final farewell performance in 1870, five months before he died.

Dickens's reputation did not suffer in the long term. The success of the readings shows that the public was ready to overlook the complexities and failings of his private life. With the ever-popular *Carol* reading, moreover, he was able to reaffirm his commitment to the vision of Christmas he had so triumphantly constructed in 1843. But he must have seen the unwisdom of placing too great a strain on the public's tolerance. He must have seen the risk of writing new works casting himself once again as spokesman for the great family festival. Add to this his having taken his exploration of the theme as far as it could go, and it is not difficult to understand why he wrote no more about Christmas, as a topic to be explored for its own sake.

Those who suppose that he simply became weary with the festival, though, can point to a couple of pieces of evidence, arguably lending support to their case. Dickens explored the theme of Christmas no more. He wrote no more works, long or short, devoted to the festival. But he used Christmas settings for episodes in two of his later novels. One of them, *Great Expectations*, was published in weekly parts in *All the Year Round*, between December 1860 and August 1861. Six monthly parts of the other, *The Mystery of Edwin Drood*, appeared between April and September 1870, but Dickens had died in June, without having written the remaining six parts. In both novels, the Christmas scenes are predominantly cheerless.

This is no reflection of a change in Dickens's attitude towards the festival, however. A careful analysis of the Christmas episode in *Great Expectations* shows it to be a triumphant exploitation of the attitude evolved in the *Carol, The Haunted Man,* and "A Christmas Tree." No incontestable conclusion can be drawn from studying the episode in the incomplete *Edwin Drood,* but what we find in the fragment, what we know of Dickens's feelings about Christmas, and what we know of his art more generally, all point to his being in the process of constructing something very similar in that book too.

In both novels, to be sure, a dark and brooding mood prevails. In both, it is difficult not to note, marriage, thoughts of marriage, thoughts of coupling of any kind, yield more problems than they do solutions. The catastrophe of Miss Havisham's aborted marriage is a potent source of evil in *Great Expectations.* And the book presents us with a series of deficient marriages: those of Joe and Mrs. Joe, of Matthew and Belinda Pocket, of Bentley Drummle and Estella, of Magwitch and his common-law wife, Molly. The end of the novel, moreover, leaves us in no state of certainty about Pip and Estella.[5] *The Mystery of Edwin Drood* is full of the single and the widowed. Sexual desire, aversion, and indifference, all stir up trouble equally. But in *Great Expectations,* at any rate, although Christmas is not untouched by the prevailing darkness, although it offers no freedom from marital tension, it hints powerfully at something better.

The Christmas episode of *Great Expectations* is contained in chapters 4, 5, and 6. Chapter 4 appeared in the issue of *All the Year Round* published on 8 December 1860, chapter 5 in the issue of 15 December, and chapter 6 in the issue of 22 December, the last before Christmas Day. For all that he had stopped doing so in the special Christmas numbers, Dickens was writing about the festival itself once again, as its date approached. But he was writing about it differently. He was making use of Christmas instrumentally and allusively. There is no suggestion of the narrator – the novel's protagonist, Pip – setting up as a spokesman for the festival. Dickens avoided that. But he was not just obeying the dictates of prudence. He was discovering something new to do with Christmas, something to yield writing as powerful, touching, and funny as anything he ever produced.

Great Expectations is Dickens's masterpiece.[6]   Morally, it is extraordinarily complex.   Readings of it often lay emphasis upon authenticity and inauthenticity, sympathy and indifference, altruism and selfishness, or similar binaries.   There is plenty of inauthenticity, indifference, and selfishness, certainly, but the book does not hinge upon simple binaries.   A mark of its profundity is the way few of the moral judgments we find ourselves making about the central characters can be uncoupled from tricky qualifications.   This, to my mind, is the chief source of the book's greatness.   Pip goes wrong, yes.   But what chance does he have, tutored by Mrs. Joe and Uncle Pumblechook, deceived by Miss Havisham?   He has Joe, to be sure, but Joe is scarcely good at getting his point across.   Magwitch is a wrong-doer, yes.   But what chance did Magwitch have, cast adrift as a child, manipulated by a wrong-doer much worse?   He loves Pip, yes, but self-indulgently – to begin with at any rate.   How is Magwitch's wrong-doing to be disentangled from his capacity for love?   Much more could be said in this vein.

We can resolve these complexities, though, when we understand that the novel is about transgression and redemption. For Dickens, by 1860, this was a theme inextricably coupled to Christian teaching on the subject. We have seen how he reviewed his Christian commitment in 1846, in *The Life of Our Lord.* We have seen how his Christmas writings gradually became more explicitly Christian. It must have been that much more of a shock to him, therefore, when he found his own conduct less easy to reconcile than before, with Christian moral teaching. The turmoil and irregularity of his private life from the early 1850s onwards, I suggest, yielded different responses in his private life and in his art. In his private life, evidence suggests, it yielded frantic rationalization. In his art it yielded an ever deepening concern with redemption of the transgressor. It may be that *The Mystery of Edwin Drood* was designed to reconcile these responses, but that is an hypothesis beyond the scope of this study.

It is not necessary, it should be said, to share Dickens's religious faith in order to respond to *Great Expectations*. It is enough broadly to sympathise with the western understanding of human beings as imperfect creatures, prone to transgression, but capable of redemption through repentance. If you are reading these words, you will almost certainly be interested in the novel as a literary form, and will be aware of the extent to which this understanding underpins the form. Much will be missed in *Great Expectations*, however, by readers insufficiently alert to implications specifically Christian, and much will be missed in chapters 4, 5 and 6, by readers unaware of what Christmas means.

One of the principal structural motifs of *Great Expectations* is unmistakeably Christian. There is a pattern in it of transgression, of scourging, of forgiveness being asked for, and of forgiveness being granted. In chapter 35, Pip attends the funeral of his sister, Mrs. Joe. Head injuries received at the hand of an assailant, as yet unknown, had profoundly disabled her, and Pip finds himself softened towards her, despite her hard treatment of him during his childhood. The text generates a powerful sense of peace and forgiveness:

> And now the range of marshes lay clear before us, with the sails of the ships on the river growing out of it; and we went into the churchyard, close to the graves of my unknown parents, Philip Pirrip, late of this parish, and Also Georgiana, Wife of the Above. And there, my sister was laid quietly in the earth while the larks sang high above it, and the light wind strewed it with beautiful shadows of clouds and trees. (*Great Expectations* 250–51)

Biddy tells Pip his sister had emerged from a bad episode just before she died, uttering the name, "Joe." Joe had sat by her, and put her arms around his neck, and laid her head on his shoulder. "And so she presently said 'Joe' again, and once 'Pardon,' and once 'Pip.' And so she never lifted her head up any more, and it was just an hour later when we laid it down on her own bed, because we found she was gone" (252–53).

Look for it, and you will find this pattern of transgression, scourging and forgiveness repeated in the fates of Miss Havisham, Estella, Magwitch, and of course Pip himself. It is Pip who asks forgiveness for Magwitch, as he dies "humble and contrite." Echoing Luke 18.13, he prays, "Oh Lord, be merciful to him, a sinner!" (411). Having betrayed those who love him, Pip too is scourged: by burns incurred trying to save the life of Miss Havisham, by injuries at the hand of Orlick, his sister's assailant, and by a fever resulting from the accumulation of his troubles. All this brings him to ask forgiveness of Joe, whom he has neglected shamefully. It is granted. "O dear old Pip, old chap," Joe responds. "God knows as I forgive you, if I have anythink to forgive!" (428).

The Christmas chapters of *Great Expectations* suggest that forgiveness is something needed, something elusive, but, for all that, something cryptically promised. In them, the adult Pip, our narrator, relates the events of a Christmas Day during his childhood – probably round about the year 1803 we are encouraged to suppose (Paroissien 423–34). What I have already demonstrated makes it unsurprising that these chapters show us the family of a skilled artisan of that era, celebrating elaborately with others of like social standing. The boy Pip, however, does not enjoy the festivities. He is tormented by anxiety about a file and some "wittles" – provisions for the Christmas dinner – that he has been bullied into stealing for a convict at large on the nearby marshes. Because of this anxiety, and other afflictions, the occasion of the dinner is excruciating for Pip.

Chapter 4 begins with an account of his return home, early on Christmas morning, after a clandestine meeting with the convict, one of two escaped from the prison hulk on the river. The opening words filter the anxiety of Pip the child through the wit of Pip the adult: "I fully expected to find a Constable in the kitchen," we are told, "waiting to take me up." Great matters are touched on lightly here. The narrator's affectionately ironic remembrance of his troubled younger self is an indication of how the chapter is organized. And the chapter is an indication of how the book is organized. The chapter, the three chapters, the entire book, bring into confrontation two systems: one in which transgression merits only punishment; one in which transgression, whatever else it merits, may be followed by redemption.

Pip hides what he has been up to, by telling his sister he has been "down to hear the Carols" (*Great Expectations* 17). We now know this was no anachronism – no case of Dickens looking back from the vantage point of 1860, and misrepresenting Christmas customs early in the century. There is no departure from verisimilitude. Carols were indeed popular then. But we do perhaps need to remind ourselves what the chief burden was, of the carols people were singing. Judging by the frequency with which it appeared in broadside form, "A Virgin Most Pure" was among the most popular. It was first published in the seventeenth century, probably written in the sixteenth, and probably acquired its first stanza during the eighteenth (Bradley 10–11). This is how the stanza appears in the version collected by Davies Gilbert in 1822, more than likely from a contemporary broadside:

> A virgin most pure, as the prophets do tell,
> Hath brought forth a baby, as it hath befell,
> To be our Redeemer from death, hell and sin,
> Which Adam's transgression hath wrapped us in. (12)

Carols, as this stanza shows, reiterate the Christmas promise of redemption from a system in which transgression merits only punishment. This Christmas promise is latent throughout the three chapters, although it is more often invoked by blatant flouting than by honor done to it.

The prevailing bad temper of Pip's sister is mollified by his lie about carols. "You might ha' done worse," she snaps. And the adult narrator remembers his taking her at her word: "Not a doubt of that, I thought" (*Great Expectations* 18). But neither Pip nor his sister, it seems, are attentive to the promise of redemption in carols. They think of them only as an innocent diversion from the perpetual tendency towards transgression and its desert – punishment.

The young Pip, in fact, is fixated upon transgression and punishment. Why he is becomes clearer as the chapter unfolds. They substantially shape his home life. To get her husband and Pip out of the way of her Christmas preparations, Mrs. Joe sends them off to church. Remembering this prompts the narrator to expatiate on his sister's religious convictions and their application to his childish self:

> ... I think my sister must have had some general idea that I was a young offender whom an Accoucheur Policeman had taken up (on my birthday) and delivered over to her, to be dealt with according to the outraged majesty of the law. (19)

The midwife and the policeman are one, that is to say. To be born is to be culpable – or so Mrs. Joe supposes in Pip's case, at any rate. Could the meaning of Adam's transgression be more neatly encapsulated? The preposterous conflation is wonderfully funny, of course, but it joins Pip's expectation of a constable in the kitchen. It is another carefully planted reminder of the novel's theme. And it shows how the notion of redemption is alien to Pip's sister at this stage in her life. Looking at him, she can see only a proneness to do wrong, and to deserve punishment. Little wonder he feels about himself as he does.

The theme is embodied in the supremely comic account of the Christmas dinner itself. At the table, Pip joins Joe and Mrs. Joe; Mr. Wopsle, the parish clerk; Joe's relation, Uncle Pumblechook, a corn and seed merchant; and Mr. Hubble the wheelwright, accompanied by Mrs. Hubble.

The conversation turns to the moral shortcomings of children in general, Pip in particular. Mr. Wopsle's grace, before dinner, brings up the subject of gratitude:

> Mrs Hubble shook her head, and contemplating me with a mournful presentiment that I should come to no good, asked, "Why is it that the young are never grateful?" This moral mystery seemed too much for the company until Mr Hubble tersely solved it by saying, "Naterally wicious." Everybody then murmured "True!" and looked at me in a particularly unpleasant and personal manner.
>
> Joe's station and influence were something feebler (if possible) when there was company, than when there was none. But he always aided and comforted me when he could, in some way of his own, and he always did so at dinner-time by giving me gravy, if there were any. There being plenty of gravy to-day, Joe spooned into my plate, at this point, about half a pint. (21)

Up to now, in fact, Pip has displayed no ingratitude. The topic is just an excuse for adults to preen themselves on their superiority, and to float the idea that the young are "naterally wicious." Somewhere in the background, clearly, the notion of Adam's transgression is lurking. Gratitude, however, and lack of it, are to be Pip's undoing. He will lack proper gratitude towards those who deserve it, feel it in abundance towards those who do not. And he will find it difficult to disentangle gratitude from other emotions. There is irony, needless to say, in Joe alone disregarding the imputation of Adam's transgression. It is Joe who will endure Pip's basest ingratitude.

Talk eventually turns to the Christmas morning sermon, the subject of which, it is generally agreed, was ill-chosen. Inspired by the feast in front of him, Mr. Pumblechook proposes a better: "Look at Pork alone. There's a subject! If you want a subject, look at Pork!"

> "True, sir. Many a moral for the young," returned Mr Wopsle; and I knew he was going to lug me in, before he said it; "might be deduced from that text."
> ("You listen to this," said my sister to me, in a severe parenthesis.)
> Joe gave me some more gravy.

Such gestures are lost on Mr. Pumblechook, however, who admonishes Pip to be thankful. Had Pip been born a piglet, he would not have been

> " . . . enjoying himself with his elders and betters, and improving himself with their conversation, and rolling in the lap of luxury. Would he have been doing that? No, he wouldn't. And what would have been your destination?" turning on me again. "You would have been disposed of for so many shillings according to the market price of the article, and Dunstable the butcher would have come up to you as you lay in your straw, and he would have whipped you under his left arm, and with his right he would have tucked up his frock to get a pen-knife out of his waistcoat pocket, and he would have shed your blood and had your life. No bringing up by hand then. Not a bit of it!"
> Joe offered me more gravy, which I was afraid to take.
> (22–23)

This is Dickens's art at its best. Opposites are vigorously united. We are given a dazzlingly funny account of an utterly dismal experience. And it is profoundly suggestive. This Christmas cameo is a precisely calculated prelude to *Great Expectations*. It vividly dramatizes the conflict between a system of values dwelling upon moral error and unyielding doom, and a system of values in which love and compassion play the chief part. To be more specific, it dramatizes the conflict between an Old Testament and a New Testament dispensation.[7]

All but one of the adults are comfortable with a view of things attributable to a reading of the Old Testament characteristic of Calvinism at its harshest. They believe in original sin, but look for its signs in others, not in themselves. Pip's sister is a great advocate of punishment, and Mr. Pumblechook gloats at the thought of Pip suffering the fate of the piglet. But it is Christmas, the season of redemption, commemorating the historic moment when the Old Testament dispensation gave way to the New. And one adult at the table acts in the spirit of the New Testament dispensation – the meek and loving Joe, consoling with gravy.

Chapter 4 ends with the transgression about which Pip feels so guilty all but discovered. Mr. Pumblechook chokes on tar-water from the brandy bottle. Stealing brandy for the convict, Pip had improvised a way of remedying the deficiency. But everyone is distracted by the arrival of a party of soldiers searching for the convicts. One of them holds out a pair of handcuffs to Pip, with the words, "Here you are, look sharp, come on!" (25). Once again, Pip is reminded – and so are we – of punishment.

Chapter 5 encapsulates the Old Testament dispensation. It dwells intently upon guilt and punishment. Pip remains anxious about the stolen "wittles." Much is made of the handcuffs, which Joe, a blacksmith by profession, is commissioned to repair. The soldiers are brutally indifferent to their quarry, accommodating themselves comfortably to a harsh system. Even the convicts – Magwitch himself, we later learn, and Compeyson his betrayer – internalise the system, thinking and speaking in the terms it imposes. They are found on the marshes, fighting. "Mind!" Magwitch tells the soldiers; "*I* took him! *I* give him up to you! Mind that!" And Compeyson gasps, "He tried – he tried – to – murder me. Bear – bear witness" (30–31).

Fittingly, the chapter ends with a powerful image of human subjugation to an indifferent system. Magwitch is put into the boat which is to return him to the prison hulk:

No one seemed surprised to see him, or interested in seeing him, or glad to see him, or sorry to see him, or spoke a word, except that somebody in the boat growled as if to dogs, "Give way, you!" which was the signal for the dip of the oars. By the light of the torches, we saw the black Hulk lying out a little way from the mud of the shore, like a wicked Noah's ark. Cribbed and barred and moored by massive rusty chains, the prison-ship seemed in my young eyes to be ironed like the prisoners. We saw the boat go alongside, and we saw him taken up the side and disappear. Then, the ends of the torches were flung hissing into the water, and went out, as if it were all over with him. (34)

Unquestioning acceptance of an inflexible sequence of crime and punishment is subverted just three times in chapter 5. Watching Joe at work on the handcuffs in his forge, Pip finds himself out of sympathy with almost everyone else present. The fire, the hammering, the sparks, the flickering shadows, all seem to menace the fugitives, but "the pale afternoon outside," Pip relates, "almost seemed in my pitying young fancy to have turned pale on their account, poor wretches."

Later he discovers that Joe too is of his persuasion. They accompany the soldiers onto the marshes:

When we were all out in the raw air and were steadily moving towards our business, I treasonably whispered to Joe: "I hope, Joe, we shan't find them." And Joe whispered to me: "I'd give a shilling if they had cut and run, Pip." (28)

When the convicts are taken, Pip signals to Magwitch that he has not betrayed him. In return, "to prevent some persons laying under suspicion alonger me," Magwitch declares he stole the file and the "wittles" unaided (33). It is Joe again who is the voice of mercy and compassion. It is Joe who reminds us of the tradition of feeding those in want and misery at Christmas time. He forgives Magwitch for eating the festive pork pie:

"God knows you're welcome to it – so far as it was ever mine," returned Joe, with a saving remembrance of Mrs Joe. "We don't know what you have done, but we wouldn't have you starved to death for it, poor miserable fellow-creatur. – Would us, Pip?"

At this point, Pip is made to sense the suffering and moral complexity which his training has taken little account of. He had sensed these things earlier, when giving the provisions to the convict, and assuring him he had told no one. Now he senses them once more: "The something that I had noticed before, clicked in the man's throat again, and he turned his back" (34).

Chapter 6 completes the story of Pip's Christmas Day, by indicating what it is in the New Testament dispensation, that is important to believers and unbelievers alike. Neither the young, nor human beings in general, are "naterally wicious." For the most part, they are frail. It is the complexity of moral choice that makes transgression inevitable and forgiveness necessary. We are tested more severely by the need to choose between conflicting values, than by the need to choose between good and bad.

The adult narrator reflects upon the conflict of values his younger self was exposed to, after the adventure with the convicts. "My state of mind regarding the pilfering from which I had been so unexpectedly exonerated," he confesses, "did not impel me to frank disclosure; but I hope it had some dregs of good at the bottom of it" (34). He was untroubled at the thought of deceiving Mrs. Joe, he explains, but fearful of telling Joe what had really happened, and of forfeiting his love:

> I morbidly represented to myself that if Joe knew it, I never afterwards could see him at the fireside feeling his fair whisker, without thinking that he was meditating on it. That, if Joe knew it, I never afterwards could see him glance, however casually, at yesterday's meat or pudding when it came on to-day's table, without thinking that he was debating whether I had been in the pantry. That, if Joe knew it, and at any subsequent period of our joint domestic life remarked that his beer was flat or thick, the conviction that he suspected Tar in it, would bring a rush of blood to my face. In a word, I was too cowardly to do what I knew to be right, as I had been too cowardly to avoid doing what I knew to be wrong.

The humor itself is a kind of forgiveness – forgiveness extended by the older Pip, narrating his sad story, to his younger self, discovering the human moral condition and struggling with it; forgiveness detectable in the largeness of sympathy and accommodation of divergent views humor permits. The narrator's irony can at once blame the cowardice of his younger self, and mitigate it with a sense of proportion: "I had had no intercourse with the world at that time, and I imitated none of its many inhabitants who act in this manner. Quite an untaught genius, I made the discovery of the line of action for myself" (35).

The humor, though, is not used to hide other values to which Pip is exposed. Chapter 6 finishes with his being brought home by Joe, utterly fatigued, after the taking of the convicts. He soon finds once again that what is natural in him is likely to be deemed culpable. His sister deplores his sleepiness, and he is consigned to bed as "a slumberous offence to the company's eyesight" (36).

In the Christmas episode of *Great Expectations*, we are made to see the law as a merciless instrument – both the law of the land, and the moral law, as widely understood. This vision of the law, however, is countered, precisely and formally, by another. Some of Pip's confused instincts, and the steady example set by Joe, place before the reader what, in "A Christmas Tree," Dickens calls "the law of love and kindness, mercy and compassion."

Recognition of this law sanctifies Pip's memories of that far-off Christmas Day, however cheerless it might have been. The story is told in retrospect, remember, by the penitent adult Pip, and Christmas past does for him what it does for Scrooge in the *Carol*. He recollects unkindness at Christmas time, but kindness too. His redemption is confirmed by his recognition of the blessings conferred upon him that day, which he was unable to learn from at the time, but which he has learned from since. Once again, Dickens emphasizes the role of memory in moral growth. Looking back, Pip is able to see grace abounding in gravy abounding.

The Christmas episode in *The Mystery of Edwin Drood* is not merely cheerless. It is permeated by a sense of ending. Expectations are disappointed, relationships are destabilized, a loss is sustained. We witness misunderstanding, calumny, rivalry, persecution, fear, regret, and rage. The episode closes with a disappearance, a suspicion of violence, a suspicion indeed of murder.

It is contained in parts 3 and 4 of the novel, chapters 10 to 16. These tell of the decision by Edwin Drood and Rosa Bud neither to pledge themselves to each other at Christmas, as had been planned, nor indeed to marry at all, as their fathers, long dead, had hoped they would. The story of a complex relationship is continued, between Edwin and his uncle, John Jasper, choirmaster of Cloisterham Cathedral. Apparently devoted to Edwin, Jasper is in truth jealous of him, and sexually obsessed with Rosa. We learn of a Christmas Eve dinner, at which an attempt is made – uncertain in outcome – to settle a quarrel between Edwin and Neville Landless. We are told of Edwin's disappearance after the dinner, of Neville's apprehension on Christmas Day on suspicion of his murder, and of Edwin's watch and shirt-pin being recovered from a nearby weir.

The narrative voice relating all this is unlike the voice we hear in any other Dickens novel. Its accents are adjusted to the book's status as a mystery. The third-person narrator is often uneasy, sad, or wistful, often demonstratively reticent. He indicates that he is in possession of more information than he releases, some of it disturbing. He admits us to the minds of characters selectively. Little is hidden from us about the thoughts and feelings of Edwin, of the Rev. Septimus Crisparkle, Neville's tutor, or of Mr. Grewgious, Rosa's guardian. We are allowed to know much, but not all, about Neville's thoughts and feelings. Those of most other characters we have chiefly to infer from what they say and do. And what we infer is often troubling.

Throughout the book, we sense the narrator allowing his language to become colored by what it is that he is keeping back, what it is that accounts for his melancholy. In the Christmas episode, he makes evidence of seasonal festivities seem trifling, absurd, tawdry or dispiriting:

> Seasonable tokens are about. Red berries shine here and
> there in the lattices of Minor Canon Corner; Mr and Mrs Tope
> are daintily sticking sprigs of holly into the carvings and sconces
> of the Cathedral stalls, as if they were sticking them into the
> coat-buttonholes of the Dean and Chapter. Lavish profusion is
> in the shops: particularly in the articles of currants, raisins,
> spices, candied peel, and moist sugar. An unusual air of
> gallantry and dissipation is abroad; evinced in an immense

bunch of mistletoe hanging in the greengrocer's shop doorway, and a poor little Twelfth Cake, culminating in the figure of a Harlequin – such a very poor little Twelfth Cake, that one would rather call it a Twenty-fourth Cake or a Forty-eighth Cake – to be raffled for at the pastrycook's, terms one shilling per member. Public amusements are not wanting. The Wax-Work which made so deep an impression on the reflective mind of the Emperor of China is to be seen by particular desire during Christmas Week only, on the premises of the bankrupt livery-stablekeeper up the lane; and a new grand comic Christmas pantomime is to be produced at the Theatre: the latter heralded by the portrait of Signor Jacksonini the clown, saying "How do you do tomorrow?" quite as large as life, and almost as miserably. (*The Mystery of Edwin Drood* 143–44)

Readers are made to feel that Christmas is contaminated – in the narrator's mind at any rate – by a setting in which so much is amiss.

But this is instrumental. The book is not about Christmas. The bleak events of the Christmas episode, the forlorn language in which festivities are described, serve the story, and say nothing of Dickens's own feelings towards the festival. A better indication of these is probably to be found in the thoughts of Neville's sister, about his plan for a period of reflection during a walking tour to begin on Christmas Day: "She is inclined to pity him, poor fellow, for going away solitary on the great Christmas festival" (146–47).

This affirmative attitude towards the festival seems all the more appropriate, because we are left in little doubt that the contamination was to have been lifted. There is enough in what we have of *The Mystery of Edwin Drood* to indicate that, like *Great Expectations*, it was intended as a story about transgression and redemption. Had Dickens finished it, I submit, we should find the mood changed. The sense of ending would be replaced by a sense of new beginning. A vision of Christmas as it should not be would be succeeded by a vision of everything once again as it should be.

There is much in the book of transgression, much foreshadowing of redemption. The fate Dickens intended for Edwin has been furiously debated ever since it was first published, but a study of the development of his character indicates, by itself, that some sort of healing resolution was planned.[8]   It may have been the kind of resolution we find in tragedy. In that case, the completed novel would enable us to see Edwin as a fundamentally decent young man, spoiled by a tragic flaw or misled by a tragic error, and doomed because of that. But to my mind, it is more likely that Dickens planned the kind of resolution we find in a bildungsroman. In that case, the completed novel would enable us to see him as a young man who makes mistakes, but learns from them and survives, all the better for his ordeal. Either model would have yielded a healing resolution. The tragic model would have led to others learning from Edwin's fate, and setting things right. The bildungsroman model would have led to what indeed we see in the six parts of the novel we have: Edwin at first in need of a sentimental education, and then starting to acquire it. The six parts of the novel that Dickens failed to write would have revealed how he completes that education.

There is a dynamic in the presentation of Edwin's character, away from transgression towards redemption. He is "always kindly," we are told (149). He has an open and easy manner. But he has a fault: he is full of himself, and insensitive to the feelings of others. He patronizes his uncle, for instance: "What a dreadfully conscientious fellow you are, Jack!"; "Have you lost your tongue, Jack?"   And he speaks carelessly of Rosa without noticing Jasper's pain (13).

Yet he is not without self-knowledge, and can contemplate changing. Without going into particulars, Jasper confides his discontent to Edwin, whose response is frankly to pinpoint both his deficiency, and what mitigates it:

> "I am afraid I am but a shallow, surface kind of fellow, Jack, and that my headpiece is none of the best. But I needn't say I am young; and perhaps I shall not grow worse as I grow older. At all events, I hope I have something impressible within me, which feels – deeply feels – the disinterestedness of your painfully laying your inner self bare, as a warning to me." (16)

Mr. Grewgious's admonition about making "a plaything of a treasure" (113), and Rosa's encouragement, enable Edwin to play an equal part in resolving their difficult situation. They break off their engagement without recrimination, without loss of respect:

> This pure young feeling, the gentle and forbearing feeling of each towards the other, brought with it its reward in a softening light that seemed to shine on their position. The relations between them did not look wilful, or capricious, or a failure, in such a light; they became elevated into something more self-denying, honourable, affectionate, and true. (137)

But Edwin's sentimental education is incomplete. He remains insensitive to Jasper's torment. He is unconcerned about his quarrel with Neville, who is attracted to Rosa, resentful over Edwin's cavalier attitude towards her, and indignant at Edwin's disparagement of his Asian upbringing (71). Edwin has yet to learn to take responsibility for his mistakes, without help from the likes of Mr. Grewgious or Rosa. At the end of the sixth part, he has vanished, a transgressor unredeemed.

The text, however, unmistakably promises redemption of some sort, in terms positively religious. A page or so before the novel breaks off, we find this famous passage about the city of Cloisterham, in which so much of the action takes place:

> A brilliant morning shines on the old city. Its antiquities and ruins are surpassingly beautiful, with a lusty ivy gleaming in the sun, and the rich trees waving in the balmy air. Changes of glorious light from moving boughs, songs of birds, scents from gardens, woods, and fields – or, rather, from the one great garden of the whole cultivated island in its yielding time – penetrate into the Cathedral, subdue its earthy odour, and preach the Resurrection and the Life. The cold stone tombs of centuries ago grow warm; and flecks of brightness dart into the sternest marble corners of the building, fluttering there like wings. (255)

Whether or not we suppose Edwin was to survive and achieve personal redemption, this passage plainly foreshadows a new beginning – a setting right of what has been amiss. It calls upon us to see the cheerless Christmas of parts 3 and 4 as the kind of sign such a Christmas is so often in Dickens's works – a sign not of his own feelings about the festival, but of a need for change.

One episode in particular, in part 3, underlines continuity between Christmas as we see it in *Drood*, and Christmas as we see it in the early works. In chapter 12, a week before Christmas, Jasper joins Durdles on a midnight expedition into the cathedral buildings (122–31). Readers reach this point in the novel deeply suspicious of Jasper. They know him to be an opium addict who suffers from strange fits, and moments of savage passion. They are aware of his ambiguous relationship with Edwin, his predatory attitude towards Rosa. And they have seen him spreading calumnies about Neville. Durdles is a drunken, surly stonemason, who lives a solitary life, and is at odds with boys of the neighborhood. He is employed to maintain the fabric of the cathedral, to search out ancient graves, and to assist with modern interments. He keeps a stock of quicklime, and carves inscriptions on monuments.

The object of the expedition is mysterious. The hour, and Cloisterham misgivings about ghosts, ensure that the two men are alone. They visit the crypt of the cathedral, where Durdles points to suspected cavities, housing "old 'uns" he proposes to disinter. He is unmoved by thoughts of their ghosts appearing but, emboldened perhaps by the contents of a wicker bottle supplied by Jasper, asks the choirmaster whether he thinks there might be such a thing as ghostly sounds:

> " . . . Now I'll tell you, Mr Jarsper. Wait a bit till I put the bottle right." Here the cork is evidently taken out again, and replaced again. "There! *Now* it's right! This time last year, only a few days later, I happened to have been doing what was correct by the season, in the way of giving it the welcome it had a right to expect, when them town-boys set on me at their worst. At length I gave 'em the slip, and turned in here. And here I fell asleep. And what woke me? The ghost of a cry. The ghost of one terrific shriek, which shriek was followed by the ghost of the howl of a dog: a long, dismal, woeful howl, such as a dog gives when a person's dead. That was *my* last Christmas Eve." (126)

They climb the tower and descend it again, Durdles refreshing himself repeatedly from the bottle. Overcome by its contents, he takes a nap once they have returned to the crypt. Half waking, half dreaming, he senses his companion wandering about the crypt, and briefly relieving him of its key. It is not until the cathedral clock strikes two in the morning that Jasper rouses him, and they both return home.

Where have we seen something like this before? Where have we seen a church functionary – drunken, surly, friendless, unsuperstitious –

visit a place of burial at night, just before Christmas? Where have we seen such a functionary meet with the uncanny, thanks perhaps to the contents of a wicker bottle? Where but in *Pickwick Papers*? The story of Gabriel Grub is being recycled here.

There are crucial differences of course, as well as incidental ones. The expedition of Jasper and Durdles is no Gothic interlude, but an integral part of the story.   Durdles's experience of the previous Christmas Eve was no bizarre vision of goblins. His half-waking dream in the crypt is not of the supernatural at all, but only of Jasper prowling about.

However, it is a final instance, in Dickens's works, of the superabundance of the miraculous at Christmas time, made discreetly compatible with a story otherwise naturalistic. By mysterious means, things that should be known are made known – to Durdles obscurely, to readers somewhat less obscurely. We see that Durdles's Christmas Eve experience was a premonition. Searching for meaning, both at this stage in our reading and retrospectively, we are apt to interpret it as a pointer to events of the Christmas Eve soon to come, a forewarning of violence and despair. Durdles's half-waking dream, during the joint expedition, alerts us to Jasper's sinister interest in the crypt and its secrets. Christmas is working its old magic, divulging truth against the grain of nature.

The Mystery of Edwin Drood does not call to mind the sacred significance of Christmas as *Great Expectations* does, but it does evoke at least one tradition associated with the festival, of which Dickens had previously made much. It is not enough to dwell upon surface effect in either novel. Each features a cheerless Christmas, but Scrooge, we learn, has endured Christmases at least as cheerless. It is necessary to ask, in each case, what the cheerless Christmas means.

8

"THE INVENTION OF CHRISTMAS"

Dickens, then, was not the inventor of Christmas – or of the modern Christmas, or of "Christmas as we celebrate it today." He was a writer who used his love of a popular but unfashionable festival to shape texts which helped to make it fashionable once again. They are texts which have delighted generation after generation; some of them are among his finest achievements; and writing them had a profound effect on the development of his craft. That is what is important about Dickens and Christmas.

We know why the supposition that he invented Christmas arose. There is evidence to suggest it, which convinced Dickens scholars. But there is plenty of evidence to the contrary, and plenty of evidence that Dickens himself supposed nothing of the kind. The puzzling question is not why such a supposition was entertained, but why it was entertained by so many, for so long, with so little dissent. Why, we need to ask, did otherwise meticulous scholars adhere to it? The wish to be thought waggish, of course, moves scholars no less than journalists, but we allow ourselves to hope that scholars are better able to resist such temptation when it impedes judgment.

The declaration that Dickens invented Christmas, I submit, cast the spell it did because it belongs to a class of statements which people wanted to hear, wanted to agree with, and wanted to repeat. It was adopted as a slogan fit to demonstrate a twentieth-century sensibility.

An encapsulation of that sensibility can be found in Hemingway's novel, *A Farewell to Arms* (1929). Just as Hemingway himself had been, Frederic Henry, the protagonist and narrator, is a volunteer ambulance driver on the Italian front during the First World War. He articulates an attitude, widespread among those who served in the war, towards a kind of discourse ill-adapted to the realities he and his comrades face:

> I was always embarrassed by the words sacred, glorious, and sacrifice and the expression in vain. We had heard them, sometimes standing in the rain almost out of earshot, so that only the shouted words came through, and had read them, on proclamations that were slapped up by billposters over other proclamations, now for a long time, and I had seen nothing sacred, and the things that were glorious had no glory and the sacrifices were like the stockyards at Chicago if nothing was done with the meat except to bury it. There were many words that you could not stand to hear and finally only the names of places had dignity. Certain numbers were the same way and certain dates and these with the names of the places were all you could say and have them mean anything. Abstract words such as glory, honour, courage, or hallow were obscene beside the concrete names of villages, the numbers of roads, the names of rivers, the numbers of regiments and the dates. (ch. 27)

This was not an attitude born in 1929, or indeed during the First World War, but it was the war which made it the default setting for twentieth-century thinkers.

The twentieth-century sensibility arranged itself around doubt. Influential thinkers, including some who finally submitted to belief, were transfixed by the difficulty of discerning order and meaning in a world which seemed ever more complex and harsh, and were convinced that delusions of the past are perpetuated in language. This they saw as opaque, not transparent. It interposes itself between reality and perception, many felt. Language was to be at once warily respected, and distrusted. When it seems to describe, it in fact persuades. When it seems disinterested, it in fact promotes an interest. Questions of value, it was generally agreed, cannot be decided apart from questions of language.

We can see this sensibility expressed in diverse forms: in the poetry of T. S. Eliot, in the philosophy of Wittgenstein, in the ethics of the logical positivists, in the principles of the New Critics, in innumerable dramas of the absurd, and in the cogitations of French literary theorists.

Some thinkers agreed with Frederic Henry, that the most important task was to isolate and reject the delusive elements of language, to cleanse perception by stringent economy of discourse.   Others believed the delusion to be radical and comprehensive, capable of exposure only through forensic deconstruction of discourse. Retrospectively, the shift of attention marked by this concentration upon language has been called the "linguistic turn."

Thanks to this shift, confidence in empiricism waned. What once had been seen as interpretation of objective fact began to be seen as intellectual construction – unverifiable, always at a remove from objective fact. The idea of reality itself, late in the century, began to give way before ideas of social and cultural construction.

Nowhere was the change in sensibility more noticeable than in the way literature was studied. Interest in the way texts affect perception began to rival interest in the way perception affects texts. What writers impose on their times – and on posterity – became a subject of inquiry, every bit as much as what their times impose on writers. Roland Barthes followed innumerable British and American critics in his reluctance to consider the personal experience traditionally looked to for explanation of an author's work. The author does not exist prior to or outside of language, he argued in "The Death of the Author." It is writing which makes the author. The author becomes an object worthy of consideration, that is to say, only in so far as he precipitates a change in understanding, objectified in writing.

It is not difficult to see how such a shift in sensibility made the notion of invention fashionable. By the 1930s, it had become a sign of intellectual boldness to dwell upon changes of understanding precipitated by writing, and to speak of invention in connection with intangibles once thought to be scarcely affected by human agency. It is a fashion that has yielded a surprising list of phenomena declared to have been invented.

On it we find romantic love, childhood, race, masculinity, femininity, personal identity, Britain, America, the nation state itself, tradition itself, history itself. Studies expanding the list, and affirming what is already on it, are still appearing in the twenty-first century at an ever faster rate. The year 2003 alone saw the publication both of Gore

Vidal's *Inventing a Nation*, and of Ian Buruma's *Inventing Japan*, about the roots of American and Japanese national identity respectively. Little wonder, then, that F. G. Kitton's modest proposal about Dickens and Christmas – a hundred years earlier, and well ahead of its time – so caught the imagination of succeeding generations. Little wonder that so many Dickens scholars, during the twentieth century, were captivated by it.

It is wrong to claim that Dickens invented Christmas, or to subscribe to some qualified variant of the proposition, but for most of the twentieth century it was harmless. Dickens profoundly affected the way people thought and felt about the festival. Discriminating scholars were able to overlook the claim as innocent hyperbole. Current thinking, however, is insisting upon it. It is being absorbed into a reductive understanding of literature which needs to be challenged.

This understanding is especially damaging to Victorian studies. Judgment is being coarsened by it. Despite the sound work of many scholars in the field, the condescension towards the Victorians which infected twentieth-century thought is hardening into dogma. A subtext repeatedly manifests itself in much that is written on the subject: "God, I thank thee, that I am not as the Victorians were." There is a growing determination to see the Victorians only as a rum lot, blinkered and venal. Lytton Strachey's *Eminent Victorians* (1918) was a *jeu d'esprit*. Now his way of thinking – less his wit – is earnestly displayed as a banner proclaiming intellectual allegiance.

The Victorians were a rum lot. Every generation is, more or less. The twentieth century cannot be supposed exceptional. It blithely fashioned its own blinkers, and pursued its own sordid objectives. But in highlighting the failings of the Victorians, we are in danger of forgetting how astonishingly vital and creative they were. The old-fashioned way of seeing the era, as an age of innovation and reform, is no more partial than the fashionable way of seeing it, as an age of power-grabbing and oppression. Victorian modes of thinking and feeling deserve more than derisive denunciation. This is something that needs to be reasserted now, particularly within the academy.

Students of Dickens and Christmas, to be sure, were for a long time spared the more abrasive kind of derision. If inventing Christmas was held up as an example of Victorian rumness, it was also generally viewed as an innocent achievement, even as a commendable one – the imposition upon readers of a vision encouraging criticism of institutions and action in favor of the dispossessed. Now, however, there is a growing tendency to find the criticism too shallow, and the action proposed inadequate. There is a growing tendency to attribute the entire vision to a hidden agenda which must be deplored.

This is misguided and unjust. The charges are not inconceivable, of course. Dickens was not infallible. What is wrong is the reductive mindset that so predictably yields such charges. We are now confronted with an attitude – not just to Dickens, not just to the Victorians, but to all literature of the past – that is not merely pharisaical: it is Philistine as well. Literature is being studied so that what is found in it may be denounced. "Invention" is deemed a smokescreen. Readers are urged not to be duped. Delight in literature is reduced to a shameful eagerness to be duped. And it is the Victorians who are getting the worst treatment.

This would not be so bad were there a sound intellectual foundation for it, but there is not. The history of literature, it is argued, is a history of powerful groups imposing their views on others less powerful, through the invention of master narratives. This understanding is justified – when it is justified at all – by reference to what is usually called postmodern literary theory, although late modern literary theory is the more accurate term. It is unmistakably a product of the twentieth-century sensibility, and contributes little more to it than an appetite for sophistry.

The writer, according to such theory, is not a creature inhabiting a distinct world, recoverable through scholarship and the exercise of the imagination. He is the creator of his own world, or a collaborator in the creation of a world, beyond which it is scarcely possible to penetrate.

All such theory hinges upon an epistemology attributed to the Swiss linguist Ferdinand de Saussure (1857–1913). I say attributed, because Saussure's *Course in General Linguistics* (1916), from which the epistemology is deduced, was compiled posthumously from students' lecture notes. There are doubts about whether the epistemology can be fairly deduced from that, let alone from what Saussure himself might have said.

There is no dispute, however, about his central doctrines. He argued that language is constructed from signs. Signs are arbitrary, he declared: there is no necessary connection between word and thing, name and object. Language, he taught, is a system of differences, socially produced and governed by convention alone.

This looks like a useful rule of thumb for linguistics, although "governed by convention alone" is a phrase that calls out for closer scrutiny. However, when Saussure's doctrines are understood as a formal epistemology, and when that epistemology is adopted as a tool in the study of literature, their inadequacy to these tasks becomes apparent. Perception is a topic which has always excited philosophical debate. No sound conclusion to it is offered by Saussure. Language may be a system of differences, socially produced. Supposing that may lead us to see perception itself in the same way. But it does not follow that either is governed by convention alone. That is a notion smuggled in. It would be possible to argue that the system is governed partly by convention – even substantially by convention – but there are no grounds for supposing it governed by convention alone.

Jorge Luis Borges was as keenly aware of the "linguistic turn" as any postmodern theorist, but much wittier. The inhabitants of Borges's imaginary planet Tlön, readers may remember, are congenitally idealist. Because of this, their conjectural *Ursprache* is deemed to have contained no nouns. It lacked words, scholars suppose, for a sentence like "The moon rose above the river." Speakers had to say something equivalent to "Upward behind the on-streaming it mooned" (*Labyrinths* 8). Borges wrote "Tlön, Uqbar, Orbis Tertius" at the end of the 1930s. He called the postmodernist bluff with his elegant *reductio ad absurdum*, more than twenty years before there were any postmodernists to theorize.

However much language shapes perception, Borges realised, it has to be useful. It has to work. The system of differences has to support practical discrimination and decision-making. The Inuit have more words for snow than the rest of us, not just because of some arbitrary convention, but because they need them. Those who doubt this should be obliged to construct a new language, eliminating whatever represents stuff they do not care for in experience – eliminating nouns, for instance, out of philosophical distaste for what nouns imply.

The fact is, we cannot dispense with the notion of reality as something distinct from its representation in language. The Saussure epistemology, such as it is, raises too many questions. How does it account for the infant's learning of his mother tongue? How does it account for the evolution of language among *Homo sapiens*, once without it? What account can it provide of perception in species without language – perception in animals?

When we recognize how imprecise and questionable postmodern epistemology is, we can get the fashion for finding "invention" in texts into proportion. We can speak once again of influence, as well as intertextuality. We can appreciate once more that stab of recognition which makes a generation favor a new mode of writing over an old. We can see how often it arises out of a sense of fit between writing and what lies beyond writing.

Doubt is currently being expressed about the survival of literary history in defiance of postmodern epistemology. My doubts are about the survival of postmodern epistemology in defiance of literary history. Postmodern epistemology will be forgotten, I predict, not only because of its defects, but also because literary history reveals more. One writer on Dickens, some years ago, commended Philip Collins for "doing the donkey work" in his study of crime in Dickens's books, but reproached him for being "very undertheorised." The donkey work of literary history, I submit, will not only outlast the muddled thinking of postmodern theorists. By providing examples of unmuddled thinking, it will hasten its demise.

My primary purpose in this book has been to correct error in what has been said about Dickens and Christmas – to show how his interest in the festival grew out of fascination with a popular tradition, to evaluate his Christmas writings as a product of that fascination, and to assess the effect of composing them upon his career. My secondary purpose, not entirely distinct from the first, has been to demonstrate the value of donkey work – to show what study of the inconsequential data of history and biography can reveal about literature.

It reveals what ought to be revealed, I believe. If I have confirmed your conviction, reader, that it does, or if I have persuaded you that it does, or if I have aroused in you a suspicion, however slight, that it does, then I have not written this book in vain. And I can allow myself to feel you have not read it in vain.

NOTES

Preface (pp. v–viii)

[1] Formerly known as the Dickens House Museum, renamed in 2003.

Chapter One (pp. 1–20)

[1] Wong does not mention this, but I have seen it for myself in Singapore.

[2] Hathorn (335) is among those who question the origin of tragedy in Dionysiac festivals. He speculates about an origin in mourning ceremonies, or at Panhellenic festivals.

[3] Doctrine tends to be posterior to ritual. Durkheim defines a cult as "a system of diverse rites, festivals and ceremonies which all have this characteristic, that they reappear periodically" (Durkheim 63).

[4] Within two months of the publication of *A Christmas Carol*, in December 1843, at least eight productions of it had been staged in London (Bolton 234).

Chapter Two (pp. 21–54)

[1] I speak of Christmas in England. During Dickens's lifetime, Great Britain consisted of England, Wales, Scotland, and all of Ireland. For the purposes of this book, however, it is the English Christmas that is important. It is the English Christmas to which Dickens responded, the English Christmas which he changed, however much his writings subsequently affected Christmas celebrations of other communities and other nations. Needless to say, there are Christmas customs in Ireland, Wales, and Scotland unique to those nations, as well as ones they share with the English. The Irish custom of whitewashing the house, the Welsh Plygain, the Scottish Cailleach, are all topics worth studying, but not here.

[2]   Not all authorities agree with the claim that Augustine converted King Aethelberht himself. See Kirby 31–37.

[3]   Pedantically speaking, it was 3 January 1624. Until the calendar reform of 1752, the New Year began on Lady Day, 25 March.

[4]   Sandys transcribes some characteristic entries (Sandys ci).

[5]   Sandys declares this to be from Barnabe Googe's 1570 translation of Thomas Naogorg's *Popish Kingdome*. The book is very rare, and I have not seen a copy.

[6]   Pimlott does not include the last two lines which, together with the rest, were quoted in the London *Sunday Telegraph* of 18 December 1994. I have not managed to trace the original source.

Chapter Three (pp. 55–108)

[1]   Quoted from Phelips family papers at the Somerset Record Office, Taunton. I am indebted to Barbara Powlesland for this information.

[2]   Instances of this, remembered from her childhood, are recorded by Mrs. Archibald Campbell Swinton, born Georgiana Caroline Sitwell (1824), daughter of Sir George and Lady Sitwell (Sitwell 4). I am indebted to Sir Reresby Sitwell for drawing my attention to her memoirs.

[3]   In the parish of Kingston-on-Thames, Surrey, for example, the custom of decorating the church at Christmas was not resumed until 1857 (Cowie 67).

[4]   For information about the Tempest family at Broughton Hall, I am indebted to Henry Tempest.

[5]   For information about the Digby family at Sherborne, I am indebted to Anne Smith, archivist of the Sherborne Castle Estates.

[6]   See British Library Add Mss 40663, f.43 (7 January 1774) and f.156 (10 January 1788). I am indebted to Rosemary Baird, Curator of the Goodwood Collections, for drawing my attention to these letters.

[7]   The social customs of the *ton* are nowhere better shown than in the life of Georgiana, Duchess of Devonshire (1757–1806), by Amanda Foreman (passim).

[8]   Bodleian Library Broadside Ballads. 4o Rawl. 566(144).

[9]   The first recorded publication of this poem was as a prologue to *Round about our Coal Fire* (c. 1730). I do not know whether poorer readers would have been able to afford this book (see Watt 42–44). In style, sentiment, and subject matter, however, the poem differs markedly from the main body of the text. I treat it as a distinct composition, therefore, by a distinct author, writing for a select audience.

[10]   I am indebted to Lord Neidpath for this information.

[11]   I am indebted to Nick Ralls of the National Trust for this information.

[12]   I am grateful to him for answering my inquiries on the topic.

[13]   For this information I am indebted to Alison McCann of the West Sussex Record Office.

[14]   Bodleian Library Broadside Ballads.   Harding B 17(52a).   The broadside is known to have been printed between 1819 and 1844. The line, "God save great George our King," makes it reasonable to suppose it was written before the death of George IV in 1830.

[15]   Christmas Day, that is, when it would have fallen had Britain adhered to the Julian calendar, and not exchanged it for the Gregorian in 1752.

[16]   For information about Pepys not to be found in the diary itself, I have relied upon Tomalin 1–269.

[17]   According to the Julian calendar then still in use, these were the Twelfth Nights of, respectively, 1662, 1664, and 1665. Twelfth Night customs such as Pepys describes persisted at least until the early nineteenth century (Hone 1: 47-53).

[18]   Bodleian Library Broadside Ballads. Harding B 25(375a).

[19]   Attributed by the *Oxford English Dictionary* (1971) to the naturalist, Edward Jesse (1780–1868).

[20]   Republished separately in *Old Christmas.*

[21]   Dickens suggests such intentions were realized after a fashion. In *The Chimes* (1844), Sir Joseph Bowley is an admirer of "the good old times." On New Year's Day he entertains at Bowley Hall. During "a great dinner in the Great Hall," poor tenants, who have been fed "in another Hall first," are brought in to hear his speech (*Christmas Books* 145–46). Sir Joseph is himself Neo-Gothic, and so presumably is his great hall.

[22]   My chief source for data about the American Christmas has been the web version of DeSimone.

[23]   I have relied upon the text of this poem, and upon the critical apparatus, supplied by the University of Toronto Representative Poetry On-line website.

[24]   In "Ceremony upon Candlemas Eve" (Herrick 297).

[25]   To trawl for early sources referring to this custom, I made use of the admirable email bulletin board, the Dickens List, operated by Patrick McCarthy of the University of California, Santa Barbara. Many subscribers came up with suggestions. Particularly useful ones came from Robert P. Davis, Marylu Hill, Eve M. Lynch, and Deborah A. Thomas.

[26]   See Chas. T. Tallent-Bateman, "The 'Forget-Me-Not'"; and Glenn Dibert-Himes, "Early Nineteenth-Century Gift Books and Annuals: Bibliography."

[27]   Hood was also the author of a poem, "The Pauper's Christmas Carol," published in the 1843 Christmas number of *Punch*, three days before Dickens's *Christmas Carol* was published.

Chapter Four (pp. 109–54)

[1]   There are exceptions. Prominent among them is Michael Slater. See his introduction to *A Christmas Carol and Other Christmas Writings*.

[2]   My sources for information about Dickens's paternal grandparents are Johnson 1: 5–6; Kaplan 20; MacKenzie 4-5; Schlicke 169; and advice given me by Michael Allen (see note 3 below).

[3]   My information on this subject comes from *Barthomley*, a book about the parish of which Crewe formed a part, published privately in 1856 by the author, Edward Hinchliffe, a native of the parish, and rector there for fourteen years. Michael Allen, who is writing a history of the Crewe family, generously drew my attention to this source.

[4]   The phrase is Hinchliffe's (Hinchliffe 307).

[5]   Charles Fawcett, Hinchliffe explains, a member of Charles Stanton's touring company, which played a circuit including Newcastle-under-Lyme, Nantwich, Ludlow, and Bridgenorth (Hinchliffe 308).

[6]   "Drury" is shorthand for the Theatre Royal, Drury Lane.   The dramatization of *Barnaby Rudge* alluded to was *Barnaby Rudge: or, The Riots of London in 1780*, an anonymous piece produced at the Adelphi in December 1841 and January 1842.

[7]   He republished it only in a volume entitled *Reprinted Pieces* (1858). It is others who, since his death, have included it in collections entitled *Christmas Stories*.

[8]   When, in 1822, his family moved from Chatham to London, for an unknown reason the ten-year-old Charles stayed behind for about three months, living with his schoolmaster, William Giles. The school was not a boarding school, however, and this seems to have been a exceptional arrangement. He probably travelled to London to join the rest of the family in early autumn rather than just before Christmas (Ackroyd 54–55).

[9]   During most of Dickens's lifetime, the presentation of gifts to adults at Christmas was not a universal practice. They were given chiefly to small children, servants, and tradespeople, and by tradespeople to their patrons.

[10]   Catherine Waters sees these opening words as a "lament for a lost tradition" (Waters 60). There is no instance of Dickens lamenting a lost tradition that I can think of, but there are many of his scoffing at such

lamentation. It is, anyway, a self-evident misreading, to see lamentation in the denunciation of an exceptional and purely hypothetical misanthrope.

[11] Theirs is "the kind of home to which Dickens's parents would have aspired," Slater astutely remarks (*Christmas Carol* xv).

[12] See Shaftesbury's *Characteristics of Men, Manners, Opinions, Times* passim; Smith's *Theory of Moral Sentiments* passim.

[13] Michael Slater spells it out, but takes the view that, in this sketch, Dickens urges his readers "not to suppress all painful memories . . . , nor seek to expunge them . . . , but simply to put them to one side" (*Christmas Carol* xv). Dickens does not advocate utter forgetfulness, to be sure, but the proscription of such memories at Christmas time was something he would quickly abandon.

[14] I am indebted to Michael Allen for advice on dating these deaths. Three Portsmouth newspapers reported Alfred's death, and there is a record of his burial at Widley, just north of Portsmouth, on 10 September 1814. The evidence about Harriet's death is conflicting. One source declares she died before the Dickens family moved from Chatham to London in 1822, another that she died after their move.

[15] Irony notwithstanding, it may be that Dickens is acknowledging a decline in the observance of Christmas customs here. Among the fashionable, there had been such a decline, if not elsewhere.

[16] Bodleian Library Broadside Ballads. Harding B 38(12).

[17] This was first noted by John Butt in "Dickens's Christmas Books" (*Pope, Dickens and Others* 134).

[18] Frightening toys also make a guest appearance in *The Cricket on the Hearth* (1845). Tackleton, the misanthropic toy merchant, delights in selling ugly toys, including "demoniacal Tumblers who wouldn't lie down, and were perpetually flying forward, to stare infants out of countenance" (*Christmas Books* 205).

[19] We could of course suppose the error Mr. Wardle's. It is he who tells the story. But if Dickens intended that, he makes nothing of it. Readers are in no way invited to reflect upon Mr. Wardle's shortcomings as a storyteller.

[20] Information about Queen Victoria and Christmas is taken from the Royal Insight webpage, "A Royal Christmas: Queen Victoria's Christmas."

Chapter Five (pp. 155–220)

[1] Waters, too, draws attention to the influence of the annuals on the finish of *A Christmas Carol* (Waters 72).

[2] My source for much of the following information on this topic is the "Introduction to *The Keepsake*," by Hoagwood, Ledbetter, and Jacobsen.

[3]   Paul Davis observes that at five shillings a copy – a third of Bob Cratchit's weekly wage – the *Carol* was too expensive for the poorest readers. He sees this as a reason for supposing Dickens "wrote to confirm his position as the voice for his established middle-class audience," and as something at odds with his wish "to speak for the urban poor" (Davis 11). But you do not have to speak to the urban poor in order to speak for them.

[4]   Dickens took care to ensure that the *Carol* was in print for potential buyers during subsequent Christmas seasons (*Letters* 4: 121). Soon, though, his intervention would not be needed. The book has in fact never been out of print since its first publication (Slater, *Christmas Carol* xi).

[5]   Quoted by Slater (*Christmas Carol* xii).

[6]   For evidence of the magnitude of Dickens's problems, see his letter to Thomas Mitton of 4 December 1843 (*Letters* 3: 604).

[7]   This was eventually set to music by Sir Frederick Bridge, and published, as *A Christmas Song*, in 1913.

[8]   The 1841 census indicates 51.7 per cent of the population lived in rural areas. The 1851 census puts the figure at 46.3.

[9]   Some commentators struggle to justify Dickens's use of supernatural elements in the *Carol* and other Christmas books. Sally Ledger sees it as "an index of Dickens's anti-materialistic ethos" (*Christmas Books* xxxiv). Catherine Waters declares it to be "part of a larger epistemological enquiry generated by the fragmented experience of urban life" (Waters 75). There is a simpler explanation: it was something that Dickens, a stout defender of the fanciful and no slave to literary tradition, was happy to take from models he used for his first Christmas book – from the carol, and from the ghost story.

[10]   Scrooge is arguably a development of Master Humphrey, Master Humphrey's *pièce noir*. Both are old, unprepossessing, and solitary, both sit by the fire and have visions, both enter into the life of others through imagination. Master Humphrey does this instinctively, however.   Scrooge, more interestingly, has to be taught.

[11]   Some critics evidently feel *A Christmas Carol* has too little in common with the Beveridge Report (the document assembled by Sir William Beveridge in 1942, laying the foundations of Britain's welfare system). Waters, for instance, is condescending. Dickens's message, she says, "is the need for Christian *caritas*, for the spread of goodwill amongst all men, so that social misery might be alleviated by a national conversion to the Christmas spirit" (Waters 76). It is true that Dickens failed to anticipate the spirit of the 1940s in the 1840s, true that he urged no practical remedy for poverty beyond charitable giving. But he did not call for this as a thoughtless duty. For him charity was nothing without compassion. He demanded that readers look at the

poor, and recognize them as fellow creatures with fellow needs. Those who suppose writers can express little beyond the interests of their own class will be unimpressed by this. Others will see it as a reply to utilitarian complacency.

[12]   The words are in fact a conflation of Matthew 18.2 and Luke 9.47.

[13]   Dickens did see his story in a Christian context. The allusions to Christian myth and doctrine in the *Carol* are few and scattered, but Dickens chose to end it by repeating Tiny Tim's words, "God Bless Us, Every One" (85). Scrooge's redemption certainly conforms to Christian doctrine. It can stand apart from such doctrine, however.

[14]   The *Carol*, Waters notes, speaks not only for the domestic hearth, and all that that implies, "but *from* the hearth, situating the reader – and the listener – in a domestic context that is projected by the tone and facilitated by the length of the work" (75).

Chapter Six (pp. 221–82)

[1]   See Miller 247–48; James 70. The most important collection of plagiarisms and piracies of Dickens's works, Christmas books included, is the Lesley Staples Collection, at the Charles Dickens Museum, London.

[2]   See Collins, "'*Carol* Philosophy, Cheerful Views,'" 161-62.

[3]   Most publishers and most Dickens scholars adhere to the convention, encouraged by Dickens himself, of calling the little books he wrote during the 1840s "Christmas books," his Christmas contributions to *Household Words* and *All the Year Round* "Christmas stories." All of the Christmas books tell stories. Not all of the periodical contributions do. But it is a convention which prevents more confusion than it causes, so I observe it.

[4]   There had been disputes about when the New Year begins. The adoption of the Gregorian calendar, in 1752, fixed 1 January as New Year's Day in England. Before that, 25 March – Lady Day – jostled with it. Even so, documents of a much earlier date associate the New Year with Christmas: the fourteenth-century *Sir Gawain and the Green Knight*, for instance.

[5]   See the preface to the Cheap Edition (1850) of *Oliver Twist* (xlii–xliii).

[6]   See *Letters* 4: 209; Slater, "Dickens (and Forster) at work on *The Chimes*."

[7]   John Kucich has revealing things to say about this subject, although he is impressed by thinkers who do not impress me. The introduction to his *Repression in Victorian Fiction* (1–33) invites a lively debate.

[8]   Forster declares Dickens wrote the account in 1847. It is possible he wrote it a little earlier, but not much (Burgis xviii–xxi).

⁹   Dickens may have been familiar with the use made of it by James Hogg in *The Confessions of a Justified Sinner* (1824). Among the contents of his library, after his death, was the six-volume edition of Hogg's *Tales and Sketches, by the Ettrick Shepherd*, published in 1837 (Stonehouse 59).

¹⁰   The college is evidently a conflation of the Charterhouse and Gresham College. Originally a Carthusian priory, the Charterhouse, in Clerkenwell, was refounded in 1611 by Thomas Sutton, as a school, and as a refuge for decayed bachelors or widowers. Damaged by bombing in 1941, its buildings in the early nineteenth century included a fifteenth century gatehouse, courts and cloisters, and a splendid sixteenth-century great hall, used by the brethren for dining. Gresham College was established in the City of London in 1579, by the will of Sir Thomas Gresham, for the delivery of free public lectures on divinity, astronomy, music, geometry, physic, law, and rhetoric. Closely associated with the Royal Society, it has always been responsible for the dissemination of scientific ideas.

¹¹   Also called "Molech" in the Authorized Version. See Leviticus 18.21, 20.2–4; Jeremiah 32.35; 2 Kings 23.10.

¹²   See Matthew 19.13–15.

¹³   It is hard to say whether Dickens was simply using a familiar phrase for the inscription, or consciously quoting. It can be found in texts with which he was familiar. In *Hamlet*, Claudius uses the trope cynically, excusing his hasty marriage to his sister-in-law,

> Though yet of Hamlet our dear brother's death
> The memory be green . . . . (I.ii)

Thomas Moore's "Oh! Breathe Not His Name" is a song about a dead man mourned only in private. Secret tears, the singer reflects, "Shall long keep his memory green in our souls" (*Complete Poems*).

¹⁴   There are no by-lines in this issue, it should be said, and rarely any at all in *Household Words*. We know who wrote what, thanks chiefly to collections of their own contributions published by Dickens and other writers, and to the survival of the *Household Words* office book (see Lohrli passim).

¹⁵   The references are to an adaptation of *Le Chien de Montargis* by René-Charles Pixérécourt, first produced in London in 1814; Nicholas Rowe's play *Jane Shore* (1714), about the mistress of Edward IV; and George Lillo's play *The London Merchant, or the History of George Barnwell* (1731).

¹⁶   The language in fact echoes that of *The Life of Our Lord*.

Chapter Seven (pp. 283–306)

[1] Quoted by Glancy (ed.), *Christmas Stories* xxxi–xxxii.

[2] See Parker, *The Doughty Street Novels* 47–56. My chief sources of information about Maria are Dickens, *Letters* 1: 5–29; Slater, *Dickens and Women* 49–59; Kaplan 50–54; and Ackroyd 130–49.

[3] See Parker, *The Doughty Street Novels* 56–69. My chief sources of information about Catherine are Dickens, *Letters* 1: 60–143; Slater, *Dickens and Women* 103–62; Ackroyd passim; and Kaplan passim.

[4] My chief sources of information about Ellen Ternan are Slater, *Dickens and Women* 202–17; Ackroyd 830–1140; and Kaplan 367–555.

[5] There were two endings, of course, the one Dickens originally wrote, and the one Edward Bulwer-Lytton persuaded him to substitute for it (see "Appendix: The Two Endings," *Great Expectations* 445–47). The first makes it clear they do not marry, the second only suggests they might.

[6] My characterization of the novel as a whole, here, is derived in part from what I wrote of it in the final chapter of *The Doughty Street Novels* (221–26).

[7] I do not infer this distinction fancifully. It was one which Dickens consciously made in thinking about his later fiction. "Set the darkness and vengeance against the New Testament," he reminded himself in his working notes for *Little Dorrit* (Stone 310–11).

[8] My views on this subject are set out at greater length in my paper "Drood Redux." Some saw this as an uncompromising "survivalist" reading of the novel. It was not intended as such. My purpose was only to show how hard it is to deduce the ending Dickens intended for *Drood*, without imagining Edwin completing the reformation of character we see him beginning.

WORKS CITED

Dickens's Works

Barnaby Rudge. Ed. Donald Hawes. London: Everyman Paperback,1996.

Bleak House. Ed. Andrew Sanders. London: Everyman Paperback, 1994.

*A Child's History of England. Holiday Romance and Other Writings for
       Children*. Ed. Gillian Avery. London: Everyman Paperback, 1995.
       1–395.

Christmas Books. Ed. Sally Ledger. London: Everyman Paperback, 1999.

Christmas Stories. Ed. Ruth Glancy. London: Everyman Paperback, 1996.

Dombey and Son. Ed. Valerie Purton. London: Everyman Paperback, 1997.

Great Expectations. Ed. Robin Gilmour. London: Everyman Paperback, 1994.

Hard Times. Ed. Grahame Smith. London: Everyman Paperback, 1994.

The Letters of Charles Dickens. Ed. Madeline House, Graham Storey,
       Kathleen Tillotson, et al. The Pilgrim/British Academy Edition. 12
       vols. Oxford: Clarendon, 1965–2002.

The Life of Our Lord. Holiday Romance and Other Writing for Children. Ed.
       Gillian Avery. London: Everyman Paperback, 1995. 441–74.

Little Dorrit. Ed. Angus Easson. London: Everyman Paperback, 1999.

Martin Chuzzlewit. Ed. Michael Slater. London: Everyman Paperback, 1994.

Master Humphrey's Clock and Other Stories. Ed. Peter Mudford. London:
       Everyman Paperback, 1997.

Memoirs of Joseph Grimaldi [edited and introduced by Dickens]. Ed.
       Richard Findlater. London: MacGibbon, 1968.

The Mudfog Papers. Sketches by Boz. The Oxford Illustrated Dickens.
       Oxford: Oxford UP, 1957. 607–88.

The Mystery of Edwin Drood. Ed. Steven Connor. London: Everyman
       Paperback, 1996.

Nicholas Nickleby. Ed. David Parker. London: Everyman Paperback, 1994.

Oliver Twist. Ed. Steven Connor. London: Everyman Paperback, 1994.

The Pickwick Papers. Ed. Malcolm Andrews. London: Everyman Paperback,
       1998.

Sketches by Boz. The Oxford Illustrated Dickens. Oxford: Oxford UP, 1957.

The Speeches of Charles Dickens. Ed. K. J. Fielding. Oxford: Clarendon, 1960.

A Tale of Two Cities. Ed. Norman Page. London: Everyman Paperback, 1994.

The Uncommercial Traveller and Reprinted Pieces. The Oxford Illustrated Dickens. London: Oxford UP, 1956.

Other Works

Ackroyd, Peter. *Dickens.* London: Sinclair-Stevenson, 1990.

"An American's Reminiscences of Charles Dickens." *Literary Opinion & Readers' Miscellany* 1 Feb. 1889: 359-361.

Andrews, William. *Bygone England.* London, 1892.

Aristotle. *Poetics. Aristotle's Poetics, Demetrius on Style, Longinus on the Sublime.* Trans. John Warrington. London: Dent, 1963. 1–60.

The Arraignment, Conviction, and Imprisoning, of Christmas. [London?], 1646.

Aubrey, John. *Remaines of Gentilisme and Judaisme.* Ed. James Britten. Publications of the Folk-Lore Society 4. London, 1881.

Austen, Jane. *Emma.* Oxford: Oxford UP, 1999.

Barthes, Roland. "The Death of the Author." *Image-Music-Text.* Trans. Stephen Heath. London: Fontana, 1977. 142–48.

Beavin, Hugh. "Hinckley in the Hungry Forties." *Hinckley Online.* 29 June 2004.
<www.hinckley-online.co.uk/histor11.shtml>

Bede. *The Ecclesiastical History of the English People.* Ed. Judith McLure and Roger Collins. Oxford: Oxford UP, 1994.

Bentham, Jeremy. *Pauper Management Improved.* London, 1812.

Billington, Sandra. "Butchers, and Fishmongers: Their Historical Contribution to London's Festivity." *Folklore* 101 (1990): 97-103.

Blackall, Offspring. *The Lawfulness and the Right Manner of Keeping Christmas and Other Festivals: A Sermon Preach'd at the Parish Church of St. Dunstan in the West upon Christmas Day, 1704.* London, 1707.

Bland, D. S., ed. *Three Revels from the Inns of Court.* Amersham: Avebury, 1984.

Bodleian Library Broadside Ballads. 27 September 1999. Bodleian Library, U of Oxford. 29 June 2004.
<www.bodley.ox.ac.uk/ballads/ballads.htm>

Bolton, H. Philip. *Dickens Dramatized*. Boston, Mass.: Hall, 1987

Booth, Bradford Allen. *A Cabinet of Gems*. Berkeley: U of California P, 1938.

Borges, Jorge Luis. "Tlön, Uqbar, Orbis Tertius." *Labyrinths*. Ed. Donald A. Yates and James E. Irby. New York: New Directions, 1964. 3–18.

Bradley, Ian, ed. *The Penguin Book of Carols*. London: Penguin, 1999.

Brand, John. *Observations on Popular Antiquities*. With the additions of Sir Henry Ellis. London: Chatto, 1900.

Bridge, Sir Frederick. *A Christmas Song*. London: Chappell, 1913.

Brooks-Davies, Douglas, ed. *Christmas Please!* London: Phoenix, 2000.

Burgis, Nina. Introduction. *David Copperfield*. By Charles Dickens. Ed. Burgis. Oxford: Clarendon, 1981.

Buruma, Ian. *Inventing Japan: From Empire to Economic Miracle, 1853–1964*. London: Weidenfeld, 2003.

Butt, John. *Pope, Dickens and Others*. Edinburgh: Edinburgh UP, 1969.

Campbell, Oscar James, ed. *A Shakespeare Encyclopaedia*. London: Metheun, 1966.

Cantacuzino, Marina, ed. *A London Christmas*. Gloucester: Sutton, 1989.

Carlyle, Jane Welsh. *Jane Welsh Carlyle: A New Selection of her Letters*. Ed. Trudy Bliss. London: Gollancz, 1949.

The Catholic Encyclopaedia. Ed. Edward A. Pace, James J. Walsh, Peter Guilday, John J. Wynne, Blanche M. Kelly, et al. New York: Gilmary Society, 1936.

Cawley, A. C, ed. *The Wakefield Pageants in the Towneley Cycle*. Manchester: Manchester UP, 1958.

Chadwick, Edwin. *Report on the Sanitary Condition of the Labouring Population of Great Britain*. Edinburgh: Edinburgh UP, 1965.

Checkland, S. G., and E. A. O. Checkland. *The Poor Law Report of 1834*. Harmondsworth, Middlesex: Penguin, 1974.

Clare, John. *The Shepherd's Calendar*. Ed. Eric Robinson and Geoffrey Summerfield. London: Oxford UP, 1964.

Clery, E. J. *The Rise of Supernatural Fiction, 1762-1800*. Cambridge: Cambridge UP, 1995.

Collins, Philip. "'*Carol* Philosophy, Cheerful Views.'" *Etudes Anglaises* 23 (1970): 158–67.

---, ed. *Charles Dickens: The Public Readings*. Oxford: Oxford UP, 1975.

---. *Dickens and Crime*. London: Macmillan, 1962.

---. "Dickens and the Whiston Case." *The Dickensian* 58 (1962): 47–49.

---, ed. *Dickens: The Critical Heritage*. London: Routledge, 1971.

Conder, Edward, Jr. *Records of the Hole Craft and Fellowship of Masons*. London, 1894.

Cowie, Leonard W. *A History of the Parish Church of Kingston upon Thames.* Kingston upon Thames: All Saints' Parish Church, n.d.

Crewdson, H. A. F. *The Worshipful Company of Musicians.* London: Knight, 1971.

Croquis, Alfred [Daniel Maclise]. "Christmas Revels: An Epic Rhapsody in Twelve Duans." *Fraser's Magazine* 17 (1838): 635–644.

Davis, Paul. *The Lives and Times of Ebenezer Scrooge.* New Haven: Yale UP, 1990.

Dawson, W. F. *Christmas: Its Origins and Associations.* London: Elliot Stock, 1902.

Dearmer, Percy, R. Vaughan Williams, and Martin Shaw, eds. *The Oxford Book of Carols.* Oxford: Oxford UP, 1964.

DeSimone, David. "Another Look at Christmas in the Eighteenth Century." *The Colonial Williamsburg Interpreter* 16 (1995-96). 2004. The Colonial Williamsburg Foundation. 29 June 2004. <www.history.org/Almanack/life/xmas/xmasqa.cfm>

Dibert-Himes, Glenn. "Early Nineteenth-Century Gift Books and Annuals: Bibliography." *British Gift Books and Annuals Web Site.* Ed. Dibert-Himes. 29 June 2004. <www.shu.ac.uk/annuals/bibliographic/annbib/biblio.htm>

Dickens, Mamie. *My Father as I Recall Him.* Westminster: [1897].

Dowden, Edward. *Life of Shelley.* 2 vols. London, 1886.

Durkheim, Emile. *The Elementary Forms of the Religious Life.* Oxford: Oxford UP, 2001.

Easterling, P. E. "A Show for Dionysus." *The Cambridge Companion to Greek Tragedy.* Ed. P. E. Easterling. Cambridge: Cambridge UP, 1997. 36-53.

Eliot, George. *Middlemarch.* Oxford: Oxford UP, 1999

Eliot, Simon. Introduction to "Publishing." *Aspects of the Victorian Book.* The British Library. 29 June 2004. <www.bl.uk/collections/early/victorian/pu_intro.html>

Emmison, F. G. *Tudor Secretary: Sir William Petre at Court and Home.* London: Longman, 1961.

Engels, Frederick [Friedrich]. *The Condition of the Working Class in England.* London: Lawrence, 1973. The Electric Book Company Ltd. 1998. 29 June 2004. <www.elecbook.com>

Espriella, Manuel Alvarez. See Southey, Robert.

Evelyn, John. *The Diary of John Evelyn.* Ed. E. S. Beer. 6 vols. Oxford: Clarendon, 1955.

The Feast of Feasts. [By Edward Fisher.] Oxford, 1644.

Fielding, Henry. *The History of Tom Jones, a Foundling.* London: Everyman, 1998

Fitzgerald, Percy. "Christmas at Gadshill; The Home of Charles Dickens." *The Free Lance* 22 Dec. 1903: 277–79

---. "Dickens in his Books." *Harper's Monthly Magazine* Apr. 1902: 700–07

Forby, Robert. *The Vocabulary of East Anglia.* 2 vols. London, 1830.

Forde Abbey. Forde Abbey, Somerset, 2001.

Foreman, Amanda. *Georgiana, Duchess of Devonshire.* London: Harper, 1998.

Forster, John. *The Life of Charles Dickens.* Ed. J. W. T. Ley. London: Palmer, 1928.

Foster, Don. *Author Unknown: On the Trail of the Anonymous.* New York: Holt, 2000.

Francillon, R.A. "English Men and Women of Letters of the 19th Century: VI. Charles Dickens." *Atlanta Scholarship and Reading Union* Mar. 1888: 349-353.

Galbraith, John Kenneth. "How to Get the Poor off our Conscience." *Harper's Magazine* Nov. 1985. U of Mississippi. 4 August 2004.
<http://home.olemiss.edu/~jmitchel/class/poor.htm>

Gay, John. *The Poetical Works of John Gay.* Ed. G. C. Faber. London: Oxford UP, 1926.

Gewertz, Ken. "Professor Brought Christmas Tree to New England." *The Harvard University Gazette* 12 Dec. 1996.   1998.   President and Fellows of Harvard College. 29 June 2004.
<www.news.harvard.edu/gazette/1996/12.12/ProfessorBrough.html>

Ghost Stories. London: Ackermann, 1823.

Gilbert, Davies, ed. *Some Ancient Christmas Carols, with the Tunes to which they were Formerly Sung in the West of England.* London, 1822.

Girouard, Mark. *Life in the English Country House.* New Haven: Yale UP, 1978.

Goldhill, Simon. "The Language of Tragedy: Rhetoric and Communication." *The Cambridge Companion to Greek Tragedy.* Ed. P. E. Easterling. Cambridge: Cambridge UP, 1997. 127-150.

Goldsmith, Oliver. *The Vicar of Wakefield.* Oxford: Oxford UP, 1974.

Happé, Peter, ed. *Mediaeval English Drama.* London: Macmillan, 1984.

Hathorn, Richmond Y. *The Handbook of Classical Drama.* London: Barker, 1967.

Hemingway, Ernest. *A Farewell to Arms.* Harmondsworth, Middlesex: Penguin, 1935.

Herrick, Robert. *The Poetical Works of Robert Herrick*. Ed. F. W. Moorman. London: Oxford UP, 1921.

Hervey, Thomas K. *The Book of Christmas*. London, 1836.

Hey, David, ed. *The Oxford Companion to Local and Family History*. Oxford: Oxford UP, 1996.

Hinchliffe, Edward. *Barthomley*. Newcastle-under-Lyme, 1856.

Hoagwood, Terence, Kathryn Ledbetter, and Martin M. Jacobsen. "Introduction to *The Keepsake*." *L. E. L.'s "Verses" and the Keepsake for 1829*. Romantic Circles/Electronic Editions. U of Maryland. 30 June 2004. <www.rc.umd.edu/editions/contemps/lel/intro.htm>

Hogg, James. *The Private Memoirs and Confessions of a Justified Sinner*. Oxford, Oxford UP, 1999.

Holland, William. *Paupers and Pig Killers: The Diary of William Holland a Somerset Parson 1799-1818*. Ed. Jack Ayres. Gloucester: Sutton, 1984.

Hone, William. *The Every-Day Book*. 2 vols. London, 1826.

Hotson, Leslie. *The First Night of Twelfth Night*. London: Hart-Davis, 1954.

Huelin, Gordon. "Christmas in the City." *Guildhall Studies in London History* 3 (1978): 164-174.

Hutton, Ronald. *The Rise and Fall of Merry England*. Oxford: Oxford UP, 1994.

---. *The Stations of the Sun*. Oxford: Oxford UP, 1996.

Inwood, Stephen. *A History of London*. London: Macmillan, 1998.

[Irving, Washington]. *A History of New York*. By Diedrich Knickerbocker [pseud.]. New York, 1809.

---. *The Legend of Sleepy Hollow and Other Tales*. London: Bloomsbury, 1994.

---. *Old Christmas*. London, 1876.

---. *The Sketchbook*. By Geoffrey Crayon, Gent [pseud.]. Oxford: Oxford UP, 1996.

James, Louis. *Fiction for the Working Man*. London: Oxford UP, 1974.

Johnson, Edgar. *Charles Dickens: His Tragedy and Triumph*. 2 vols. New York: Simon, 1952.

Johnson, Richard. *The Famous Historie of the Seaven Champions of Christendome*. London, 1670.

Jones, Philip E. *The Butchers of London*. London: Secker, 1976.

---. *The Worshipful Company of Poulters of the City of London*. Oxford: Oxford UP, 1981.

Kaplan, Fred. *Dickens: A Biography*. London: Hodder, 1988.

Keble, John. *The Christian Year*. London, 1898.

King, William. *Miscellanies in Prose and Verse*. 2 vols. London, [1705-12?].

Kirby, D. P. *The Earliest English Kings*. London: Unwin, 1991.

Kightly, Charles. *The Customs and Ceremonies of Britain: an Encyclopaedia of Living Traditions*. London: Thames, 1986.

Kitton, F. G. Introduction. *The* [sic] *Christmas Carol*. By Charles Dickens. London, 1890. iii-viii.

---. "The Man who 'Invented' Christmas." *V. C.* 17 Dec. 1903: 223-24.

Kucich, John. *Repression in Victorian Fiction*. Berkeley: U of California P, 1987.

Lacy, Norris. J, ed. *The Arthurian Encyclopaedia*. Woodbridge, Suffolk: Boydell, 1986.

Lai Ming. *A History of Chinese Literature*. London: Cassell, 1964.

Levi, Peter. *A History of Greek Literature*. Harmondsworth, Middlesex: Viking, 1985

Ley, J. W. T. "The Apostle of Christmas," *Dickensian* 2 (1906): 324–26.

Lithgow, William. *Lithgow's Nineteen Years Travels*. London, 1682.

Livingston, Major Henry, Jr. "Account of a Visit from St. Nicholas." *Author Unknown: On the Trail of Anonymous* by Don Foster. New York: Holt, 2000. *Representative Poetry Online*. Ed. Ian Lancashire, 18 April 2002. Web Development Group, Information Technology Services, U of Toronto Libraries. 30 June 2004. <http://eir.library.utoronto.ca/rpo/display/poem1312.html>

Lloyd, Albert Lancaster, ed. *Folk song in England*. London: Lawrence, 1967

Lohrli, Anne. *Household Words. A Weekly Journal, 1850-1859, Conducted by Charles Dickens. Table of Contents, List of Contributors and their Contributions*. Toronto: U of Toronto P, 1973.

Lovefun, A. G. [pseud.]. *A New Cure for the Spleen*. London, 1778.

MacKenzie, Norman, and Jeanne MacKenzie. *Dickens: A Life*. Oxford: Oxford UP, 1979.

Maclise, Daniel. See Croquis, Alfred.

Malthus, Thomas. *An Essay on the Principle of Population*. London, 1798.

Mayhew, Henry. *London labour and the London poor*. Introd. John D. Rosenberg. 4 vols. New York: Dover, 1968.

Miles, Clement. *Christmas Customs and Traditions*. New York: Dover, 1976.

Miller, William. *The Dickens Student and Collector*. London: Chapman, 1944.

Milton, John. *Paradise Lost. The Poems of John Milton*. Ed. John Carey, and Alastair Fowler. London: Longmans, 1968. 419-1060.

Moore, Sir Thomas. *The Complete Poems of Sir Thomas Moore. Project*

Gutenberg. Ed. Charles Aldarondo, Tiffany Vergon, Robert Connal, et al. 2003. 30 June 2004.
<http://textual.net/access.gutenberg/1/Thomas.Moore>

"The Novelist of Christmas." *The Pictorial Magazine* 3 Dec. 1904: 50-52.

Palmer, Geoffrey, and Noel Lloyd. *A Year of Festivals: A Guide to British Calender Customs.* London: Frederick Warne, 1972.

Parker, David. *The Doughty Street Novels.* New York: AMS, 2002.

---. "Drood Redux: Mystery and the Art of Fiction." *Dickens Studies Annual* 24 (1995): 185-195.

---. "John Dickens to George Franklin." *The Dickensian* 99 (2003): 223–30.

Parker, David, and Michael Slater. "The Gladys Storey Papers. *The Dickensian* 76 (1980): 3–16.

Parley's Magazine. New York, 1833–44.

Paroissien, David. *The Companion to Great Expectations.* Robertsbridge, East Sussex: Helm, 2000.

Patten, Robert L. *Charles Dickens and his Publishers.* Oxford: Clarendon, 1978.

Pattison, Bruce. "Music and Masque." William Shakespeare. *The Complete Works.* Ed. C. J. Sisson. London: Odhams, 1953. xlvii-lii.

Peacock, Thomas Love. *Crochet Castle. The Novels of Thomas Love Peacock.* Ed. David Garnett. 2 vols. London: Hart-Davis, 1963. 2: 639-761.

Pepys, Samuel. *The Diary of Samuel Pepys.* Ed. Robert Latham and William Matthews. 11 vols. London: Bell, 1970.

Pimlott, J. A. R. *The Englishman's Christmas: A Social History.* Hassocks, Sussex: Harvester, 1978.

Pindar. *Odes. Perseus Digital Library.* Trans. and ed. Diane Svarlien. 1990. Tufts U. 30 June 2004.
<www.perseus.tufts.edu/cgi-bin/ptext?lookup=Pind.+O.+1.5>

Pliny the Elder. *Naturalis Historia.* Bill Thayer's Website. 26 June 2004. 30 June 2004.
<www.ukans.edu/history/index/europe/ancient_rome/E/Roman/Texts/Pliny_the_Elder/home.html>

Pope, Alexander. *The Correspondence of Alexander Pope.* Ed. George Sherburn. 5 vols. Oxford: Clarendon, 1956.

Powderham Castle. By Lady Paulina Hadley, et al. Exeter: Powderham Castle, n.d.

Prest, Wilfred R. *The Inns of Court Under Elizabeth I and the Early Stuarts, 1590-1640.* London: Longman, 1972.

Prickett, Stephen. *Victorian Fantasy.* Hassocks, Sussex: Harvester, 1979.

Prynne, William. *Histrio-Mastix.* London, 1633.

Round about our Coal Fire. London, [1730?].

"A Royal Christmas: Queen Victoria's Christmas." *Royal Insight.* Dec. 2003.
    30 June 2004.
    <www.royal.gov.uk/output/page2821.asp>

Sandys, William, ed. *Christmas Carols, Ancient and Modern.* London, 1833.

Saussure, Ferdinand de. *Course in General Linguistics.* Trans. Wade Baskin.
    New York: McGraw-Hill, 1966.

Schlicke, Paul, ed. *Oxford Reader's Companion to Dickens.* Oxford: Oxford
    UP, 1999.

Scholes, Percy A. *The Oxford Companion to Music.* Rev. John Owen Ward.
    Oxford: Oxford UP, 1970

Scott, Sir Walter. *The Poetical Works.* London, [1880].

---. *Waverley.* The Waverley Novels, vol. 1. Edinburgh, 1889.

Segal, Charles. "Choral Lyric in the Fifth Century." *The Cambridge History
    of Classical Literature.* Ed. P. E. Easterling, and B. M. W. Knox. 2
    vols. Cambridge: Cambridge UP, 1985. 1: 222-244.

Selander, Helen Wilcox. "The Boar's Head." *mymerrychristmas.com.* Ed. Jeff
    Westover. 14 June 2004. 30 June 2004.
    <www.mymerrychristmas.com/legends/x2000lg06.html>

Shaftesbury. Anthony Ashley Cooper. Earl of. *Characteristics of Men,
    Manners, Opinions, Times.* Ed. Lawrence. E. Klein. Cambridge:
    Cambridge UP, 1999.

Shakespeare, William. *The Complete Works.* Ed. C. J. Sisson. London:
    Odhams, 1953.

Shijing. Zhong Hua Xue Yi She. Shanghai, 1936. *University of Virginia
    Library Electronic Text Center.* Ed. Xuepen Sun and Xiaoqian Zheng.
    1998. U of Virginia. 30 June 2004.
    <http://etext.lib.virginia.edu/chinese/shijing/>

Sir Gawain and the Green Knight. Ed. J. R. R. Tolkien, and E. V. Gordon.
    Oxford: Clarendon, 1930.

Sitwell, Osbert, ed. *Two Generations.* London: Macmillan, 1940.

Skinner, John. *The Journal of a Somerset Rector, 1803-1834.* Ed. Howard
    Coombs, and Peter Coombs. Oxford: Oxford UP, 1984.

Slater, Michael. "The Christmas Books." *The Dickensian* 65 (1969): 17–24.

---, ed. *A Christmas Carol and Other Christmas Writings.* By Charles
    Dickens. Harmondsworth, Middlesex: Penguin, 2003.

---. "Dickens (and Forster) at work on *The Chimes.*" *Dickens Studies* 2
    (1966), 106–40.

---. *Dickens and Women.* London: Dent, 1983.

Smith, Adam. *The Theory of Moral Sentiments.* Ed. D. D. Raphael, and A. L.
    Macfie. Oxford: Clarendon, 1976.

Southey, Robert. *Letters from England.* By Manuel Alvarez Espriella
[pseud.]. Ed. Jack Simmons. Gloucester: Sutton, 1984.

---. *Poems, 1799. Project Gutenberg.* Ed. Jonathan Ingram, Clytie Siddall,
Charles Franks, et al. 2003. 30 July 2004.
<http://mirrors.xmission.com/gutenberg/etext05/8spm210h.htm>

The Spectator. By Joseph Addison, Richard Steele, et al. 4 vols. London:
Dent, 1945.

Stone, Harry (ed.). *Charles Dickens' Working Notes for His Novels.* Chicago:
U of Chicago P, 1987.

Stonehouse. J. H. (ed.). *Catalogues of the Libraries of Charles Dickens and
W. M. Thackeray.* London: Piccadilly Fountain Press, 1935.

Storey, Gladys. *Dickens and Daughter.* London: Muller, 1939.

Strachey, Giles Lytton. *Eminent Victorians.* London: Chatto, 1974.

Strutt, Joseph. *The Sports and Pastimes of the People of England.* Ed. J.
Charles Cox. London: Methuen,1903.

Stukeley, William. *The Medallic History of Marcus Aurelius Valerius
Carausius.* 2 vols. London, 1757–59.

Sutton, Denys. *Westwood Manor.* London: The National Trust, 1978.

Tallent-Bateman, Chas. T. "The 'Forget-Me-Not.'" *Manchester Quarterly,*
1912. *British Gift Books and Annuals Web Site.* Ed. Glenn
Dibert-Himes. 30 June 2004.
<www.shu.ac.uk/annuals/intro/Bateman.html>

[Taylor, Edgar, trans.] *Grimm's Goblins.* Trans. from the *Kinder und Haus
Marchen* by Edgar Taylor. London, 1876. [I have not seen a copy of
the original edition of this book: *German Popular Stories.* London,
1823.]

Taylor, John. *The Complaint of Christmas.* Oxford, [2 May 1646].

Tennyson, Alfred. *The Poems of Tennyson.* Ed. Christopher Ricks. London:
Longmans, 1969.

Thackeray, William Makepeace. *The Works of William Makepeace
Thackeray.* 13 vols. London, 1894.

Thorn, Romaine Joseph. *Christmas. A Poem.* Bristol, 1795.

Thornton, Peter. *Authentic Decor.* London: Weidenfeld, 1984.

Tiddy, R. J. E. *The Mummers' Play.* Oxford: Clarendon, 1923.

Tomalin, Claire. *Samuel Pepys: The Unequalled Self.* London: Penguin,
2003.

Tusser, Thomas. *Five Hundred Points of Good Husbandry.* London, 1812.

Vaughan, Henry. *The Complete Poems.* Ed. Alan Rudrum. New Haven: Yale
UP, 1976.

Vidal, Gore. *Inventing a Nation: Washington, Adams, Jefferson.* New Haven:
Yale UP, 2003.

Walder, Dennis. *Dickens and Religion*. London: Allen, 1981.

Walpole, Horace. *Horace Walpole's Correspondence with Sir Horace Mann IV*. London: Oxford UP, 1960. Vol. 20 of *Horace Walpole's Correspondence*. Ed. W. S. Lewis, et al. 48 vols. New Haven: Yale UP, Oxford UP, 1937–83.

Waters, Catherine. *Dickens and the Politics of the Family*. Cambridge: Cambridge UP, 1997.

Watt, Ian. *The Rise of the Novel*. Harmondsworth, Middlesex: Penguin, 1963.

Wells, Stanley, ed. *A Midsummer Night's Dream*. By William Shakespeare. London: Penguin, 1995.

Weston, Jessie L. *From Ritual to Romance*. Garden City: Doubleday, 1957.

Winnington-Ingram, R. P. "The Origins of Tragedy." *The Cambridge History of Classical Literature*. Ed. P. E. Easterling, and B.M. W. Knox. 2 vols. Cambridge: Cambridge UP, 1985. 1: 258-345.

Wither, George. "A Christmas Carol." *Fair-virtue, the Mistresse of Philarete*. London, 1622. *Representative Poetry Online*. Ed. N. J. Endicott. 6 February 2002. Web Development Group, Information Technology Services, U of Toronto Libraries. 30 June 2004. <http://eir.library.utoronto.ca/rpo/display/poem2324.html>

Wong, C. S. *A Cycle of Chinese Festivities*. Singapore: Malaysia Publishing House, 1967.

Wood, Anthony. *Nineteenth Century Britain, 1815–1914*. 2nd ed. Harlow, Essex: Longman, 1982.

Woodforde, James. *The Diary of a Country Parson 1758-1802*. Ed. John Beresford. Oxford: Oxford UP, 1978.

Woolf, Rosemary. *The English Mystery Plays*. London: Routledge, 1972.

INDEX

[Entries relating to Dickens and other authors, to their works, and to fictional characters in those works, are dispersed throughout the index, rather than assembled under single headings. Parenthetical clues are supplied where I judge readers are likely to need help.]